ACCA
NEW SYLLABUS
PRACTICE & REVISION KIT

Paper 3.7

Strategic Financial Management

BPP Publishing
January 2002

First edition 2001
Second edition January 2002

ISBN 0 7517 0525 X (Previous edition 0 7517 0798 8)

British Library Cataloguing-in-Publication Data
A catalogue record for this book
is available from the British Library

Published by

BPP Publishing Limited
Aldine House, Aldine Place
London W12 8AW

www.bpp.com

Printed in Great Britain by Ashford Colour Press

We are grateful to the Association of Chartered Certified Accountants for permission to reproduce past examination questions. The answers to past examination questions have been prepared by BPP Publishing Limited.

CONTENTS

Page number

Question search tools

    Question and answer checklist/index   (v)

    Topic index   (viii)

Revision

    Effective revision   (x)

    Revising with this kit   (xi)

    Revision programme   (xiii)

The exam

    The exam paper   (xix)

Background

    Current issues   (xxi)

    Useful websites   (xxv)

    Syllabus mindmap   (xxvi)

    Oxford Brookes Bsc in Applied Accounting   (xxvii)

    Oxford Institute of International Finance MBA   (xxvii)

Question practice

    Questions   3

    Answers   79

Exam practice

    Mock exam 1   259
    • **Questions**   261
    • **Plan of attack**   269
    • **Answers**   271

    Mock exam 2 (Pilot paper)   289
    • **Questions**   291
    • **Plan of attack**   301
    • **Answers**   303

BPP PUBLISHING

Contents

Mathematical tables and exam formulae   321

Order form

Review form & free prize draw

QUESTION AND ANSWER CHECKLIST/INDEX

The headings in this checklist/index indicate the main topics of questions, but questions often cover several different topics.

Preparation questions, listed in italics, provide you with a firm foundation for attempts at exam-standard questions.

Questions preceded by ⋆ are **key questions** which we think you must attempt in order to pass the exam. Tick them off on this list as you complete them.

Note that questions 31 (real options), 46 (Greeks), 47 and 48 (Black-Scholes model) and 54 (Delta hedge) cover topics not examined under the equivalent old syllabus paper *Financial Strategy*.

Questions set under the old syllabus *Financial Strategy* paper are included because their style and content are similar to those which will appear in the Paper 3.7 exam. Some of the questions have been amended to reflect the new syllabus exam format.

			Marks	Time allocation Mins	Page number Question	Answer
PART A: OBJECTIVES AND STRATEGY FORMULATION						
		Objectives				
	1	*Preparation question: Conflict*	–	–	3	79
⋆	2	Stakeholders (FS, 6/96 amended)	15	27	3	80
⋆	3	International differences (FS, 6/97 amended)	15	27	3	81
⋆	4	ESOPs (FS, 12/98 amended)	15	27	4	83
⋆	5	Share ownership (FS, 12/99 amended)	15	27	4	84
		Strategy formulation				
	6	*Preparation question: Potren*	–	–	5	85
⋆	7	Steps (FS, 6/98 amended)	15	27	6	86
	8	Pulfer (FS, 12/94)	30	54	6	87
	9	Noifa Leisure	30	54	7	91
⋆	10	Cedarlodge (FS, 12/98)	30	54	9	94
⋆	11	Hanme (FS, 6/99)	40	72	10	97
⋆	12	Muton	30	54	11	101
PART B: INVESTMENT DECISIONS AND RISK ANALYSIS						
	13	Mover (FS, 6/99 amended)	15	27	14	105
⋆	14	Utopia Hotels (FS, 12/97)	40	72	14	106
	15	Tovell (FS, 6/94)	30	54	16	112
⋆	16	Zedland Postal Services	15	27	17	116
	17	Market efficiency (FS, 12/00 amended)	15	27	17	118
⋆	18	Bonds (FS, 6/98 amended)	15	27	18	119
⋆	19	Fuelit (FS, 12/00)	40	72	18	121
	20	*Preparation question: Rodfin*	–	–	20	125
	21	Phantom (FS, 6/98 amended)	15	27	21	128
	22	Bartoo (FS, 12/96 amended)	15	27	21	130
⋆	23	Wonpar (FS, 12/97 amended)	15	27	22	132
⋆	24	Munxay (FS, 12/99 amended)	15	27	23	134
⋆	25	Berlan and Canalot	15	27	24	135
	26	Netra (FS, 6/97 amended)	15	27	24	137
⋆	27	Daron (FS, 12/96)	40	72	25	139
⋆	28	Kulpar (FS, 12/00)	30	54	27	145

BPP PUBLISHING

Question and answer checklist/index

			Marks	Time allocation Mins	Page number Question	Answer
*	29	Your company (FS, 6/99 amended)	40	72	28	148
*	30	Progrow	30	54	31	153
*	31	Husoc	15	27	33	156

PART C: CORPORATE EXPANSION AND REORGANISATION

			Marks	Time allocation Mins	Page number Question	Answer
	32	*Preparation question: Bid calculations*	–	–	35	157
	33	Peden and Tulen (FS, 6/99 amended)	15	27	36	159
	34	Oakton (FS, 6/98 amended)	30	54	36	161
*	35	Demast (FS, 6/94)	30	54	38	164
	36	Airgo (FS, 6/97)	30	54	39	168
*	37	Dricom (FS, 12/97)	30	54	41	171
*	38	Planetspan (FS, 12/98)	40	72	43	177
	39	Grocas (FS, 6/95)	30	54	44	182

PART D: FOREIGN EXCHANGE AND INTEREST RATE RISK

			Marks	Time allocation Mins	Page number Question	Answer
	40	*Preparation question: Herler*	–	–	47	185
	41	*Preparation question: Financial futures*	–	–	47	187
*	42	Vertid (FS, 6/95)	40	72	48	188
*	43	Lanvert (FS, 6/98 amended)	30	54	49	191
*	44	KYT (FS, 6/99 amended)	15	27	50	193
*	45	USA options (FS, 12/00 amended)	15	27	50	195
*	46	RCB	15	27	51	197
*	47	Cathlyn	15	27	51	199
*	48	Sarhall	30	54	52	200
*	49	Murwald (FS, 12/94)	30	54	53	202
*	50	HYK (FS, 12/99)	30	54	54	206
*	51	Tayquer (FS, 6/96 amended)	15	27	55	210
*	52	Projections (FS, 12/98 amended)	15	27	56	212
*	53	Somax (FS, 6/96)	40	72	57	213
*	54	PZP (FS, 12/97 amended)	15	27	58	216

PART E: THE GLOBAL ENVIRONMENT

			Marks	Time allocation Mins	Page number Question	Answer
	55	*Preparation question: Exchange rate systems*	–	–	60	218
	56	Axelot	15	27	60	219
	57	*Preparation question: Risk data*	–	–	61	221
	58	Rippentoff	15	27	62	222
*	59	FDI (FS, 12/98, amended)	15	27	63	224
*	60	Dialtous (FS, 12/95)	30	54	63	226
*	61	Omnikit (FS, 6/97 amended)	30	54	65	229
*	62	Valtick (FS, 12/99)	40	72	67	234
*	63	Forun (FS, 6/94 amended)	40	72	68	238
	64	Axmine	40	72	70	244
*	65	VTW (FS, 6/98 amended)	15	27	71	249
*	66	Centralisation (FS, 6/97 amended)	15	27	72	251
	67	Debois (FS, 6/98 amended)	15	27	73	253
	68	Tax haven (FS, 12/00 amended)	15	27	74	255

		Marks	Time allocation Mins	Page number Question	Answer
PART F: CORPORATE DIVIDEND POLICY					
69	*Preparation question: Electronics*	–	–	75	256
* 70	Divs	15	27	75	257

MOCK EXAM 1

Questions 71 to 76

MOCK EXAM 2 (PILOT PAPER)

Questions 77 to 82

BPP
PUBLISHING

TOPIC INDEX

Listed below are the key Paper 3.7 syllabus topics and the numbers of the questions in this Kit covering those topics.

If you need to concentrate your practice and revision on certain topics or if you want to attempt all available questions that refer to a particular subject (be they preparation or exam-standard questions), you will find this index useful.

The New Syllabus *Strategic Financial Management* paper differs from the Old Syllabus *Financial Strategy* in a number of ways. Some of the questions in this kit are on topics which were not covered under the Old Syllabus, and these are marked with an asterisk (*).

> RETAKE STUDENTS SHOULD PAY PARTICULAR ATTENTION TO THE QUESTIONS ON THE TOPIC AREAS MARKED WITH A *. THESE ARE BEING EXAMINED FOR THE FIRST TIME UNDER THE NEW SYLLABUS.

Syllabus topic	Question numbers
Adjusted present value	15, 27, 29, 30, 38, 53 Mock 1 - Q1
Alpha values	22 – 24
Arbitrage pricing theory	14
Balance of payments	Mock 2 - Q6
Barriers to trade	61, Mock 1 - Q5
Basis	46, Mock 1 - Q2
* Black-Scholes model	47, 48
Bonds	18, 21
Capital asset pricing model	14, 20, 23 – 24, 27 – 30, 39
Collars	45, 49, 51
Corporate governance	3, 35
Currency futures	41, 44, 46, 63, Mock 1 - Q2
Currency options	42, 43, 45, 47, 63, Mock 2 - Q3
Debt problem	64
Debt valuation	17
* Delta hedge	54
Divestment	39, Mock 1 - Q1
* Dividend policy	5, 17, 69, 70, Mock 2 - Q5
Dividend remittance	62, 65, Mock 2 - Q1
Efficient market hypothesis	17, Mock 1 - Q3
* Ethical issues	Mock 2 - Q1
Euro	61, Mock 1 - Q2
Exchange rates	55
Financial planning	8, 10
Financing	9, 10, 27, 28, 36, 38, 42, 53, 56, 60, 68
Forecasts	8
Foreign investment	58, 59, 61 – 65, Mock 1 - Q4, Mock 2 - Q1
Forward market	43, 49, 51, 63, Mock 1 - Q2
Free cash flow	28, Mock 1 - Q6

Syllabus topic	Question numbers
Goal congruence	4
★ Greeks	46, 54
Interest rate futures	41, 49 – 51, 50, 51, Mock 2 - Q4
Interest rate options	49 – 52
Interest rate parity	63, Mock 2 - Q3
International Monetary Fund	Mock 2 - Q6
Investment appraisal	13 – 16, 19, 30, 39, 58, 60 – 62
Less developed countries	64
Management buy-out	36
Modigliani and Miller	25 – 27, 70
Money market hedge	42, Mock 1 - Q2
Multilateral netting	63, 65
Multinationals	59, 64, 68, Mock 2 - Q6
Objectives	1
Political risk	57, 58
Portfolio theory	20 – 23
Post-audits	34
Purchasing power parity	40, 42, 56, 62, 64, Mock 2 - Q3
Ratio analysis	6, 9, 11, 12
★ Real options	19, 31
Reconstruction	37, 39, Mock 1 - Q1
Remuneration policy	4, 48
Share options	4, 48
Share ownership	5
Share repurchase	70, Mock 2 - Q5
Share valuation	21, 27, 32 – 35, 38, 56, Mock 1 - Q3, Mock 2 - Q2
★ Shareholder value analysis	Mock 1 - Q6
Social responsibilities	3
Stakeholders	2
Strategic planning	7, 9, 11, 12, 15, 27, 61, Mock 1 - Q1
Swaps	49, 53, 54, 60
Swaptions	49, 52, Mock 2 - Q4
Synergy	33
Takeovers and mergers	32 – 36, 38, Mock 2 - Q2
Tax haven	68
Trade blocs	Mock 1 - Q5
Transaction exposure	44, 45
Transfer prices	67, Mock 1 - Q4, Mock 2 - Q1
Translation exposure	44, 63
Treasury management	66, 67
Weighted average cost of capital	14, 19, 25 – 30, 34, 53

EFFECTIVE REVISION

This is a very important time as you approach the exam. You must remember three things.

> **Use time sensibly**
> **Set realistic goals**
> **Believe in yourself**

Use time sensibly

1   **How much study time do you have**? Remember that you must EAT, SLEEP, and of course, RELAX.

2   **How will you split that available time between each subject?** What are your weaker subjects? They need more time.

3   **What is your learning style?** AM/PM? Little and often/long sessions? Evenings/ weekends?

4   **Are you taking regular breaks?** Most people absorb more if they do not attempt to study for long uninterrupted periods of time. A five minute break every hour (to make coffee, watch the news headlines) can make all the difference.

5   **Do you have quality study time?** Unplug the phone. Let everybody know that you're studying and shouldn't be disturbed.

Set realistic goals

1   Have you set a **clearly defined objective** for each study period?

2   Is the objective **achievable**?

3   Will you **stick to your plan**? Will you make up for any **lost time**?

4   Are you **rewarding yourself** for your hard work?

5   Are you leading a **healthy lifestyle**?

Believe in yourself

Are you cultivating the right attitude of mind? There is absolutely no reason why you should not pass this exam if you adopt the correct approach.

- **Be confident** – you've passed exams before, you can pass them again

- **Be calm** – plenty of adrenaline but no panicking

- **Be focused** – commit yourself to passing the exam

REVISING WITH THIS KIT

Here is some **general guidance** about how to get the most out of this Kit. In the following section we set out a detailed revision plan which you may find useful.

A confidence boost

To boost your morale and to give yourself a bit of confidence, **start** your practice and revision with a topic that you find **straightforward**.

Diagnosis

First look through the Paper 3.7 Passcards and do some revision. Then attempt any **preparation questions** included for the syllabus area. These provide you with a firm foundation from which to attempt exam-standard questions.

Key questions

Then try as many as possible of the **exam-standard questions**. Obviously the more questions you do, the more likely you are to pass the exam. But at the very least you should attempt the **key questions** that are highlighted in the following section. Even if you are short of time, you must prepare answers to these questions if you want to pass the exam - they incorporate the key techniques and concepts underpinning *Strategic Financial Management* and they cover the principal areas of the syllabus.

No cheating

Produce **full answers** under **timed conditions**; practising exam technique is just as important as recalling knowledge. Don't cheat by looking at the answer. Look back at your notes or at your BPP Study Text instead. Produce answer plans if you are running short of time. In the guidance below we have distinguished between questions that should be answered in full and those for which you can prepare a plan.

Imagine you're the marker

It's a good idea to actually **mark your answers**. Don't be tempted to give yourself marks for what you meant to put down, or what you would have put down if you had time. And don't get despondent if you didn't do very well. Refer to the **topic index** and try another question that covers the same subject.

Ignore them at your peril

Always read the **Tutor's hints** in the answers. They are there to help you.

Trial run for the big day

Then, when you think you can successfully answer questions on the whole syllabus, attempt the **two mock exams** at the end of the Kit. You will get the most benefit by sitting them under strict exam conditions, so that you gain experience of the four vital exam processes.

- Selecting questions
- Deciding on the order in which to attempt them
- Managing your time
- Producing answers

Key skills and topics

The examiner for Paper 3.7 is Scott Goddard, previously the examiner of the old syllabus Paper 14 *Financial Management*. He will expect you to display the following skills.

- **Flexible thinking.** Questions will often not spell out the techniques you can use. You will need to select the appropriate techniques yourself. Often, more than one technique is valid, and there may be no single right answer. (Remember this last point when you review our answers: if your answer is different from ours, it does not necessarily mean that it is wrong.)

- **Strategic awareness.** You will be tested in different questions on your ability to **understand strategic implications** of problems you are faced with.

- **Knowledge of current issues.** Be prepared for topical questions on **recent events**, eg developments on the Euro; corporate governance; World Trade Organisation.

The following areas of the syllabus will be particularly important.

- Investment decisions under conditions of uncertainty including portfolio theory, CAPM, the cost of capital, adjusted present value and interactions between investment and financing decisions

- Mergers, acquisitions and other forms of corporate reorganisation including any associated valuation, financing and corporate governance effects

- Risk management. The management of foreign exchange risk and interest rate using options, futures, swaps and other risk management techniques

- The evaluation of foreign investment and financing decisions and the control of operations within an internal group of companies.

You will improve your chances significantly by practising questions in all of these areas. You do need to be comfortable with advanced techniques such as ungearing and regearing betas, and also the calculations relating to futures and options.

Discursive parts of questions are also important, as there will be sub-sections within longer questions asking for discussion, perhaps about the assumptions or limitations of the models or techniques used. Some of the optional questions may not involve any calculations.

- When answering discussion questions that relate to a specific organisation, you need to consider the implications of the situation described in the question and apply your knowledge to that situation. The examiner has complained in the past that answers are often not related to the information given in the question.

- Some discussion questions will be more general in nature, and these can represent the easiest marks on the paper.

Mark guides are given at the end of a number of the longer questions in the Kit. Study these carefully as they will show you what you need to do to achieve the pass mark of 50%.

REVISION PROGRAMME

Below is a suggested **step-by-step revision programme**. Please note that this is not the only approach – you may prefer to do your revision in a different order, and your college may suggest a different approach. However, **as a minimum you must do the key questions if you want to pass the exam.**

The BPP programme requires you to devote a **minimum of 35 hours** to revision of Paper 3.7. Any time you can spend over and above this should only increase your chances of success.

Suggested approach

1   For the topics covered in each revision period, **review** your notes and the relevant summaries in the **Paper 3.7 Passcards**.

2   Then do the **key questions** for that section. These are **shaded** in the table below, and, as we indicated earlier, are the questions you must attempt, even if you are short of time. Try to complete your answers without referring to our solutions.

3   Once you have worked through all of the syllabus sections, **attempt at least one of the Mock Exams under strict exam conditions**. Mock Exam 1 is BPP's prediction of the topics likely to come up in June 2002. Mock Exam 2 is the Pilot Paper for this subject. If you don't have time to do both under exam conditions, have a look at the exam you didn't do to get an idea of the style of questions and the likely topics.

Topic	2001 Passcard Chapters	Questions in this Kit	Comments	Done ✓
Revision period 1				
Objectives of organisations	1	2	A good introduction to the wider considerations that you may need to include when discussing the desirability of a particular investment.	
Corporate governance	2	3	This question emphasises the strong international dimension of this paper, and also covers environmental issues, which are often brought into longer investment appraisals.	
		4	This question tests the ramifications of a key financial decision, how to reward staff.	
		5	You have to think here about the implications of different shareholding patterns on directors' actions.	
Strategy formulation	3	7	Tactical and strategic issues may be brought into longer questions, for example investment appraisal, or mergers and acquisitions.	
Revision period 2				
Financial planning and forecasting	4	10	This question provides good coverage of financial planning, and also illustrates how the financial sources used affect growth.	
		11	This is an example of a question that quite commonly comes up in exams, being presented with an (optimistic) analysis of a situation, and then having to assess what the true financial picture really is.	
		12	This shows how a difficult decision can be resolved by comparisons between different entities.	

Topic	2001 Passcard Chapters	Questions in this Kit	Comments	Done ✓
Revision period 3				
Investment decisions	5	16	This is a good investment appraisal question that gets you into this section of the syllabus.	
		19	A tough investment appraisal question that also involves consideration of the increasingly important topic of real options.	
Valuation of companies	6	24	This question gets you to think about valuation issues, which will also be important when you cover chapters 12 and 13.	
Valuation of debt and market efficiency	7	18	The issues relating to bonds are good topics for shorter optional questions.	
The cost of capital	8	25	This question requires knowledge of the theories of capital structure that you may need to use in longer questions.	
Revision period 4				
Portfolio theory	9	23	This question will focus you on the main issues involved in international portfolio diversification.	
The capital asset pricing model	10	14	A good example of a question that combines a general FM topic with an unusual investment appraisal (of a hotel).	
		29	The format of this question is unusual, but it does provide good coverage of a number of very important issues.	
Revision period 5				
Capital structure and advanced valuation techniques	11	27	A tough question, and you will learn a lot from reviewing the answer.	
		28	As well as demonstrating how different capital structures can affect company valuation, you also need knowledge of the increasingly important free cash flow methods.	

BPP PUBLISHING

Topic	2001 Passcard Chapters	Questions in this Kit	Comments	Done ✓
		31	Real options are likely to come up regularly in 3.7.	
		30	A good question to finish off revision of this part of the syllabus, showing how investment appraisal and capital structure interact.	
Revision period 6				
Mergers and acquisitions	12	35	This is an important revision session as expansion and reorganisation will often be examined as compulsory questions. This question is a good one on acquisitions; note how the calculations are used to support the written analysis.	
		38	Another good assessment of the likely effects of an acquisition.	
Corporate reorganisation	13	37	As an alternative to acquisition, you may be asked to discuss how a company with problems can reorganise, and this question thoroughly covers reconstruction.	
Revision period 7				
Foreign exchange risk	14	42	Hedging foreign exchange and interest rate risks are key topics in this paper, and you must give yourself a lot of practice on the techniques involved.	
		43	This question allows you to practice various ways of hedging foreign currency risk.	
		44	Although a short question, this question covers a number of important issues that may be brought into foreign currency exposure questions.	
Foreign exchange risk: options	15	45	This illustrates the foreign currency options available.	

Topic	2001 Passcard Chapters	Questions in this Kit	Comments	Done ✓
Revision period 8				
Interest rate risk	16	46	This question is similar to a question set in the mock exam.	
		47	This question provides practice at using the Black-Scholes model.	
		48	This is a longer question on Black-Scholes, covering similar issues to a question in the December 2001 exam.	
Revision period 9				
Interest rate risk	16	49	A thorough test of the various ways that interest rate risk can be countered.	
		50	This is a good illustration of the interest rate options available.	
		51	Part (b) tests your understanding of collars.	
Revision period 10				
Swaps	17	52	Part (b) tests your understanding of swaptions.	
		54	This question provides thorough revision on swaps.	
The international financial system	19	53	As well as testing your understanding of swaps, this question is a good test of your understanding of international finance.	
Revision period 11				
The global economic environment	18	59	This question introduces foreign direct investment issues, which may also form the discussion part of a longer question on international investment appraisal.	

Topic	2001 Passcard Chapters	Questions in this Kit	Comments	Done ✓
Appraisal of overseas investment decisions	20	61	A good complicated investment appraisal, but one that also requires thought about the figures you are using.	
		62	A test of your ability to carry out an international investment appraisal, but a question that also has a significant written element.	
		65	This question covers two significant international cash management issues, blocks on dividends and multilateral netting.	
Revision period 12				
Raising capital overseas	21	60	This question is a good test of your understanding of how overseas subsidiaries may be financed.	
Financial control within multinationals	22	66	An illustration of how treasury management may be examined.	
Management of international trade	23	63	A good question to finish your revision of international issues, covering a number of international management issues.	
Corporate dividend policy	24	70	This question ranges well over dividends and share buybacks.	

THE EXAM PAPER

Approach to examining the syllabus

The examination is a **three hour paper** comprising a mix of computational and discursive elements. The core questions will normally be in the form of a case study or case scenario.

Key areas of the syllabus will always be tested in the compulsory questions, and may be tested in the elective questions.

		Number of Marks
Section A:	2 compulsory questions	70
Section B:	Choice of 2 from 4 questions (15 marks each)	30
		100

Additional information

The Study Guide provides more detailed guidance on the syllabus.

Analysis of past papers

The analysis below shows the topics which were examined in the first sitting of the new syllabus and in the pilot paper.

December 2001

Section A

1   Financial performance analysis; divestment
2   Black – Scholes; share options

Section B

3   Weighted average cost of capital; capital structure
4   Hedging interest rate risk
5   Overseas investment; political risk
6   Share repurchases and splits

Pilot paper

Section A

1   Investment appraisal; block on dividend remittance; ethical issues
2   Assessment of takeover bid; tactics used to fight against bid

Section B

3   Forecasts of exchange rates; exchange rate hedging
4   Interest rate risk hedging; swaptions
5   Dividend policy
6   Reduction in current account deficit; role of International Monetary Fund

Formulae to learn

Share price valuation, where company expected to pay dividend increasing at a constant rate of month g

$$P_0 = \frac{D_1}{Ke - g} = \frac{D_0(1+g)}{Ke - g}$$

Irredeemable undated debt, paying after-tax interest, I in perpetuity

$$P_0 = \frac{I(1-t)}{Kdnet}$$

Redeemable debt, paying after-tax interest I to time to n

$$P_0 = \frac{I(1-t)}{1+Kd} + \frac{I(1-t)}{(1+Kd)^2} + \ldots\ldots + \frac{I(1-t)}{(1+Kd)^n} + \frac{Pn \times R}{(1+Kd)^n}$$

where P_n is market value of ordinary share, R is conversion ratio

Multi-asset portfolios with no correlation

$$\sigma = \sqrt{\sigma_a^2 x_a^2 + \sigma_b^2 x_b^2 + \sigma_c^2 x_c^2 + \sigma_d^2 x_d^2}$$

where σ is risk of relevant asset in percentage terms
         x is proportion of portfolio held in each asset

Cost of capital in a geared company

$$Ke_g = Ke_u + [(Ke_u - Kd)\frac{D(1-t)}{E}]$$

Modigliani and Miller adjusted cost of equity

$$Ke_{adj} = Ke_u(1 - tL)$$

where L is marginal contribution of the project to the debt capacity of the firm.

Beta factor of equity in geared company

$$\beta_e = \beta_a \frac{E + D(1-t)}{E}$$

assuming β_d is zero.

International Fisher effect

$$\frac{1+r_f}{1+r_h} = \frac{1+i_f}{1+i_h}$$

Formula for put-call parity

value of put + value of share = value of call + present value of exercise price

CURRENT ISSUES

A new timetable for paying corporation tax is currently being introduced in the UK. It may be included in investment appraisal questions, so you need to read the questions, so you need to read the questions very carefully to see what are taxation payment method is using. Details of the new system are given below.

Corporation tax

Under the new UK system currently being introduced, corporation tax is **payable** by companies **quarterly**.

- In the seventh and tenth months of the year in which the profit is earned
- In the first and fourth months of the following year

This simply means that **half the tax is payable in the year in which the profits are earned** and **half in the following year.**

> **Exam focus point**
>
> This payment timetable is not difficult to remember but details will be given in the exam question anyway.

EXAMPLE: PAYMENT OF CORPORATION TAX

If a project increases taxable profits by £10,000 in year 2, there will be tax payments of £10,000 × 30% × 50% = £1,500 in both year 2 and in year 3 (assuming a tax rate of 30%). It is these tax payments (that are a direct result of the project) that need to be included in a DCF analysis.

As half the tax on profit is paid in the year to which the profits relate, and half in the following year, the **benefit of the capital or writing down allowance** is also felt **half in the year to which it relates** and **half in the following year.**

EXAMPLE: WDAs

Suppose a company purchases plant costing £80,000. The rate of corporation tax is 30% and WDAs are given on a 25% reducing balance basis. Here are the WDAs and reductions in tax payable for years 1 to 4.

	Reducing balance £	Tax saved £	Yr 1 £	Yr 2 £	Yr 3 £	Yr 4 £
				Benefit received		
Purchase price	80,000					
Yr 1 WDA (25%)	(20,000)	6,000	3,000	3,000		
Value at start year 2	60,000					
Yr 2 WDA (25%)	(15,000)	4,500		2,250	2,250	
Value at start year 3	45,000					
Yr 3 WDA (25%)	(11,250)	3,376			1,688	1,688
Value at start year 4	33,750					
Yr 4 WDA (25%)	(8,438)	2,532				1,266
Value at start year 5	25,312					

Points to note

- The tax saved is 30% of the WDA.
- Half of the tax saved is a benefit in the year in question, half in the following year.

EXAMPLE: TAXATION

A company is considering whether or not to purchase an item of machinery costing £40,000. It would have a life of four years, after which it would be sold for £5,000. The machinery would create annual cost savings of £14,000.

The machinery would attract writing down allowances of 25% on the reducing balance basis. A balancing allowance or charge would arise on disposal. The rate of corporation tax is 30%. Tax is payable quarterly in the seventh and tenth months of the year in which the profit is earned and in the first and fourth months of the following year. The after-tax cost of capital is 8%.

Should the machinery be purchased?

SOLUTION

Step 1. WDAs and balancing charges / allowances

We begin by calculating the WDAs and balancing charge / allowance.

Year		Reducing balance £
0	Purchase	40,000
1	WDA	(10,000)
	Value at start of year 2	30,000
2	WDA	(7,500)
	Value at start of year 3	22,500
3	WDA	(5,625)
	Value at start of year 4	16,878
4	Sale	(5,000)
	Balancing allowance	11,875

Step 2. Calculate tax savings / payments

Having calculated the allowances each year, the **tax savings** can be computed. The tax savings effect two years, the year for which the allowance is claimed and the following year.

Year of claim	Allowance	Tax saved	Tax saving				
	£	£	Yr 1	Yr 2	Yr 3	Yr 4	Yr 5
			£	£	£	£	£
1	10,000	3,000	1,500	1,500			
2	7,500	2,250		1,125	1,125		
3	5,625	1,688			844	844	
4	11,875	3,562				1,781	1,781
	35,000 *		1,500	2,625	1,969	2,625	1,781

* Net cost £(40,000 – 5,000) = £35,000

These tax savings relate to capital allowances. We must also take **the tax effects of the annual savings** of £14,000 into account.

The savings increase taxable profit (costs are lower) and so extra tax must be paid. Each saving of £14,000 will lead to extra tax of £14,000 × 30% × 50% = £2,100 in the year in question and the same amount in the following year.

Step 3. Calculate NPV

The **net cash flows and the NPV** are now calculated as follows.

Year	Equipment	Savings	Tax on savings	Tax saved on capital allowances	Net cash flow	Discount factor	Present value of cash flow
	£	£	£	£	£	8%	£
0	(40,000)				(40,000)	1.000	(40,000)
1		14,000	(2,100)	1,500	13,400	0.926	12,408
2		14,000	(4,200)	2,625	12,425	0.857	10,648
3		14,000	(4,200)	1,969	11,769	0.794	9,345
4	5,000	14,000	(4,200)	2,625	17,425	0.735	12,807
5			(2,100)	1,781	(319)	0.681	(217)
							4,991

The NPV is positive and so the purchase appears to be worthwhile.

An alternative and quicker method of calculating tax payments or savings

In the above example, the tax computations could have been combined, as follows.

Year	1	2	3	4	5
	£	£	£	£	£
Cost savings	14,000	14,000	14,000	14,000	
Capital allowance	10,000	7,500	5,625	11,875	
Taxable profits	4,000	6,500	8,375	2,125	
Tax (paid)/received at 30%	(1,200)	(1,950)	(2,512)	(638)	
Yr of (payment)/saving	(600)	(600)			
		(975)	(975)		
			(1,256)	(1,256)	
				(319)	(319)
(Payment)/saving	(600)	(1,575)	(2,231)	(1,575)	(319)

The net cash flows would then be as follows.

Year	Equipment £	Savings £	Tax £	Net cash flow £
0	(40,000)			(40,000)
1		14,000	(600)	13,400
2		14,000	(1,575)	12,425
3		14,000	(2,231)	11,769
4	5,000	14,000	(1,575)	17,425
5			(319)	(319)

The net cash flows are exactly the same as calculated above.

The Euro

The Euro was introduced as the common currency of the following countries on 1 January 2002: France, Germany, Republic of Ireland, Italy, Greece, Belgium, Netherlands, Luxembourg, Spain, Portugal, Austria and Finland.

Recent articles

The content of any relevant articles, published before February 2001 is reflected in the BPP Study Text for *Strategic Financial Management*. Articles published since then, which are of direct relevance to the syllabus, are listed below.

The Greeks are coming, Steve Jay, *Student Accountant*, November/December 2001

A question of values, Steve Jay, *Student Accountant*, October 2001

USEFUL WEBSITES

The websites below provide additional sources of information of relevance to your studies for *Strategic Financial Management.*

- **www.ft.com**

  This website provides information about current international business. You can search for information and articles on specific industry groups as well as individual companies.

- **www.economist.com**

  Here you can search for business information on a week-by-week basis, search articles by business subject and use the resources of the Economist Intelligence Unit to research sectors, companies or countries.

- **www.bpp.com**

  Our website provides information about BPP products and services, with a link to the CIMA website.

- **www.strategy-business.com**

  This website includes articles from *Strategy & Business.*

- **www.invweek.co.uk**

  This site carries business news and articles on markets from Investment Week and International Investment.

- **www.pwcglobal.com/uk**

  The PricewaterhouseCoopers website includes UK Economic Outlook.

- **www.bbc.co.uk**

  The website of the BBC carries general business information as well as programme-related content.

- **www.accaglobal.com**

  ACCA's website. Includes student section.

SYLLABUS MINDMAP

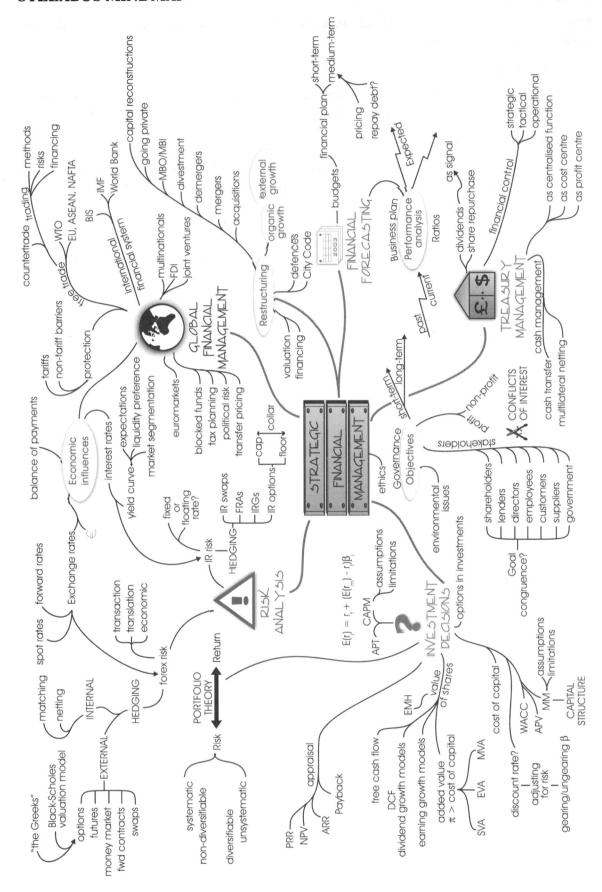

OXFORD BROOKES BSc IN APPLIED ACCOUNTING

The standard required of candidates completing Part 2 is that required in the final year of a UK degree. Students completing Parts 1 and 2 will have satisfied the examination requirement for an honours degree in Applied Accounting, awarded by Oxford Brookes University.

To achieve the degree, you must also submit two pieces of work based on a **Research and Analysis Project.**

- A 5,000 word **Report** on your chosen topic, which demonstrates that you have acquired the necessary research, analytical and IT skills.

- A 1,500 word **Key Skills Statement**, indicating how you have developed your interpersonal and communication skills.

BPP was selected by the ACCA and Oxford Brookes University to produce the official text *Success in your Research and Analysis Project* to support students in this task. The book pays particular attention to key skills not covered in the professional examinations.

> AN ORDER FORM FOR THE NEW SYLLABUS MATERIAL, INCLUDING THE OXFORD BROOKES PROJECT TEXT, CAN BE FOUND AT THE END OF THIS STUDY TEXT.

OXFORD INSTITUTE OF INTERNATIONAL FINANCE MBA

Plans for a new joint MBA have been announced by the ACCA and Oxford Brookes University, who have set up the Oxford Institute of International Finance as a partnership. BPP has been appointed the provider of materials and electronic support. This new qualification will be available worldwide from January 2002.

The MBA is available to those who have completed the professional stage of the ACCA qualification (subject to when this was achieved), as the ACCA's Professional exams contribute credits towards the MBA award.

The qualification features an introductory module (*Markets, Management and Strategy*) followed by modules on *Global Business Strategy*, and *Organisation Change and Transformation*. The MBA is completed by a **research dissertation** and a programme of **self-development**.

For further information, please see the Oxford Institute's website: www.oxfordinstitute.org

Questions

OBJECTIVES AND STRATEGY FORMULATION

Questions 1 to 12 cover Objectives and strategy formulation, the subject of Part A of the BPP Study Text for Paper 3.7

1 PREPARATION QUESTION: CONFLICT

Discuss whether or not the objectives of directors of a quoted company are likely to conflict with those of the company's shareholders.

Approaching the question

Think about the directors' personal goals and the scrutiny and checks over directors' activities. Remember that sanctions against directors can take a number of different forms. You also need to suggest how goal congruence between directors and shareholders might be achieved.

2 STAKEHOLDERS (FS, 6/96 amended)   *27 mins*

(a) Many decisions in financial management are taken in a framework of conflicting stakeholder viewpoints. Identify the stakeholders and some of the financial management issues involved in the situation of a private company converting into a public company.   (4 marks)

(b) You have been summoned to a meeting with your new managing director. He states that as maximisation of the company's share price depends upon the level of earnings per share that is achieved, it is vital to improve profits next year. He gives you a list of suggested ways to achieve this. The list includes the following.

   (i)   Minimise capital investment to reduce depreciation charges.

   (ii) Increase wages and salaries by less than the level of inflation and sell the land that is currently used as a staff sports field.

   (iii) Reduce overdraft charges by delaying payments to creditors.

   (iv) Delay expenditure on new equipment that will reduce pollution levels from the company's factory.

Required

Prepare a memo to the managing director discussing the possible effects on relevant stakeholders of the managing director's suggestions and whether or not they are likely to result in an increased share price.   (11 marks)

                                                                              (15 marks)

3 INTERNATIONAL DIFFERENCES (FS, 6/97 amended)   *27 mins*

(a) Briefly explain what is meant by corporate governance and discuss the major differences that exist between corporate governance practice in the UK and USA.

                                                                              (6 marks)

(b) XYZ plc is a medium-sized company operating in the chemical industry. It is a profitable business, currently producing at below maximum capacity. It has one large factory located on the outskirts of a small industrial town. It is the region's main employer. The company is evaluating a project which has substantial environmental implications.

Required

Discuss the inclusion of environmental costs and benefits into the investment appraisal procedure and explain how this might be done.   (9 marks)

(15 marks)

4   ESOPs (FS, 12/98 amended)   *27 mins*

(a) Discuss the importance and limitations of ESOPs (executive share option plans) to the achievement of goal congruence within an organisation.   (9 marks)

(b) A company is considering improving the methods of remuneration for its senior employees. As a member of the executive board, you are asked to give your opinions on the following suggestions:

  (i)   A high basic salary with usual 'perks' such as company car, pension scheme etc but no performance-related bonuses

  (ii) A lower basic salary with usual 'perks' plus a bonus related to their division's profit before tax

Required

Discuss the arguments for and against *each* option from the point of view of both the company and its employees. Detailed comments on the taxation implications are *not* required.   (6 marks)

(15 marks)

5   SHARE OWNERSHIP (FS, 12/99 amended)   *27 mins*

(a) The pattern of share ownership in the United Kingdom in 1980 and 1995 is illustrated below.

	1980	1995
	%	%
Insurance companies	21	26
Pension funds	28	32
Investment trusts	6	2
Unit trusts (mutual funds)	4	9
Individuals	27	17
Others, including unidentified	14	14
	100	100

Required

Discuss the possible implications of the above changes in share ownership patterns for financial managers of quoted companies.   (9 marks)

(b) The table below shows earnings and dividends for XYZ plc over the past five years.

Year	Net earnings per share £	Net dividend per share £
20X0	1.40	0.84
20X1	1.35	0.88
20X2	1.35	0.90
20X3	1.30	0.95
20X4	1.25	1.00

There are 10,000,000 shares issued and the majority of these shares are owned by private investors. There is no debt in the capital structure.

It is clear from the table that the company has experienced difficult trading conditions over the past few years. In the current year, net earnings are likely to be £10 million, which will be just sufficient to pay a maintained dividend of £1 per share.

Required

Comment on the company's dividend policy between 20X0 and 20X4 and on its possible consequences for earnings.   (6 marks)

(15 marks)

6   PREPARATION QUESTION: POTREN

The directors of two divisions of Potren plc were each asked last year to improve their division's performance.

Summarised financial data at that time for the two divisions is shown below.

	Division A £'000	Division B £'000
Turnover	840	610
Operating profit	95	78
Interest	6	8
Taxable profit	89	70
Fixed assets	580	430
Current assets	290	250
Current liabilities	210	180
Medium and long-term debt	40	55
Shareholders' equity	620	445
Capital employed	660	500

The results for the current year have just been announced as:

	Division A £'000	Division B £'000
Turnover	1,000	650
Operating profit	122	94
Interest	18	8
Taxable profit	104	86
Fixed assets	680	440
Current assets	350	240
Current liabilities	260	170
Medium and long-term debt	140	55
Shareholders' equity	630	455
Capital employed	770	510

Required

Analyse the performance of the two divisions, and from the perspective of the future strategic development of Potren suggest what controls the directors of Potren might introduce to influence the future development of the divisions.

Approaching the question

You need to discuss how both divisions have achieved any boosts in performance and what Potren needs to do to achieve long-term growth.

7 STEPS (FS, 6/98 amended)   *27 mins*

(a) Explain the difference between tactical and strategic decisions in the corporate planning process.   (4 marks)

(b) Describe the steps that a company will normally have to follow in order to develop a strategic financial plan.   (11 marks)

    (15 marks)

8 PULFER (FS, 12/94)   *54 mins*

Pulfer Ltd is a small company that has been operating for five years. It now employs 40 people, and turnover during the last financial year was £875,000. The board of directors has been asked by the company's bank to provide medium-term financial plans for each of the next three years and to clarify the company's financial objectives. The board has decided that the primary financial objectives should be to achieve a return on capital employed (defined as earnings before interest and tax related to shareholders' equity) of 20% per year for each of the first two years, rising to 25% per year in year three, and also to increase dividends per share by 10% per year. The current dividend per share is 2.5 pence.

Statistical analysis by one of the company's managers has produced the following relationships for the last two financial years.

Cost of goods sold	75% of sales
Other expenses (excluding interest)	£5,000 + 18% of sales
Cash (at year end)	minimum 1% of sales
Debtors (at year end)	£10,000 + 20% of sales
Stock (at year end)	£12,000 + 25% of sales
Creditors (at year end)	35% of sales

Net fixed assets are currently £410,000, and cash £9,000. Sales, at current prices, are expected to increase by 15% per year for two years and by either 15% or 25% in year three depending upon how quickly the economy recovers from a recession.

Existing machinery can only satisfy a demand of up to £1.1 million per year (current prices), and the purchase of new machinery at a cost of £200,000 (current prices) would be necessary to satisfy higher levels of demand.

The company's current capital structure is:

	£'000
Ordinary shares (50 pence par value)	200
Reserves	149
12% bank loan	180
	529

No overdraft finance is currently used, but a £50,000 facility exists for short-term financing. The current overdraft interest rate is 10% per year, and interest on any new longer-term debt would be 11% per year.

Other information

(a) Corporation tax is at the rate of 25%.

(b) If external finance is required debt will be used wherever possible as the existing shareholders, who are mainly directors, do not have the funds to subscribe to further equity capital. Any new equity that was necessary would be sought from venture capital organisations.

(c) Restrictive covenants on the existing bank loan limit the current ratio to a minimum of 1.3 to 1, and gearing (total loans to shareholders' equity) to a maximum of 80%.

(d) Cash is kept in a non-interest bearing current account.

Required

As a consultant to Pulfer you have been asked to use the above information to produce *pro forma* profit and loss accounts and a schedule of funding requirements for the next three years. This should be incorporated into a report for the board of directors which also:

(a) Highlights your major findings; and

(b) Discusses any concerns that you have about:

    (i) The financial relationships used by the company as the basis for its forecasts, and

    (ii) The company's financial objectives

Inflation may be ignored in your forecasts. Depreciation/capital allowances may be assumed to equal the cash flows required for the replacement of existing fixed assets. Interest may be assumed to be paid or received at the year end. State clearly any other assumptions that you make.   **(30 marks)**

9   NOIFA LEISURE   *54 mins*

Extracts from the 20X9 annual report of Noifa Leisure plc are shown below.

Chairman's report

'The group's financial position has never been stronger. Turnover has risen 209% and the share price has almost doubled during the last four years. Since the end of the financial year the company has acquired Beddall Hotels for £100 million, financed at 9% per year by a euro floating rate loan which has little risk. Our objective is to become the largest hotel group in the United Kingdom within five years.'

PROFIT AND LOSS ACCOUNT SUMMARIES
FOR THE YEARS ENDING 31 DECEMBER

	20X6	20X7	20X8	20X9
	£m	£m	£m	£m
Turnover	325	370	490	680
Operating profit	49	60	75	92
Investment income	18	10	3	1
	67	70	78	93
Interest payable	14	16	24	36
Profit before tax	53	54	54	57
Taxation	23	19	19	16
Profit attributable to shareholders	30	35	35	41
Dividends	12	12	12	12
Retained earnings	18	23	23	29

[1] Loss/gain on disposal of fixed assets

BALANCE SHEET SUMMARIES AS AT 31 DECEMBER

	20X6 £m	20X7 £m	20X8 £m	20X9 £m
Fixed assets				
Tangible assets	165	260	424	696
Investments	120	68	20	4
	285	328	444	700
Current assets				
Stock	40	45	70	110
Debtors	56	52	75	94
Cash	2	3	4	5
	98	100	149	209
Less current liabilities				
Trade creditors	82	94	130	176
Taxation	18	19	19	20
Overdraft	-	-	42	68
Other	15	24	28	42
	115	137	219	306
Total assets less current liabilities	268	291	374	603
Financed by				
Ordinary shares (10 pence nominal value)	50	50	50	50
Share premium	22	22	22	22
Revaluation reserve	-	-	-	100
Revenue reserves	74	97	120	149
Shareholders' funds	146	169	192	321
Bank loans	42	42	102	102
13% debenture 20Y6-8	80	80	80	180
	268	291	374	603

Analysis by type of activity

	20X6 Turnover £m	20X6 Profit[1] £m	20X7 Turnover £m	20X7 Profit £m	20X8 Turnover £m	20X8 Profit £m	20X9 Turnover £m	20X9 Profit £m
Hotels	196	36	227	41	314	37	471	45
Theme park	15	(3)	18	(2)	24	3	34	5
Bus company	24	6	28	8	38	14	46	18
Car hire	43	7	45	8	52	12	62	15
Zoo[2]	5	(1)	6	(1)	9	0	10	(1)
Waxworks	10	1	11	3	13	4	14	5
Publications	32	3	35	3	40	5	43	5
	325	49	370	60	490	75	680	92

[1]Operating profit before taxation.   [2]The zoo was sold during 20X9.

	20X6	20X7	20X8	20X9
Noifa Leisure plc average share price (pence)	82	104	120	159
FT 100 Share Index	1,500	1,750	1,800	2,300
Leisure industry share index	178	246	344	394
Leisure industry P/E ratio	10:1	12:1	19:1	25:1

Required

In his report the chairman stated that 'the group's financial position has never been stronger'. From the viewpoint of an external consultant appraise whether you agree with the chairman. Discussion of the group's financing policies and strategic objective, with suggestions as to how these might be altered, should form part of your appraisal. Relevant calculations must be shown.

(30 marks)

10   CEDARLODGE (FS, 12/98)   *54 mins*

(a)   Briefly discuss the nature, and advantages, of top-down and bottom-up financial
       planning.   (6 marks)

(b)   Cedarlodge Chemicals has a current turnover of £300 million. Each additional £1 of
       sales is believed to require a total investment in fixed assets, stock and debtors of £1.50,
       but this will also result in the provision of additional finance of 40 pence per £1 of
       additional sales, as various creditors will automatically increase with the increase in
       sales.

       The net profit margin, after tax, of Cedarlodge is 12% and dividends are typically 25%
       of after tax income.

       CEDARLODGE PLC
       SUMMARISED PROFIT AND LOSS ACCOUNT

	£million
Turnover	300
Profit before tax	54
Taxation	18
Profit after tax	36
Dividend	9
Retained earnings	27

       SUMMARISED BALANCE SHEET

	£million
Fixed assets (net)	190
Current assets	146
Current liabilities	(103)
	233
Financed by:	
Issued ordinary shares	50
Reserves	90
Medium and long-term debt	93
	233

       Required

       (i)   Cedarlodge wishes to increase sales by 15% during the next year. Based upon the
              above information, estimate how much external finance will be needed in order
              to achieve this growth rate.   (3 marks)

       (ii)   Estimate the maximum sales growth that can be achieved if only internal funds
              are used.   (5 marks)

       (iii) Estimate the maximum growth that can be achieved if the company does not
              wish to increase its current level of financial gearing. Assume that financial
              gearing is measured by book value of debt:equity.   (6 marks)

       (iv)   Briefly comment upon the likely accuracy of your estimates in (i) to (iii) above.
                                                                            (4 marks)

(c)   Explain the meaning of gap analysis and discuss how gap analysis might be of use to
       Cedarlodge in its financial planning.   (6 marks)

                                                                        (30 marks)

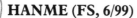

11   HANME (FS, 6/99)   *72 mins*

Hanme plc is a UK based multinational company with subsidiaries in two countries. These subsidiaries, producing biscuits and clothing, are located in Denmark and Turkey respectively. Hanme also produces biscuits and clothing in its UK factories. The company's other activities focus upon the manufacture of electronic products.

Extract from the latest chairman's report.

'I am delighted to report that once again we have had an excellent year with our profit before tax increasing by 22% and the ordinary share price increasing by 30%. All three major product areas showed a growth in profitability, with particularly strong performance from clothing manufacture. Our strong financial position has allowed the company to successfully develop its operations in textiles, food processing and electronics, and plans exist to double turnover within five years in all areas of operation. The management team has the skills to unlock full shareholder value and has every confidence in the future.'

Extracts from the company's financial statements. Data are for full calendar years ending 31 December.

| | Biscuits | | | | Clothing | | | | Group | |
| | UK(£m) | | Denmark(DKr) | | UK(£m) | | Turkey(TL000m) | | £m | |
	20X7	20X8	20X7	20X8	20X7	20X8	20X7	20X8	20X7	20X8
Turnover	25	28	109	120	31	36	1,040	1,650	410	460
Operating exps	15	17	70	74	22	25	480	660	300	328
Net interest	1	1	4	5	-	-	50	80	20	22
Profit before tax	9	10	35	41	9	11	510	910	90	110
Taxation	2.7	3	10.5	12.3	2.7	3.3	204	364	27	33
Profit after tax	6.3	7	24.5	28.7	6.3	7.7	306	546	63	77
Dividends	3.0	4	12.0	14.0	3.0	4.0	306	546	20	25
Retentions	3.3	3	12.5	14.7	3.3	3.7	0	0	43	52
Fixed assets										
Tangible assets	34	39	80	95	33	38	950	950	320	380
Other investments	-	-	-	-	-	-	-	-	12	18
	34	39	80	95	33	38	950	950	332	398
Stock	10	10	42	47	13	14	250	360	185	215
Debtors	8	8	15	18	14	16	280	400	75	80
Cash	-	-	1	1	-	-	20	20	15	17
Current liabilities										
Borrowings	4	4	8	10	-	-	30	60	40	50
Other creditors	13	14	17	19	12	14	280	360	95	112
Net current assets	1	0	33	37	15	16	240	360	140	150
Term loans	8	8	60	60	-	-	70	70	210	225
Net assets	27	31	53	72	48	54	1,120	1,240	262	323
Capital & reserves										
Ordinary shares	5	6	10	14	10	12	300	420	110	119
Reserves	22	25	43	58	38	42	820	820	152	204
	27	31	53	72	48	54	1,120	1,240	262	323

Note. UK shares are £1 par value.

Hanme's share price: End of 20X7   End of 20X8
                        690 pence   897 pence

Hanme's equity beta is 1.32 and the risk free rate is 6%

Comparative industry data:

	Biscuits	Clothing	Electronics
Dividend yield	2.9%	4.3%	5.2%
P/e ratio	11:1	8:1	18:1
Gearing (total loans to equity)	0.85	0.65	0.43

Economic data

	20X7	20X8
FTSE 100 share index (year end)	4,219	5,634
Dividend yield of FTSE 100 shares	4.5%	4.0%
Inflation: UK	3%	3%
Denmark	2%	1%
Turkey	75%	100%

Average exchange rates

	20X7	20X8
Danish kroners /£	8.60	9.50
Turkish lire/£	280,000	350,000

Required

Acting as an external consultant prepare a report which:

(a) Analyses the financial health of Hanme plc and, where appropriate, of its subsidiaries. The analysis should include:

  (i)   An evaluation of the return, in terms of share price and dividends, that Hanme has provided to its shareholders over the last calendar year.

  (ii) Determination of the expected P/E ratio of Hanme.

  (iii) Calculation of, and comment on, relevant growth rates and financial ratios for the group and for individual subsidiaries.

  Highlight any aspects of the group's or subsidiaries' performance which might be of concern to an external investor, and state clearly any assumptions that you make.

(b) Discuss the validity of **all** of the chairman's comments. Your discussion should include comment on the stated strategy of doubling turnover in all areas of operation within five years.

Approximately 20 marks are available for calculations and 20 marks for analysis/discussion.

(40 marks)

12 MUTON   *54 mins*

Muton plc is a textile producer based in the UK, with manufacturing subsidiaries in Thailand, Switzerland and Slovenia. Production in Switzerland and Slovenia is mainly for markets in Europe and in Thailand for the ASEAN (Association of South East Asian Nations) trade bloc and Europe.

A confidential internal memo has just been sent from the managing director to senior managers of the company. Its contents include the following.

'Our medium-term strategic aim is to rationalise and to consolidate our position in the textile industry in the face of strong overseas competition. This may mean the closure of one of our overseas manufacturing subsidiaries. Any subsidiary that does not meet the desired benchmark return on capital employed applied to our UK operations of 25% per year, or a productivity of £10,000 turnover per employee, must be considered as a candidate for closure.' The financial results for the last financial year ending 31 October 20X6 have just been made available, and the managing director has requested their analysis. These results are summarised below.

11

	Thailand	Switzerland	Slovenia
		Swiss Francs	
	Baht million	million	Tolars million
	20X6	20X6	20X6
Profit and loss account			
Turnover	420 9.88	39.1	2,780
Operating profit	42	4.8	240
Net interest payable	10	0.3	70
Profit before tax	32 0.79	4.5	170
Taxation	13	1.6	51
Profit after tax	19 0.47	2.9	119
Balance sheet			
Tangible fixed assets	110 2.72	22.0	710
Current assets			
Stock	52	4.0	480
Debtors	42	4.0	270
Cash	2	0.5	15
Less current liabilities			
Loans and other borrowings	32	1.6	210
Other creditors	45	3.8	320
Net current assets	19	3.1	235
Creditors: amounts falling due			
after more than one year			
Loans and other borrowings	30	2.2	150
	99	22.9	795
Capital and reserves			
Ordinary shares	40	10.0	500
Reserves	59	12.9	295
Total shareholders' funds	99 2.45	22.9	795
Number of employees	2,450	520	1,090
Annual growth in turnover			
(local currency)	15%	3%	8%

19.90%

Notes

(i)   All share capital of the subsidiaries is owned by Muton plc.

(ii) Return on capital employed is based upon earnings before interest and tax.

Exchange rates	*Baht/£*	*SFr/£*	*Tolars/£*
Year end	42.52	2.25	256
Average during the year	40.46	2.30	245

Muton's bank has recently supplied economic data on the three countries where the subsidiaries are located and the UK.

	UK	*Thailand*	*Switzerland*	*Slovenia*
Population (million)	56	58	80	10
Real growth in GDP (annual %)	2	6	1	4
Main bank base rate (%)	6	18	4	12
Inflation (annual %)	3	20	1	9
Balance of payments surplus/				
(deficit) £billion	(15)	(6)	6	(3)

Required

Prepare a report discussing which, if any, of the three overseas subsidiaries should be considered for closure. Include in your report, or as an appendix to it,

(a) An appraisal of the key elements in the financial health of each of the three overseas subsidiaries

(b) Discussion of the benchmarks used by the managing director, and

(c)   The factors that the board of directors of Muton plc should consider before reaching their decision

State clearly any assumptions that you make.

(30 marks)

(Approximately 12 marks will be allocated for calculations and 18 marks for discussion/analysis.)

INVESTMENT DECISIONS AND RISK ANALYSIS

Questions 13 to 31 cover Investment decisions and risk analysis, the subject of Part B of the BPP Study Text for Paper 3.7

---

13 MOVER (FS, 6/99 amended) *27 mins*

(a) You have been asked to provide preliminary advice on whether or not your company's pension fund should make an investment in the shares of Mover plc, a large construction company which is leading a consortium that is proposing to build a rail tunnel between Gibraltar and Morocco. The tunnel is scheduled to open in 20X4. The only information available to you at this time is the cash flow projections published by the tunnel consortium.

Projected cash flows of the tunnel project

	£million
20X0	-450
20X1	-500
20X2	-550
20X3	-650
20X4	-200
20X5	200
20X6	300
20X7	320
20X8	340
20X9	360
20Y0	400
Each year after 20Y0	400

All projections exclude inflation, which is expected to remain at approximately 4% per year.

Required

Undertake an analysis of the proposed tunnel project and advise on whether or not the pension fund should invest in shares of Mover plc. Relevant calculations must be shown.

State clearly all assumptions that you make. In this question *only* reasoned assumptions regarding a discount rate are encouraged. (10 marks)

(b) Explain how inflation affects the rate of return required on an investment project, and the distinction between a real and a nominal (or 'money terms') approach to the evaluation of an investment project under inflation. (5 marks)

(15 marks)

14 UTOPIA HOTELS (FS, 12/97) *72 mins*

It is currently December 20X7. The Utopia hotel group is considering building a new luxury hotel in the English resort of Torquay. The hotel would have a cost of £50 million, ten percent of which is payable immediately, fifty percent payable in one year's time and the balance on completion in approximately two years' time. This expenditure is eligible for tax allowable depreciation on a straight line basis at the rate of 2.5% per year. Corporate taxes are levied at the rate of 33% per year, payable in the year that income arises. Working capital of £1.5 million will be required from the start of year three.

14

The hotel is planned with 300 bedrooms. On average, when a bedroom is occupied, 1.4 people per night are expected to occupy a room. The average room charge per night is expected to be £100, which is valid whether one or more persons use the room. In addition on average £40 per person per day is expected to be spent on food and drink, and £15 per person per day on other hotel facilities. Based upon previous experience the profit margin on food and drink is expected to be 40%, and on other facilities, 30%.

Non-resident guests are expected to provide an annual contribution to cash flow of £1 million per year.

Annual outlays are expected to be:

	£'000
Staff	4,000
Services (gas, electricity, water, local building taxes etc)	1,800
Maintenance and other costs	400

Every five years the hotel would require major redecoration and refurbishment, at a cost of approximately £10 million. These costs are tax allowable in the year incurred.

The group evaluates its hotels over a fifteen operating years time horizon. At the end of fifteen years of operation the hotel is expected to have an after tax value of £60 million, before any end of period refurbishment, and excluding working capital.

All revenues, costs and values are estimated at current prices, and take no account of inflation.

The group is not sure what occupancy rate (the percentage of rooms occupied per night) the hotel would have.

Utopia Hotels - summarised capital structure as at December 20X7

	£m
Net assets	740
Financed by:	
Issued ordinary shares (25 pence par)	120
Reserves	270
12% debenture, redeemable at the par of £100 in Dec 20Z0	200
Bank floating rate term loans	150
	740

The ordinary shares are currently trading at 345 pence per share, and the debentures at £114.

The group believes that it can issue new long dated debentures at a gross yield of 3% above the risk free rate. The systematic risk of the group's shares is 80% of that of the market, and the market return is estimated to be 15%. The new hotel is not expected to significantly affect the group's business risk or financial risk.

The current level of inflation is 3.8% per year and this is expected to continue for the foreseeable future.

Required

(a) Evaluate what occupancy rate the hotel would need to achieve in order to be financially viable, and comment upon your findings.

State clearly any assumptions that you make.   (25 marks)

(b) Discuss how accurate your evaluation is likely to be and explain which parts of your evaluation could be subject to significant error.   (7 marks)

(c) One of the directors of Utopia is concerned about the use of the capital asset pricing model (CAPM) in the evaluation of the proposed hotel, as she has heard that many of the model's assumptions are unrealistic. She suggests the use of the arbitrage pricing theory as an alternative to CAPM.

Prepare a brief report for the board of directors of Utopia which discusses this suggestion, and advise whether or not it should be agreed. (8 marks)

(40 marks)

15 TOVELL (FS, 6/94)   *54 mins*

The selection of appropriate discount rates for capital investments has frequently been a problem for the finance director of Tovell plc. The company has adopted a strategy of diversification into many different industries, in order to reduce risk for the company's shareholders. This has resulted in frequent changes in the company's gearing level and widely fluctuating risks of individual investments.

The current project under appraisal, an investment in the fast food industry where Tovell has no other investments, is expected to generate pre-tax operating cash flows of £420,000 in the first year, rising by 5% per year for the five year expected life of the project. After five years the land and buildings are expected to have a realisable value of £1,250,000 (after any tax effects), the same as their original cost, but in order to continue operations major new investment in equipment would be required at that time. Other fixed assets would have negligible value after five years. The total initial outlay of the project (net of issue costs) is £2.3 million, and all but the land and buildings attracts a 25% per year capital allowance on a reducing balance basis.

The project would be financed by a £800,000 fixed rate loan from a regional development agency at a subsidised interest rate of 6% per year, 3% less than Tovell could borrow at in the capital market. The remainder of the finance would be provided by an underwritten rights issue at a 10% discount on current market price, with total underwriting and issue costs of 5% of gross proceeds. The investment is believed to add £1 million to the company's debt capacity.

Current financial data for Tovell and the fast food industry includes the following.

	Tovell plc	Fast food industry (average)
P/E ratio	12	20
Dividend yield	5%	3%
Equity beta	1.1	1.4
Debt beta	0.2	0.25
Gearing (debt/equity):		
Book values	1.1 to 1	1.6 to 1
Market values	0.4 to.1	1 to 1
Share price	470 pence	n/a
Number of ordinary shares	3.5 million	n/a

The corporate tax rate is currently 30% per year, and tax is payable half in the year profits are earned, half one year in arrears. Treasury bills are currently yielding 5% per year after tax, and the return required by well diversified investors is 12.5% per year.

Required

(a) Provide a reasoned explanation as to whether you would support the company's strategy of diversifying into many different industries. (8 marks)

(b) Prepare a report for the finance director of Tovell plc advising on the financial viability of the proposed fast food investment. Include in the report an assessment of the limitations of the method of appraisal that you have used. Supporting calculations should form an appendix to your report. (22 marks)

(30 marks)

16   ZEDLAND POSTAL SERVICES   *27 mins*

The general manager of the nationalised postal service of a small country, Zedland, wishes to introduce a new service. This service would offer same-day delivery of letters and parcels posted before 10am within a distance of 150km. The service would require 100 new vans costing $8,000 each and 20 trucks costing $18,000 each. 180 new workers would be employed at an average annual wage of $13,000 and five managers at average annual salaries of $20,000 would be moved from their existing duties, where they would not be replaced.

Two postal rates are proposed. In the first year of operation letters will cost $0.525 and parcels $5.25. Market research undertaken at a cost of $50,000 forecasts that demand will average 15,000 letters each working day and 500 parcels each working day during the first year, and 20,000 letters a day and 750 parcels a day thereafter. There is a five day working week. Annual running and maintenance costs on similar new vans and trucks are estimated in the first year of operation to be $2,000 a van and $1,000 a truck. These costs will increase by 20% a year compound (excluding the effects of inflation). Vehicles are depreciated over a five year period on a straight line basis. Depreciation is tax allowable and the vehicles will have negligible scrap value at the end of five years. Advertising in year one will cost $1,300,000 and year two $250,000. There will be no advertising after year two. Existing premises will be used for the new service but additional costs of $150,000 a year will be incurred.

All the above data are based on price levels in the first year and exclude any inflation effects. Wage and salary costs and all other costs are expected to rise because of inflation by approximately 5% a year during the five year planning horizon of the postal service. The government of Zedland will not permit annual price increases within nationalised industries to exceed the level of inflation.

Nationalised industries are normally required by the government to earn at least an annual after tax return of 5% on average investment and to achieve, on average, at least zero net present value on their investments.

The new service would be financed half with internally generated funds and half by borrowing on the capital market at an interest rate of 12% a year. The opportunity cost of capital for the postal service is estimated to be 14% a year. Corporate taxes in Zedland, to which the postal service is subject, are at the rate of 30% for annual profits of up to $500,000 and 40% for the balance in excess of $500,000. Tax is payable one year in arrears. The postal service's taxable profits from existing activities exceed $10,000,000 a year. All transactions may be assumed to be on a cash basis and to occur at the end of the year with the exception of the initial investment which would be required almost immediately.

Required

Acting as an independent consultant prepare a report advising whether the new postal service should be introduced. Include in your report a discussion of other factors that might need to be taken into account before a final decision is made on the introduction of the new postal service.

State clearly any assumptions that you make.   **(15 marks)**

17   MARKET EFFICIENCY (FS, 12/00 amended)   *27 mins*

Your managing director has just returned from a business school seminar on market efficiency. He is puzzled as he was told in the seminar that if markets are efficient all investments have an expected NPV of zero, yet his finance director has told him that it is essential for the company to maximise its expected NPV. He also wonders how recent stock market volatility can be explained if the market is efficient, and how important dividend announcements by companies to the stock market are.

Required

You have been asked to produce a brief report for the managing director discussing his concerns, and the importance of market efficiency to capital investment decisions and dividend policy.

(15 marks)

18 BONDS (FS, 6/98 amended)   *27 mins*

It is 20X8. The following data is taken from a leading financial newspaper, and relates to UK government bonds.

	Yield (%)	
	Interest	*Redemption*
Exchequer 13.5% 20Y0	12.75	10.10
Treasury 7% 20Y2	7.64	9.62
Treasury 8% 20Y6	8.49	9.00
Exchequer 12% 20Z3	8.94	8.00
Consols 4%	7.95	-

Required

(a) Explain what the above data reveals about the current shape of the yield curve, and whether or not this data is consistent with the liquidity preference hypothesis for yield curves.   (5 marks)

(b) You have been asked to advise a company that will need to borrow £10 million in the near future for a period of seven years. Prepare a brief memo, including relevant calculations, which discusses whether or not a zero coupon bond redeemable at the par value of £100 and issued at £55 would be a good way for the company to raise the £10 million. Your advice should take into account the data presented in part (a).   (5 marks)

(c) A financial manager wishes to invest surplus funds in government bonds for a period of one year. If the manager does not expect interest rates to change during the next year, use the following data relating to two bonds of similar risk to recommend how the investment should be undertaken in order to maximise expected yield. Interest is paid annually on the bonds, and annual interest has just been paid.

Coupon	*Maturity*	*Price*	*Redemption yield*
11 ¾%	One year	£103.06	8.43%
11 ¼%	Two years	£103.94	9.01%

(5 marks)

(15 marks)

19 FUELIT (FS, 12/00)   *72 mins*

Fuelit plc is an electricity supplier in the UK. The company has historically generated the majority of its electricity using a coal fuelled power station, but as a result of the closure of many coal mines and depleted coal resources, is now considering what type of new power station to invest in. The alternatives are a gas fuelled power station, or a new type of efficient nuclear power station.

Both types of power station are expected to generate annual revenues at current prices of £800 million. The expected operating life of both types of power station is 25 years.

Financial estimates:

	£ million	
	Gas	Nuclear
Building costs	600	3,300
Annual running costs (at current prices)		
Labour costs	75	20
Gas purchases	500	-
Nuclear fuel purchases	-	10
Customer relations	5	20
Sales and marketing expenses	40	40
Interest expense	51	330
Other cash outlays	5	25
Accounting depreciation	24	132

Other information:

(i)   Whichever power station is selected, electricity generation is scheduled to commence in three years' time.

(ii) If gas is used most of the workers at the existing coal fired station can be transferred to the new power station. After tax redundancy costs are expected to total £4 million in year four. If nuclear power is selected fewer workers will be required and after tax redundancy costs will total £36 million, also in year four.

(iii) Both projects would be financed by Eurobond issues denominated in Euros. The gas powered station would require a bond issue at 8.5% per year. The bond for the nuclear project would be at 10%, reflecting the impact on financial gearing of a larger bond issue.

(iv) Costs of building the new power stations would be payable in two equal instalments in one and two years' time.

(v)   The existing coal fired power station would need to be demolished at a cost of £10 million in three years time.

(vi) The company's equity beta is expected to be 0.7 if the gas station is chosen and 1.4 if the nuclear station is chosen. Gearing (debt to equity plus debt) is expected to be 35% with gas and 60% with nuclear fuel.

(vii) The risk free rate is 4.5% per year and the market return is 14% per year. Inflation is currently 3% per year in the UK and an average of 5% per year in the member countries of the Euro bloc in the European Union.

(viii) Corporate tax is at the rate of 30% payable in the same year that the liability arises.

(ix) Tax allowable depreciation is at the rate of 10% per year on a straight line basis.

(x)   At the end of twenty-five years of operations the gas plant is expected to cost £25 million (after tax) to demolish and clean up the site. Costs of decommissioning the nuclear plant are much less certain, and could be anything between £500 million and £1,000 million (after tax) depending upon what form of disposal is available for nuclear waste.

Required

(a)   Estimate the expected NPV of each of investment in a gas fuelled power station and investment in a nuclear fuelled power station.

State clearly any assumptions that you make.

(NB. It is recommended that annuity tables are used wherever possible)   (20 marks)

(b)   Discuss other information that might assist the decision process.   (8 marks)

(c)   An external advisor has suggested that the discount rate for the costs of decommissioning the nuclear power station should be adjusted because of their risk. Discuss whether or not this discount rate should be increased or decreased.   (4 marks)

(d)   Explain the significance of the existence of real options to the capital investment decision, and briefly discuss examples of real options that might be significant in the power station decision process.   (8 marks)

(40 marks)

20   PREPARATION QUESTION: RODFIN

Rodfin plc is considering investing in one of two short-term portfolios of four short-term financial investments in diverse industries. The correlation between the returns of the individual components of these investments is believed to be negligible.

Portfolio 1

Investment	Beta	Expected return	Standard deviation of return	Amount invested
		%	%	£million
a	1.4	16	7	3.8
b	0	6	2	5.2
c	0.7	10	5	6.1
d	1.1	13	13	2.9
				18.0

Portfolio 2

Investment	Beta	Expected return	Standard deviation of return	Amount invested
		%	%	£ million
a	1.2	14	9	7.1
b	0.8	11	4	2.7
c	0.2	7	3	5.4
d	1.5	17	14	2.8
				18.0

The managers of Rodfin are not sure of how to estimate the risk of these portfolios, as it has been suggested to them that either portfolio theory or the capital asset pricing model (CAPM) will give the same measure of risk. The market return is estimated to be 12.5%, and the risk free rate 5.5%.

Required

(a)   Discuss whether or not portfolio theory and CAPM give the same portfolio risk measure.

(b)   Using the above data estimate the risk and return of the two portfolios and recommend which one should be selected.

Approaching the question

1   In (a) you should explain the reasons for any differences.

2   You can either answer (b) using portfolio theory or the CAPM. You need to explain what would normally determine which one would be used. If you are using CAPM, the formula $E(r_j) = r_f + (E(r_m) - r_f) \beta_j$ is important; if you decide to use portfolio theory, the appropriate formula is:

$$\sigma_p = \sqrt{\sigma_a^2 x_a^2 + \sigma^2 x_b^2 + \sigma_c^2 x_c^2 + \sigma_d^2 x_d^2}$$

21 PHANTOM (FS, 6/98 amended)   *27 mins*

Phantom plc wishes to buy £1 million of shares in each of two companies from a choice of three companies that it might wish to acquire at some future date. The companies are in different industries. Historic five year data on the risk and returns of the three companies are shown below.

	Average annual returns	*Standard deviation of returns*
Mangeit Foods	11%	17%
Altalk Communications	20%	29%
Legi Printers	14%	21%

	Correlation coefficients between returns
Mangeit and Altalk	0.00
Altalk and Legi	0.40
Mangeit and Legi	0.62

An adviser to Phantom plc has suggested that the decision about which shares to buy should be based upon selecting the most efficient portfolio of two shares.

Required

(a) Estimate which of the possible portfolios is the most efficient.   (4 marks)

(b) Discuss whether or not Phantom plc's strategy should be to purchase the most efficient portfolio of two shares.   (5 marks)

Phantom has a number of other long-term fixed interest financial investments. The company's treasury team has received data on two bonds and is considering whether or not to replace its current investment in the bonds of Magnacorp with either bonds of Suprafirm or Grandit. It is now 1 January 20X0.

	Magnacorp	**Suprafirm**	**Grandit**
Annual coupon	8.125%	6.5%	7.8%
Maturity date	31.12.20X9	31.12.20X9	31.12.20X3
Credit rating	A–	BBB+	A–
Market price (£)	107.8	93.1	105.83
Yield to redemption	7.0%	7.5%	6.0%
Redemption price (£)	100	100	100

Required

(c) Prepare reasoned advice to Phantom plc as to whether or not the bonds of Magnacorp should be replaced.   (3 marks)

(d) Evaluate whether or not the market price of Grandit's bonds in the above table is what would be expected from the company's other data.   (3 marks)

                                                                              (15 marks)

22 BARTOO (FS, 12/96 amended)   *27 mins*

(a) Bartoo Ltd has had a very successful year and has generated a cash surplus of £500,000 which will be used for a factory extension in one year's time. The managing director of Bartoo is considering investing in UK equities. A short-list of eight equities has been selected. Details of these are given below.

	Equity beta	Specific risk (as a % of total risk)
ATTA Petroleum	0.90	60%
Flyit Airways	1.32	80%
Mapet Telecom	0.73	62%
Kippa Hotels	1.14	84%
Swapit Bank	0.98	65%
Safer Insurance	1.08	71%
NSH Foods	0.91	68%
Sparket Electric Company	0.78	58%

The managing director wishes to keep risk below that of the market as a whole, but is unsure whether it is better to invest equal amounts in the five lowest beta companies or in all eight companies.

Required

Acting as a consultant to the managing director of Bartoo give reasoned advice on how the £500,000 might be invested. (10 marks)

(b) You have purchased the following data from a merchant bank.

Company	Forecast total equity return %	Standard deviation of total equity return %	Covariance with market return %
Dedton	16	6.3	32
Paralot	12	4.8	19
Sunout	14	4.7	24
Rangon	19	6.9	43

The market return and the market standard deviation are 14.5% and 5% respectively and the risk free rate is 6%. Returns and all other data relate to a one year period.

Required

Estimate the 'alpha' values for each of these companies' shares and explain what use alpha values might be to financial managers. (5 marks)

(15 marks)

23 WONPAR (FS, 12/97 amended)   *27 mins*

(a) Wonpar plc wishes to invest £5 million in ordinary shares for a period of up to five years. The company's directors are debating in which country(ies) to invest.

Director 1 suggests investing in France because it has a relatively high expected return and a low standard deviation of returns.

Director 2 suggests Singapore, as it has the lowest correlation coefficient with the UK stock market.

	\multicolumn{6}{c}{Correlation coefficients between stock market returns}

	UK	USA	France	Japan	Singapore	Hong Kong
UK	-					
USA	0.62	-				
France	0.74	0.49	-			
Japan	0.36	0.43	0.37	-		
Singapore	0.25	0.32	0.41	0.56	-	
Hong Kong	0.44	0.52	0.49	0.67	0.71	-

	Average return (%)	Standard deviation (%)	Beta
UK	12.8	6.3	0.94
USA	11.9	7.2	0.98
France	13.0	4.6	1.06
Singapore	12.9	10.3	1.17
Hong Kong	15.3	14.2	1.32

Notes

(a)   The world beta is 1.

(b)   Average returns have been adjusted for currency changes relative to the pound.

Required

Prepare a brief report that:

(i)   Discusses the possible benefits of international portfolio investment

(ii)   Comments upon the validity of each of the two directors' suggestions   (11 marks)

(b)   The following table shows the quarterly returns of the shares of Graltune plc during the last two years.

	20X8 %	20X9 %
January – March	5.00	4.75
April – June	4.55	4.25
July – September	4.40	4.25
October – December	4.30	4.15

The annual Treasury Bill rate during the same period was:

	%
January 20X8	7.5
July 20X8	7.0
October 20X8	6.75
April 20X9	6.25
October 20X9	6.00

The annual market risk premium is believed to be constant at 8.5%.

Graltune's equity beta is 1.25.

Required

Calculate whether or not the quarterly returns of Graltune in the table are those that might have been expected, and briefly discuss your findings.   (4 marks)

(15 marks)

 24   MUNXAY (FS, 12/99 amended)   *27 mins*

(a)   Briefly discuss reasons for the existence of alpha values and whether or not the same alpha values should be expected to exist in a year's time.   (4 marks)

(b)   Munxay plc is comprised of only four major investment projects, details of which are as follows.

Project	% of company market value	Annual % return during the last 5 years	Risk % standard deviation	Correlation with the market
1	28	10	15	0.55
2	17	18	20	0.75
3	31	15	14	0.84
4	24	13	18	0.62

The risk free rate is expected to be 5% per year, the market return 14% per year, and the standard deviation of market returns 13%.

Required

Assume that Munxay plc's shares are currently priced based upon the assumption that the last five years' experience of returns will continue for the foreseeable future. Evaluate whether or not the share price of Munxay plc is undervalued or overvalued.

(6 marks)

(c) Discuss why your results in (b) above might not correctly identify whether or not the share price of Munxay plc is undervalued or overvalued.   (5 marks)

(15 marks)

25   BERLAN AND CANALOT   *27 mins*

(a) Berlan plc has annual earnings before interest and tax of £15 million. These earnings are expected to remain constant. The market price of the company's ordinary shares is 86 pence per share cum div and of debentures £105.50 per debenture ex interest. An interim dividend of six pence per share has been declared. Corporate tax is at the rate of 31% and all available earnings are distributed as dividends.

Berlan's long-term capital structure is shown below.

	£'000
Ordinary shares (25 pence par value)	12,500
Reserves	24,300
	36,800
16% debenture 31.12.X4 (£100 par value)	23,697
	60,497

Required

Calculate the cost of capital of Berlan plc according to the traditional theory of capital structure. Assume that it is now 31 December 20X1.   (8 marks)

(b) Canalot plc is an all equity company with an equilibrium market value of £32.5 million and a cost of capital of 18% per year. The company proposes to repurchase £5 million of equity and to replace it with 13% irredeemable loan stock.

Canalot's earnings before interest and tax are expected to be constant for the foreseeable future. Corporate tax is at the rate of 31%. All profits are paid out as dividends.

Required

Using the assumptions of Modigliani and Miller explain and demonstrate how this change in capital structure will affect:

(i)   The market value
(ii) The cost of equity
(iii) The cost of capital

of Canalot plc.   (7 marks)

(15 marks)

26   NETRA (FS, 6/97 amended)   *27 mins*

The finance director of Netra plc, a company listed on the AIM (Alternative Investment Market) wishes to estimate what impact the introduction of debt finance is likely to have on the company's overall cost of capital. The company is currently financed only by equity.

Netra plc. Summarised capital structure

	£'000
Ordinary shares (25 pence par value)	500
Reserves	1,100
	1,600

The company's current share price is 420 pence, and up to £4 million of fixed rate five year debt could be raised at an interest rate of 10% per annum. The corporate tax rate is 33%.

Netra's current earnings before interest and tax are £2.5 million. These earnings are not expected to change significantly for the foreseeable future.

The company is considering raising either:

(a) £2 million in debt finance, or

(b) £4 million in debt finance.

In either case the debt finance will be used to repurchase ordinary shares.

Required

(a) Using Miller and Modigliani's model in a world with corporate tax, estimate the impact on Netra's cost of capital of raising:

    (i)   £2 million, or

    (ii) £4 million in debt finance

    State clearly any assumptions that you make.   (6 marks)

(b) Briefly discuss whether or not the estimates produced in part (a) are likely to be accurate.   (4 marks)

(c) Explain any weaknesses of the traditional theory of capital structure and discuss how useful it might be in the determination of the appropriate capital structure for a company.   (5 marks)

                                                             (15 marks)

27   DARON (FS, 12/96)   *72 mins*

The senior managers of Daron, a company located in a European country, are reviewing the company's medium-term prospects. The company is in a declining industry, and is heavily dependent on a single product. Sales volume is likely to fall for the next few years. A general election will take place in the near future and the managers believe that the future level of inflation will depend upon the result of the election. Inflation is expected to remain at approximately 5% if political party A wins the election, or will quickly move to approximately 10% per year if party B wins the election. Opinion polls suggest that there is a 40% chance of party B winning. An increase in the level of inflation is likely to reduce the volume of sales of Daron.

Projected financial data for the next five years, including expected inflation where relevant, are shown below.

Political party A wins, inflation 5% per year

	\$million				
	20X7	*20X8*	*20X9*	*20Y0*	*20Y1*
Operating cash flows:					
Sales	28	29	26	22	19
Variable costs	17	18	16	14	12
Fixed costs	3	3	3	3	3
Other financial data:					
Incremental working capital*	-	(1)	(2)	(3)	(3)
Tax allowable depreciation	4	3	3	2	1

BPP PUBLISHING

Political party B wins, inflation 10% per year

	$million				
	20X7	*20X8*	*20X9*	*20Y0*	*20Y1*
Operating cash flows:					
Sales	30	26	24	20	16
Variable costs	18	16	15	12	11
Fixed costs	3	3	4	4	4
Other financial data:					
Incremental working capital*	1	(2)	(2)	(3)	(3)
Tax allowable depreciation	4	3	3	2	1

* A bracket signifies a decrease in working capital.

Tax allowable depreciation will be negligible after 20Y1 in both cases. Cash flows after year 20Y1, excluding tax savings from tax allowable depreciation, are expected to be similar to year 20Y1 cash flows for a period of five years, after which substantial new fixed investment would be necessary in order to continue operations.

Working capital will remain approximately constant after the year 20Y1. Corporation taxation is at a rate of 30% per year, and is expected to continue at this rate. Tax may be assumed to be payable in the year that the income arises.

Daron's current ordinary share price is 92 centos. (100 centos = $1)

Summarised balance sheet of Daron as at 31 March 20X6

	$ million
Tangible fixed assets	24
Net current assets	12
Total assets less current liabilities	36
Loans and other borrowings falling due after one year	14
Capital and reserves:	
Called up share capital (25 centos par value)	5
Reserves	17
	36

The company can currently borrow long-term from its bank at an interest rate of 10% per year. This is likely to quickly rise to 15.5% per year if the political party B wins the election. The real risk free rate (ie excluding inflation) is 4% and the real market return is 10%.

Daron's equity beta is estimated to be 1.25. This is not expected to significantly change if inflation increases.

Three alternatives are available to the managers of Daron.

(i) Recommend the sale of the company now. An informal, unpublicised, offer of $20 million for the company's shares has been received from a competitor.

(ii) Continue existing operations, with negligible capital investment for the foreseeable future.

(iii) If the political party A wins the election, diversify operations by buying a going concern in the hotel industry at a cost of $9 million. The purchase would be financed by the issue of 10% convertible debentures. Issue costs are 2% of the gross sum raised. Daron has no previous experience of the hotel industry.

Financial projections for the hotel purchase

	$million				
	20X7	*20X8*	*20X9*	*20Y0*	*20Y1*
Turnover	9	10	11	12	13
Variable costs	6	6	7	7	8
Fixed costs	2	2	2	2	2
Other financial data:					
Incremental working capital	1	-	-	1	-

Tax allowable depreciation is negligible for the hotel purchase. The after tax realisable value of the hotel at the end of year 20Y1 is expected to be $10 million, including working capital. The systematic risk of operating the hotels is believed to be similar to that of the company's existing operations.

Required

(a) Using the above data, prepare a report advising the managers of Daron which, if any, of the three alternatives to adopt. Include in your report comment on any weaknesses/limitations of your data analysis. Relevant calculations, including:

  (i)   Estimates of the present values of future cash flows from existing operations, and
  (ii) The estimated adjusted present value of diversifying into the hotel industry

  should form appendices to your report.

  The book value and market value of debt may be assumed to be the same. State clearly any other assumptions that you make.   (32 marks)

  (Approximately 20 marks are available for calculations and 12 for discussion.)

(b) Details of the possible convertible debenture issue for the purchase of the hotel are shown below.

  10% $100 convertible debentures 20Z0, issued and redeemable at par. The debentures are convertible into 60 ordinary shares at any date between 1 January 20Y0 and 31 December 20Y4. The debentures are callable for conversion by the company subject to the company's ordinary share price exceeding 200 centos between 1 January 20Y2 and 31 December 20Y4, and puttable for redemption by the debenture holders if the share price falls below 100 centos between the same dates.

  Discuss the implications for Daron if the diversification is financed with convertible debentures with these terms.   (8 marks)
                                                                                        (40 marks)

28 KULPAR (FS, 12/00)   *54 mins*

The finance director of Kulpar plc is concerned about the impact of capital structure on the company's value, and wishes to investigate the effect of different capital structures.

He is aware that as gearing increases the required return on equity will also increase, and the company's interest cover is likely to decrease. A decrease in interest cover could lead to a change in the company's credit rating by the leading rating agencies.

He has been informed that the following changes are likely.

Interest cover	Credit rating	Cost of long term debt
More than 6.5	AA	8.0%
4.0 – 6.5	A	9.0%
1.5 – 4.0	BB	11.0%

The company is currently rated A.

Summarised financial data:

	£ million
Net operating income	110
Depreciation	20
Earnings before interest and tax	90
Interest	22
Taxable income	68
Tax (30%)	20.4
Net income	47.6
Capital spending	20

BPP PUBLISHING

Market value of equity is £458 million, and of debt £305 million.

Kuplar's equity beta is 1.4. The beta of debt may be assumed to be zero.

The risk free rate is 5.5% and the market return 14%.

The company's growth rate of cash flow may be assumed to be constant, and to be unaffected by any change in capital structure.

Required

(a) Determine the likely effect on the company's cost of capital and corporate value if the company's capital structure was:

(i)   80% equity, 20% debt by market values

(ii) 40% equity, 60% debt by market values

Recommend which capital structure should be selected.

Any change in capital structure would be achieved by borrowing to repurchase existing equity, or by issuing additional equity to redeem existing debt, as appropriate.

The current total firm value (market value of equity plus market value of debt) is consistent with the growth model ($CF_1/(k - g)$) applied on a corporate basis. CF_1 is next year's free cash flow, k is the weighted average cost of capital (WACC), and g the expected growth rate. Company free cash flow may be estimated using EBIT $(1 - t)$ + depreciation – capital spending.

State clearly any other assumptions that you make.   (20 marks)

(b) Discuss possible reasons for errors in the estimates of corporate value in part (a) above.
                                                                          (10 marks)
                                                                          (30 marks)

29 YOUR COMPANY (FS, 6/99 amended)   *72 mins*

(a) Your company has produced a draft guidance manual to assist in estimating the cost of capital to be used in capital investment appraisal. Extracts from the manual, which includes worked examples, are reproduced below.

Guidance manual for estimating the cost of capital

(i)   It is essential that the discount rate used reflects the weighted average cost of capital of the company.

(ii)   The cost of equity and cost of debt should always be estimated using market values.

(iii) Inflation must always be included in the discount rate.

(iv)   The capital asset pricing model or the dividend valuation model may be used in estimating the cost of equity.

(v)   The cost of debt is to be estimated using the redemption yield of existing debt.

(vi)   Always round the solution up to the nearest whole percentage. This is a safeguard if the cost of capital is underestimated.

Illustrative examples

The current date is assumed to be June 20X9, with four years until the redemption of the debentures.

Relevant data

	Book values (£m)	Market values (£m)
Equity (50 million ordinary shares)	140	214
Debt 10% bank loans £40m,		
10% debentures 20Y3 £40m	80	85

	Per share	Annual growth rates
Dividends	24 pence	6%
Earnings	67 pence	9%

The beta value of the company (asset beta) is 1.1

Other information

Market return	14%
Risk free rate	6%
Current inflation	4%
Corporate tax rate	30%

Illustration 1 - When the company is expanding existing activities

Cost of equity

Dividend valuation model: $\dfrac{D}{P} + g = \dfrac{24}{428} + 0.09 = 0.146$ or 14.6%

Capital asset pricing model:

$$ke = Rf + (Rm - Rf) \text{ beta}$$
$$= 6\% + (14\% - 6\%)\ 1.1$$
$$= 14.8\%$$

Cost of debt

To find the redemption yield, with four years to maturity, the following equation must be solved.

Debt is assumed to be redeemed at par value and interest to be payable annually. Estimates are based upon total interest payments of £80m at 10% or £8m per year.

$$85 = \frac{8}{(1+kd)} + \frac{8}{(1+kd)^2} + \frac{8}{(1+kd)^3} + \frac{88}{(1+kd)^4}$$

By trial and error

At 9% interest

8 × 3.240 =	25.92
80 × 0.708 =	56.64
	82.56

9% discount rate is too high

At 7% interest

8 × 3.387 =	27.10
80 × 0.763 =	61.04
	88.14

Interpolating:

$$7\% + \frac{3.14}{3.14 + 2.44} \times 2\% = 8.13\%$$

The cost of debt is 8.13%

Market value of equity £214m
Market value of debt £85m

Weighted average cost of capital:

(CAPM has been used in this estimate. The dividend valuation model would result in a similar answer.)

$$14.8\% \times \frac{214}{299} + 8.13\% \times \frac{85}{299} = 12.90\%$$

Inflation of 4% must be added to the discount rate.

The discount rate to be used in the investment appraisal is 12.90% + 4% = 16.90% or 17% rounded up to the nearest whole percentage.

Illustration 2 - When the company is diversifying its activities

The asset beta of a similar sized company in the industry in which your company proposes to diversify is 0.90.

Gearing of the similar company

	Book values (£m)	Market values (£m)
Equity	165	230
Debt	65	60

Cost of equity

The beta of the comparator company is used as a measure of the systematic risk of the new investment. As the gearing of the two companies differs, the beta must be adjusted for the difference in gearing.

Ungearing

$$\text{Beta equity} = \text{beta assets} \times \frac{E}{E + D(1 - t)}$$

$$\text{Beta equity} = 0.90 \times \frac{230}{230 + 60(1 - 0.3)} = 0.76$$

Using the capital asset pricing model:

$$\begin{aligned} ke &= Rf + (Rm - Rf)\,\text{beta} \\ &= 6\% + (14\% - 6\%)\,0.76 \\ &= 12.08\% \end{aligned}$$

Cost of debt

This remains at 8.13%

Market value of equity £214m
Market value of debt £85m

Weighted average cost of capital:

$$12.08\% \times \frac{214}{299} + 8.13\% \times \frac{85}{299} = 10.96\%$$

The discount rate to be used in the investment appraisal when diversifying into the new industry is 10.96% + 4% inflation, 14.96% or 15% rounded up to the nearest %.

Required

Produce a revised version of the draft manual for estimating the cost of capital. Revisions, including amended calculations, should be made, where appropriate to both written guidance notes and illustrative examples. Where revisions are made to any of the six guidance notes, or to the illustrations, brief discussion of the reason for revision should be included. State clearly any assumptions that you make.   (30 marks)

(14 marks are available for guidance notes and 16 marks for illustrative examples.)

(b) Your company is considering the possible effect on its cost of capital if conversion of a convertible debenture occurs. Stock market prices have recently been very volatile, and could easily rise or fall by 10% or more during the next two months. The convertible is a £20 million 8% debenture with four years to maturity, which was originally issued at its par value (face value) of £100. The debenture may be converted into 20 ordinary shares during the next two months only. The debenture's current market price is £110. Redemption in four years' time would be at the par value of £100. The company has other debts with a market value of £23 million.

Your company could currently issue straight debt at par of £100 with a redemption yield of 9%.

The company's current share price is 520 pence, the market value of ordinary shares is £180 million, and financial gearing 80% equity to 20% debt (by market values).

The systematic risk of the company's equity is similar to that of the market, and is thought to be unlikely to change in the near future.

The market return is 15%.

The corporate tax rate is 30%.

Required

Assuming that no major changes in interest rates occur during the next two months, estimate the impact on the company's cost of capital if:

(i) The company's share price in two months' time is 470 pence, and no conversion takes place.

(ii) The company's share price in two months' time is 570 pence, and conversion takes place.

State clearly any other assumptions that you make.

Comment on your findings. (10 marks)

(40 marks)

30 PROGROW

54 mins

It is currently 20X5. Progrow plc is a company with 350 employees located in Southern England. The company has two main products, a manually operated lifting jack for cars, and a range of high quality metal gardening tools. the products are sold in car accessory shops, garden centres and 'do it yourself' superstores.

The company's production manager has just learned that a new process incorporating new machines could be used in the manufacture of the jacks. The process would require some extra factory space which is currently surplus to the company's needs (and could not be rented to an external user), and would require 25% less direct labour than current jack production techniques. No expansion in jack production from the current level of 250,000 units per year is proposed. The cost of the new machines would total £535,000, and the machines would require incremental annual maintenance costing approximately £45,000 in current prices. The existing machinery could be sold for £125,000 (after any tax effects including the balancing allowance on disposal). This amount would be received in one year's time. If the new machines are not purchased, the existing machinery is expected to be kept for a further five years after which time the after tax scrap value is expected to be negligible.

Prices and costs currently associated with the company's products are as follows.

	Jacks £	*Garden tools (average)* £
Selling price (per unit)	11.20	7.80
Direct costs (per unit):		
Skilled labour	1.80	0.50
Unskilled labour	2.30	2.80
Materials	3.60	2.40
Indirect costs:		
Apportionment of management salaries	0.43	0.26
Apportionment of head office overhead	0.54	0.44

Incremental annual interest costs associated with the finance of the new machines are £10,000.

As the company is located in a government approved development area, expenditure on any new machinery would be eligible for first year tax allowable depreciation of 50%, with a 25% reducing balance thereafter. The expected working life of the machines is five years, and at that time they are expected to have a scrap value of £40,000.

If the machines are purchased 26 skilled and 24 unskilled workers would be made redundant. Redundancy costs are on average £9,000 for skilled workers, and £5,000 for unskilled workers. Twenty of the remaining skilled workers would need to retrain to use the new machines at a cost of £750 per person. These are all tax allowable costs.

As an alternative to buying the new machines the company could use the spare factory space to expand garden tool production. For a capital equipment expenditure of £200,000 the existing annual production of 400,000 garden tools could be increased by 70,000 units per year. Expenditure on this capital equipment is also eligible for 50% first year tax allowable depreciation, and a 25% reducing balance thereafter. This new equipment would have a scrap value of £14,000 after five years.

The managing director of Progrow is concerned that failure to invest in the new jack manufacturing process might lead to the company losing significant market share in the jack market if competitors were able to reduce their prices in real terms as a result of introducing the new process.

If the new jack manufacturing process is introduced Progrow proposes that prices of jacks would be kept constant for the next few years. Garden tool prices are expected to increase by an average of 5% per year, wage and material costs by 6% per year. All other production and maintenance costs are expected to increase by 4% per year.

The financial gearing of Progrow is not expected to change with either the adoption of the new jack production process, or expansion of garden tool production.

The company is listed on the AIM, and its overall beta equity is 1.30. The average beta equity of other garden tool manufacturers is 1.4, but no data is available for jack manufacturers. The average market weighted gearing of other garden tool manufacturers is 50% equity and 50% debt. The appropriate risk free rate is 7% and the estimated market return 14%. Corporate taxation is at the rate of 25% and is payable one year in arrears. It is now late in the current tax year.

Summarised balance sheet of Progrow as at 31 March 20X5

	£'000
Fixed assets	2,800
Current assets	2,400
Less current liabilities	(1,950)
	3,250
Creditors: amounts payable after more than one year	
Clearing bank term loan	400
15% secured bond 20Y5 (redeemable at par of £100)	1,000
Issued share capital (25 pence par)	700
Reserves	1,150
	3,250

The company's ex-div share price is 162 pence, and bond price £125. Garden tool and jack manufacture represent 60% and 40% respectively of the company's total market value. All cash flows may be assumed to occur at year ends. Corporate debt may be assumed to be risk free.

Required

Prepare a report advising the directors of Progrow whether to purchase the new machines or to expand garden tool production. Highlight in your report any further information requirements, or other factors that might influence the decision process. Relevant calculations, including expected net present values, should form an appendix to your report. State clearly any assumptions that you make.   **(30 marks)**

(Approximately 20 marks are available for calculations, and 10 for discussion.)

31   HUSOC   *27 mins*

Husoc Ltd publishes textbooks for schools and further education colleges. It specialises in humanities and business subjects. In this market Husoc has one main competitor, Isecon Ltd. Generally however over the last few years Husoc's results have been much better than Isecon; many schools and colleges buy books for the relevant subjects only from Husoc.

Recent government concern over the level of business awareness possessed by school-leavers has resulted in the launch of a new business diploma. This qualification has three levels taken over three years; assessment is by a variety of different means.

Husoc decided to invest in this market two years ago by publishing a series of textbooks; Isecon decided not to publish material when the qualification was initially available. Husoc's projected costs and revenues for the first five years of the project were as follows.

Year	Revenues	Costs		Other production
		Authorship		
		New material	Updating	
	£'000	£'000	£'000	£'000
1	-	100	-	50
2	180	125	30	90
3	450	225	75	150
4	710	-	90	160
5	960	-	100	180

Textbooks for the lowest qualification level were published a year ago. Sales however were disappointing as far fewer students than expected enrolled. Husoc has amended cost and revenue estimates for years 3 to 5. The revised revenue and other (non-authorship) production cost figures for years 2 to 5 are expected to be as follows:

Year	Revenues	Other production costs
	£'000	£'000
2	90	75
3	360	110
4	520	130
5	900	160

Textbooks for the second level of qualification are now (at the end of year 2) in final draft stage. Husoc is currently deciding whether to go ahead with publication of this material and to commission authors to write material for the final level of qualification, or whether to abandon plans to produce material for the two higher levels and just bring out updated textbooks for the lowest level each year. If Husoc does the latter, it will save £30,000 of non-authorship costs for year 2, and costs and revenues for years 3 to 5 would be expected to be as follows:

Year	Revenues	Costs		Other production
		Authorship		
		New material	Updating	
	£'000	£'000	£'000	£'000
3	300	-	15	45
4	370	-	25	45
5	390	-	25	55

Husoc uses a 10% pre-tax cost of capital to appraise its investments.

Required

(a) Calculate the net present value from now until the end of year 5 of the project if Husoc decides to:

   (i) Publish textbooks for the two higher levels of the qualification (use the revised year 3-5 figures for revenues and other production costs and the original estimates for authorship costs).

   (ii) Abandon plans to publish books for those levels and only publish updated textbooks for the lowest level.   (4 marks)

(b) Discuss the other factors that might influence the process of deciding whether to undertake further investment and indicate how these factors might be incorporated into DCF calculations.   (11 marks)

(15 marks)

34

CORPORATE EXPANSION AND REORGANISATION

Questions 32 to 39 cover Corporate expansion and reorganisation, the subject of Part C of the BPP Study Text for Paper 3.7.

32 PREPARATION QUESTION: BID CALCULATIONS

Provincial plc is contemplating a bid for the share capital of National plc. The following statistics are available.

	Provincial plc	*National plc*
Number of shares	14 million	45 million
Share price	840p	166p
Latest equity earnings	£11,850,000	£9,337,500

Provincial plc's plan is to reduce the scale of National plc's operations by selling off a division which accounts for £1,500,000 of National plc's latest earnings, as indicated above. The estimated selling price for the division is £10.2 million.

Earnings in National plc's remaining operations could be increased by an estimated 20% on a permanent basis by the introduction of better management and financial controls. Provincial plc does not anticipate any alteration to National plc's price/earnings multiple as a result of these improvements in earnings.

To avoid duplication, some of Provincial plc's own property could be disposed of at an estimated price of £16 million. Rationalisation costs are estimated at £4.5 million.

Required

(a) Calculate the effect on the current share price of each company, all other things being equal, of a two for nine share offer by Provincial plc, assuming that Provincial plc's estimates are in line with those of the market.

(b) Offer a rational explanation of why the market might react to the bid by valuing National plc's shares at (i) a higher figure and (ii) a lower figure than that indicated by Provincial plc's offer even though the offer is in line with market estimates of the potential merger synergy.

(c) Assume that Provincial plc is proposing to offer National plc shareholders the choice of the two for nine share exchange or a cash alternative. Advise Provincial plc whether the cash alternative should be more or less than the current value of the share exchange, giving your reasons.

(d) Assume now that Provincial plc, instead of making a two for nine share exchange offer, wishes to offer an exchange which would give National plc shareholders a 10% gain on the existing value of their shares. Calculate what share exchange would achieve this effect, assuming the same synergy forecasts as before.

Approaching the question

1 The first part of the question requires the calculation of the theoretical market capitalisation of the new group post merger. This can be derived by calculating the new level of equity earnings in National plc and applying the P/E ratio to find the new value of the earnings.

2 The capital inflows and outflows arising from acquisition can then be included to arrive at the total post merger capitalisation. Since the number of shares in the new group is known, this can then be used to find the theoretical share prices.

3 Parts (b) and (c) require an understanding of the way in which the market reacts to bids in practice, and of factors influencing the way in which investors will react to cash and paper offers.

35

33   PEDEN AND TULEN (FS, 12/99 amended)   *27 mins*

(a) The total values (equity plus debt) of two companies, Peden and Tulen are expected to fluctuate according to the state of the economy.

	Economic state		
	Recession	*Slow growth*	*Rapid growth*
Probability	0.15	0.65	0.20
Total values			
Peden (£m)	42	55	75
Tulen (£m)	63	80	120

Peden currently has £45 million of debt, and Tulen £10 million of debt.

Required

If the two companies were to merge, and assuming that no operational synergy occurs as a result of the merger, calculate the expected value of debt and equity of the merged company. Explain the reasons for any difference that exists from the expected values of debt and equity if they do not merge.   (10 marks)

(b) Explain why synergy might exist when one company merges with or takes over another company.   (5 marks)

(15 marks)

34   OAKTON (FS, 6/98 amended)   *54 mins*

(a) It is 20X8. Oakton plc, a company quoted on the London Stock Exchange, has cash balances of £23 million which are currently invested in short-term money market deposits. The cash is intended to be used primarily for strategic acquisitions, and the company has formed an acquisition committee with a remit to identify possible acquisition targets. The committee has suggested the purchase of Mallard plc, a company in a different industry that is quoted on the AIM (Alternative Investment Market). Although Mallard is quoted, approximately 50% of its shares are still owned by three directors. These directors have stated that they might be prepared to recommend the sale of Mallard, but they consider that its shares are worth £22 million in total.

Summarised financial data

	Oakton plc £'000	Mallard plc £'000
Turnover	480,000	38,000
Pre tax operating cash flow	51,000	5,300
Taxation (33%)	16,830	1,749
Post tax operating cash flow	34,170	3,551
Dividend	11,000	842
Fixed assets (net)	168,000	8,400
Current assets	135,000	4,700
Current liabilities	99,680	3,900
	203,320	9,200

Financed by

Ordinary shares (25 pence par)	10,000	(Mallard 10 pence par)	500
Reserves	158,320		5,200
12% Debentures 20Y6	20,000		
10% Bank term loan	15,000		
		Recent 11% bank loan	3,500
	203,320		9,200

Current share price	785 pence	370 pence
Earnings yield	10.9%	19.2%
Average dividend growth during the last five years	7% p.a.	8% p.a.
Equity beta	0.95	0.8
Industry data:		
Average P/E ratio	10:1	6:1
Average P/E of companies recently taken over, based upon the offer price	12:1	7:1

The risk free rate of return is 6% per annum and the market return 14% per annum.

The rate of inflation is 2.4% per annum and is expected to remain at approximately this level.

Expected effects of the acquisition would be:

(i)   50 employees of Mallard would immediately be made redundant at an after tax cost of £1.2 million. Pre-tax annual wage savings are expected to be £750,000 (at current prices) for the foreseeable future.

(ii)   Some land and buildings of Mallard would be sold for £800,000 (after tax).

(iii)   Pre-tax advertising and distribution savings of £150,000 per year (at current prices) would be possible.

(iv)   The three existing directors of Mallard would each be paid £100,000 per year for three years for consultancy services. This amount would not increase with inflation.

Required

Estimate the value of Mallard based upon:

(i)   The use of comparative P/E ratios
(ii)   The dividend valuation model
(iii)   The present value of relevant operating cash flows over a 10 year period

and critically discuss the advantages and disadvantages of *each* of the three valuation methods.

Recommend whether or not Oakton should offer £22 million for Mallard's shares.

(20 marks; approximately 8 marks are available for discussion)

(b)   Briefly discuss the factors that might influence whether or not Oakton plc uses its *cash balances* rather than shares or bonds, to make payment for Mallard.   (5 marks)

(c)   Discuss the importance of financial post-audits following a merger or takeover.

(5 marks)

(30 marks)

35   DEMAST (FS, 6/94)   *54 mins*

Demast Ltd has grown during the last five years into one of the UK's most successful specialist games manufacturers. The company's success has been largely based on its Megaoid series of games and models, for which it holds patents in many developed countries. The company has attracted the interest of two plcs, Nadion, a traditional manufacturer of games and toys, and BZO International, a conglomerate group that has grown rapidly in recent years through the strategy of acquiring what it perceives to be undervalued companies.

Summarised financial details of the three companies are shown below.

DEMAST LTD
SUMMARISED BALANCE SHEET AS AT 31 DECEMBER 20X3

	£'000	£'000
Fixed assets (net)		8,400
Current assets		
Stock	5,500	
Debtors	3,500	
Cash	100	
		9,100
Less *current liabilities*		
Trade creditors	4,700	
Tax payable	1,300	
Overdraft	1,200	
		7,200
		10,300
Medium and long-term loans		3,800
Net assets		6,500
		£'000
Financed by		
Ordinary shares (25 pence nominal)		1,000
Reserves		5,500
		6,500

SUMMARISED PROFIT AND LOSS ACCOUNT FOR THE YEAR
ENDED 31 DECEMBER 20X3

	£'000
Turnover	27,000
Profit before tax	4,600
Taxation	1,380
	3,220
Dividend	1,500
Retained earnings	1,720

Additional information

(a)   The realisable value of stock is believed to be 90% of its book value.
(b)   Land and buildings, with a book value of £4 million, were last revalued in 20W9.
(c)   The directors of the company and their families own 25% of the company's shares.

	Demast	Nadion	BZO Int
Turnover (£m)	27	112	256
Profit before tax (£m)	4.6	11	24
Fixed assets (£m net)	8.4	26	123
Current assets (£m)	9.1	41	72
Current liabilities (£m)	7.2	33	91
Overdraft (£m)	1.2	6	30
Medium and long-term liabilities (£m)	3.8	18	35
Interest payable (£m)	0.5	3	10
Share price (pence)	-	320	780
EPS (pence)	80.5	58	51
Estimated required return on equity	16%	14%	12%
Growth trends per year:			
Earnings	12%	6%	13%
Dividends	9%	5%	8%
Turnover	15%	10%	23%

Assume that the following events occurred shortly after the above financial information was produced.

7 September. BZO makes a bid for Demast of two ordinary shares for every three shares of Demast. The price of BZO's ordinary shares after the announcement of the bid is 710 pence. The directors of Demast reject the offer.

2 October. Nadion makes a counter bid of 170 pence cash per share plus one £100 10% convertible debenture 20Y8, issued at par, for every £6.25 nominal value of Demast's shares. Each convertible debenture may be exchanged for 26 ordinary shares at any time between 1 January 20X7 and 31 December 20X9. Nadion's share price moves to 335 pence. This offer is rejected by the directors of Demast.

19 October. BZO offers cash of 600 pence per share. The cash will be raised by a term loan from the company's bank. The board of Demast are all offered seats on subsidiary boards within the BZO group. BZO's shares move to 680 pence.

20 October. The directors of Demast recommend acceptance of the revised offer from BZO.

24 October. BZO announces that 53% of shareholders have accepted its offer and make the offer unconditional.

Required

(a) Discuss the advantages and disadvantages of growth by acquisition. (7 marks)

(b) Discuss whether or not the bids by BZO and Nadion are financially prudent from the point of view of the companies' shareholders. Relevant supporting calculations must be shown. (17 marks)

(c) Discuss problems of corporate governance that might arise for the shareholders of Demast Ltd and BZO plc. (6 marks)

(30 marks)

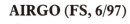

36   AIRGO (FS, 6/97)   *54 mins*

The directors of ASTER plc have decided to concentrate the company's activities on three core areas, bus services, road freight and taxis. As a result the company has offered for sale a regional airport that it owns. The airport handles a mixture of short-haul scheduled services, holiday charter flights and air freight, but does not have a runway long enough for long-haul international operations.

The existing managers of the airport, along with some employees, are attempting to purchase the airport through a leveraged management buy-out, and would form a new unquoted company, Airgo plc. The total value of the airport (free of any debt) has been independently assessed at £35 million.

The managers and employees can raise a maximum of £4 million towards this cost. This would be invested in new ordinary shares issued at the par value of 50p per share. ASTER plc, as a condition of the sale, proposes to subscribe to an initial 20% equity holding in the company, and would repay all debt of the airport prior to the sale.

EPP Bank is prepared to offer a floating rate loan of £20 million to the management team, at an initial interest rate of LIBOR plus 3%. LIBOR is currently at 10%. This loan would be for a period of seven years, repayable upon maturity, and would be secured against the airport's land and buildings. A condition of the loan is that gearing, measured by the book value of total loans to equity, is no more than 100% at the end of four years. If this condition is not met the bank has the right to call in its loan at one month's notice. Airgo would be able to purchase a four year interest rate cap at 15% for its loan from EPP Bank for an up-front premium of £800,000.

A venture capital company, Allvent plc, is willing to provide up to £15 million in the form of unsecured mezzanine debt with attached warrants. This loan would be for a five year period, with principal repayable in equal annual instalments, and have a fixed interest rate of 18% per year.

The warrants would allow Allvent to purchase 10 Airgo shares at a price of 100 pence each for every £100 of initial debt provided, at any time after two years from the date the loan is agreed. The warrants would expire after five years.

Most recent annual profit and loss account of the airport

	£'000
Landing fees	14,000
Other turnover	8,600
	22,600
Labour	5,200
Consumables	3,800
Central overhead payable to ASTER	4,000
Other expenses	3,500
Interest paid	2,500
	19,000
Taxable profit	3,600
Taxation (33%)	1,188
Retained earnings	2,412

ASTER has offered to continue to provide central accounting, personnel and marketing services to Airgo for a fee of £3 million per year, with the first fee payable in year one. All revenues and cost (excluding interest) are expected to increase by approximately 5% per year.

Required

(a) Prepare a report for the managers of the proposed Airgo plc discussing the advantages and disadvantages for the management buy-out of the proposed financing mix. Include in your report an evaluation of whether or not the EPP Bank's gearing restriction in four years' time is likely to be a problem. All relevant calculations must be shown. State clearly any assumptions that you make.   (22 marks)

(b) As a possible alternative to obtaining finance from Allvent, assume that a venture capital company that you are employed by has been approached by the management buy-out team for a £10 million loan. Discuss what information, other than that provided above, would be required from the MBO team in order to decide whether or not to agree to the loan.

(8 marks)

(30 marks)

37   DRICOM (FS, 12/97)   *54 mins*

It is currently December 20X7. Dricom plc is a manufacturer of mobile phones. The company was successful in the early 20X0s, and established a small chain of retail shops in major UK cities. In 20X5-X6 the company's new products experienced reliability problems and competition from technologically superior products, causing sales to fall by forty percent from 20X4-X5 levels. This led to substantial losses being made in both 20X5-X6 and 20X6-X7.

The company's managers are confident that the technical problems can be overcome, but this will require an investment of £2.25 million for new automated equipment and quality monitoring machinery. Dricom's bank, BXT Bank, is concerned about the company's recent performance, and a new debt or equity issue on the stock market is not possible. Without the new investment Dricom is unlikely to be competitive, and might not survive the next financial year. With the new investment profits before interest and tax are forecast to be at least £750,000 per year from 20X8-X9 for at least five years.

Dricom plc
Summarised balance sheet as at 30 September 20X7

	£'000
Land and buildings	1,500
Plant and machinery (net)	2,100
	3,600
Current assets	
Stocks	1,340
Debtors	1,090
Cash at bank and in hand	35
Total current assets	2,465
Creditors: amounts falling due within one year	
Overdraft	620
Other creditors	940
	1,560
Total assets less current liabilities	4,505
Creditors: amounts falling due after more than one year	
Term loan (from BXT Bank)	800
9% debenture 20Z0	500
8% convertible debenture 20X9	1,000
10% loan stock 20Y5	500
	2,800
Capital and reserves	
Called up share capital (£1 par value)	1,000
Share premium account	945
Revenue reserves	(240)
Total shareholders' funds	1,705
Total capital employed	4,505

Notes

(a)   The 9% straight debenture is secured by a fixed charge on the company's main factory building, the convertible debenture and term loan by a floating charge on fixed assets. The loan stock and overdraft are unsecured.

41

(b) The land and buildings are believed to have a realisable value 20% less than their net book value.

(c) If the company ceased trading stocks would be sold at 50% of their book value.

(d) The new equipment would result in fifty staff being made redundant, with an immediate after tax cost of £500,000. If the company were to be liquidated after tax redundancy payments would total £1 million. Redundancy payments may be assumed to rank before unsecured creditors.

(e) Obsolete machinery with a net book value of £800,000 will be sold for £300,000 irrespective of whether or not the new investment takes place. The remainder of the plant and machinery could be disposed of at net book value. All disposal values are after tax.

(f) The overdraft currently costs 10% per year and the bank term loan 12% per year.

(g) The company's current share price is 23 pence, loan stock price £78, straight debenture price £90 and convertible debenture price £94. All marketable debt has a par and redemption value of £100.

Dricom's finance directors believes that a corporate restructuring could solve the company's problems, and has made the following proposals.

(a) Existing shareholders are to be offered 28 pence per share to redeem their shares, which would then be cancelled.

(b) £1 million would be provided by a venture capital organisation in return for 700,000 new 25 pence par value ordinary shares.

(c) The company's directors and employees would subscribe to 500,000 new 25 pence ordinary shares at a price of 150 pence per share.

(d) The convertible debenture is to be replaced by new ordinary shares (par value 25 pence), with 60 ordinary shares for every £100 nominal value loan stock.

(e) The term loan is to be renegotiated with the bank and the total amount of the loan increased to £2 million. This would have an expected interest charge of 13% per annum. A floating charge on fixed assets would be offered on the overdraft.

(f) All other long-term loans would remain unchanged.

Apart from the directors, none of the above parties have yet been consulted regarding the proposed reconstruction.

Following a reconstruction no corporate tax is expected to be paid for at least two years. The corporate tax rate is 33%.

The average price/earnings ratio in Dricom's industry is 12:1.

Required

Acting as a consultant to Dricom plc prepare a report evaluating whether or not the suggested scheme of reconstruction is likely to succeed.

A full pro forma balance sheet is not required as part of your evaluation.

State clearly any assumptions that you make.   **(30 marks)**

38   PLANETSPAN (FS, 12/98)   *72 mins*

The chairman of Planetspan plc has asked two executives to produce press releases that might be sent to newspapers in order to justify the acquisition of LSER plc, a company in the same industry.

The executives were provided with the following information.

	Planetspan	*LSER*
Turnover	£168 million	£110 million
Share price (£1 par value shares)	220 pence	387 pence
Earnings per share	14 pence	36 pence
Number of issued shares	125 million	19.44 million
Gearing by market value	Debt 40%, Equity 60%	Debt 20%, Equity 80%
Corporate tax rate	33%	33%
Equity beta	1.25	1.1

Other information

The acquisition is not expected to have a significant effect on the equity beta or cost of equity of Planetspan.

Planetspan can currently borrow funds at an interest rate of 10% per year.

The acquisition would increase the debt capacity of Planetspan by £20 million.

LSER currently possesses £3 million of marketable securities.

LSER has £20.35 million par value of 8% debt which matures in five years' time. This debt obligation would be taken over by Planetspan. Interest on this debt is payable annually. LSER can currently issue new debt at an interest rate of 12% per year. An expected £1 million per year after tax would be saved in the operating costs of LSER if it was to be taken over by Planetspan.

The acquisition would be wholly financed by an issue of new shares by Planetspan.

The expected premium over the current share price that will be necessary to purchase LSER is 25%.

Advertising, legal and other expenses associated with the purchase are expected to be £6 million, payable almost immediately.

The risk free rate is 6% per year, and the market return 14% per year.

Expected after tax operating cash flows for the next 10 years with current operations:

Year	Planetspan	LSER
1	£21.6m	£8m
2	£26m	£9m
3	£28m	£10m
4	£34m	£11m
5	£40m	£12m
6-10	£48m	£14m

Note. These are the cash flows from operations and do not reflect financing costs or income from marketable securities.

Summarised press release one

The proposed acquisition is likely to lead to an *immediate* increase in earnings per share for the new company, and a potential post acquisition market price of 230 pence per share.

The new company will be less risky for both bondholders and shareholders as the volatility of cash flows will be reduced, which should lead to a reduction in the company's cost of finance.

Synergies from the acquisition will increase cash flows which should eventually increase the share price even further.

Summarised press release two

The key factor determining the success or failure of an acquisition is the effect of the acquisition on the group's future cash flows. Based upon Planetspan's assessment of future discounted cash flows, using the widely accepted adjusted present value technique, the acquisition is likely to result in an adjusted present value of approximately £10 million, and to significantly increase shareholder wealth.

Required

Provide relevant calculations to confirm or dispute the figures contained within the two summarised press releases to the likely post-acquisition earnings per share, share price and adjusted present value, and discuss the validity of *all* of the statements within the press releases.

State clearly any assumptions that you make.

(Approximately 25 marks are available for calculations and 15 marks for discussion.)

(40 marks)

39   GROCAS (FS, 6/95)   *54 mins*

The finance director of Grocas plc has ordered a strategic review of the company's operating subsidiaries. Assume that it is now early in 20X6. A summary of the subsidiaries is provided below.

	Turnover £m	Operating profit £m	Group charges £m	Profit before tax £m
Subsidiary 1: Textile industry				
20X2	28.3	1.2	0.8	0.4
20X3	30.5	1.5	1.0	0.5
20X4	29.3	0.8	1.0	(0.2)
20X5	28.1	1.0	1.0	0
Subsidiary 2: Engineering				
20X2	35.8	(1.3)	1.2	(2.5)
20X3	38.5	0.6	1.4	(0.8)
20X4	40.7	1.5	1.4	0.1
20X5	39.6	2.1	1.4	0.7
Subsidiary 3: Food processing				
20X2	55.8	6.2	2.8	3.4
20X3	66.9	6.8	3.4	3.4
20X4	87.3	7.0	3.8	3.2
20X5	93.6	7.4	4.0	3.4
Subsidiary 4: Printing				
20X2	18.3	2.6	1.4	1.2
20X3	28.6	4.8	3.6	1.2
20X4	40.3	8.4	4.8	3.6
20X5	51.4	12.3	6.1	6.2

Group charges relate to depreciation, which is not tax allowable, and to directly attributable overhead. The overhead has stayed almost constant for each of the subsidiaries during the last four years and, because of efficiency gains, is expected to remain at similar levels for the next four years.

Other current data for the subsidiaries include:

	Annual overhead (directly attributable, included in group charges)
Textiles	£0.5 million
Engineering	£0.5 million
Food processing	£1.0 million
Printing	£1.0 million

	Estimated after tax realisable value (as a going concern)	
	Currently	At end of 20X9
Textiles	£5.2 million	£6.5 - 7 million
Engineering	£14 million	£18 - 20 million
Food processing	£28 million	£30 - 33 million
Printing	£45 million	£45 - 50 million

During the next four years pre-tax operating profits are expected to increase by 5% per year for the engineering subsidiary, by 2% per year for food processing, by 10% per year for printing and to remain approximately constant for textiles.

Inflation rates

20X2	8%
20X3	6%
20X4	3%
20X5	3%

Expected inflation rates 20X6 - 20X9: 4% per year.

Industry asset beta values and price/earnings ratios for companies of similar gearing levels to Grocas are:

	Asset beta	P/E ratio
Textiles	0.86	4.3
Engineering	1.29	6.4
Food processing	0.57	12.0
Printing	1.43	20.4

The risk free rate is 6% (after tax) and the expected market return is 13% (after tax).

The summarised balance sheet of Grocas is shown below.

	£m
Net fixed assets	34.6
Net current assets	8.4
	43.0
Financed by	
Ordinary shares (50 pence par value)	10.0
Reserves	23.0
Long-term debt	10.0
	43.0

The market value of the company's ordinary shares is currently 360 pence per share. The weighted average cost of capital of Grocas is estimated to be 14%.

Corporation tax is at the rate of 30%, payable in the same year that income arises. The company may be assumed to have negligible amounts of debtors and creditors at the year end.

Required

(a) Prepare a report discussing whether or not Grocas should dispose of any of its subsidiaries, and if so when. Your report must be supported by relevant calculations.

Include in your report discussion of the possible implications of changes in the group's level of diversification that would result from the disposal of one or more subsidiaries.

(23 marks)

(b) As an alternative to disposing of any subsidiaries a partial demerger of the printing subsidiary has been suggested whereby the company floats 25% of the shares of the subsidiary on the London Stock Exchange. Discuss the possible reasons for this suggestion, and estimate the possible financial effects for Grocas if this partial demerger occurs. (7 marks)

(30 marks)

FOREIGN EXCHANGE AND INTEREST RATE RISK

Questions 40 to 54 cover Foreign exchange and interest rate risk, the subject of Part D of the BPP Study Text for Paper 3.7.

Revise.

40 PREPARATION QUESTION: HERLER

It is December 20X8. Herler plc has agreed to undertake an eighteen-month construction project in the country of Surkaya. Payments to Herler will be made 25% as an immediate down payment, 25% in six months time, 15% in one year's time and the balance upon completion. The purchaser in Surkaya has no access to sterling or other leading currencies as the country is experiencing balance of payments problems, cannot readily borrow internationally, and has only small foreign currency reserves. Payment for the project is therefore to be made in the local currency, the Surkayan franc. The total price of the construction is 8 billion (8,000 million) Surkayan francs.

Inflation in Surkaya is currently at the rate of 250 percent per year, which is not expected to change significantly in the near future. Inflation in the UK is 5 percent per year.

The management of Herler plc when costing the construction project allowed for a 100% contribution to variable costs at each payment stage, at 1 December 20X8 spot exchange rates. Almost all variable costs are incurred in sterling. Fixed costs are negligible. The company's discount rate for this construction project is 12%.

Spot rate 1 December 20X8

2,400 Surkayan francs/£1

No forward market exists beyond three months, and Herler has no access to Surkayan money or capital markets.

Required

(a) Estimate the likely financial result for Herler plc of the construction project. State clearly any assumptions that you make.

(b) Suggest what actions Herler plc might have taken prior to agreeing the contract to reduce foreign exchange risk.

Approaching the question

1   In (a) you need to consider purchasing power parity and the significance of cash flows being at six-monthly intervals.

2   In (b) you should ignore on this occasion the possibility of derivative product hedging.

41 PREPARATION QUESTION: FINANCIAL FUTURES

As a result of the Barings Bank collapse early in 1995 the board of directors of your company is proposing to ban the use of financial futures within the company. Prepare a brief report for the board of directors outlining the possible advantages of financial futures for a large manufacturing company, and how any risks of using financial futures might be minimised.

Approaching the question

1   Think of the variety of uses of futures.

2   Whilst you do need to discuss risks, consider also how risks can be reduced by control and scrutiny.

42   VERTID (FS, 6/95)   *72 mins*

In an attempt to recover from the economic recession, Vertid Ltd, a company employing 30 workers in the UK Midlands, is starting to trade with two foreign countries, Werland and Thodia. Competitively priced components have been purchased from Werland, with payment of 3,000,000 Werland francs due in three months time. Goods have been sold to Thodia and receipts of 3,500,000 Thodian pesos are due to be received in six months time.

The managing director of Vertid is concerned that the company cannot afford to lose money on the two deals, as the company's poor cash flow situation has been the subject of recent discussions with the company's bank. Vertid's overdraft is currently approaching its agreed limit, and the bank has indicated that it is unlikely that the overdraft facility will be increased in the near future.

The managing director asked his sales manager for a brief report discussing the likely foreign exchange risk to be faced when trading with Werland and Thodia. The sales manager has stated that there is likely to be a substantial foreign exchange risk in trading with Werland, but little risk in trading with Thodia, whose currency is directly linked to the US dollar. The US dollar in recent months has been quite stable relative to sterling.

Exchange rates

Spot market

290 - 294 Werland francs/£
1.4640 - 1.4690 $US/£
220 - 228 Thodian pesos/$US

Forward market $US/£

| 3 months forward | 0.98 - 1.15 cents discount |
| 6 months forward | 1.70 - 1.86 cents discount |

No forward market exists for the Werland franc or Thodian peso.

Current inflation rates

United Kingdom	3%
USA	6%
Werland	12%
Thodia	20%

Current annual interest rates that are available to Vertid

	Investing	*Borrowing*
£ Sterling	4.5%	10%
$US	6%	12%
Werland francs	12.5%	-
Thodian pesos	15%	-

OTC European currency call options are available for Werland francs at a premium of 25 francs/£ with an exercise price of 300 francs/£ and a three month maturity date.

The managing director of Vertid wishes to develop a strategy for:

(i)   Protecting against *any form* of risk that these deals involve
(ii) Financing the overseas trade deals

Required

You have been asked as a consultant to:

(a) Explain whether or not the views of the sales manager regarding exchange risk are likely to be correct.   (9 marks)

48

(b) Prepare a report discussing how the managers of Vertid might protect the company against *all* of the risks of each of the foreign deals. Relevant calculations should support your report.   (25 marks)

(c) Outline what alternatives might be available to Vertid Ltd to finance the two trade deals.   (6 marks)

    (40 marks)

43   LANVERT (FS, 6/98 amended)   *54 mins*

(a) Lanvert SA is a French company which trades frequently with Switzerland and the USA.

Transactions to be completed within the next six months are as follows.

	Receipts	*Payments*
3 months time	$4.8m	$7.6m
6 months time	SF4.5m	SF2.8m

Exchange rates in Paris

	Euro/SFr	*Euro/$*
Spot	0.6250 – 0.6260	1.0610 – 1.0661
3 months forward	0.6221 – 0.6231	1.0656 – 1.0715
6 months forward	0.6197 – 0.6208	1.0683 – 1.0740

Current bank prime rates (per annum)

	3 month	*6 month*
France	6%	6.25%
Switzerland	8%	8.30%
USA	4%	4.25%

Lanvert can borrow at prime plus 1% in France, and prime plus 1.5% in Switzerland, and can invest at 1% below prime in France and Switzerland.

Euro market traded option prices (62,500 euro contract size) in the USA

(The options relate to the purchase or sale of euros)

Exercise price ($/€)	*June contracts*		*September contracts*	
	Calls	*Puts*	*Calls*	*Puts*
0.936	1.65	0.41	2.38	0.71
0.938	0.56	1.20	1.01	1.57
0.940	0.17	2.65	0.48	3.45

Option premia are in cents per euro and are payable up front. The options are American style.

Assume that it is now 1 June and that option contracts mature on the 15th of the month.

Lanvert currently has an overdraft of €1.3m.

Required

Discuss, with supporting calculations, how Lanvert should hedge its foreign exchange risk during the next six months. Include in your discussion comment about which currency options contracts might be best for Lanvert. The company does not wish to take significant risk and wishes to accumulate as high a cash flow as possible from its foreign trade transactions. Transaction costs may be ignored.

State clearly any assumptions that you make.   (26 marks)

(b) Briefly discuss the possible foreign exchange consequences for Lanvert if its Swiss customer defaults on its payment in six months time.   (4 marks)

(30 marks)

44   KYT (FS, 6/99 amended)   *27 mins*

(a) Explain the meaning of transaction and translation exposure and discuss their importance to the financial manager.   (5 marks)

(b) Assume that it is now 30 June. KYT Inc is a company located in the USA that has a contract to purchase goods from Japan in two months time on 1 September. The payment is to be made in yen and will total 140 million yen.

The managing director of KYT Inc wishes to protect the contract against adverse movements in foreign exchange rates and is considering the use of currency futures. The following data are available.

Spot foreign exchange rate

Yen/$ 128.15

Yen currency futures contracts on SIMEX (Singapore Monetary Exchange)

Contract size 12,500,000 yen, contract prices are $US per yen.

Contract prices:

  September 0.007985
  December 0.008250

Assume that futures contracts mature at the end of the month.

Required

(i)   Illustrate how KYT might hedge its foreign exchange risk using currency futures.   (3 marks)

(ii) Show what basis risk is involved in the proposed hedge.   (2 marks)

(iii) Assuming the spot exchange rate is 120 yen/$ on 1 September and that basis risk decreases steadily in a linear manner, calculate what the result of the hedge is expected to be. Briefly discuss why this result might not occur. Margin requirements and taxation may be ignored.   (5 marks)

(15 marks)

45   USA OPTIONS (FS, 12/00 amended)   *27 mins*

(a) Your UK based company has won an export order worth $1.8 million from the USA. Payment is due to be made to you in dollars in six months time. It is now 15 November. You wish to protect the exchange rate risk with currency options, but do not wish to pay an option premium of more than £10,000.

Your bank has suggested using a particular currency option which has no premium. The option would allow a worst case exchange rate at which the option could be exercised of $1.65/£. If the contract moved in your favour then the bank would share (participate in) the profits, and would take 50% of any gains relative to the current spot exchange rate.

You also have access to currency options on the Philadelphia Stock Exchange.

Current option prices are:

Sterling contacts, £31,250 contract size. Premium is US cents per £.

Exercise price	Calls			Puts		
	Dec	*March*	*June*	*Dec*	*March*	*June*
1.55	6.8	7.9	10.1	0.2	0.5	0.9
1.60	2.1	3.8	5.3	1.9	3.1	4.0
1.65	0.6	0.9	1.1	5.1	7.2	9.6
1.70	0.1	0.2	0.4	10.1	12.3	14.1

The current spot rate is $1.6055 – 1.6100/£. Any option premium would be payable immediately.

Required

Evaluate whether a participating option or traded option is likely to offer a better foreign exchange hedge.   (10 marks)

(b) Your company is trading in and with developing countries and has a subsidiary in a country with no developed capital or currency markets. Your company is now about to invoice a customer in that country in the local currency. Advise your treasurer about ways in which the risk can be managed in these circumstances.   (5 marks)

(15 marks)

46 RCB

27 mins

RCB plc is committed to borrowing £3 million in five months time for a period of four months. The directors of the company are concerned interest rates will rise in the meantime.

RCB can currently borrow at LIBOR + 2%. Three months LIBOR is at 7.5%.

Current LIFFE £500,000 sterling three months futures prices are:

December   92.30
March   91.80

Assume that it is now the end of September and that future contracts mature at the end of the relevant month.

Required

(a) Illustrate how RCB plc could use a futures hedge to protect against its potential interest rate risk. The type and number of contracts must be included in your illustration.

(5 marks)

(b) Estimate the basis risk for this hedge both now and at the time the contract is likely to be closed out. Comment upon the significance of your estimates for RCB plc. Illustrate your answer with reference to the impact of a 2% increase in LIBOR.

(5 marks)

(c) Discuss the importance of the 'Greeks' in determining holdings of options.   (5 marks)

(15 marks)

47 CATHLYN

27 mins

(a) The current share price of Cathlyn plc is £3.50. Using the Black-Scholes model, estimate the value of a European call option on the shares of the company that has an exercise price of £3.30 and 3 months to run before it expires. The risk free rate of interest is 8% and the variance of the rate of return on the share has been 12%.

Note: The Black-Scholes formula shows call price for a European option C_o, where

$$C_o = Ps\ N(d_1) - Xe^{-rT}\ N(d_2)$$

where $N(d)$ = cumulative distribution function

$$d_1 = \frac{\ln(Ps/X) + rT}{\sigma\sqrt{T}} + 0.5\sigma\sqrt{T}$$

$$d_2 = d_1 - \sigma\sqrt{T}$$

Ps = share price

e = the exponential constant 2.7183

X = exercise price of option

r = annual (continuously compounded) risk free rate of return

T = time of expiry of option in years

σ = share price volatility, the standard deviation of the rate of return on shares

$N(d_x)$ = delta, the probability that a deviation of less than d_x will occur in a normal distribution with a mean of zero and a standard deviation of one

$\ln$ = natural log

Normal distribution tables

	0.00	0.01	0.02	0.03	0.04	0.05	0.06	0.07	0.08	0.09
0.0	.0000	.0040	.0080	.0120	.0160	.0199	.0239	.0279	.0319	.0359
0.1	.0398	.0438	.0478	.0517	.0557	.0596	.0636	.0675	.0714	.0753
0.2	.0793	.0832	.0871	.0910	.0948	.0987	.1026	.1064	.1103	.1141
0.3	.1179	.1217	.1255	.1293	.1331	.1368	.1406	.1443	.1480	.1517
0.4	.1554	.1591	.1628	.1664	.1700	.1736	.1772	.1808	.1844	.1879
0.5	.1915	.1950	.1985	.2019	.2054	.2088	.2123	.2157	.2190	.2224
0.6	.2257	.2291	.2324	.2357	.2389	.2422	.2454	.2486	.2517	.2549
0.7	.2580	.2611	.2642	.2673	.2704	.2734	.2764	.2794	.2823	.2852
0.8	.2881	.2910	.2939	.2967	.2995	.3023	.3051	.3078	.3106	.3133
0.9	.3159	.3186	.3212	.3238	.3264	.3289	.3315	.3340	.3365	.3389
1.0	.3413	.3438	.3461	.3485	.3508	.3531	.3554	.3577	.3599	.3621

(10 marks)

(b)   Discuss the main limitations of the Black-Scholes model.

(5 marks)

(15 marks)

48   SARHALL   *54 mins*

(a)   Explain how the price of a call option might alter as a result of an increase in the value of the determinants of the option price in the Black-Scholes option pricing model for European options.

(6 marks)

The directors of Sarhall plc are considering the introduction of a new remuneration scheme for the company's senior employees. Two alternatives have been suggested:

(i)   A basic salary plus a bonus related to the pre-tax profit of the employees' department

(ii)   A basic salary plus a share option scheme

Required

(b) Ignoring tax and the data about the schemes given below, discuss the advantages and disadvantages of these schemes to both the shareholders and the employees.

(11 marks)

Details of the two schemes are as follows:

(i) If based on the profits for the last three years, bonuses would vary as follows.

20X4 £5,000 - £6,000
20X5 £6,500 - £7,500
20X6 £7,000 - £8,000

(ii) For the share option scheme, employees would be allowed to purchase 6,000 shares at a price of 450 pence per share when the options had been held for two years, as allowed by current tax regulations. The options will lapse if not exercised at that time.

The ex div price of the shares is 650 pence. The directors have just declared a dividend of 35p per share. They plan to pay the next dividend in twelve months, and annually thereafter. They are expecting to maintain, but not increase, dividend payments over the next few years.

Over the last year the standard deviation of the company's share price has been 35%.

The current short-term risk-free interest rate is 7%.

Required

(c) Evaluate whether, on the data given, senior employees are likely to prefer the bonus or option schemes.

(9 marks)

One of the directors has asked whether put options would be worth more to employees than call options.

Required

(d) Respond to the director by calculating whether put or call options would be more valuable to employees.

Use the put-call parity equation:

Price of put option = Price of call option $- Ps + Xe^{-rT}$

where Ps, X, e, r and T are as defined in the formula given in Question 47.   (4 marks)

(30 marks)

49   MURWALD (FS, 12/94)   *54 mins*

The corporate treasury team of Murwald plc are debating what strategy to adopt towards interest rate risk management. The company's financial projections show an expected cash deficit in three months time of £12 million, which will last for a period of approximately six months. Base rate is currently 6% per year, and Murwald can borrow at 1.5% over base, or invest at 1% below base. The treasury team believe that economic pressures will soon force the Swiss central bank to raise Swiss interest rates by 2% per year, and similar pressures could also lead to a rise in UK interest rates..

In the UK, the economy is recovering from a recession and representatives of industry are calling for interest rates to be cut by 1%. Opposing representations are being made by pensioners, who do not wish their investment income to fall further due to an interest rate cut.

BPP
PUBLISHING

The corporate treasury team believes that interest rates are more likely to rise than to fall, and does not want interest payments during the six month period to increase by more than £10,000 from the amounts that would be paid at current interest rates. It is now 1 December.

LIFFE prices (1 December)

Futures: LIFFE £500,000 three month sterling interest rate (points of 100%)

December	93.75
March	93.45
June	93.10

Options: LIFFE £500,000 short sterling options (points of 100%)

Exercise Price	Calls June	Puts June
9200	3.33	-
9250	2.93	-
9300	2.55	0.92
9350	2.20	1.25
9400	1.74	1.84
9450	1.32	2.90
9500	0.87	3.46

Required

(a) Illustrate results of futures and options hedges if, by 1 March:

    (i)   Interest rates rise by 2%. Futures prices move by 1.8%.
    (ii)   Interest rates fall by 1%. Futures prices move by 0.9%.

    Recommend with reasons how Murwald plc should hedge its interest rate exposure. All relevant calculations must be shown. Taxation, transactions costs and margin requirements may be ignored. State clearly any assumptions that you make.

(22 marks)

(b) Discuss the advantages and disadvantages of other derivative products that Murwald might have used to hedge the risk. (8 marks)

(30 marks)

HYK (FS, 12/99) *54 mins*

The monthly cash budget of HYK Communications plc shows that the company is likely to need £18 million in two months' time for a period of four months. Financial markets have recently been volatile, due to uncertainties about the impact of a major computer bug. If computer problems occur in January 20X0, the finance director of HYK plc fears that short term interest rates could rise by as much as 150 basis points. If few problems occur then short term rates could fall by 50 basis points. LIBOR is currently 6.5% and HYK plc can borrow at LIBOR + 0.75%.

The finance director does not wish to pay more than 7.50%, including option premium costs, but excluding the effect of margin requirements and commissions.

LIFFE £500,000 3 month futures prices. The value of one tick is £12.50

December	93.40
March	93.10
June	92.75

LIFFE £500,000 3 months options prices (premiums in annual %)

Exercise Price	Calls			Puts		
	December	*March*	*June*	*December*	*March*	*June*
92.50	0.33	0.88	1.04	-	-	0.08
93.00	0.16	0.52	0.76	-	0.20	0.34
93.50	0.10	0.24	0.42	0.18	0.60	1.93
94.00	-	0.05	0.18	0.36	1.35	1.92

Assume that it is now 1 December and that exchange traded futures and options contracts expire at the end of the month. Margin requirements and default risk may be ignored.

Required

(a) Estimate the results of undertaking *each of* an interest rate futures hedge and an interest rate options hedge on the LIFFE exchange, if LIBOR

    (i)   Increases by 150 basis points, and
    (ii)   Decreases by 50 basis points.

    Discuss how successful the hedge would have been.

    State clearly any assumptions that you make.   (18 marks)

(b) Discuss the relative advantages of using exchange traded interest rate options and over-the-counter (OTC) interest rate options.   (6 marks)

(c) Your finance director has received some quotations for over-the-counter (OTC) interest rate options and wonders whether or not they are too expensive. Outline the main determinants of interest rate option prices, and comment upon whether or not the OTC options are likely to be expensive.   (6 marks)

       (30 marks)

51   **TAYQUER (FS, 6/96 amended)**   *27 mins*

(a) Explain the term 'risk management' in respect of interest rates and discuss how interest rate risk might be managed by forward rate agreements, futures and options.   (7 marks)

(b) The directors of Tayquer plc are considering the use of options to protect the current interest yield from their company's £9.75 million short-term money market investments. Having made initial enquiries they have been discouraged by the cost of the option premium. A member of the treasury staff has suggested the use of a collar as this would be cheaper. Protection is required for the next eight months. Assume that it is now 1 June.

LIFFE interest rate options on three month money market futures

Contract size is £500,000, premium cost is in annual %.

	Calls		Puts	
	Dec	*March*	*Dec*	*March*
9100	0.90	1.90	-	0.02
9150	0.56	1.45	0.05	0.06
9200	0.27	1.04	0.17	0.13
9250	0.09	0.68	0.45	0.24
9300	0.01	0.20	0.83	0.32
9350	-	0.05	1.13	0.54

Tick size is 0.01%, and tick value £12.50.

The current interest rate received on Tayquer's short-term money market investments is 7.5% per annum. Assume that Tayquer can buy or sell options at the above prices. Commission, taxation and margins may be ignored.

Required

Discuss how, and estimate at what cost, collars may be used to protect against the interest yield risk. Recommend at which exercise price(s) the collar should be arranged.

(8 marks)

(15 marks)

52   **PROJECTIONS (FS, 12/98 amended)**   *27 mins*

(a) Financial projections show that your company is likely to have a cash flow deficit of approximately £2 million for a period of five months commencing 1 May next year. It will be necessary for your company to borrow short-term funds during this period. The company can currently borrow at LIBOR + 1.5%.

Short-term interest rates are believed to be more likely to increase than to decrease although, if there is a fall in the retail price index during the next few months, interest rates could decrease. Experts at your company's bank believe that LIBOR could increase by up to 1% or decrease by up to 0.75% during the next four months. LIBOR is currently 7%.

LIFFE three month Sterling futures, £500,000 contract size, £12.50 tick size

March	92.75
June	92.50

LIFFE option price on three months Sterling futures. £500,000 contract size, £12.50 tick size

	Premium (%)			
	Calls		*Puts*	
Exercise price	*March*	*June*	*March*	*June*
92.00	0.94	1.19	0.22	0.37
93.00	0.28	0.36	0.44	0.59
94.00	0.10	0.20	1.30	1.45

Required

Using interest rate *options*, suggest a hedging strategy to manage short-term interest rate risks, and calculate the likely impact of your suggested strategy if interest rates were to move to each of the extremes suggested by the experts at the bank.

Assume that it is now 31 December and that contracts mature at the month end.

Basis risk and margin requirements may be ignored.

State clearly any assumptions that you make.   (9 marks)

(b) Noswis plc borrowed three million Swiss Francs in five year floating rate Euro-Swiss Franc funds three months ago at an interest rate LIBOR plus 2%, in an attempt to reduce the level of interest paid on its loans. At that time Euro-Swiss Franc LIBOR was 7%. Unfortunately Euro-Swiss Franc LIBOR interest rates have increased since that time to 8.5%. The company wishes to protect itself from further interest rate volatility, but does not wish to lose the benefit of probable interest rate reductions that are likely to occur in a few months time. An adviser has suggested the use of a six month American style SFr swaption at 9.5% with a premium of SFr100,000, commencing in nine months time and with a maturity date the same as the floating rate Euro-Swiss Franc loan.

Required

Define a swaption, and illustrate how this proposed swaption might benefit Noswis. Ignore the time value of money. (6 marks)

(15 marks)

53 SOMAX (FS, 6/96)   *72 mins*

(a) Somax plc wishes to raise 260 million Swiss Francs in floating rate finance for a period of five years. Discuss the advantages and disadvantage of raising such funds through:

   (i)   Direct borrowing from a domestic banking system such as the Swiss domestic banking system. (Detailed knowledge of the Swiss banking system is not required)

   (ii)   The Euromarket   (10 marks)

(b) The funds are to be used to establish a new production plant in the eastern region of Switzerland. Somax evaluates its investments using NPV, but is not sure what cost of capital to use in the discounting process. The company is also proposing to increase its equity finance in the near future for UK expansion, resulting overall in little change in the company's market weighted capital gearing. The summarised financial data for the company before the expansion are shown below.

PROFIT AND LOSS ACCOUNT FOR THE YEAR ENDING 31 MARCH 20X6

	£m
Turnover	1,984
Gross profit	432
Profit after tax	81
Dividends	37
Retained earnings	44

BALANCE SHEET AS AT 31 MARCH 20X6

	£m
Fixed assets (net)	846
Working capital	350
	1,196
Medium and long-term loans[1]	(210)
	986
Shareholders' funds	
Issued ordinary shares (50 pence par)	225
Reserves	761
	986

[1]Including £75m 14% fixed rate bonds due to mature in five years time and redeemable at £100. The current market price of these bonds is £119.50. Other medium and long-term loans are floating rate UK bank loans at base rate plus 1%.

Corporate rate tax may be assumed to be at the rate of 33% in both the UK and Switzerland. The company's ordinary shares are currently trading at 376 pence.

Somax's equity beta is estimated to be 1.18. The systematic risk of debt may be assumed to be zero. The risk free rate is 7.75% and market return 14.5%. Bank base rate is currently 8.25%.

The estimated equity beta of the main Swiss competitor in the same industry as the new proposed plant in the eastern region of Switzerland is 1.5, and the competitor's capital gearing is 35% equity, 65% debt by book values, and 60% equity, 40% debt by market values.

Exchange rates

Spot	SFr2.3245 - 2.3300/£
6 months forward	SFr2.2955 - 2.3009/£

Somax can borrow in SFr at a floating rate of between 5.75% and 6% depending upon which form of borrowing is selected (ie in the Euromarkets or the Swiss domestic market). SFr LIBOR is currently 5%.

The interest rate parity theorem may be assumed to hold.

Required

Estimate the *sterling* cost of capital that Somax should use as the discount rate for its proposed investment in eastern Switzerland. State clearly any assumptions that you make.   (12 marks)

(c) Somax's bank has suggested a five year interest rate swap as an alternative to direct SFr borrowing. Somax would issue a five year sterling fixed rate bond, and make the following swap with a Swiss company that is also a client of the bank.

Somax would pay the Swiss company SFr LIBOR + 1% per year. The Swiss company would pay Somax 9.5% per year.

A 0.2% per year fee would also be payable by each company to the bank. There will be an exchange of principal now, and in five years time, at today's middle spot foreign exchange rate. The Swiss company can borrow fixed rate sterling at 10.5% per annum, and floating rate SFr finance at SFr LIBOR + 1.5%.

Required

(i)   Estimate the annual interest cost to Somax of issuing a five year sterling fixed rate bond, and calculate whether the suggested swap would be of benefit to both Somax plc and the Swiss company.   (10 marks)

(ii) Excluding cheaper finance, discuss the possible benefits and the possible risks of such a swap for the two companies and the intermediary bank.   (8 marks)

(40 marks)

54 **PZP (FS, 12/97 amended)**   *27 mins*

PZP plc wishes to raise £15 million of floating rate finance. The company's bankers have suggested using a five year swap. PZP has an AAB rating and can issue fixed rate finance at 11.35%, or floating rate at LIBOR plus 60 basis points. Foreten plc has only a BBC credit rating and can raise fixed rate finance at 12.8%, or floating rate at LIBOR + 1.35%.

A five year interest rate swap on a £15 million loan could be arranged with Gigbank acting as an intermediary for a fee of 0.25% per annum. PZP will only agree to the swap if it can make annual savings of at least 40 basis points. LIBOR is currently 10.5%.

Required

(a) Evaluate whether or not the swap is likely to be agreed.   (3 marks)

(b) Estimate the present value of the differences in cash flow that would exist for PZP from using a floating rate swap rather than borrowing fixed rate directly in the market if:

(i)   LIBOR moves to 11.8% after one year and then remains constant.
(ii) LIBOR moves to 8.8% after three years and then remains constant.

The market may be assumed to be efficient and the discount rate to be the prevailing effective floating rate swap rate for PZP. Interest may be assumed to be paid annually at the end of the year concerned.

Comment upon your findings, and discuss whether they would be likely to influence PZP's decision to undertake a swap.   (7 marks)

(c) Discuss the main purpose of a delta hedge and illustrate the impact on the number of shares held if the delta of options changed from 0.8 to 0.5 for a previously delta-hedged option holding of 200 contracts. The standard option contract size is 1,000 shares.

                                                                                        (5 marks)

                                                                                    (15 marks)

THE GLOBAL ENVIRONMENT

Questions 55 to 68 cover The global environment, the subject of Part E of the BPP Study Text for Paper 3.7.

55   PREPARATION QUESTION: EXCHANGE RATE SYSTEMS

Describe the main types of foreign exchange rate system.

Approaching the question

Remember that 'pure' fixed and floating systems are not the only systems that have been operated.

56   AXELOT   *27 mins*

It is June 20X1 and Mr Axelot has just inherited the controlling interest in IXT plc. At his first board of directors meeting an item for discussion is the financing of a £5 million expansion scheme. Mr Axelot has read that debt finance is normally cheaper than equity finance and suggests that all external finance during the next five years should be in the form of debt. For the expansion scheme he has suggested using either:

(a)   A fixed rate 10 year Swiss Franc bond for 12.25 million francs issued in Zurich at an interest rate of 8% per year, or

(b)   A 13% debenture 20Y4-20Y6 issued at par of £100 with warrants to purchase ordinary shares in five years time at a price of 450 pence per share.

A director has challenged Mr Axelot's five year financing strategy, saying that it would be too risky, and has suggested that the £5 million expansion scheme be financed using a placing of new ordinary shares at a price of 245 pence per share.

Financial details of IXT are summarised below. Earnings before interest payable and tax are expected to increase by 20% per year for the next five years, during which time approximately £5 million per year will be required from external financing sources. The company normally uses a dividend payout ratio of 40% and corporate tax rates are not expected to change. IXT's current share price is 250 pence ex div.

The level of inflation in Switzerland is 2% per year and in the United Kingdom 8% per year. The current spot exchange rate is SF2.445-2.450/£.

SUMMARISED BALANCE SHEET AS AT 31 MARCH 20X1

	£'000	£'000
Fixed assets		
Tangible fixed assets		33,000
Investments		4,500
		37,500
Current assets		
Stocks	12,400	
Debtors	9,200	
Bank	1,400	
		23,000
Current liabilities		
Short-term loans	(4,200)	
Overdrafts	(6,400)	
Trade creditors	(10,100)	
Other	(1,800)	
		(22,500)
Creditors falling due after more than one year		
Debentures and loan stock	(5,000)	
Unsecured bank loans	(8,400)	
		(13,400)
		24,600
Capital and reserves		
Called up share capital (25 pence par value)		4,000
Share premium account		3,500
Revaluation reserve		3,900
Profit and loss account		13,200
		24,600

SUMMARISED PROFIT AND LOSS ACCOUNT
FOR THE YEAR ENDING 31 MARCH 20X1

	£'000
Turnover	53,500
Trading profit	13,400
Investment income	350
Interest payable	(3,000)
Taxable income	10,750
Taxation	(3,762)
Profit attributable to ordinary shareholders	6,988
Dividend	(2,795)
Profit retained for year	4,193

Required

(a) Appraise Mr Axelot's suggested strategy that all external financing during the next five years should be in the form of debt. (8 marks)

(b) Discuss whether IXT plc should finance the *current* £5m expansion project with the Swiss franc bond, the 13% debenture or the placing. (7 marks)

(15 marks)

57 **PREPARATION QUESTION: RISK DATA**

Your company has purchased the following data which provide scores of the political risk for a number of countries in which the company is considering investing in a new subsidiary.

	Total	Economic performance	Debt in default	Credit ratings	Government stability	Remittance restrictions	Access capital
Weighting	100	25	10	10	25	15	15
Gmala	37	13	4	5	5	10	0
Forland	52	5	10	9	16	8	4
Amapore	36	12	2	3	9	5	5
Covia	30	9	3	2	15	1	0
Settia	39	15	4	3	11	4	2

Countries have been rated on a scale from 0 up to the maximum weighting for each factor (eg 0-15 for remittance restrictions). A high score for each factor, as well as overall, reflects low political risk.

A proposal has been put before the company's board of directors that investment should take place in Forland.

Required

Prepare a brief report for the company's board of directors discussing whether or not the above data should form the basis for:

(a) The measurement of political risk, and

(b) The decision about which country to invest in

Approaching the question

1   Consider what you can ascertain about the basis of the weightings, and also what other factors might have been included in the weightings.

2   When discussing the decision, you need to mention how important political risk is at an individual or firm level.

58   RIPPENTOFF   *27 mins*

Rippentoff Inc is an American multinational which is considering an investment in a subsidiary company in Penuria, a developing country.

The investment would require capital of 50 million local currency units (LCUs) and the current rate of exchange is LCU 5 = $1. Rippentoff would supply capital of LCU 30 million and the remainder would be borrowed locally at a 15% rate of interest. The subsidiary would invest its capital in machinery costing LCU 40 million and inventory of LCU 10 million. Of the machinery, LCU 30 million would be purchased from Rippentoff, consisting of three machines costing LCU 10 million each. One of these machines was scheduled for sale for scrap at $100,000, one would need to be replaced by a machine costing $1.5 million, and one would be bought new for $2.0 million, less a discount of 10%.

One half of the opening inventory and of all subsequent purchases of materials would be bought from Rippentoff, which obtains a 25% contribution on all sales of materials. It is forecast that the annual income statement of the subsidiary for the foreseeable future will be as follows.

	LCU million	LCU million
Sales		40
Less: Materials	20	
Labour	7	
Interest	3	
Management fee to Rippentoff	5	
		35
Net profit (all paid as dividend)		5

The management fee does not involve Rippentoff in any additional cost. The cost of equity of the subsidiary is 20%, while Rippentoff's overall cost of capital is 15%. There is no taxation in Penuria.

Required

(a) Calculate whether the proposed investment is worthwhile from the viewpoint of Rippentoff.   (8 marks)

(b) Explain the additional factors that Rippentoff would take into account in the appraisal of the investment.   (7 marks)

                                                                                                                                                    (15 marks)

59   FDI (FS, 12/98 amended)   *27 mins*

(a) In the late 1990s the global turnover of the largest multinational companies is greater than the gross national product of many countries.

    Discuss factors that might explain the successful growth of large multinational companies.   (8 marks)

(b) Discuss the potential advantages and disadvantages for the overseas host country of foreign direct investment by multinational companies.   (7 marks)

                                                                                                                                                    (15 marks)

60   DIALTOUS (FS, 12/95)   *54 mins*

It is currently December 20X5. Dialtous plc, a UK based company, is a leading manufacturer of portable telephones. The company's board of directors have decided to expand the operations of the existing South Korean subsidiary where there is ample land for new development, and a relatively cheap skilled labour supply. The expected working life of the new factory is seven years, but further development may be possible at that time with major investment in new equipment. The expanded South Korean factory will supply all of the Middle and Far East. Almost all of its cash flows are in South Korean Wons.

The company's finance director has been asked to suggest three alternative means of raising external finance for the 100,000 million lire project. He believes that any finance used by the South Korean subsidiary should be debt finance, and makes the following suggestions.

(i) The parent company borrows from a UK clearing bank for a seven year period at LIBOR plus 1.5%. LIBOR is currently 7% and UK interest rates have been stable for the past few months. This sum would then be converted into wons and loaned to the South Korean subsidiary. Floating charge security would be required for this loan from Dialtous, and an initial arrangement fee of 0.5% would be payable in sterling.

(ii) A 10 year 7% convertible Eurobond loan denominated in US$, which could be converted into 50 Dialtous ordinary shares for every $1,000 nominal value bond held anytime between 1 January 20X8 and 31 December 20Y0. Total issue costs associated with the Eurobond are expected to be 2%.

(iii) A 10 year fixed rate 4.75% Swiss franc bond issue on the Swiss domestic market where Dialtous has a high credit rating. Ten years is the period that gives the most attractive cost within the current Swiss term structure of interest rates. The loan could be swapped into a fixed rate South Korean won loan at 11.75% per annum interest. The initial arrangement fee of the loan would be 1%, and the swap fee 2%, payable immediately in Swiss francs.

63

The South Korean subsidiary would be responsible for all interest payments on the loan and repayment of the principal for all three loans.

Summarised financial accounts of the Dialtous Group of companies and its South Korean subsidiary Itdial are shown below.

Dialtous plc

Group profit and loss account for the year ended 31 March 20X5

	£million
Turnover	465
Operating costs	389
Operating profit	76
Interest receivable	2
Interest payable	14
Profit on ordinary activities before tax	64
Tax	21
Profit attributable to shareholders	43
Dividends	18
Retained profit for the financial year	25

Group consolidated balance sheet as at 31 March 20X5

	£million	£million
Fixed assets		162
Current assets		
Stocks	123	
Debtors	87	
Investments	46	
Cash at bank and in hand	4	
Total current assets	260	
Creditors: amounts falling due within one year		
Loans and other borrowings	50	
Other creditors	126	
	176	
Net current assets		84
Total assets less current liabilities		246
Creditors: amounts falling due after more than one year		
Loans and other borrowings		75
		171
Capital and reserves		
Called up share capital (50 pence par)		20
Share premium account		62
Profit and loss account		89
Total capital and reserves		171

Dialtous ordinary shares are currently trading at 760 pence.

Itdial

Profit and loss account for the year ended 31 March 20X5

	Won '000m
Turnover	144
Operating costs	106
Operating profit	38
Interest receivable	-
Interest payable	18
Profit on ordinary activities before tax	20
Tax	6
Profit attributable to shareholders	14
Dividends	14
Retained profit for the financial year	-

Balance sheet as at 31 March 20X5

	Won '000m	Won '000m
Fixed assets		150
Current assets		
Stocks	124	
Debtors	98	
Investments	-	
Cash at bank and in hand	5	
Total current assets	227	
Creditors: amounts falling due within one year		
Loans and other borrowings	70	
Other creditors	65	
	135	
Net current assets		92
Total assets less current liabilities		242
Creditors: amounts falling due after more than one year		
Loans and other borrowings		100
		142

	Won '000m
Capital and reserves	
Called up share capital	100
Share premium account	-
Profit and loss account	42
Total capital and reserves	142

Foreign exchange rates

	Won/£	*Swiss franc/£*	*US$/£*	*Won/US$*
Spot	2404-2420	2.0440-2.0610	1.5456-1.5490	1552-1566
1 year forward	2456-2474	2.0135-2.0178	1.5267-1.5304	1605-1620

These foreign exchange rate trends are expected to continue for the foreseeable future.

Required

(a) Discuss the merits and disadvantages of the suggestion of the finance director that any finance provided to the South Korean subsidiary should be debt finance. Support your explanation with brief calculations where relevant. (10 marks)

(b) Discuss the advantages and disadvantages of *any two* of the three suggested financing sources, and recommend which source should be used. Support your discussion with any relevant calculations, including estimates of the cost of the financing sources, and state clearly any assumptions that you make. Taxation may be ignored in any calculations. (17 marks)

(c) Suggest, and briefly discuss, *one* other type of debt financing that may be attractive to Dialtous in this situation. (3 marks)

(30 marks)

61   **OMNIKIT (FS, 6/97 amended)**   *54 mins*

Omnikit plc is a manufacturer of kitchen furniture. The company's senior management have believed for several years that there is little opportunity to increase sales in the UK market and wish to set up a manufacturing subsidiary in Switzerland or the USA. Because of high transportation costs, exporting from the UK is not financially viable.

The Swiss subsidiary would involve the construction of a new factory on a 'green field' site. The projected costs are shown below.

Swiss subsidiary

	Now	*Year 1*
	SFr'000	SFr'000
Land	2,300	-
Building	1,600	6,200
Machinery	-	6,400
Working capital	-	11,500

Production and sales in year two are estimated to be 2,000 kitchens at an average price of SFr20,000 (at current prices). Production in each of years 3-6 is forecast at 2,500 units. Total local variable costs in Switzerland in year two are expected to be SFr11,000 per unit (at current prices). In addition a fixed royalty fee of £750,000 per year would be payable to the UK parent company. Tax allowable depreciation in Switzerland on machines is at 25% per year on a reducing balance basis. No tax allowable depreciation exists on other fixed assets.

The US investment would involve the purchase, via a takeover bid, of an existing kitchen furniture manufacturer based in Boston. The cost is not precisely known but Omnikit's managers are confident that a bid within the range $8m-10m will be successful. Additional investment of $2 million in new machines and $4 million in working capital would immediately be required, resulting in forecast pre-tax net cash flows (after tax savings from depreciation) in year one of $2 million (at current prices) rising to $3 million (at current prices) in year two and subsequent years.

All prices and costs in Switzerland and the USA are expected to increase annually by the current rate of inflation. The after-tax realisable value of the investments in six years' time is expected to be approximately SFr16.2 million and US$14.5 million at price levels then ruling, excluding working capital.

Inflation rates for each of the next six years are expected to be:

USA	6%
UK	3%
Switzerland	5%

Exchange rates

	SFr/£	$/£
Spot	2.3140-2.3210	1.5160-1.5210

Omnikit can borrow funds for the investment at 10% per year in the UK. The company's cost of equity capital is estimated to be 15%. After either proposed investment Omnikit's gearing will be approximately 50% debt, 50% equity by book value, and 30% debt, 70% equity by market value.

Corporate tax in Switzerland is at 40%, in the UK 33% and the USA 30%, Full bilateral tax treaties, exist between the UK and both Switzerland and the USA. Taxation is payable, and allowances are available, one year in arrears.

Required

(a) Discuss the advantages and disadvantages of organic growth and growth by acquisition. (6 marks)

(b) Evaluate which, if either, of the two subsidiaries should be established by Omnikit. Include discussion of the limitations of your evaluation. State clearly any assumptions that you make. (24 marks)

(30 marks)

62   VALTICK (FS, 12/99)   *72 mins*

Valtick plc is a company located in Wales which specialises in the production of digital clocks. A slump in demand during the last two years has meant that the company has moved into a loss-making situation. Prospects for the future are poor, unless the company can find new markets. Valtick's managing director has been to South America where she has been discussing a possible joint venture in the country of Marantinta. A company in Marantinta would like to use the technical expertise and patent rights of Valtick, and set up a manufacturing operation in Marantinta, which would sell clocks to the South American market, an area to which Valtick has never exported. Due to differences in labour costs the Marantintan company expects to manufacture the clocks for 40% less than it costs to manufacture in Wales. The Marantintan company has agreed that it would not export to Europe within the next four years.

Valtick would be required to:

(i)   Provide 30% of the total capital of 45 million pesos required to establish production in Marantinta. 5 million pesos of the total capital would be for working capital the remainder for depreciable fixed assets

(ii) Grant full patent rights to produce the clocks in Marantinta. The patent has six years until it expires

(iii) Provide technical expertise to assist in setting up the joint venture

(iv) Provide ongoing technical aid

The joint venture agreement would be for a period of four years, after which time a new agreement would be negotiated, or the Marantintan company would guarantee to buy Valtick's share of the venture, including future patent rights to produce the clocks for a sum of 30 million pesos, after any tax liabilities. The joint venture agreement would provide for equal share of profits or losses from the venture.

The clocks are expected to sell in South America for a price in year 1 of 480 pesos per unit. Prices will then increase by the expected rate of inflation in Marantinta. 40,000 units are expected to be sold in South America in the first year, rising by 10% per year for the next three years. The joint venture would also sell an expected 10,000 units per year to the USA at a constant price of $30 per unit. Valtick currently exports similar clocks to the USA, providing a pre-tax contribution of £80,000 per year. Because of the cheaper price of clocks manufactured in Marantinta it is expected that 40% of these exports would be lost.

Provision of initial technical assistance would cost Valtick £105,000, and ongoing aid would cost £50,000 per year in salaries, at current prices. Neither would be tax allowable expenses in Marantinta, although the salaries would be tax allowable in the UK. Use of the patent would have no cash cost, but would mean that the patent could not be sold to another South American company which was willing to pay a constant £40,000 per year for the patent.

Direct costs in Marantinta are expected to be an initial 200 pesos per unit, and fixed costs 4 million pesos per annum; both are expected to increase by the inflation rate in Marantinta. Tax allowable depreciation in Marantinta is available at 50% per year on a reducing balance basis. The corporate tax rate in Marantinta is 20% and in the UK 30%. A bilateral tax agreement exists between Marantinta and the UK. Tax is payable one year in arrears.

Expected inflation rates (%):

	UK	Marantinta	USA
Year 1	3	20	5
Year 2	3	20	5
Year 3	3	15	5
Year 4	3	15	5
Year 5	3	15	5

Spot exchange rates:

Marantintan pesos	32.78/£
Marantintan pesos	18.32/US$

Valtick's current after tax cost of capital is 14%. Because of the risk of operating in South America Valtick's finance director is proposing to use 18% as the cost of capital for the joint venture. Valtick would finance its capital needs for the new venture with a 9% convertible debenture.

Required

(a) Discuss the advantages and disadvantages of establishing international operations by means of joint ventures. (10 marks)

(b) Evaluate whether or not Valtick plc should participate in the joint venture in Marantinta. Include as part of your evaluation discussion of:

(i) The proposed financial contribution of Valtick and the Marantintan company to the joint venture, and

(ii) Any other factors that you consider to be relevant to the decision

State clearly any assumptions that you make.

Relevant calculations should be included as part of your evaluation. (30 marks)

Approximately 20 marks are available for calculations, and 10 marks for discussion.

(40 marks)

63   FORUN (FS, 6/94 amended)   *72 mins*

(a) Forun plc, a UK registered company, operates in four foreign countries, with total foreign subsidiary turnover of the equivalent of £60 million. The managing director is conducting a strategic review of the company's operations, with a view to increasing operations in some markets, and to reducing the scale of operations in others. He has assembled economic and other data on the four countries where subsidiaries are located which he considers to be of particular interest. His major concern is foreign exchange risk of overseas operations.

	UK	Country 1	Country 2	Country 3	Country 4
Inflation rate (%)	4	8	15	9	6
Real GDP growth (%)	1	–2	3	2	2
Balance of payments ($bn)	–12	3	–14	5	–2
Base rate (%)	6	10	14	10	8
Unemployment rate (%)	12	8	17	4	9
Population (million)	56	48	120	29	9
Currency reserves ($bn)	35	20	18	26	3
IMF loans ($bn)	-	4	20	5	5

On the basis of this information the managing director proposes that activity is concentrated in countries 1 and 4, and operations are reduced in countries 2 and 3.

A non-executive director believes that the meeting should not be focusing on such long-term strategic dimensions, as he has just read the report of the finance director who has forecast a foreign exchange loss on net exposed assets on consolidation of £15 million for the current financial year. The non-executive director is concerned with the detrimental impact he expects this loss to have on the company's share price. He further suggests a number of possible hedging strategies to be undertaken by Forun's foreign subsidiaries in order to reduce the exposure and the consolidated loss. These include:

(i)   Early collection of foreign currency receivables
(ii) Early repayment of foreign currency loans
(iii) Reducing stock levels in foreign countries

Required

(i)   Discuss whether or not you agree with the managing director's proposed strategy with respect to countries 1 to 4.   (8 marks)

(ii) Give reasoned advice as to the benefit to Forun plc of the non-executive director's suggested hedging strategies.   (10 marks)

(b) Forun has a number of intra-group transactions with its four foreign subsidiaries in six months time, and several large international trade deals with third parties. These are summarised below. Intra-group transactions are denominated in US dollars. All third party international trade is denominated in the currency shown. It is now 1 June.

Intra-group transactions

$US'000

		Paying company			
Receiving company	*UK*	*Sub 1*	*Sub 2*	*Sub 3*	*Sub 4*
UK	-	300	450	210	270
1	700	-	420	-	180
2	140	340	-	410	700
3	300	140	230	-	350
4	560	300	110	510	-

Exports to third parties

Receipts due in six months:

   £2,000,000 from Australia
   A$3,000,000 from Australia
   $12 million from the USA
   £1,800,000 from Switzerland

Receipts due in some time between three and six months:

   32 billion wons from South Korea

Imports from third parties

Payments due in six months:

   £3,000,000 to the USA
   A$3,000,000 to Australia
   13 million Swiss Francs to Switzerland
   £2,000,000 to Denmark

Foreign exchange rates

	Spot	3 mths forward	6 mths forward
US$/£	1.4960 - 1.4990	1.4720 - 1.4770	1.4550 - 1.4600
Australian$/£	2.1460 - 2.1500	2.1780 - 2.1840	2.2020 - 2.2090
Danish Kroners/£	7.7050 - 7.7090	7.9250 - 7.9490	8.0750 - 8.0990
Swiss Francs/£	2.4560 - 2.4590	2.4140 - 2.4180	2.3830 - 2.3870
South Korean Wons/£	2203 - 2208	2217 - 2224	2225 - 2232

Futures market rates

Sterling £62,500 contracts

	$/£	SFr/£
September	1.4820	2.4510
December	1.4800	2.4480

Minimum price movements are: $/£ 0.01 cents, SFr/£0.01 cents

Foreign currency option rates

Sterling £31,250 contracts (cents per £)

	Calls		Puts	
Exercise price	September	December	September	December
$1.450/£	3.50	5.75	4.80	7.90
$1.475/£	1.86	3.42	6.95	9.08
$1.500/£	0.82	1.95	9.80	11.53
$1.525/£	0.38	0.90	12.16	14.70

Required

(i)   Explain and demonstrate how multilateral netting might be of benefit to Forun plc.   (5 marks)

(ii)   Recommend, with supporting calculations, alternative hedging strategies that the company might adopt to protect itself against short-term foreign exchange exposure. The company is risk averse with respect to short-term foreign exchange risk.   (17 marks)

                                                                                                    (40 marks)

64   AXMINE   *72 mins*

(a)   The managers of Axmine plc, a major international copper processor are considering a joint venture with Traces, a company owning significant copper reserves in a South American country with a significant overseas debt problem. If the joint venture were not to proceed Axmine would still need to import copper from the South American country. Axmine's managing director is concerned that the government of the South American country might impose some form of barriers to free trade which put Axmine at a competitive disadvantage in importing copper. A further director considers that this is unlikely due to the existence of the WTO (formerly known as GATT).

Required

Briefly discuss possible forms of non-tariff barrier that might affect Axmine's ability to import copper, and how the existence of the WTO might influence such barriers.

                                                                                                    (8 marks)

(b)   The proposed joint venture with Traces would be for an initial period of four years. Copper would be mined using a new technique developed by Axmine. Axmine would supply machinery at an immediate cost of 800 million pesos and ten supervisors at an annual salary of £40,000 each at current prices. Additionally, Axmine would pay half of the 1,000 million pesos per year (at current prices) local labour costs and other expenses in the South American country. The supervisors' salaries and local labour and other expenses will be increased in line with inflation in the United Kingdom and the South American country respectively.

Inflation in the South American country is currently 100% per year, and in the UK 8% per year. The government of the South American country is attempting to control inflation, and hopes to reduce it each year by 20% of the previous year's rate.

The joint venture would give Axmine a 50% share of Traces' copper production, with current market prices at £1,500 per 1,000 kilogrammes. Traces' production is expected to be 10 million kilogrammes per year, and copper prices are expected to rise by 10% per year (in pounds sterling) for the foreseeable future. At the end of four years Axmine would be given the choice to pull out of the venture or to negotiate another four year joint venture, on different terms.

The current exchange rate is 140 pesos/£. Future exchange rates may be estimated using the purchasing power parity theory.

Axmine has no foreign operations. The cost of capital of the company's UK mining operations is 16% per year. As this joint venture involves diversifying into foreign operations the company considers that a 2% reduction in the cost of capital would be appropriate for this project.

Corporate tax is at the rate of 20% per year in the South American country and 35% per year in the UK. A tax treaty exists between the two countries and all foreign tax paid is allowable against any UK tax liability. Taxation is payable one year in arrears and a 25% straight-line writing down allowance is available on the machinery in both countries.

Cash flows may be assumed to occur at the year end, except for the immediate cost of machinery. The machinery is expected to have negligible terminal value at the end of four years.

Required

Prepare a report discussing whether Axmine plc should agree to the proposed joint venture. Relevant calculations must form part of your report or an appendix to it.

State clearly any assumptions that you make.   (18 marks)

(c) If the South American government were to fail to control inflation, and inflation were to increase rapidly during the period of the joint venture, discuss the likely effect of very high inflation on the joint venture.   (4 marks)

(d) Outline the main methods that have been suggested to reduce the debt problem of less developed countries (LDCs).   (6 marks)

(e) Explain the potential significance of the LDC debt problem to multinational companies.   (4 marks)

                                                                         (40 marks)

---

65 **VTW (FS, 6/98 amended)**   *27 mins*

The managers of VTW plc are discussing whether or not to set up a foreign subsidiary in a South American country. The government of the country has recently changed, and the country's new leaders have stated that they intend to introduce economic policies to improve the balance of payments. VTW is concerned that one of these measures could be to block the remittance of dividends from the South American country to the UK. VTW expects to remit about 180 million pesos per year to the UK if the government does not intervene. Blocked funds may be invested internally within the South American country, but the government is likely to control domestic interest rates.

The investment in the South American subsidiary has an expected NPV of £2 million. The peso is expected to devalue by approximately 10% per year relative to the pound. VTW used a discount rate of 20% per year in the appraisal of its South American capital investment. The current spot exchange rate is 20 pesos/£.

Required

(a) Assuming that the government blocks the remittance of dividends for a period of three years, estimate the approximate interest rate that would have to exist in the South American country for the proposed investment to remain financially viable. Taxation may be ignored. (6 marks)

(b) Briefly discuss methods by which VTW might try to avoid the block on the remittance of dividends. (4 marks)

(c) Tandem plc is registered in England and is listed on the London Stock Exchange. It has four subsidiaries in foreign countries, A, B, C and D, with a total turnover equivalent in sterling to £110 million. Tandem is risk-averse in respect of short-term currency risks.

It is now 1 December 20X5. Tandem and its subsidiaries have a number of intercompany balances held with each other, all of which are US dollar balances as follows.

Balances on intergroup accounts

Debtor's country	Creditor's country	$'000
UK	A	621
UK	B	751
UK	C	147
A	UK	1,024
A	B	682
A	C	329
B	UK	671
B	A	518
B	C	568
B	D	56
C	A	229
C	B	247
D	UK	200
D	B	121

Required

Explain briefly what is meant by multilateral netting and, giving relevant calculations, show how Tandem can take advantage of this procedure. (5 marks)

(15 marks)

66   CENTRALISATION (FS, 6/97 amended)   *27 mins*

(a) Touten plc is a UK registered multinational company with subsidiaries in 14 countries in Europe, Asia and Africa. The subsidiaries have traditionally been allowed a large amount of autonomy, but Touten plc is now proposing to centralise most of the group treasury management operations.

Required

Acting as a consultant to Touten plc prepare a memo suitable for distribution from the group finance director to the senior management of each of the subsidiaries explaining:

(i) The potential benefits of treasury centralisation; and

(ii)   How the company proposes to minimise any potential problems for the subsidiaries that might arise as a result of treasury centralisation   **(9 marks)**

(b)   Gotop plc has large subsidiaries in Malaysia and Hong Kong. The chief accountant at Gotop is concerned about the size of cash bank balances that are held by each of the companies and would like to reduce these balances to make more funds available for capital investment.

	Expected average cash need	*One standard deviation from expected average cash need*
Gotop (UK)	£5.5 million	£0.5 million
Malaysia	8 million Ringgit	1 million Ringgit
Hong Kong	HK$18 million	HK$2.7 million

Exchange rates

Ringgit/£	*HK$/£*
3.95	11.98

The three cash bank balances are currently independent of each other. Gotop's chief accountant suggests combining the accounts of all three companies into one UK based account. In order to meet unforeseen need Gotop has a policy of requiring actual cash balances to be three standard deviations higher than the average cash need.

Required

Estimate by how much the total balances might be reduced, without altering the current policy of keeping cash to meet unforeseen needs.   **(6 marks)**

(15 marks)

---

67   DEBOIS (FS, 6/98 amended)   *27 mins*

(a)   What factors should a company consider when deciding how to arrange the international transfer of cash?   **(5 marks)**

(b)   Debois, a Danish multinational company, has subsidiaries in the United Kingdom and Germany. The UK subsidiary produces components that are transferred to Germany and for final production.

The components are sold by the UK subsidiary to the German subsidiary for a unit price of 144 Danish kroners, with annual sales of 125,000 units. Total production expenses are 80% of the sales price. The finished goods are sold in the German market for the equivalent of 350 Danish kroners, yielding a taxable profit per unit in Germany of the equivalent to 70 Danish kroners.

Tax rates are as follows.

	Denmark	*UK*	*Germany*
Corporate tax on profits	33.3%	25%	40%
Withholding tax on dividends	10%	-	8%

Bilateral double tax treaties exist between each of the countries which allow credit for foreign tax paid against any domestic liability. It is the policy of Debois to remit annually all profit from foreign subsidiaries to the parent company in the form of dividends.

Required

(i)   Illustrate how the tax liability of Debois might be reduced by a 20% increase in the transfer price between the UK and German subsidiaries.   **(6 marks)**

(ii)   Discuss briefly the possible practical problems of such a change in transfer price.   **(4 marks)**

(15 marks)

73

68   **TAX HAVEN (FS, 12/00 amended)**   *27 mins*

(a) Outline the main factors that a multinational company should consider before deciding whether or not to use a tax haven.   (5 marks)

(b) Retro plc has manufacturing subsidiaries in three overseas countries.

	Country	Corporate tax rate	Proposed net dividend (£000)
Subsidiary 1	Mopia	40%	600
Subsidiary 2	Blueland	35%	800
Subsidiary 3	Saddonia	20%	1,500

The UK corporate tax rate is 30%. There are no taxes in the tax haven country.

Bilateral tax treaties exist between the UK and the countries where each of the subsidiaries are located, which allow a tax credit against UK corporate tax liability up to a maximum of the UK tax liability. This tax credit may be assumed to be available even when dividends are channelled via a tax haven. UK corporate taxation on overseas earnings may be assumed to be based upon the total dividends remitted to the UK (grossed up by one minus the relevant national tax rate(s)), from each overseas country).

Required

Evaluate whether or not Retro would benefit from using a tax haven holding company through which dividends would be channelled.   (5 marks)

(c) Describe the factors that the financial manager of a multinational company would consider when deciding whether to borrow funds on the domestic market or the Euro currency or Eurobond markets.   (5 marks)

(15 marks)

Answers

1   PREPARATION QUESTION: CONFLICT

> **Tutor's hint**. Points to be covered are: What are shareholders objectives? What are directors' objectives? Where are the potential conflicts? Are conflicts taken care of automatically by the law and the market system or do shareholders need to use motivating techniques?

Assuming they are not also involved in the management of the company, the main **objective of shareholders** is to increase their wealth as much as possible, subject to various constraints, the main one being the risk they are prepared to bear. Shareholders' **attitude to risk** is very much affected by the fact that they can reduce it by diversifying their holding into a range of different companies.

Other constraints on the wealth objective include the extent to which they are prepared to invest in companies which engage in activities which are socially, politically or environmentally undesirable.

In the UK, directors have a **legal duty** to run their company on behalf of the shareholders. Most successful directors realise, however, that 'rewarding shareholders' is not by itself an objective that can be translated into action plans, rather it is a natural consequence of building a successful company. Most successful companies recognise that a whole range of stakeholders are involved.

Conflicts between shareholders and directors arise when directors pursue personal goals at the expense of shareholders' wealth, whether through greed, fear or ignorance. Typical **personal goals** include:

(a)   **Payment** of **excessive remuneration** and fringe benefits

(b)   Attempts to **improve job security** (eg excessively long service contracts)

(c)   **Reduction** in the **company's risk level** (eg by diversification of the company's activities, which does not necessarily reduce the risk of diversified shareholders, but which will reduce the directors' personal risk position)

(d)   **Power and prestige** (eg building a large 'empire' with diminishing returns to shareholders)

In extreme cases directors may even engage in **illegal acts** (eg using their company position to make personal profits).

Do directors need any special incentives to bring their goals into line with those of shareholders? One school of thought says 'No' because there are already sufficient adverse consequences for directors who do not reward shareholders, as follows:

(a)   Shareholders have the right to **remove directors** if they are not satisfied with the company's performance.

(b)   In an efficient market, a company which does not reward shareholders will suffer from a **falling share price** and will ultimately be taken over, resulting in the directors losing their jobs.

(c)   The external auditor provides an **independent report** on the validity of the financial statements.

(d)   **Voluntary codes** such as the Combined Code and the City Code on Takeovers and Mergers prevent further abuses of corporate governance.

The alternative viewpoint says that these preventive measures do not act fast enough to bring director's goals into line with those of shareholders. The best way to establish goal congruence is to reward directors for producing high shareholder returns.

This school of thought recommends **performance related pay** and other incentive schemes such as share options. The main problem with this approach is finding a suitable scheme which is fair but which cannot be manipulated by directors or encourage them to make short term profits at the expense of real wealth.

2   STAKEHOLDERS

> **Tutor's hint.** In (b) As well as evaluating each of the points raised, it is helpful to set out the wider context of the theory underlying the principles that govern the movement of the share price.
>
> **Examiner's comment.** Weaker answers often failed to discuss which stakeholders might be affected by the proposed measures.

(a)   **A private company converting into a public company**

When a private company converts into a public company, some of the existing shareholder/managers will sell their shares to outside investors. In addition, new shares may be issued. The dilution of ownership might cause loss of control by the existing management.

The stakeholders involved in potential conflicts are as follows.

(i)   **Existing shareholder/managers**

They will want to sell some of their shareholding at as high a price as possible. This may motivate them to overstate their company's prospects. Those shareholder/managers who wish to retire from the business may be in conflict with those who wish to stay in control – the latter may oppose the conversion into a public company.

(ii)   **New outside shareholders**

Most of these will hold minority stakes in the company and will receive their rewards as dividends only. This may put them in conflict with the existing shareholder/managers who receive rewards as salaries as well as dividends. On conversion to a public company there should be clear policies on dividends and directors' remuneration.

(iii)   **Employees, including managers who are not shareholders**

Part of the reason for the success of the company will be the efforts made by employees. They may feel that they should benefit when the company goes public. One way of organising this is to create employee share options or other bonus schemes.

(b)   MEMO

To: Managing Director
From: Finance Director
Date: 15 June 20X6
Subject: Proposals aimed at maximisation of the share price

Further to our recent discussions, I agree fully with your desire to seek the **maximisation of the company's share price** and therefore its **market capitalisation**. However, although I agree that a relationship does exist between reported profits, earnings per share and the share price, short-term profits are not in themselves the principal driver of the share price.

In reality, assuming a reasonably efficient market, the maximisation of the share price will be brought about by the maximisation of the present value of the future cash flows. The most effective way to increase the share price therefore is to concentrate on making investments that generate a positive net present value (NPV) when discounted at the cost of capital. I believe that some of the current proposals could damage the position of some of the groups of stakeholders in the firm and could even have a negative impact on the share price.

(i)   As explained above, it is necessary to undertake investments that generate a **positive NPV** in order to maximise the share price. Minimising capital expenditure in order to boost short-term profits could therefore mean that some important **opportunities** are **missed**. This in turn means that the value of the company will be lower than it could be, which will impact badly on the share price. It could also adversely affect the position of other stakeholders such as employees and suppliers.

(ii)   **Reducing real wages and employee benefits** is likely to damage the **morale** of the employees, and could result in good employees being lost, while at the same time making it harder to recruit the right people. If morale is badly affected this could also affect both quality and the efficiency of production.

(iii)   **Delaying payments to creditors** beyond the terms allowed could have a number of damaging effects.

    (1)   **Valuable discounts** may be **lost** and credit charges incurred.

    (2)   The **credit rating** of the company could be **damaged making** it difficult to obtain further credit from new suppliers in the future, or from other sources of finance.

    (3)   **Supplies of materials** could be **jeopardised** if the company's orders are moved down the priority list or even placed 'on stop'.

(iv)   Stringent controls on pollution exist, and the company must be certain that any **delay in expenditure on measures to reduce pollution** will not result in environmental standards such as discharge consents being breached. If this does happen then the company will be liable for financial penalties, and again the standing in the local community will be damaged. If the problems are severe, then the company could come under pressure from environmental pressure groups which could result in more widespread damaging publicity.

I would be pleased to discuss these issues with you further, and to consider some alternative approaches to increasing the share price.

3   INTERNATIONAL DIFFERENCES

> **Tutor's hint**. Corporate governance in the USA is a topic which is specifically included in the syllabus, along with the development of corporate governance in the UK. It is not an easy topic to write about in the time available.
>
> **Examiner's comment**. Answers were often disappointing for two reasons:
> * Some candidates wrote only about the Cadbury report.
> * Many candidates ignored the discussion about the USA.

(a) A **definition of corporate governance** is 'the system by which an organisation is directed and controlled'. It is concerned with systems, processes, controls, accountability and decision making at the heart of and at the highest level of an organisation. It is therefore concerned with the way in which top managers execute their responsibilities and authority and how they account for that authority to those who have entrusted them with assets and resources. In particular it is concerned with the potential abuse of power and the need for openness, integrity and accountability in corporate decision making.

In both the **UK** and **USA**, the shareholders appoint a board of directors and an external auditor and need to satisfy themselves that an appropriate governance structure exists. The board of directors is responsible for running the company on behalf of shareholders, considering the interests of other stakeholders such as employees, and reporting to shareholders on the company's progress. The auditor provides an independent examination of the company's financial statements.

A major difference between UK and US governance is that there is far more emphasis on legislation in the USA. In particular there are more detailed laws on directors' duties and on detailed financial reporting requirements than in the UK. The UK has a tradition of operating by voluntary codes of best practice rather than by detailed legislation and this is reflected by voluntary codes contained in the Cadbury Report on Corporate Governance, in the City Code on Takeovers and Mergers and within the Financial Services Act.

In the USA it more common for bankers, other creditors and directors of other companies to have seats on a company's board. The UK is now moving towards this position with the Cadbury requirement for non-executive directors.

(b) The way in which **environmental costs and benefits** are included in the appraisal process will depend on the nature of the environmental implications, and the way in which the company intends to approach them. One method is to include in the appraisal only those elements of environmental cost that are **directly attributable** to undertaking the project, and to evaluate any further actions that the company may wish to undertake as a separate issue. In some cases, this may be relatively simple, particularly if legislation exists that defines the environmental standards to be applied.

The company will then be faced with a variety of **technological options** that it could use to reduce the contamination to the required levels; for example, if volumes are large enough, it may be appropriate to build a treatment plant to decontaminate the effluent – alternatively it could enter into an agreement with a waste treatment company to tanker away the waste and dispose of it off site. Each of these options will have a definable cost which can be evaluated and incorporated into the overall project appraisal. In this situation, there are no quantifiable benefits as such, since the environmental issues take the form of a constraint on the project. The costs arise as a direct result of undertaking the project, and as such must be incorporated into the appraisal.

The problems arise where the company sees the opportunity to go beyond its statutory duties and to act in such a way as to **maximise** the **environmental benefits**. In the example cited above, it may be that the most cost effective method from the point of view of the company is to tanker the waste to a remote treatment plant. However, it may view this as unacceptable on the grounds that it wishes to minimise the disturbance to the area around the site, and thus not to generate high volumes of tanker traffic in the local area. In this situation, the higher cost option of on-site treatment may become more attractive, although this is not a direct requirement of the project being undertaken. The benefits that arise are difficult to quantify and will not accrue directly to the company undertaking the investment.

In this situation, two approaches are possible.

(i)   The company could decide that its own environmental standards form a financial constraint upon the project, and thus that the project should be **evaluated at its full environmental cost**.

(ii) Alternatively, it could decide that the additional costs of on-site treatment over and above the cost of meeting the statutory requirements represent a **separate environmental investment**. If the company sets aside a budget for environmental and social issues, these excess costs could then be taken away from the project and allocated against this environmental budget.

Both approaches are valid and will depend on the objectives and policies of the company with regard to environmental issues.

4   ESOPs

> **Tutor's hint**. This question calls for an understanding of the nature and limitations of share option schemes, and the way in which they interact with agency theory. It is important to discuss the ways in which such schemes may contribute to goal congruence and not just the nature of the schemes themselves.
>
> **Examiner's comment**. Most candidates showed good knowledge of ESOPs, but did not focus sufficiently upon their limitations in the achievement of goal congruence, either between managers and shareholders, or between managers and other stakeholders of the organisation.

(a) The relationship between management and shareholders is sometimes referred to as an **agency relationship**, in which managers act as agents for the shareholders, using delegated powers to run the affairs of the company in the shareholders' best interests. There is a potential **conflict of interest** that is inherent in this situation, since **shareholders** will be best rewarded by efficient performance, while **managers** may prefer a life where they don't have to work too intensively and in which they are rewarded by high salaries and perks. **Other interest groups** such as employees, suppliers, customers and the government may also have objectives that conflict with those of the shareholders.

Goal congruence occurs when the goals of the different interest groups coincide with those of the company as a whole. There have been many attempts to change the way in which managers are remunerated so as to improve the achievement of goal congruence between the managers and the shareholders, and the provision of share options form one of these methods.

In a **share option scheme**, selected employees can be given a number of share options, each of which gives the holder the right after a certain date to subscribe for shares in the company at a fixed price. The value of an option will increase if the company is successful and its share price goes up. The theory is that this will encourage managers to pursue high NPV strategies and investments, since they as shareholders will benefit personally from the increase in the share price that results from such investments. However, although share option schemes can contribute to the achievement of goal congruence, there are a number of reasons why the benefits may not be as great as might be expected, as follows.

(i)   **Managers** are **protected** from the **downside risk** that is faced by shareholders. If the share price falls, they do not have to take up the shares and will still receive their standard remuneration, while shareholders will lose money.

(ii) Many **other factors** as well as the quality of the company's performance influence share price movements. If the market is rising strongly, managers will still benefit from share options, even if performance has been worse than expected. Similarly, even though the company may have been very successful, the share price will fall if there is a downward stock market adjustment, and the managers will not be rewarded for their efforts in the way that was planned.

(iii) The scheme may encourage management to adopt '**creative accounting**' **methods** that will distort the reported performance of the company in the service of the managers' own ends.

(b) The choice of an appropriate remuneration policy by a company will depend, among other things, on:

(i) **Cost:** the extent to which the package provides value for money

(ii) **Motivation:** the extent to which the package motivates employees both to stay with the company and to work to their full potential

(iii) **Fiscal effects:** government tax incentives may promote different types of pay. At times of wage control and high taxation this can act as an incentive to make the 'perks' a more significant part of the package

(iv) **Goal congruence:** the extent to which the package encourages employees to work in such a way as to achieve the objectives of the firm - perhaps to maximise rather than to satisfice.

In this context, Option (i) is likely to be **relatively expensive** with no payback to the firm in times of low profitability. It is unlikely to encourage staff to maximise their efforts, although the extent to which it acts as a **motivator** will depend on the individual psychological make-up of the employees concerned. Many staff prefer this type of package however, since they know where they are financially. In the same way the company is also able to budget accurately for its staff costs.

Provided that the scheme qualifies, the firm may be able to gain **fiscal benefits** from operating a profit-related pay scheme (Option (ii)). It also benefits from the fact that **costs** will be lower, though not proportionately so, during a time of low profits. The effect on motivation will vary with the individual concerned, and will also depend on whether it is an individual or a group performance calculation. There is a further risk that figures and performance may be manipulated by managers in such a way as to maximise their bonus to the detriment of the overall longer term company benefit.

5   SHARE OWNERSHIP

Tutor's hint. Be careful not to get side-tracked into a discussion of why institutions are so dominant – concentrate on the implications. Four benefits and four concerns about institutional shareholders should suffice.

Examiner's comment. Most answers identified the most important trends, although some concentrated too much on one or two aspects.

(a) Institutional shareholders are insurance companies, pension funds, investment trusts and unit trusts. From the data supplied, the percentage of UK shares owned by such institutions rose from 59% in 1980 to 69% in 1995, with all institutions showing increased holdings apart from investment trusts. The reasons are well documented. They include **tax concessions** to investors, cheap and easy diversification of investors' funds and effective marketing by institutions.

The **implications** for financial managers of quoted companies are:

Benefits

(i)   Institutional investors are allegedly **better informed** and react swiftly, creating a **more efficient** market and encouraging realistic share prices.

(ii) Knowledge that intelligent investors are analysing their results and statements may encourage **more rational** longer term **decision making** by directors and fewer 'quick wins' and less creative accounting.

(iii) Large institutional shareholders can **offer advice** to company directors, though care must be taken to avoid conflicts of interest and **insider dealing**.

(iv) Fewer shareholders means **lower administrative costs** for the company.

Concerns

(i)   Institutional investors may not be as rational as they claim. In the past they have been criticised as being **too short term** in their outlook, requiring immediate consistent returns. However, there is also evidence that they follow 'fads' for example investing in 'dot.com' shares at the expense of 'conventional' businesses.

(ii) They can build up large shareholdings and distort the market price if they '**buy and hold**' leaving only small numbers of shares to be traded actively.

(iii) On the other hand they can significantly **affect** the company's **share price** in the event of a swift disposal. This does not help to create market efficiency and may contribute to bubbles and crashes in share prices, which hinder the raising of capital.

(iv) They can exert **significant influence** on **company decision making**, particularly in a merger/takeover situation.

(b) During this period, **earnings per share** have declined by 10.7% while at the same time **dividend per share** has increased by 19.0%. The **payout ratio** has increased from 60% in 20X0 to 80% in 20X4, and thus the proportion of earnings retained has fallen to 20%. If it is assumed that the capital structure has not changed over the period, then it can be seen that both **actual earnings** and the **return on capital employed** have declined over the period.

One possible implication of this policy is that insufficient earnings have been retained to finance the investment required to at least maintain the rate of return on capital employed. If this means that the company is falling behind its competitors, then this could have a serious impact on the long-term profitability of the business.

6   PREPARATION QUESTION: POTREN

Analysis of results

	Division A		Division B	
	Last yr	*This yr*	*Last yr*	*This yr*
Profitability ratios				
Return on capital employed				
(Op. profit: capital employed)	14.4%	15.8%	15.6%	18.6%
Return on sales				
(Op. profit: turnover)	11.3%	12.2%	12.8%	14.5%
Asset turnover				
(Turnover: capital employed)	1.27	1.30	1.22	1.27

	Division A		Division B	
	Last yr	*This yr*	*Last yr*	*This yr*
Liquidity ratios				
Current ratio	1.38	1.35	1.39	1.41
Financial ratios				
Gearing				
(med/long-term debt:equity)	6.45%	22.2%	12.4%	12.1%
Interest cover	15.83	6.78	9.75	11.75

	Division A	Division B
Growth rates (this yr/last yr)		
Turnover	+ 19.1%	+ 6.56%
Operating profit	+ 28.4%	+ 20.5%
Taxable profit	+ 16.9%	+ 22.9%
Fixed assets	+ 17.2%	+ 2.33%
Working capital	+ 12.5%	+ 0%

Both divisions have improved their **profitability** while maintaining adequate levels of **liquidity** and **interest cover.** However they appear to have achieved this in different ways.

Division A has made a **significant investment** in new fixed assets, this being apparently financed mainly by the increase in medium and long-term debt.

Division B on the other hand appears to have boosted performance through **improvements in operating profitability** using the existing assets and by keeping tight control over its working capital.

It is probable that Division B has taken a **more short-term approach** to the target than Division A and that as a result it may be less likely to be able to deliver a sustained improvement in performance in the longer term.

This difference in approach highlights the fact that Potren has given the divisions a **target** which is both **very general** in definition and short-term in timescale.

If Potren wishes to influence the future development of the divisions so as to assist it to meet its long-term corporate strategic objectives, its **target setting** must be more defined and measurable. Examples of areas in which targets could be established include the following.

(a) It could set **NPV parameters** for the acceptance of new investments, with all investments above a certain size being referred to Potren. This should serve to focus attention on the long-term value of the entity.

(b) It could define product and market areas with **targets for each division**.

(c) It could set **targets relating to the mix of capital and labour** that it wishes to achieve in the long term.

7   STEPS

> **Tutor's hint**. The main pitfall in answering (b) identified by the examiner is to focus too closely on the techniques of capital budgeting rather than taking a broader strategic perspective and linking the company's financial objectives to its overall corporate objectives.
>
> **Examiner's comment**. Some candidates failed to gain marks in (a) by focusing their answers too much on the financial techniques of capital budgeting rather than take a broader strategic perspective, and linking the companies financial objectives to its overall corporate objectives.

(a) **Strategic decisions** are those which concern the **objectives** or **strategic targets** of an organisation. They include such areas as the selection of products and markets, the required levels of company profitability, and the purchase and disposal of subsidiary companies.

Tactical decisions concern the **efficient** and **effective use** of an **organisation's resources** to achieve these objectives. Examples include the sourcing of raw materials and the pricing structure for the different product ranges.

(b) **Strategic plans** are those which **set or change the objectives,** or strategic targets of an organisation. They include such matters as selection of products and markets, the required levels of company profitability, the purchase and disposal of subsidiary companies or major fixed assets, and whether employees should share in company profits.

The first stage in constructing the framework for a strategic plan is that of business **review and assessment**, including the appraisal of corporate strengths and weaknesses. A **detailed appraisal** of the **market situation** and the **key competencies** needed to succeed in the chosen markets will also be made at this stage. The review will enable a forecast to be made of likely changes in sales, profitability and capital requirements. This can then be compared with the restatement of the company's objectives in order to identify the 'gap' which must be overcome strategically. This stage is very important in establishing some of the parameters that will be used in creating the financial model, including:

(i) Defining the **primary objective**, for example to achieve a given level of NPV return to equity

(ii) Establishing **initial forecasts** of sales activity, production bottlenecks, etc

(iii) Deciding the **cost of capital** to be used in evaluating new opportunities, taking account of the company's attitude to risk

(iv) **Quantifying the interrelationships** between different variables, such as price elasticity, volume/cost, and any constraints that may exist, for example in the area of technical support

(v) Evaluating the likely effect of various **external influences**, for example changes in fiscal policy and the implementation of the EU social chapter

Once the overall plan has been drawn up, it must be broken down into **shorter term tactical plans** that can be implemented and monitored at the operational level.

Strategic financial planning should not be seen as an occasional exercise. If it is to be successful, plans must be continually monitored and updated in the light of actual events, and people at all levels in the organisation must understand the aims of the plan and be committed to seeing it through in their area of activity.

8   PULFER

> **Tutor's hint**. Various approaches are possible when calculating the funding requirements. It is therefore important to be very clear about the timing of transactions and the assumptions you have made about the use of the overdraft. Although much information is available, for the sake of time you should restrict your critique of performance to a comparison of the projections with the stated objectives of the company.
>
> **Examiner's comment.** Candidates generally made satisfactory attempts to produce pro forma profit and loss accounts. There were fewer satisfactory attempts at a schedule of funding requirements that is necessary to highlight potential cash flow problems.

REPORT

To: Board of Directors, Pulfer Ltd
From: Consultant
Date: 17 December 20X4
Subject: Three year financial projections

Introduction

1   This report seeks to analyse the **projected financial performance** for the next three years in the context of the company's stated financial objectives. An appraisal of estimated funding requirements is made, and the final part of the report deals with the forecasting techniques that have been used. Detailed numerical analysis can be found in the appendices to this report.

Projected financial performance

2   The projections in Appendix 2 show that **earnings before interest and tax (EBIT)** should rise gradually over the period in question from the current level of £57,000 to either £88,000 or £96,000 in year 3 depending on the speed with which the economy pulls out of recession. The **return on capital figures** are as follows:

	Yr 1	Yr 2	Yr 3 15% growth	Yr 3 25% growth
	£'000	£'000	£'000	£'000
EBIT	65	76	88	96
Ordinary shares	200	239	239	239
Reserves	170	184	205	212
Total equity	370	423	444	451
Return on equity	17.6%	18.0%	19.8%	21.3%

3   It can be seen that for the majority of the period, the **primary financial objective** of 20% return on equity in years one and two, and 25% in year three is **unlikely to be achieved**. If the company wishes to achieve the target return on capital it will need to consider making cost savings. While there is very little operational information available on which to make suggestions, it is noted that the number of people employed in relation to turnover is high, the current level of sales per employee being only £21,875 per year. This is very little given the current level of UK employment costs and savings in this area could significantly improve financial performance.

4   The other objective of **increasing dividend payments by 10% per annum** has been incorporated into the financial projections.

Funding requirements

5   The **critical funding issue** arises in year 2 when additional investment in fixed assets is needed to meet the level of demand. It is assumed that the new machinery will be purchased at the start of the year ahead of the increase in sales, and that the additional funding is negotiated at the same time. The restrictive covenants on the existing bank loan mean that it will not be possible to raise the whole of the required amount in the form of debt, but that some additional equity will also be required. In making the projection for this year it has been assumed that advantage will be taken of the existing overdraft facility to fund the working cash requirement. However, the maximum size of new loan that can be taken out is restricted. This means that a further £23,000 will need to be raised in the form of equity.

6   Although the directors wish to source new equity finance from venture capital organisations, it may be difficult to raise such a **relatively small amount of money** in this way. In practice, the directors may have to choose between making personal

borrowings to subscribe for the new shares, finding a new personal investor to take a stake in the company, or raising a higher proportion of the additional funds in the form of equity so as to be able to take advantage of venture capital funds. An alternative approach would be to restrict dividend payments for the next three years in order to ease the demands for finance.

7   It is noted that at present surplus cash is kept in a **non-interest bearing current account**. It is suggested that the cash position is monitored weekly or even daily, and funds transferred to interest bearing accounts as available.

Forecasting techniques

8   The financial projections have been based upon the assumption that existing historical statistical relationships between items of revenue and expenditure will continue into the future. In practice this is likely to be **unrealistic** due to changes in the pattern of demand, differing levels of price change between the factors of production, cyclical influences and economies of scale. For example, it should not be necessary to increase the level of stockholding at the same rate as the level of sales.

9   It would be more appropriate to construct the forecasts on the basis of units of resource consumed and goods produced, and to calculate the financial budget using a '**bottom up**' approach. If this approach is taken, it will be easier to discover why actual performance differs from projections and to take action to improve the position.

10 It is recommended that a **computerised financial planning** model be used, to allow the effects of various different relationships and assumptions to be shown.

Conclusions

11 Pulfer will be **unable to meet its financial targets** without making savings in costs. **Additional fixed capital** will be needed in year 2, and it is suggested that the directors consider some of the alternatives to venture capital as discussed above. Besides the problem of the sum required being too low to interest most venture capital funds, the cost of arranging this form of finance is likely to be high and there is likely to be a loss of control by the directors since most funds will require a seat on the board.

APPENDIX 1: OPENING BALANCE SHEET

	£'000	£'000
Fixed assets		410
Current assets		
Stock	231	
Debtors	185	
Cash	9	
	425	
Less current liabilities		
Creditors	(306)	
Net current assets		119
Total assets employed		529
Financed by		
Ordinary shares (50p par value)		200
Reserves		149
Bank loan (12%)		180
		529

Note: Whilst not strictly necessary, showing the opening balance sheet helps with subsequent workings.

APPENDIX 2: THREE YEAR FINANCIAL PROJECTIONS

Profit and loss account	*Year 0*	*Year 1*	*Year 2*	*Year 3* 15% growth	*Year 3* 25% growth
	£'000	£'000	£'000	£'000	£'000
Sales	875	1,006	1,157	1,331	1,446
Cost of goods sold (75%)	(656)	(755)	(868)	(999)	(1,085)
Gross profit	219	251	289	332	361
Other expenses	(162)	(186)	(213)	(244)	(265)
EBIT	57	65	76	88	96
Interest (see below)	(22)	(22)	(22)	(39)	(39)
	35	43	54	49	57
Tax at 25%	(9)	(11)	(13)	(12)	(14)
	26	32	41	37	43
Dividend	(10)	(11)	(12)	(15)	(15)
Retained earnings	16	21	29	22	28

Interest is calculated as follows.

		£'000
Existing interest		22
Additional interest:	Overdraft (£15,000 × 10%)	1
	Term loan (142,000 × 11%)	16
		39

The projection assumes that there will be 46,000 new shares issued, ie at par. In practice, a premium is likely, which would affect the size of the dividend.

The restriction on the current ratio is satisfied by the above projections. Projected current ratios are as follows.

Year	*Current ratios*
1	1.40
2	1.37
3 (15% growth)	1.37
3 (25% growth)	1.36

New machinery will be required in Year 2.

	Year 1	*Year 2*	*Year 3* 15% growth	*Year 3* 25% growth
	£'000	£'000	£'000	£'000
Schedule of funding needs				
Change in fixed assets	0	200	0	0
Change in working capital excluding cash (see below)	12	15	18	30
Cash from retentions	(21)	(29)	(22)	(28)
Funding needs after use of existing cash	(9)	186	(4)	2
Cash movement	9	(6)	4	(2)
	-	180*	-	-
Cash balance (0.1% minimum)	(9 + 9) 18	(18 – 6) 12	(12+4) 16	(16 – 2) 14
Shareholder's funds	(200+149+21) 370	(370+29) 399	(399+22+23) 444	(399+28+23) 450
Change in working capital				
Stock	263	301	345	374
Debtors	211	241	276	299
Less creditors	(352)	(405)	(466)	(506)
	122	137	155	167
Existing	(110)	(122)	(137)	(137)
Change in working capital	12	15	18	30

* Funding is likely to be £15,000 (overdraft) for working capital. However, the amount of debt which can be used is restricted due to the covenant.

A maximum 80% for debt/shareholders equity is allowed by the covenant.

Shareholder's equity in Year 2 is estimated at £399,000. The £180,000 required can be financed by £157,000 of debt and £23,000 of equity to maintain gearing at 80%. Such a small amount of equity is unlikely to be attractive to a venture capitalist.

New debt $\dfrac{180,000 + 157,000}{399,000 + 23,000} = \dfrac{337,000}{422,000} = 0.799$

9   NOIFA LEISURE

> **Tutor's hint**. This question has a fairly brief requirement, not divided into sections, and so careful planning of your answer is vital. Several different answers could be equally good, but any good answer will make good use of the detailed information given in the question, supporting general conclusions with specific calculations. Weaker candidates will tend to focus on ratio analysis of the group only, and not use the data in the group's various activities.

Strategic objective

The Chairman appears to be emphasising **growth as the primary company objective**. The annual growth in turnover over the past four years has been impressive (averaging $\sqrt[3]{(680/325)} - 1 = 28\%$). However, the primary objective of the company should be **shareholder wealth maximisation**. Although growth may be compatible with this objective, it can be detrimental to shareholder wealth maximisation if it is achieved either by excessive increases in financial risk or at the cost of the efficient utilisation of assets.

Basic ratio analysis

	Formula		20X6		20X9
Profitability					
Return on capital employed	$\dfrac{\text{PBIT}}{\text{Capital}}$	$\dfrac{67}{268}$	25%	$\dfrac{93}{603}$	15.4%
Net profit % before interest and tax	$\dfrac{\text{PBIT}}{\text{Turnover}}$	$\dfrac{67}{325}$	20.6%	$\dfrac{93}{680}$	13.7%
Asset turnover	$\dfrac{\text{Turnover}}{\text{Assets}}$	$\dfrac{325}{285 + 98}$	0.85 ×	$\dfrac{680}{700 + 209}$	0.75 ×
Debt and gearing					
Gearing	$\dfrac{\text{Total loans}}{\text{Equity}}$	$\dfrac{42 + 80}{146}$	83.6%	$\dfrac{68 + 102 + 180}{321}$	109%
Debt ratio	$\dfrac{\text{Total debt}}{\text{Total assets}}$	$\dfrac{115 + 42 + 80}{285 + 98}$	61.9%	$\dfrac{306 + 102 + 180}{700 + 209}$	64.7%
Interest cover	$\dfrac{\text{PBIT}}{\text{Interest payable}}$	$\dfrac{67}{14}$	4.8	$\dfrac{93}{36}$	2.6
Liquidity					
Current ratio	$\dfrac{\text{Current assets}}{\text{Current liabilities}}$	$\dfrac{98}{115}$	85.2%	$\dfrac{209}{306}$	68.3%
Quick ratio	$\dfrac{\text{CAs less stock}}{\text{Current liabilities}}$	$\dfrac{58}{115}$	50.4%	$\dfrac{99}{306}$	32.4%
Shareholders' ratios					
P/E ratio	$\dfrac{\text{Share price} \times \text{issued shares}}{\text{Earnings}}$	$\dfrac{0.82 \times 500}{30}$	13.7	$\dfrac{1.59 \times 500}{41}$	19.4

Analysis at the level of the group

From the drop in **ROCE** it can be seen that the group's apparent strategic objective has been achieved at the expense of profitability. This drop in profitability is apparently due to a fall in net profit before tax rather than asset turnover.

Gearing has increased on the above figures, indicating higher levels of financial risk, while interest cover has decreased markedly.

Current and quick ratios have deteriorated from what appeared to be an inadequate base in the first place. It is usual to expect at least a ratio of 1 for the quick ratio to ensure continued solvency. However, given that hotels presumably have a high cash element to their turnover, this might not be significant. In addition, the inclusion of the bank overdraft as a current liability, while legally correct, may disguise the fact that this overdraft is available on a long-term basis.

The **price earnings ratio** has indeed increased, by approximately 1.41 times. However, P/E ratios in the industry as a whole have increased by 2.5 times, so the group appears to be underperforming relative to its sector. Similarly the share price has increased by approximately 159/82 = 1.94 times, whereas the sector-wide increase has been 394/178 = 2.21 times.

However, this analysis ignores several **additional factors**.

(a) The company originally derived a substantial amount of income from investments, which represented a significant asset in 20X6.

(b) There has been a revaluation of the fixed assets.

(c) The company is involved in a number of businesses other than the hotel industry.

(d) Since the end of the financial year, significant developments have occurred, which might impact significantly on the above ratios, especially via share price.

Analysis after allowing for investment income and investment assets

Adjusting ratios to remove the 'business' of investments from the company shows the following.

	Formula	*20X6*		*20X9*	
Profitability					
Return on capital employed	$\dfrac{\text{PBIT}}{\text{Capital} - \text{investments}}$	$\dfrac{49}{268 - 120}$	33.1%	$\dfrac{92}{603 - 4}$	15.4%
Net profit % before interest and tax	$\dfrac{\text{PBIT}}{\text{Turnover}}$	$\dfrac{49}{325}$	15.1%	$\dfrac{92}{680}$	13.5%
Asset turnover	$\dfrac{\text{Turnover}}{\text{Assets}}$	$\dfrac{325}{383 - 120}$	1.24 ×	$\dfrac{680}{909 - 4}$	0.75 ×

This analysis reveals a substantial drop in **ROCE**. The drop could be due to a deterioration in the profitability of existing assets, the acquisition of under performing assets or subsidiaries, or a combination of both.

Net profit percentage has also dropped, although not by as large a percentage. The problem appears to be due to a lack of growth in turnover to match the assets acquired. This is demonstrated by the fall in asset turnover.

Revaluation of fixed assets

Adjusting ratios for both the investment income and the valuation of fixed assets shows the following.

	Formula	20X6		20X9
Profitability				
Return on capital employed	$\dfrac{\text{PBIT} - \text{interest rec'd}}{\text{Capital} - \text{invmts.} - \text{revaln.res}}$	33.1%	$\dfrac{92}{603 - 4 - 100}$	18.4%
Asset turnover	$\dfrac{\text{Turnover}}{\text{Assets} - \text{invmts.} - \text{revaln.res}}$	1.24 ×	$\dfrac{680}{909 - 4 - 100}$	0.84 ×
Debt and gearing				
Gearing	$\dfrac{\text{Total loans}}{\text{Equity} - \text{reva ln. res.}}$	83.6%	$\dfrac{68 + 102 + 180}{321 - 100}$	158%

The revaluation of the group's assets has altered the ratios significantly, especially the **gearing ratio**. Whether this alteration makes the ratios more or less comparable with 20X6 it is difficult to say. It depends on how close to market values the 20X6 values are, and whether the revaluation made was to a realistic market value. This in turn depends on the basis of the revaluation, and whether it was carried out by an independent person.

The company is involved in a number of businesses other than the hotel industry. An analysis of the figures given for other businesses shows the following.

Net profit percentage

		20X6		20X8
		%		%
Hotels	36/196	18.4	45/471	9.6
Bus company	6/24	25	18/46	39
Car hire	7/43	16	15/62	24
Waxworks	1/10	10	5/14	36
Publications	3/32	9	5/43	12

Percentage of total turnover

		%		%
Hotels	196/325	60	471/680	69
Bus company	24/325	7	46/680	7
Car hire	43/325	13	62/680	9
Waxworks	10/325	3	14/680	2
Publications	32/325	10	43/680	6

From the above analysis it can be seen that the drop in group profitability can be attributed to a change in the mix of turnover to the hotel business, with its lower profit percentage. This was exacerbated by a drop in the actual level of profitability achieved by this business.

It is impossible to say which business caused the deterioration in the **asset turnover** figure without information on the breakdown of assets by business.

Post balance sheet events

The managing director has indicated that the company has expanded further into the hotel industry via the acquisition of Beddall Ltd. This is likely to **further depress group profitability** (because of the greater emphasis on this sector). The actual effect of the deal will depend on the levels of profitability achieved by Beddall's assets and business.

This deal has been **financed by debt,** which will further increase gearing levels, something of major concern. The debt is in the form of euros, exposing the group to potential losses due to the fluctuation of the euro against the pound. If the reason for taking out the loan in euros was purely to take advantage of the lower interest rate, then this was unwise, since it is likely to be compensated for by currency depreciation in the future.

However, it is possible that the group's business is associated with the **strength** of **other European currencies** (perhaps a large proportion of business is with EU countries), in which case the loan could act as a hedge against company profit fluctuations. Whether it is wise for the company to remove this risk depends on the ability of the company's shareholders to achieve this objective individually at lower cost.

Conclusion

From the information given, the company is performing worse than would be expected in comparison with other companies in the same sector. There has been a **significant deterioration in profitability, liquidity and stability**. The company appears to have expanded in the area in which it has the lowest level of profitability (hotels), and has not maintained the profit margins in this area. The assets it has acquired, and/or the profitability of its existing assets, have fallen dramatically.

I would disagree with the Chairman's statement, and advise the company to concentrate on fundamental improvements to existing business assets before further growth is pursued.

10   CEDARLODGE

> **Tutor's hint**. This question examines financial planning, the concepts of top-down and bottom-up planning, and gap analysis. You will need to formulate your own simple equations based on the information provided to estimate the growth rates in parts (b)(ii)-(iii). This is not difficult provided that you have specified your calculations clearly in part (b)(i).
>
> **Examiner's comment**. The most frequent error in part (b)(i) was the addition of the increase in creditors to the funds required rather than their subtraction from it. Some candidates ignored the potential role of retained earnings in meeting financing needs, despite the fact that they are the most important single source of finance for most companies. Answers to parts (b)(ii) and (iii) tended to depend upon the level of success in part (b)(i). Many made little attempt at these sections if they perceived their solution to (b)(i) to be incorrect. Even incorrect attempts at parts of questions can earn marks, and candidates making sensible attempts to estimate the growth rates normally earned some marks.

(a)   In '**bottom-up' planning**, information is accumulated at **lower levels of the enterprise** and consolidated as it is passed up through the organisation, with a summary covering the overall position being prepared for top management. This process can be **difficult** to **control** and lead to the feeling that the organisation lacks strategic direction. There is also the further risk that management might make decisions based only on the basis of the **limited options** that seem to be available using the information presented to them. Another problem with this method is that each layer of the organisation who contribute to the plan may be tempted to **specify more resources** than they actually **need,** which can result in an unrealistic overall picture. The main benefit of the bottom-up approach is that managers feel 'bought in' to the plans that result since they have been involved in their formulation, and not had them imposed from above.

In contrast, a '**top-down' planning** system is based on the idea that **directives** emanating from the top management flow down through the organisational structure for implementation. Financial planning often has to be top-down in nature because only the centralised financial departments are in a position to make choices that will make financial sense across the company or group as a whole. However, as far as the broader planning process is concerned, many companies will use a **combination of the two approaches** in an attempt to ensure that staff at lower levels are consulted, while at the same time gaining the benefits of co-ordination and wider vision that result from the top-down approach.

(b) (i) The growth in sales will require an increase in the level of **investment in assets**. However, this will be partially offset by the increases in the level of liabilities and of retained earnings:

			£million
Increase in assets:	£300m × 15% × 1.5		67.50
Increase in liabilities:	£300m × 15% × 0.40		(18.00)
Total retained earnings for the year:			
Sales	£300m × 115%	£345.0m	
Profit after tax	£345m × 12%	£41.4m	
Retained earnings	£41.4m × 75%		(31.05)
Additional external funds that will be required			18.45

(ii) If **only internal funds** are used, the level of increase in assets less liabilities must be equal to the level of increase in retained earnings. Using the calculations above, this can be expressed as follows.

Let 'g' = rate of growth required

$$(300g \times 1.5) - (300g \times 0.40) = 300 \times (1 + g) \times 0.12 \times 0.75$$

Dividing both sides by 300:

$$1.5g - 0.40g = 0.09 + 0.09g$$

$$1.1g - 0.09g = 0.09$$

$$g = 0.0891 \, (= 8.91\%)$$

The maximum rate of growth that could be achieved using internal funds is therefore **8.91%**.

(iii) The current level of gearing can be calculated as:

Debt:Equity = 93:140 = 0.6643

If this ratio is to remain constant, for every £100 of additional earnings that are retained, the company must take on an additional £66.43 of debt. The expression used in (b)(ii) above can be adjusted to allow for this as follows:

$$(300g \times 1.5) - (300g \times 0.40) = (300 \times (1+g) \times 0.12 \times 0.75) + (300 \times (1+g) \times 0.12 \times 0.75 \times 0.6643)$$

Dividing both sides by 300:

$$1.5g - 0.40g = 0.09 + 0.09g + 0.0598 + 0.0598g$$

$$g = 0.1577$$

The company could therefore achieve a growth rate of **15.77%** if the gearing was kept at a constant level.

(iv) The estimates produced above are likely to be inaccurate for the following reasons.

(1) Forecasts of financing needs must be based upon the **expected cash flows** that will result from the increases in sales. The calculations above have used retained earnings as a surrogate for cash flow, but in practice, the two figures are likely to be quite different due to the inclusion of significant non-cash items such as depreciation and accrued expenses in the retained earnings figure.

(2)   It is likely that the company may have to **reduce prices** in order to increase sales by as much as 15%. This would **depress the profit margin** and introduce errors into the above calculations. Similarly, other elements in the profit and loss account are likely to change proportionately as the level of sales increases.

(3)   It is simplistic to assume a **simple rate of increase in assets** and liabilities that varies directly with additional sales.

(4)   In practice, companies try to **maintain a stable or slowly rising level of dividends per share**. However, the question assumes that it is the payout ratio that will remain constant, and this is unlikely to be the case.

(c)   **Gap analysis** is 'the comparison of an entity's ultimate objective with the sum of projections and already planned projects'. The purpose of gap analysis is to establish the following.

(1)   What are the organisation's **targets** over the planning period?

(2)   What would the organisation be expected to achieve if it '**did nothing**' - in other words, did not develop any new strategies, but simply carried on in the current way with the same products and selling to the same markets.

There will be a difference between the **targets** and the **expected achievements** thus defined. This difference is known as the '**gap**'. New strategies will then have to be developed which will close this gap, so that the organisation can expect to achieve its targets over the planning period.

Cedarlodge has identified its financial target of increasing sales by 15% during the next year. However, there is **no estimate** of what the **expected profit and loss account and balance sheet** would look like next year if the company took no action - we have only the historic information for the last accounting period. The use of **gap analysis** would allow Cedarlodge to identify the changes that are required, not only in terms of sales, but also in terms of profits and financing. It could then evaluate alternative strategies, for example raising prices or introducing new products, in a quantitative manner.

Marking guide				Marks
(a)	Top-down planning			3-4
	Bottom-up planning			3-4
			Max	6
For full marks financial planning rather than general planning should be discussed.				
(b)	(i)	Investment		1
		Increased liabilities		1
		Retained earnings		1
				3
	(ii)	A number of different approaches. Key element is discussion of the relationships involved.	Max	5
	(iii)	As (ii) with up to three for gearing estimates/discussion	Max	6
	(iv)	One mark for each point, but two marks for comments about the use of cash flows rather than retained earnings		4
(c)	Gap analysis			2
	Actions if gaps occur and financial planning			4
				30

11 HANME

> **Tutor's hint**. Do the computations first, and put them in the appendix to the report. There are some clear computation requirements in the question (shareholders' return and P/E ratio) but other ratios shown in our appendix are illustrative. You may have chosen other similar ratios. Half the marks are available for discussion (not just repetition of the figures in words!) so make sure you allocate enough time for this and answer the specific questions asked. Our answer follows the numbering system in the question.
>
> **Examiner's comment**. In part (a) high marks were scored by getting at least 6 correct ratios, a selection of group and subsidiary ratios and some growth rates and trends (less figures than in our answer). Some candidates however made errors in ratio calculations. However in addition even correct ratio calculations are not enough, and many candidates did not produce the required interpretation and analysis of the ratios. Foreign exchange risk was frequently ignored. Candidates also failed to discuss the importance of the electronics industry to the group, and use the beta to assess the expected level of return.
>
> Comments in part (b) were expected on market and industry comparisons, financial health of the group and subsidiaries, including comments on the exchange rates, identification of problems and specific discussion on all the points in the chairman's report. However few candidates discussed all the chairman's comments, and discussion of whether the company should focus on cash flows rather than turnover was particularly poor.

Analysis of the Financial Health of Hanme plc

Prepared by: AB Consultants

This report analyses the performance of Hanme plc in 20X7 and 20X8 and draws conclusions about its financial health. We also comment, as requested, on the validity of claims made in the Chairman's 20X8 report. Detailed computations are shown in the Appendix.

(a) **Performance of Hanme plc**

    (i) **Evaluation of return to shareholders**

        Calculations of return are shown in Appendix section 4. Return to Hanme's shareholders in 20X8 was 33%. Although this is a good return, it should be evaluated against the **returns** of **other investments** with a similar risk level. Taking into account the market risk of the Hanme's shares compared with the stock market as a whole (which returned 38%) a return of 48% would have been expected from the company. Hanme's return in 20X8 was therefore **15% below** the **expected** level.

    (ii) **The expected P/E ratio of Hanme**

        Computations are shown in Appendix section 5. Group profits derive from electronics (75%), biscuits (13%) and clothing (12%). Based on 20X8 comparative industry data from these sectors, the **weighted average P/E** was 15.9. Hanme's **actual P/E ratio** was 13.9, a low result which probably indicates **below average expectations of growth** for the company.

    (iii) **Commentary on growth rates and financial ratios**

        Growth rates. Profitability of the group has **increased** by 22% from a 12% increase in sales, indicating improved profit margins. In the UK, electronics, which contributes 75% of group after tax profits, showed the best results, with profitability up 24% from a 12% sales increase. Other UK operations showed similar sales increases (biscuits 12% and clothing 16%). However, whereas profitability was up 22% for clothing, it only rose by 11% for the biscuits subsidiary, indicating reduced margins. All increases were substantial in **real terms,** as inflation remained at 3%.

The Danish biscuit subsidiary showed **better profitability growth** (17%) than its UK sister company, but with lower sales growth (10%). Unfortunately the Danish kroner depreciated during the year by 10.5% which severely depleted the results when translated into sterling, and contributed to below average results from the company's biscuit operations. This depreciation is, however, greater than expected by purchasing power parity theory, and may be reversed in the near future.

By contrast, against a background of 100% annual inflation, the Turkish clothing subsidiary showed **negative real growth** in sales and profit. However, when translated into sterling, the results were well above average for the group, because the Turkish lire depreciated by only 25%. Future results are, however, vulnerable to further TL depreciation.

Financial ratios

The company's low dividend yield is indicative of a policy of **high reinvestment** for growth, which is probably an efficient method of equity financing.

Analysis of the **profit to assets ratio** (15.5% for the group in 20X8) shows that in general **biscuits** and clothing show a better return on assets than electronics. For all subsidiaries there is a **low sales to assets ratio** but relatively **high profit margins**, probably indicating a **premium pricing** strategy. The result may be that **sales volume** is **lower** than budgeted, which is reflected in **low stock turnover** (sales/stock) and **generally high current ratios. Debtors' collection period** is approximately two months for most of the business but is significantly higher than this for the UK subsidiaries in biscuits and clothing, for reasons which are unclear.

It is difficult to compare the **gearing levels** of the subsidiaries with sector gearing averages because the group probably treats its borrowings as a pool of funds, borrowing in the most convenient location and currency. However, given that electronics accounts for most of the group's business, overall gearing does seem rather high compared with most electronics companies.

(b) **Validity of the comments in the Chairman's Report**

Although the chairman is factually correct in his statements about increased profit and share price, our analysis above shows that neither result is excellent when viewed in the light of **average stock market performance** in 20X8 and the company's **high level of systematic risk**.

He is correct in saying that all three sectors showed **profit growth**, but the strong performance in clothing has been boosted by the translated results of the Turkish subsidiary in conditions where the Turkish lire did not depreciate nearly as much as expected. He has, in fact, underplayed the profitability of the electronics business, which has grown by more than the group average.

He refers to a **strong financial position** when in fact there is scope for significant improvement in working capital management and gearing is probably too high for safety.

The objective of **doubling turnover** within 5 years is probably unachievable on the basis of the present figures, which took place against a background of high economic growth, unless more acquisitions are made. The relevance of this objective needs to be strongly questioned. Shareholder value is unlocked by perception and achievement of long term profitable returns after allowing for the risk of the business. The company has not done well in 20X8 judged by this criterion. Further pursuit of sales growth regardless of profit may make the situation worse.

Conclusion

Whilst Hanme appears to be doing reasonably well, the chairman has taken too optimistic a view of prospects. The performance of certain subsidiaries could be improved.

Appendix: Financial Analysis

1   **Results of foreign subsidiaries, at average exchange rates**

	Biscuits Denmark		Clothing Turkey	
	20X7 £m	20X8 £m	20X7 £m	20X8 £m
Average exchange rate	8.6	9.5	280.0	350.0
Turnover	12.7	12.6	3.7	4.7
Operating expenses	8.1	7.8	1.7	1.9
Net interest	0.5	0.5	0.2	0.2
Profit before tax	4.1	4.3	1.8	2.6
Tax	1.2	1.3	0.7	1.0
Profit after tax	2.9	3.0	1.1	1.6
Dividends	1.4	1.5	1.1	1.6
Retentions	1.5	1.5	-	-

2   **Growth rates in turnover and profit**

Growth rates in real terms are after subtracting the appropriate rate of inflation (which gives an acceptable approximation).

(a) **Group**

	Nominal	Real terms
Sales	12%	9%
Profit before tax	22%	19%
Profit after tax	22%	19%

(b) **Biscuits**

	UK		Denmark (Kr)		Denmark	
Inflation 20X8	3%		1%		3%	
Growth rates	Nominal	Real terms	Nominal	Real terms	Nominal	Real terms
Sales	12%	9%	10%	9%	-1%	-4%
Profit before tax	11%	8%	17%	16%	5%	2%
Profit after tax	11%	8%	17%	16%	3%	0%

(c) **Clothing**

	UK		Turkey (TL)		Turkey (£)	
Inflation 20X8	3%		100%		3%	
Growth rates	Nominal	Real terms	Nominal	Real terms	Nominal	Real terms
Sales	16%	13%	59%	-41%	27%	24%
Profit before tax	22%	19%	78%	-22%	44%	41%
Profit after tax	22%	19%	78%	-22%	45%	42%

(d) **Electronics** Computed by subtracting figures for biscuits and clothing from the group total figures

	20X7	20X8	Growth Nominal	Real terms
Sales	337.6	378.7	12%	9%
Profit before tax	66.1	82.1	24%	21%
Profit after tax	46.4	57.7	24%	21%

3 **Financial ratios**

	Group		Biscuits		Clothing	
			UK	Denmark (Kr)	UK	Turkey (TL)
	20X7	*20X8*	*20X8*	*20X8*	*20X8*	*20X8*
Sales/total assets	0.68	0.65	0.49	0.74	0.53	0.95
Profit before tax/total assets	14.8%	15.5%	17.5%	25.5%	16.2%	52.6%
Profit before tax/sales	22.0%	23.9%	35.7%	34.2%	30.6%	55.1%
Current ratio	2.04	1.92	1.00	2.27	2.14	1.86
Sales/stock	2.22	2.14	2.80	2.55	2.57	4.58
Debtors/sales x 365 days	66.77	63.00	104.00	55.00	162.00	88.00
Gearing (total loans/equity)	0.95	0.85	0.39	0.97	0.00	0.10

	Group		
	20X7	*20X8*	*Growth*
Earnings per share (pence)	57.3	64.7	12.9%
Share price (pence)	690	897	30.0%
FTSE 100 index	4,219	5,634	33.5%
P/E ratio	12.04	13.86	
Dividend yield	2.9%	2.8%	
FTSE dividend yield	4.5%	4.0%	

4 **Evaluation of return to shareholders**

Figures are extracted from the above table of financial ratios. Hanme's 20X8 percentage return to shareholders is the percentage increase in share price plus the 20X8 dividend yield. This is 30% + 2.8% = 32.8%

The percentage return on the stock market as a whole is the percentage increase in the FTSE index plus the 20X8 FTSE dividend yield: 33.5% + 4% = 37.5%

If Hanme's equity beta is 1.32 and the risk free rate is 6% per annum, the percentage return expected from the Capital Asset Pricing Model is 6% + (37.5% − 6%) 1.32 = 47.6%

On the basis of these figures, Hanme's 20X8 return is well below that expected from an investment with its level of systematic risk.

5 **Percentage makeup of company and overall expected P/E ratio**

Profit after tax	£m	£m	%	*Industry P/E*
Biscuits				
UK	7.0			
Denmark	3.0			
		10.0	13%	11
Clothing				
UK	7.7			
Turkey	1.6			
		9.3	12%	8
Electronics (balancing figure)		57.7	75%	18
		77.0	100%	

Hanme's expected P/E would be 13% × 11 + 12% × 8 + 75% × 18 = 15.9

Marking guide	Marks
Chairman's comments	
Financial condition of group, in particular market & industry comparisons	4-5
Financial condition of subsidiaries	
UK	2
Overseas, in particular exchange rates & use of economic data	3-4
Possible management/financial problems	5
Discussion of plans to double turnover	3
Discussion of unlocking of shareholder value	2
Conclusion	1
	20
Ratios, need at least six correct ratios and relevant group & subsidiary	
Ratios	8
Growth rates and trends	5
Shareholders' return	4
Price/earning and market factors	3
	20
	40

12   MUTON

> **Tutor's hint.** You may find it helpful to structure both your calculations and your discussion around the three main groups of ratios that can be used to evaluate performance, as well as the benchmark ratios. Do not ignore factors external to the firms in question when evaluating their performance and strategic position. When calculating the ratios you should be careful to define your method of calculation, since different approaches are possible.
>
> **Examiner's comment.** Candidates generally showed good ability to assess the financial health of the subsidiaries, and an awareness of the problems of using UK based benchmarks to make decisions affecting subsidiaries in different economic environments. The main weaknesses in answers were poor use of the economic data provided to assess the possible future prospects for the different countries, and unsupported conclusions as to which subsidiary to close.

REPORT

To: Managing Director
From: Company Accountant
Date: 10 December 20X6
Subject: Medium-term consolidation proposals

The purpose of this report is to provide financial analysis of the results of the three manufacturing subsidiaries with the aim of establishing which, if any, should be considered for closure.

Financial appraisal

Detailed numerical analysis is included in the Appendix. The performance of the subsidiaries will be analysed in relation to their liquidity, profitability and financial position.

(a) **Liquidity**

   None of the subsidiaries appear to be in financial difficulties, all having acceptable liquidity ratios for a manufacturing business.

(b) **Profitability**

   Although return on sales in Slovenia is lower than that of the other two companies, all three are **trading profitably** and **with a reasonable level of return**. The annual rate of

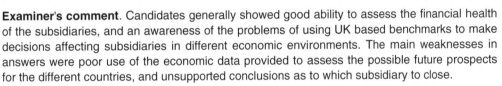

growth in turnover must also be considered and in this area performance appears to be particularly strong in Thailand and Slovenia with annual growth rates of 15% and 8% respectively. However, in both these countries, sales growth is below the rate of inflation whereas in Switzerland, although growth of 4.3% appears to be low at first sight, it is in fact above the inflation rate. **Asset turnover** is also **higher in Thailand and Slovenia,** but this reflects the fact that production is much more capital intensive in Switzerland where labour costs are relatively high, and much more labour intensive in Thailand and Slovenia where labour costs are lower. It does not necessarily reflect any fundamental weakness therefore, but merely a difference in the structure of the production process.

(c) **Financial position**

Although there are differences in the capital structures of the three companies, none of them appears to be in a **financially risky position,** with acceptable levels of gearing and interest cover. The much higher level of gearing in Thailand has presumably been adopted to take advantage of the fact that base lending rates there are currently below the rate of inflation.

Thus in financial terms, each of the subsidiaries seems to be trading successfully and to be in a financially healthy position. There are no financial indicators that would suggest that closure is required.

Performance against UK benchmarks

(a) **Return on capital employed (ROCE)**

Only the Swiss subsidiary is currently below the 25% benchmark. This can again be attributed to the **different operating structure** that has been adopted to make the most efficient use of capital and labour resources, given relative local unit costs. It does not necessarily indicate a fundamental weakness in the business.

(b) **Sales per employee**

There are significant differences in performance in this area, with the Swiss company having sales per employee of over three times the benchmark and the Slovenian company just meeting the benchmark level, while the Thai subsidiary falls well short of it. However, these differences can also be accounted for by the **different operating structures** in relation to capital and labour, and not to fundamental weaknesses. Labour costs in Thailand are much lower than those in Europe and result in a substitution of labour for capital which is reflected in the ROCE figures.

Thus although two of the three subsidiaries are failing to perform against both of the benchmarks, I suggest that has more to do with the fact that the benchmarks are set at levels geared to the relationship between capital and labour costs in the UK, rather than to any particular financial weaknesses in the companies concerned. The fact that capital and labour resources are organised differently so as to optimise profitability is not a reason for closure.

Other factors to be considered

There are a number of other factors that should be considered before any decision is reached to rationalise production in the way suggested.

(a) The **medium-term strategic aim** of **rationalising and consolidating** the group's position in the textile industry requires **further clarification** in terms of the strategic reasons for such an objective. It also needs to be more closely defined in order to establish criteria that will enable it to be met successfully.

(b) The use of **benchmark ratios** for **performance evaluation** has potential weaknesses, not least because managers in the subsidiaries may manipulate results in order to enhance the apparent performance against the benchmarks. For example, capital investment may be restricted to improve ROCE even though this is not in the best long-term interests of the business. UK operations should also be subjected to a deeper financial analysis to ensure that distortions of this type are not happening.

(c) **UK operations** should be **considered** as well as the **overseas production** before any rationalisation decisions are reached.

(d) **Relative differences** in the **rates of interest** and **inflation** that are likely to influence the exchange rates must be taken into account. Rates are much higher in Thailand than in Europe, suggesting that the Baht is likely to depreciate against sterling, and the effect of this exposure should be investigated. However, it may well be that the weakness of the Baht will enhance the performance of this subsidiary in its export markets. Exchange rate exposure is likely to be much less important in the European subsidiaries.

(e) The **political risk** of the countries in which the subsidiaries operate and in the markets that they serve must also be considered.

(f) It would be helpful to **analyse the results** given against those for similar local companies operating in the same markets.

Conclusions

On the basis of the information provided, none of the three subsidiaries is an obvious candidate for closure. In addition to the individual financial position of the companies, it has been suggested that a number of other factors should be considered. It is also important that a wider evaluation should be made of the long-term prospects of the markets in which they operate before any rationalisation decisions are reached.

Appendix: Key financial ratios (monetary amounts in millions, except where stated)

	Thailand	Switzerland	Slovenia
Year end exchange rate to sterling	42.52	2.25	256
Average exchange rate to sterling	40.46	2.30	245
Benchmark ratios			
Return on capital employed:			
Operating profit: Equity plus long-term debt			
(i) Local currency:			
Operating profit	42	4.8	240
Capital employed	129	25.1	945
ROCE	32.6%	19.1%	25.4%
(ii) Sterling:			
Operating profit at average exchange rate	1.04	2.09	0.98
Capital employed at year end exchange rate	3.03	11.16	3.69
ROCE	34.2%	18.7%	26.6%
Turnover per employee:			
Turnover/Number employed			
Turnover in local currency	420	39.1	2,780
Turnover in sterling (average exchange rate)	10.38	17.00	11.35
Number employed	2,450	520	1,090
Turnover/employee	£4,237	£32,692	£10,413

BPP PUBLISHING

	Thailand	Switzerland	Slovenia
Liquidity ratios			
Current ratio:			
Current assets: Current liabilities			
(local currency)			
Current assets	96	8.5	765
Current liabilities	77	5.4	530
Current ratio	1.25	1.57	1.44
Quick ratio:			
Current assets excluding stock	44	4.5	285
Current liabilities	77	5.4	530
Quick ratio	0.57	0.83	0.54
Profitability ratios			
Return on sales:			
Operating profit: Sales			
Operating profit	42	4.8	240
Sales	420	39.1	2,780
Return on sales	10.00%	12.28%	8.63%
Asset turnover:			
Sales/total assets			
Sales	420	39.1	2,780
Total assets	206	30.5	1,475
Asset turnover (times)	2.04	1.28	1.88
Financial ratios			
Gearing ratio:			
Prior charge debt: Equity			
Prior charge debt	62	3.8	360
Equity	99	22.9	795
Gearing ratio	62.6%	16.6%	45.3%
Interest cover:			
Operating profit: Net interest			
Operating profit	42	4.8	240
Net interest	10	0.3	70
Interest cover (times)	4.2	16.0	3.4

Marking guide		**Marks**
Financial calculations relevant to the overseas subsidiaries		
Benchmark calculations		5
(for full marks look for sensible use of exchange rates)		
Other relevant ratios		<u>7</u>
(Look for a selection of ratios that allows assessment of the performance of the subsidiaries.)		
		12
Critical discussion of benchmarks	max	5
Limitations of the data available		2 - 3
Comments on the ratios. (Do not reward mere repetition of the ratios.)		2 - 3
Use of economic data in the analysis		3 - 4
Other discussion, eg FOREX exposure, reasons for closure, UK operations, nature of the company's objectives. All factors do not have to be included for high marks	max	<u>5</u>
		<u>18</u>
		<u><u>30</u></u>

13   MOVER

Tutor's hint. Unusually in (a) you are not given a discount rate. In this case you need to fall back on the assumption that the market risk premium for shares above the risk free rate is in the range 8% to 9%. The inflation figure is not needed, as the cash flows are given in real terms, and hence a real discount rate is needed. Do not assume that because a tunnel is a very high risk project its discount rate must be extremely high. For a diversified investor, the relevant risk in the discount rate is systematic risk. However, construction as an industry does have fairly high systematic risk.

Examiner's comment. In (a) candidates needed to use a realistic (not too low) discount rate, justify the discount rate used, and treat estimates beyond year 10 in a sensible fashion. However many discount rates used were too low, and in some cases the inflation rate was used. Some candidates also failed to appreciate the difference between real and nominal rates. Most candidates also failed to discuss wider issues such as the reliability of the cash flows, or the risks, or Mover's activities other than the tunnel project.

(a)   The expected cash flows of the tunnel should be discounted at a suitable cost of capital, taking into account the **risk** of the project. Since the cash flow projections exclude inflation, the cost of capital should also be a **real rate.**

An estimate of the real rate might be as follows:

(i)   In the UK the current **risk free rate** is approximately 6% whilst inflation is approximately 2%, giving an approximate real risk free rate of 4%.

(ii)   The **market premium** is assumed to be in the range 7 – 8%, although several market commentators are using much lower rates today (closer to 4.5%).

(iii) The tunnel project is assumed to have a **high level** of **systematic risk**, say a beta of 1.3.

(iv)   The pension fund is well diversified and therefore only subject to **systematic risk.**

This implies a real discount rate of approximately 4% + (7% × 1.3) = approx. 13%

Assuming the tunnel has an indefinite life, post 20Y0 cashflows are discounted in perpetuity:

Year	£m	13% df	PV £m
20X0	(450)	0.885	(398)
20X1	(500)	0.783	(392)
20X2	(550)	0.693	(381)
20X3	(650)	0.613	(398)
20X4	(200)	0.543	(109)
20X5	200	0.480	96
20X6	300	0.425	128
20X7	320	0.376	120
20X8	340	0.333	113
20X9	360	0.295	106
20Y0	400	0.261	104
20Y1 onwards*	400	0.261/0.13	803
			(208)

*These are PVs of perpetuity cash flows.

At this estimated discount rate the NPV is **negative,** and therefore the project should be rejected. For a more comprehensive assessment **sensitivity analysis** should be used.

The pension fund trustees should also consider:

(i)   The use of NPV ignores the value of any **embedded or real options**. Such options might include the option to develop land either side of the tunnel.

(ii)   **Economic factors** may be critical to the accuracy of the forecast cashflows.

(iii) **Assumptions** concerning costs and competitive issues (the costs of alternative transport links) should be reviewed. In particular there may be a high probability that costs will be greater than forecast, and also that the project will be delayed, leading to further costs and delays in revenues. In addition the costs of **upkeep** of the tunnel have not been included in the calculations.

(iv)   The **contractual role** of the construction company should be reviewed – is the project Government supported?

(v)   Whilst the tunnel project is presumably the most important project that Mover will be undertaking over the next few years, the company's continued existence may not depend upon it. The trustees should therefore consider the likely results of the **other contracts** that Mover will be undertaking over the next few years.

On a project of this size, and dependent on the level of the pension fund investment, such factors should be modelled in more detail, perhaps using **sensitivity analysis** or **simulation**.

(b)   **Inflation erodes** the **purchasing power** of money. It therefore has an **effect** on the **returns** an investor will require, and consequently on the appraisal of capital investment decisions by companies. As the **inflation rate increases so will the minimum return required** by an investor.

A return of 5% on a sum invested of £100 will provide £105 back in one year's time. If inflation is running at 15% then at the end of one year £105 will only buy 105/1.15 = £91.30 worth of goods at today's prices. In order to be able to purchase £105 worth of goods at today's prices the investor will need a nominal return of 1.05 × 1.15 = 1.2075, ie 20.75%. Thus with inflation at 15%, a nominal rate of interest of 20.75% is required to give the investor a real return of 5%. This effect can be expressed as:

(1 + money (or nominal) rate) = (1 + real rate) × (1 + inflation rate)

Companies therefore have a **choice** of approaches when accounting for inflation in the appraisal of capital projects. They can either **inflate all the elements** of the cash flow at the appropriate rates and then **discount at the nominal (or money) rate of return**. Alternatively they can **exclude inflation** from the cash flows and **discount at the real rate**.

14   UTOPIA HOTELS

(a)

> **Tutor's hint**. The key to part (a) of this question is to decide on your approach before you jump into it. Plan what you want to do before you hit the calculator. Look at the examiner's comment shown below: it seems that some candidates ended up with an unstructured mess. Their computations may have been correct but they were unmarkable.

Your first decision is about whether to do the computation in real terms or in nominal terms, but *not* a combination of nominal discount rate and real cash flows! The 15 year time horizon should have made this decision for you. The real terms approach allows the use of annuity factors, whereas the nominal terms approach means that you will have to write down all cash flows for every year to year 17 – and you would still be sitting there when they turned out the lights! Our solution shows a convenient lay-out for questions of this type.

Examiner's comment. Answers were very variable in standard. A common weakness was that candidates discounted cash flow projections on an annual basis which is very time consuming when there is a 15 year time horizon. Annuity tables would have allowed the calculations to be undertaken much more quickly.

Some lost marks because their calculations were very difficult to follow and not presented in a logical sequence.

General approach

The minimum occupancy rate will be that which gives the project a net present value of zero when the cash flows are discounted at the appropriate cost of capital.

The general rate of inflation is 3.8%. Because details of the way inflation affects individual costs and revenues are not provided, the most convenient method of appraisal will be to discount the **real cash flows** using the **real cost of capital**.

Tutor's hint. 'Real cash flows' are cash flows expressed at today's prices. The 'real cost of capital' is the cost of capital with inflation of 3.8% removed.

You would be perfectly correct in discounting the nominal cash flows at the nominal cost of capital. However this takes much longer because annuity factors cannot be used.

Examiner's comment. A common error was the use of a nominal discount rate with real cash flows. This was unacceptable.

Since the new hotel is not expected to significantly affect the group's business risk or financial risk (ie no significant change in the nature of the business or in financial gearing) the group's existing real weighted average cost of capital (WACC) will be used as the discount rate.

Tutor's hint. A novel feature of this question is that the risk free rate of interest is not given! You must estimate it by deducting 3% from the pre-tax cost of debt and then use it in the CAPM to compute the cost of equity.

Examiner's comment. Many candidates could not estimate the risk free rate and therefore assumed one.

Tutor's comment. Well that's better than nothing, but don't be too hasty in assuming there's data missing from the question.

Pre-tax cost of the company's debt

Tutor's hint. This must be computed by trial and error, finding the IRR of the cash flows for the company's 12% debenture, redeemable in 13 year's time. Try to choose a sensible starting point for the computation. The pre-tax interest yield is 12/114 = 10.5% and over 13 years the difference between 114 and 100 is not much, but will reduce the redemption yield to slightly below the interest yield. So try 10% discount factors.

Year		£	10% factors	PV
0	Current price	(114)	1	(114.00)
1 - 13	Interest	12	7.103	85.24
13	Redemption	100	0.290	29.00
				0.24

This is so near to zero that the cost of debt pre-tax may be taken as 10%.

BPP PUBLISHING

Therefore, the risk free rate of interest is 10% – 3% = 7%

Cost of equity capital

From the capital asset pricing model (CAPM), the cost of equity is given by:

$Ke = r_f + (E(r_m) - r_f)\beta_j$

$Ke = 7\% + (15\% - 7\%)0.8 = 13.4\%$

After-tax cost of debt

> **Tutor's hint**. If pushed for time, use the quick approximate method:
>
> Kd after tax = 10%(1 – 0.33) = 6.7%.
>
> This is inaccurate for redeemable debt, where market value differs from redemption value, though not too bad when redemption is 13 years in the future! The proper method is by trial and error. To find a suitable trial discount rate, 6.7% is as good as any, so try 7% and, if that is too high, 6%.

Annual interest, after tax saved at 33%, is £12 × 0.67 = £8.04.

Year	£	7%	PV	6%	PV
0	(114)	1	(114.00)	1	(114.00)
1 - 13	8.04	8.358	67.20	8.853	71.18
13	100	0.415	41.50	0.469	46.90
			(5.30)		4.08

By interpolation, the after tax cost of debt is $6\% + \dfrac{4.08}{4.08 + 5.30} \times 1\% = 6.43\%$.

Weighted average cost of capital

Market values:			£'000
Equity	480m × £3.45		1,656
Debt			
Debenture	£200m × 114/100	228	
Term loan		150	
			378
			2,034

WACC = 13.4% × 1,656/2,034 + 6.43% × 378/2,034 = 12.10%.

Real WACC is after removing 3.8% inflation.

1 + r = 1.121/1.038 = 1.080.

The real WACC is 0.08, or 8% and will be used to discount the project cash flows.

Appraisal of the project cash flows

Assumptions

1   There is no tax delay (given).

2   Time horizon is 15 years from start of year 3 to end of year 17.

3   Working capital is returned at end of year 17.

4   Tax depreciation starts in year 1 on the year 0 expenditure.

5   No balancing allowance has been included at year 17: this is included in the estimate of after-tax value of the hotel, £60m.

6   Refurbishment takes place in years 7 and 12. No refurbishment cost has been included at year 17 as this is assumed to relate to cash flows earned beyond that point.

Year			£'000	8% d.f.	PV £'000	
0	Hotel cost	10%	(5,000)	1	(5,000)	
1	"	50%	(25,000)	0.926	(23,150)	
2	"	40%	(20,000)	0.857	(17,140)	
1	Tax saved by depreciation	(W1)	41	0.926	38	
2	"		248	0.857	213	
3 - 17	"		413	7.338	3,031	(W3)
2	Working capital		(1,500)	0.857	(1,286)	
17	Working capital released		1,500	0.270	405	
3 - 17	Annual net operating cash flows	(W2)	(3,484)	7.338	(25,566)	(W3)
7	Redecoration (after-tax cost)		(6,700)	0.583	(3,906)	
12	"		(6,700)	0.397	(2,660)	
17	After-tax value at end		60,000	0.270	16,200	
					(58,821)	

Working 1: Tax depreciation

Year		2.5% dep'n £'000	Tax saved at 33% £'000
1	2.5% × 5,000	125	41.25
2	2.5% × (5,000 + 25,000)	750	247.5
3	2.5% × (5,000 + 25,000 + 20,000)	1,250	412.5

Other points. Purists will note that this tax depreciation computation is technically wrong because we are carrying out the computation in *real* terms and should reduce the allowance by 3.8% per year. In the exam, though, you do not have time to pursue this point. Ignore it, or make a short note on the inaccuracy.

Working 2: Annual net operating cash flows	£'000
Contribution from non-residents	1,000
Staff, services, maintenance	(6,200)
	(5,200)
Tax saving at 33%	1,716
Net cash flow	(3,484)

Working 3: Discount factor

Year 3 to 17 is the annuity for year 1 to 15 at 8% set back two years:

$8.559/1.08^2 = 7.338.$

Tutor's hint. Ignoring income from hotel rooms, the hotel has a net present value of costs of £58.281 million. The break-even occupancy rate is where the income from rooms has the same net present value. Thus the *annual* contribution from rooms will have to be at least £58.281m/7.338, where 7.338 is the annuity factor at 8% for years 3 to 17.

Occupancy level to break even

Contribution per guest:		£
Food and drink	£40 × 40%	16.0
Other facilities	£15 × 30%	4.5
Contribution per guest		20.5
Contribution from 1.4 guests		28.70
Room charge		100.00
Contribution per room		128.70
After tax contribution per room (× 0.67)		86.23
Annual contribution required	£58,821,000/7.338	£8,015,944
Daily contribution required	÷ 365	£21,961
Number of rooms to break even	£21,961 ÷ 86.23	255
Occupancy to break even	255/300 =	85%

If the hotel achieves higher than an 85% occupancy rate, the project will have a positive net present value. This break-even occupancy rate would be considered too high by most hotel companies. On the basis of these figures, the project would be rejected. However, much depends on the analysis of uncertainty of estimates (see part (b)).

> **Examiner's comment**. Some candidates assumed 100% occupancy in their NPV computation. If they then went on to use or to discuss sensitivity analysis, some credit was given, but a NPV alone with 100% occupancy and no comment is not very helpful to the investment decision.

(b)

> **Tutor's hint.** Answers to open-ended questions like this must be tailored to the number of marks available. Try to tread the middle path between offering an unexplained 'list of points' and getting 'bogged down' in trying to explain just one or two problems.
>
> *Other points.* If you are tempted not to answer part (b) because you are too busy with part (a), you need to think more about your exam technique.
>
> **Examiner's comment.** Answers to this part were satisfactory with some good suggestions. Some candidates did not gain many marks as they mentioned only one or two influences on the accuracy of the calculations.

Most of the **estimates** made in the project evaluation are subject to considerable uncertainty, especially because the project covers such a long time horizon. Over this period the nature of the hotel's operations could change significantly, depending on many internal decisions and external environmental factors. The only certainty is that the world in which the hotel is operating will be significantly different in seventeen years' time!

It follows therefore that an analysis of the figures independently of an examination of overall strategic plans is likely to be very limited in scope. Nevertheless it is possible to use sensitivity analysis to identify which input figures are the ones which cause the most uncertainty in the evaluation of break-even occupancy rate.

Estimates which could be subject to significant error include:

(i)   Selling prices for rooms and services, because of:

- The seasonal nature of the English hotel trade

- The need to secure occupancy by lowering the price for advance block bookings

- Economic cycles of boom and recession

- Decisions to change the target clientele; and many other factors

(ii)   The estimate of an average of 1.4 people per room

(iii)   Refurbishment costs

(iv)   The residual value of £60 million

(v)   The company's cost of capital because of:

- Statistical errors in the estimates
- Changes to the risk profile of the hotel or to the company's financial risk
- Long-term changes to real interest rates; and other factors

In addition, the cost estimates are very rough, no details of the way in which inflation might affect specific costs have been given and there may be mistakes in the 'cost models' used (eg the split between fixed and variable costs and the use of appropriate cost drivers).

(c)

> **Tutor's hint.** 'Limitations of the CAPM' has always been a common discussion question in this paper: the question can be asked in many different ways but each requires the same basic answer. More recently the examiner has taken to asking for a discussion on whether arbitrage pricing theory is a viable alternative to the CAPM. Don't be too quick to write the CAPM off. It has stood the test of time for thirty-five years, which is longer than most City analysts!
>
> **Examiner's comment.** Most candidates displayed good knowledge of the weaknesses of the capital asset pricing model. Relatively few showed good understanding of arbitrage pricing theory. Common errors were to confuse APT with adjusted present value (APV) or with Miller and Modigliani's arbitrage proof in their theory of capital structure.

To: The Board of Directors, Utopia Group
From: I Newton, Finance Director
Date: 12 January 20X7
Subject: Use of arbitrage pricing theory as an alternative to the capital asset pricing model in evaluating the cost of equity capital

This report is in response to a question by Ms Einstein that the assumptions behind the **capital asset pricing model** (CAPM) are unrealistic and hence, by implication, that the model is unsuitable for determining the cost of our shareholders' funds.

It is certainly true that many of the assumptions behind the CAPM are unrealistic. For instance it is assumed that:

(a)   All investors hold **well-diversified portfolios** and all make the same forecasts of future performance of shares.

(b)   **Return, risk and correlation** can be **evaluated** over a **single time period**.

(c)   Risk is measured entirely by **variability of returns**.

(d)   There is a **perfect capital market**.

None of these assumptions are true and all lead to imperfections in the model. Not surprisingly there is a body of evidence concerning inaccurate predictions made by the CAPM, for example when it is applied to small companies, low beta companies, certain days of the week or months of the year.

Furthermore, the only feasible way of estimating a company's beta factor or the market risk premium $(R_m - R_f)$ is by **examining historical data** and making the assumption that the future will be the same as the past.

When applied to capital investment appraisal, the CAPM makes the additional assumption that companies **make decisions** on **behalf of shareholders only**. This ignores the position of other stakeholders who have different attitudes to risk because they find it more difficult to diversify their position than shareholders do.

It is fair to summarise the CAPM as a **simple model** which contains well documented imperfections. The model is simple in that it attempts to describe the difference in the returns of shares in terms of a single variable, systematic risk, measured by the beta factor. The beta factor represents the sensitivity of the company's shares to the risk of 'the economy'. Clearly 'the economy' is not just a single variable however.

Arbitrage pricing theory (APT), in contrast, explains return in terms of several independent economic factors, such as the rate of inflation, the level of interest rates, and the index of industrial production. Different shares will have different sensitivities to each of these factors and, if these sensitivities can be estimated, the return of the share can be predicted.

While this seems a lot more sensible, it is difficult to implement in practice because:

(a) It is not clear **how many factors** should be **used** in the model and what they should be.

(b) It is difficult to **measure the sensitivity of a company's shares** to these factors (APT is certainly not the only financial theory to fall foul of the problems of multiple regression analysis).

You can always explain the past if you make a model complex enough. The test is whether the future is properly explained. Since APT has yet to be proved significantly better than the CAPM in this respect, I suggest that we keep the matter under review, but for the moment continue to use the CAPM as the basis for estimating our cost of equity capital.

15   TOVELL

> **Tutor's hint**. Part (b) requires firstly the selection of an appropriate appraisal technique. The information permits use of the WACC as a discount rate, or alternatively the APV approach can be used. If you are confident in the use of the APV technique then this is the preferred option.
>
> When using the APV method, potential pitfalls include:
>
> - Calculating the tax savings on the basis of a loan of £800,000 rather than £1m
>
> - Using the subsidised interest rate of 6% to evaluate the tax savings rather than the market rate of 9%
>
> - Omitting the tax effects when evaluating the benefit of the discount to the interest rate
>
> - Omitting the issue and underwriting costs associated with the rights issue

(a) The stated objective that Tovell has in adopting a strategy of **diversifying** into many different industries is to reduce risk for the company's shareholders. However, except where restrictions apply to direct investments, investors can probably reduce investment risk more efficiently than companies, and they should already be seeking to be **well-diversified** in order to minimise unsystematic risk. The cost of diversifying is likely to be much higher for a company than for an individual investor, and therefore Tovell's diversification strategy is unlikely to contribute to the primary financial objective of maximising the wealth of the ordinary shareholders.

Other practical arguments against a high level of diversification by companies include the following.

(i) Managers employed by a company will normally have **acquired skills** and experience in **one or two business sectors**. If they are required to work in areas outside their direct experience their effectiveness is likely to be reduced, at least while they are going through the learning curve. Co-ordination of the different areas and effective financial control are also much harder in a fully diversified business.

(ii) For the reasons outlined above, **performance in the individual divisions** of a conglomerate is unlikely to be **much above the average** for the industry. Conglomerates may therefore be vulnerable to takeover and unbundling whereby the individual businesses are sold of one by one at a profit.

On the other hand, there may be some **benefits to shareholders** in diversification by Tovell.

(i) **Volatility in the internal cash flows** is **reduced**. This makes it possible to service a higher level of debt without undue risk than might otherwise be possible. As a result the overall cost of capital can be reduced, to the benefit of the ordinary shareholders.

(ii) Companies may be able to **diversify into areas** which are **inaccessible** to individual investors, for example in foreign countries which have exchange controls or other barriers to direct investment.

(iii) The **probability of failure** is lower in a well diversified company due to the **reduced overall level of risk**. This may be attractive to shareholders, particularly if they are risk-averse.

(b)   REPORT

To: Finance Director
From: Accountant
Date: 17 May 20X6
Subject: The financial implications of the fast food investment

Introduction

The purpose of this report is to make a financial evaluation of the proposed diversification into the fast food industry. Detailed calculations are included as an appendix to the report. The **adjusted present value (APV) technique** has been selected as being the most appropriate way of taking all the effects of the financing proposals fully into account.

Details of appraisal

The investment under consideration is in an area where Tovell has no existing activities or experience. The risk profile of the market, as defined by the **equity betas**, is different to that of Tovell's existing activities, and the project is large in relation to the size of the company (1.4 × £4.70 × 3.5m) at £23.03m. The new investment would increase the size of the company by 10% and the financing of the new investment would have an effective gearing of 51% (£800,000:£1.579m - see Appendix) which is significantly different to Tovell's existing gearing of 40%.

The difference in risk profile, the size of the project and the difference in the level of gearing all mean that the existing **weighted average cost of capital** (WACC) is **inappropriate** to use in this case. It is therefore proposed that the adjusted present value (APV) approach should be used which is a method of separating the effects of the financing method from the operating cash flows of the project.

One of the limitations of this approach is the fact that the determination of the **asset beta** assumes that the cash flows are all perpetuities, which is not the case in this example.

The calculations using this technique are shown in the Appendix. The possibility of continuing the activity beyond the end of the five year appraisal term has been ignored, and this means that the terminal value (in this case the realisable value of the land and buildings) will have a significant effect on the results of the calculations.

On the basis of the calculations shown, the investment shows a **negative APV** of £90,921 over the five year period, which suggests that it is not a financially viable proposition.

Conclusions

Although the calculations suggest that the investment should not be undertaken, it is suggested that further work is done to evaluate the effects of making additional investment in year 5 and continuing the business for a longer period. It would also be helpful to look in **more detail** at the **terminal value**. In the calculations shown, this amounts solely to the realisable value of the land and buildings. In reality, it may be able to sell the business on as a going concern, and if this is the case it would be helpful to value the future income stream as well, as a means of approximating the potential sale price.

APPENDIX

The adjusted present value (APV) of the investment is the base case NPV plus the present value of the financing effects.

The **base case NPV** is calculated assuming that the company is wholly equity financed. The first stage therefore is to calculate the appropriate discount rate to use in this event. Data from the fast food industry will be used.

It is necessary as a first step to estimate the appropriate **equity beta** to use in calculating the cost of capital.

$$\beta_a = \beta_e \frac{E}{E + D(1-t)} + \beta_d \frac{D(1-t)}{E + D(1-t)}$$

where β_a = β of equity in an ungeared company

β_e = β of equity in geared company

β_d = β of debt in geared company

E = market value of equity

D = market value of debt

t = tax rate

∴ β_a = $1.4 \times 1/(1 + 1(1 - 0.3)) + (0.25 \times 1(1 - 0.3)/(1 + 1(1 - 0.3))$

= 0.926

This can now be used to find the cost of equity in an ungeared firm.

$$E(r_j) = r_f + [E(r_m) - r_f]\,\beta_j$$

where $E(r_j)$ = cost of equity

β_j = equity beta

$E(r_m)$ = market rate of return

r_f = risk free rate of return

$E(r_j)$ = $5\% + (12.5\% - 5\%) \times 0.926$

= 11.945%, say 12%

The next step is to find the base case NPV. The annual cash flows are projected as follows. (All monetary figures are in £'000.)

	0	1	2	*Year* 3	4	5	6
Land & buildings	(1,250)					1,250	
Other fixed assets	(1,050)						
Op cash flow		420	441	463	486	511	
Tax at 30%		(63)	(129)	(136)	(142)	(150)	(77)
Tax saved on capital allowances		39	69	52	39	66	49
Net cash flow	(2,300)	396	381	379	383	1,677	(28)
Discount at 12%	1.000	0.893	0.797	0.712	0.636	0.567	0.507
Present values	(2,300)	354	304	270	244	951	(14)

Capital allowances

Year		Reducing balance £'000
0	Purchase	1,050
1	WDA	(262)
	Value at start of year 2	788
2	WDA	(197)
	Value at start of year 3	591
3	WDA	(148)
	Value at start of year 4	443
4	WDA	(111)
	Value at start of year 5	332
5	WDA	(83)
	Balancing allowance	(249)

Year of claim	Allow-ance £'000	Tax saved £'000	Yr 1 £'000	Yr 2 £'000	Yr 3 £'000	Yr 4 £'000	Yr 5 £'000	Yr 6 £'000
1	262	78	39	39				
2	197	60		30	30			
3	148	44			22	22		
4	111	34				17	17	
5	83	24					12	12
5	249	74					37	37
			39	69	52	39	66	49

Base case NPV = (£191,000)

The next stage is to calculate the **financial effects of the financing alternatives**.

(i)   Tax relief on borrowing capacity:

Annual tax benefit = £1m × 0.09 × 30% = 27,000

Remember, however, the 50:50 split

Year	£	Discount factor 9%	Present value £
1	13,500	0.917	12,380
2 – 5	27,000	(3.890 – 0.917)	80,271
6	13,500	0.596	8,046
			100,697

(ii)   Subsidised loan effects:

(1)   *Interest saved*

Year	£	Discount factor 9%	Present value £
1 – 5	3% × 800,000	3.890	93,360

(2)   *Tax shield lost*

Year	£	Discount factor 9%	Present value £
1	(3% × 800,000 × 30% × 0.5)	0.917	3,301
2 – 5	(3% × 800,000 × 30%)	(3.890 – 0.917)	21,406
6	(3% × 800,000 × 30% × 0.5)	0.596	2,146
			26,853

(iii) The issue costs of the rights issue must also be taken into account. The net proceeds of the rights issue are £2.3m less £0.8m (loan) = £1.5m. Since issue costs are 5%, the gross proceeds of the issue are £1.5m/0.95 = £1,578,947, and therefore the issue costs equal £78,947.

The APV can now be calculated.

	£
Base case NPV	(191,000)
Borrowing capacity tax relief	100,697
Subsidy benefit	93,360
Tax shield lost	(26,853)
Issue costs	(78,947)
APV	(102,743)

16 ZEDLAND POSTAL SERVICES

> **Tutor's hint**. Don't forget to discuss why your DCF calculation might not give the complete picture.

From:	A N Accountant
To:	The Board of directors
Date:	1 April 20X9
Subject:	Proposed new same day service

Introduction

This report considers whether the proposed new service will meet the two targets of a return on investment of at least 5% and a non-negative net present value. It also considers other factors which may be relevant. Calculations are set out in the Appendix.

Recommendation

The proposed new service has an annual **average return on average investment of 29%**, but it has a **negative net present value** ($36,000). Because projects must meet both targets to be acceptable, it is recommended that the service is not provided. However, this is subject to the further factors considered below.

Further factors

The proposed service might well be of **great value** to the public. It should perhaps be provided on that ground.

If the postal service's other projects have large positive net present values, it might be possible to net them off against the negative net present value here, to give an acceptable overall result. This is, of course, tantamount to **cross-subsidisation**.

It may be that charges could be increased and/or costs reduced, so that the net present value could become positive. In particular, planned staffing levels may be excessive.

Before any final decision is taken, the **reliability** of all forecasts should be reviewed, and a **sensitivity analysis** should be carried out.

APPENDIX

1   **Return on average investment**

Year	1 $'000	2 $'000	3 $'000	4 $'000	5 $'000
Revenue					
Letters	2,048	2,867	3,010	3,160	3,318
Parcels	682	1,075	1,129	1,185	1,244
	2,730	3,942	4,139	4,345	4,562
Expenses					
Staff	2,340	2,457	2,580	2,709	2,844
Premises	150	158	165	174	182
Vehicle maintenance					
Vans	200	252	318	400	504
Trucks	20	25	32	40	50
Advertising	1,300	263			
Depreciation	232	232	232	232	232
	4,242	3,387	3,327	3,555	3,812
Revenue less expenses	(1,512)	555	812	790	750
Taxation (40%)	605	(222)	(325)	(316)	(300)
Profit after tax	(907)	333	487	474	450

Total profit after tax = $837,000

Average profit after tax = $837,000/5 = $167,400

Average investment - £1,160,000/2 = $580,000

Average annual after tax return on investment = $\frac{\$167,400}{\$580,000} \times 100\% = 29\%$

2   **Net present value**

Year	0 $'000	1 $'000	2 $'000	3 $'000	4 $'000	5 $'000	6 $'000
Revenue less expenses		(1,512)	555	812	790	750	
Add depreciation		232	232	232	232	232	
Less taxation			605	(222)	(325)	(316)	(300)
Less initial investment	(1,160)						
Cash flow	(1,160)	(1,280)	1,392	822	697	666	(300)
Discount factor (14%)	1	0.877	0.769	0.675	0.592	0.519	0.456
Present value	(1,160)	(1,123)	1,070	555	413	346	(137)

Net present value = ($36,000).

3   **Assumptions made**

(a)   The **inflation rate,** for both revenue per unit and costs (excluding depreciation) will be 5%.

(b)   The cost of **preliminary research** is to be ignored, as it has already been incurred.

(c)   If the five managers were not needed for this new service, they would **remain** in their **present posts** rather than being made redundant.

(d)   **Return on average investment** is to be computed ignoring financing costs.

17 MARKET EFFICIENCY

To: Managing director
From: Accountant
Date: 2 January 20X2
Subject: Report on market efficiency

Market efficiency and NPV maximisation

Investors in any form of capital market attempt to **maximise** the **net present value** (NPV) of their investments, subject to constraints imposed by **ethical considerations** or the **needs of other stakeholders**.

In an efficient market, such as that for quoted securities (for example, stock exchange listed shares), investments can be bought and sold with ease and information is freely available. By competing to maximise the NPV of their investments, investors bid up prices until, in theory, NPVs are on average eroded to zero, which is another way of saying that each investment earns a **fair return** for its risk. This situation is correctly described in the business school's seminar.

Real capital investments are not traded in an efficient market, however. They are carried out by organisations which have often conducted **research and development** and do not divulge their knowledge to the general public. Other **competitive advantages** include location, contacts, and general 'know-how'. A real capital investment therefore gives an opportunity of exploiting these market imperfections to make a positive NPV. Only after an elapse of time will competitive forces erode these 'excess profits'.

Market efficiency and dividend policy

In a perfect capital market, with efficient flows of information, **dividend announcements** are **unimportant**. Provided companies generate a return which is at least as high as shareholders require for the risk, the actual pattern of cash dividend payouts does not matter. If companies need to cut back on dividends in order to **invest profitably**, then they should do so, paying dividends at a later stage when they have more cash available. Companies should not worry about whether the shareholders need the cash from their current dividend, runs the argument, because they can always raise cash by **selling shares**.

In the 'real world', however, capital markets are not perfect and shareholders do **not receive perfect information** about the prospects of companies. In addition **taxation** means that some shareholders prefer **reinvestment** whereas others prefer **high cash dividends**. An announcement that the dividend is to be reduced may therefore favour some shareholders more than others. Consequently a company should be very careful about suddenly changing its dividend policy. Unnecessary uncertainty might cause a **drop in the share price**.

Most financial directors take the view that the dividend announcement conveys significant information to shareholders and they therefore try to manage dividend policy by ensuring that shareholders receive as few 'surprises' as possible. This is commonly done by attempting to pay out a smooth trend of dividends. Variations from this trend are assumed to indicate **unusual prospects**.

Evidence of market efficiency

Market efficiency is identified on three levels, known as **strong, semi-strong** and **weak**. Empirical evidence suggests that for most of the time the UK stock market is **efficient** in the **semi-strong form**, which implies that share prices react very swiftly and logically to publicly available information by adjusting to appropriate values. The market is not strong form efficient, which means that those with inside information are able to make abnormal trading gains (although it is illegal to do so). This means that our company's share price is usually at an **appropriate value** given future expectations of performance. Thus by making suitable calculations, we can **estimate our cost of capital** and the **minimum return** required from our capital investments. It also means that **positive NPVs** generated by our projects will translate into **increases in shareholder wealth**.

Stock market volatility

The efficiency of stock markets has frequently been called into question during times of high volatility. Whereas high volatility (large increases and decreases in value) may simply be indicative of **uncertainty** in **general economic factors**, there do appear to be occasionally repeated patterns of **long periods of growth** followed by swift crashes. These patterns are **difficult to reconcile** with market efficiency, unless the crashes are associated with the sudden emergence of significant bad news, which does not seem to be the case. It appears that other behavioural, social or financial factors are at work which cause the **progressive over-valuation** of shares over long time periods, followed by a sudden collapse of confidence after (often relatively minor) trigger events.

18 BONDS

Tutor's hint. (a) requires a basic understanding of yield curves and the liquidity preference theory. Provided you have this knowledge, this part of the question is quite simple to answer.

(b) requires you to calculate the effective cost to the company of issuing a zero coupon bond. The calculations required are brief, and the conclusions to be drawn are quite straightforward. Be careful to do as the question instructs, and take into account the data provided in the first part of the question in making your recommendations.

Examiner's comment. This was the least popular optional question, and the standard of answers varied widely. Candidates failed to gain marks by confusing coupon yields with redemption yields in the determination of the shape of the yield curve, and/or not commenting upon the liquidity preference theory. In part (b) many candidates correctly identified the redemption yield on the zero coupon bond, but failed to use information from part (a) to analyse whether or not it might be advantageous for the company to issue such a bond.

(a) The **yield curve** is a method of describing the current term structure of interest rates, whereby the rate of interest is plotted against the term to maturity of a security. In this example, the yield curve is downward sloping since the redemption yield falls for longer dated bonds, suggesting that there is an expectation of a long-term decline in interest rates.

The **liquidity preference theory** is based on the proposition that the investor must be compensated for tying up his money in the asset for a longer period of time. Thus if the government were to make two issues of 8% bonds on the same date, one with a term of five years and one with a term of ten years, and if interest rates were expected to remain constant, the liquidity preference of investors would make them prefer the five year bond. The only way to overcome the liquidity preference of investors is to compensate them for the loss of liquidity; in other words to offer a higher rate of interest on longer dated stock.

The implication of this theory is that the yield curve will normally be **upward sloping**. However if there is an expectation that interest rates will fall, this can lead to a **downward sloping** curve. The gradient of the curve will be less than that of the expected rate of decline in interest rates, since the premium required for liquidity preference will offset some of the effect of expected lower interest rates.

(b)   **Memo: Possible use of a zero coupon bond**

The attraction of **zero coupon bonds** is that there are no annual interest payments to be made. However, the company will need to make provision for the repayment at par in seven years' time.

To evaluate the bond it is necessary to calculate the redemption yield. This can be estimated using the expression:

$$£55 = \frac{£100}{(1 + Kd)^7}$$

$$1 + Kd = \sqrt[7]{\frac{100}{55}} = 1.0892$$

$$Kd = 8.92\%$$

This **redemption yield** is just marginally lower than that on the Treasury 8% 20Y6 bonds that have eight years to go before maturity. Normally companies will have to pay a higher rate of interest than the government to compensate investors for the higher level of risk. Therefore, if the company has the opportunity to raise the funds in this way, it appears to be a very low cost way of obtaining the money. However, it is technically simplistic to compare the yield on zero coupon bonds with those of coupon-paying bonds.

(c)   The manager has **two options**. Either he can **invest in the one year bond,** or he can **invest in the two year bond** and **sell** it at the end of the first year. The expected return on the second option can be evaluated, assuming that there is no change in interest rates during the period.

At the end of the first year, since the risk of the two bonds is similar, the redemption yield on the second bond might reasonably be expected to be 8.43%. This can be used to estimate the price (p) at the end of the first year on a £100 bond, as follows.

On redemption at the end of the second year, the investor receives £100 + £11.25 (second year's interest).

$$
\begin{aligned}
p \times (1 + 8.43\%) &= £100 + £11.25 \\
p &= £111.25/1.0843 \\
&= £102.60
\end{aligned}
$$

If the bond is sold at the end of the first year the total expected return is therefore £102.60 + £11.25 (first year's interest) = £113.85. Since the current price of the bond is £103.94, this represents a yield of (113.85/103.94) − 1 = 9.53%. This is above the expected redemption yield of the one year bond of 8.43%, and is therefore the preferred investment. However, the risk is that if interest rates rise during the year the actual return will be much lower.

19   FUELIT

(a)   **NPV of the two investments**

We need to calculate a WACC and convert it to a real cost of capital to discount the real cash flows of the investments.

Gas

$$Ke = r_f + [E(r_m) - r_f] B_j$$
$$= 4.5 + [14 - 4.5] \, 0.7$$
$$= 11.15\%$$

$$Kd = 8.5 \, (1 - 0.3)$$
$$= 5.95\%$$

$$WACC = (\text{Equity weighting} \times Ke) + (\text{Debt weighting} \times Kd)$$
$$= (0.65 \times 11.15) + (0.35 \times 5.95)$$
$$= 9.33\%$$

As WACC is a nominal rate, convert to real rate.

$$\text{Real rate} = \frac{(1 + \text{nominal rate})}{(1 + \text{inflation rate})} - 1$$
$$= \frac{1.0933}{1.03} - 1$$
$$= 6.15\%, \text{ say } 6\%$$

Nuclear

$$Ke = 4.5 + (14 - 4.5) \, 1.4$$
$$= 17.8\%$$

$$Kd = 10 \, (1 - 0.3)$$
$$= 7\%$$

$$WACC = (0.4 \times 17.8) + (0.6 \times 7)$$
$$= 11.32\%$$

$$\text{Real rate} = \frac{1.1132}{1.03} - 1$$

$$= 8.08\%, \text{ say } 8\%$$

Discounted cash flow estimates: Gas

Annual operating cash flows	*First 10 years*	*Last 15 years*
Years	*4 – 13*	*14 – 28*
	£m	£m
Annual revenues	800	800
Annual costs		
Labour	75	75
Gas purchases	500	500
Sales and marketing expenses	40	40
Customer relations	5	5
Other cash outlays	5	5
Tax allowable depreciation at 10%	60	-
	685	625
Incremental taxable profit	115	175.0
Tax at 30%	44.5	52.5
After tax profit	80.5	122.5
Add back depreciation	60.0	-
Incremental cash flow	140.5	122.5
Annuity factors at 6%		
10 years × PV 3 years		
7.360 × 0.840	6.182	
15 years × PV 13 years		
9.712 × 0.469		4.555
Present value	868.6	558.0

Other cash flows

Year	1	2	3	4	28
	£m	£m	£m	£m	£m
After tax redundancy costs				4	
Building costs (2 instalments)	300	300			
Demolition of coal fired station			10		
Demolition of gas plant					25
6% factors	0.943	0.890	0.840	0.792	0.196
Present value of costs	282.9	267.0	8.4	3.2	4.9

Total net present value = 868.6 + 558.0 – (282.9 + 267.0 + 8.4 + 3.2 + 4.9)

= £ 860.2 million

Note: Interest is ignored from annual cost estimates because it (and the tax relief it attracts) is included in the after tax discount rate.

Discounted cash flow estimates: Nuclear power

Annual operating cash flows	*First 10 years*	*Last 15 years*
Years	*4 – 13*	*14 – 28*
	£m	£m
Annual revenues	800	800
Annual costs		
Labour	20	20
Nuclear fuel purchases	10	10
Sales and marketing expenses	40	40
Customer relations	20	20
Other cash outlays	25	25
Tax allowable depreciation at 10%	330	-
	445	115
Incremental taxable profit	355.0	685.0
Tax at 30%	106.5	205.5
After tax profit	248.5	479.5
Add back depreciation	330.0	-
Incremental cash flow	578.5	479.5
Annuity factors at 8%		
10 years × PV 3 years		
6.710 × 0.794	5.328	
15 years × PV 13 years		
8.559 × 0.368		3.150
Present value	3,082.2	1,510.4

Other cash flows

Year	1	2	3	4	28
	£m	£m	£m	£m	£m
After tax redundancy costs				36	
Building costs (2 instalments)	1,650	1,650			
Demolition of coal fired station			10		
Decommissioning of nuclear plant					1,000
8% factors	0.926	0.857	0.794	0.735	0.116
Present value of costs	1,527.9	1,414.1	7.9	26.5	116.0

Total net present value = 3,082.2 + 1,510.4 – (1,527.9 + 1,414.1 + 7.9 + 26.5 + 116.0)

    = **£1,500.2 million**

Note: If the lowest estimate of nuclear plant decommissioning cost was used, the net present value would be £1,558 million.

Conclusion

On the basis of net present values applied to the estimates given, the nuclear plant should be chosen.

(b) The most significant factors to affect the decision which have not been taken into account above are:

(i) **Social and political acceptability of more nuclear powered station**

If **public opinion** is heavily **against** nuclear power, the government is unlikely to risk its political majority by deciding in favour of it. Even if a vocal minority is the only opposition, construction could be severely delayed by demonstrations and sabotaging actions. **Social and political intelligence** is therefore vital information.

(ii) **Risk of a rapid change in political acceptability of nuclear plants**

Future political acceptability may be influenced by a number of events. For example a number of **small leakages** could cause a nuclear plant to abandoned at any time during its life because of a fall in public acceptability. Threat of **terrorist action** may also cause political opinion to change. **Risk scenarios** need to be constructed and **contingency plans** devised.

(iii) **Risk of a large-scale nuclear accident or gas explosion**

Such risks are not easily analysed by expected values and NPV computations, but both events have actually happened in the past. Information needs to be collected to **model** these events as **scenarios**.

(iv) **Technical information**

It would be useful to evaluate the **technical information** underlying the projected construction and operation of the plants to ensure that best practice, particularly in **safety testing,** is envisaged and that costs are realistic to achieve the necessary quality. This may indicate how likely delays are during construction. **Industry information** on current developments would aid an evaluation of **how long** the stations would be **in operation,** and the consequences if technology changes. It might also enable a narrower estimate of the rage of **decommissioning costs** to be made.

(v) **Economic information**

More details and accurate estimates could be obtained on, for example, expected future **demand** for power, annual **inflation** rate estimates (both in general and for individual cost items), and **interest rate movements.** The likelihood of the United Kingdom **joining the euro currency zone** is also significant. If the UK does not join the euro zone in the near future, there may be **uncertainties** attached to the **cost of debt,** which is denominated in euros for both projects. Based on existing predictions of inflation levels, the **euro** is likely to **depreciate** against the pound, making the cost of debt cheaper.

(vi) **Fiscal changes**

Expected **future tax rates** and **capital allowances** may have a significant impact, including the possibility of 'green' taxes or constraints on polluting industries and likely treatment of gas and nuclear power under these taxes.

(vii) **CAPM implications**

It would be useful to get more information about the **systematic risk** of the power industry, and how **different gearing levels** would affect the assessment of other projects and the company's overall valuation.

(viii) **The value of real options associated with each project**

As discussed in part (d) below, these are likely to be **higher** for the gas fuelled power station.

On the basis however of the estimates made, the NPV of the nuclear power alternative is so much higher than the gas alternative that further information on the accuracy of other general cash flow estimates is unlikely to change the decision.

(c) Perhaps the simplest way of dealing with the range of options available is to use the **highest cost estimate.**

A further way of dealing with the high uncertainty attached to the cost of decommissioning is to **decrease the discount rate** for the cost figure used.

An alternative method of handling risk is to **discount at the risk free rate** and to **convert all cash forecasts to certainty-equivalents**. The certainty-equivalent for this cost would be **higher** than the expected value.

(d) An option is a choice which need only be exercised if it is to the investor's advantage. A **'real option'** is such a **choice or opportunity** which exists because of a capital investment. The choice may involve being able to change plans once the project is underway. The opportunity also may not have been envisaged when the original plans were made, but may arise later on.

Options associated with the projects are in the main more valuable for the gas fuelled than for the nuclear power project. They include the following:

(i) **The option to abandon the project early.** This may be needed for a variety of reasons, for example because of falling demand or because of the emergence of a new technology. High decommissioning costs make this a problem for the nuclear powered project.

(ii) **The option to expand if demand increases.** This is easier for gas because of the lower investment costs.

(iii) **The option to switch power source in the future.** This is more valuable for gas, because the technology could be adapted for other fossil fuels, such as oil. Nuclear power technology has no easy power source alternatives.

The significance of these options is that they **add value** to the project and should be taken into account in the **investment appraisal.** Although the valuation is difficult, even a rough estimate is better than no estimate at all. On this basis, the gas fuelled project is likely to be relatively more valuable than shown in the original calculations.

20   PREPARATION QUESTION: RODFIN

Tutor's hint. Part (a) requires an understanding of the differences between portfolio theory and the CAPM, principally in regard to their treatment of unsystematic risk. This understanding should influence your choice of calculation method in your approach to evaluating the risk of the two portfolios for part (b), since sufficient data is provided to use either portfolio theory or the CAPM. Full marks could be gained in (b) by using either CAPM or portfolio theory, and we show alternative answers below.

(a) Portfolio theory and the CAPM are not the same, although portfolio theory provides the basis of the more sophisticated CAPM approach to making investment decisions under conditions of risk.

The principal difference in this context is that the **CAPM** is only concerned with systematic risk ie that element of risk that cannot be removed by diversification. **Portfolio theory** on the other hand is concerned with the total risk of the portfolio.

Thus it is unlikely that the two approaches will give the same portfolio risk measure unless the portfolio in question is sufficiently well diversified to eliminate fully unsystematic risk.

(b) We do not have information on whether shareholders have diversified portfolios. If the company's shareholders are not diversified, **portfolio theory** should be used. If the company's shareholders are already diversified, a **CAPM** approach should be used.

Alternative answer 1: CAPM

The expected return for each portfolio can be estimated as the weighted average of the expected return from each investment in the portfolio.

Portfolio 1

Investment	Expected return	Invested	
	%	£m	
	X	Y	X × Y
a	16	3.8	60.8
b	6	5.2	31.2
c	10	6.1	61.0
d	13	2.9	37.7
		18.0	190.7

Expected return = 190.7/18.0 = 10.59%

Portfolio 2

Investment	Expected return	Invested	
	%	£m	
	X	Y	X × Y
a	14	7.1	99.4
b	11	2.7	29.7
c	7	5.4	37.8
d	17	2.8	47.6
		18.0	214.5

Expected return = 214.5/18.0 = 11.92%

Using the **CAPM**, the weighted average portfolio betas can be found as a measure of the beta of the portfolio and this can then be used to calculate the required return for the portfolio taking into account the level of risk. This can be compared with the expected return to form the basis for an investment recommendation. The **required return for the portfolio** can be found using the following expression from the formula sheet.

$E(r_j) = r_f + [E(r_m) - r_f]\beta_j$

In this case $E(r_m) = 12.5\%$ and $r_f = 5.5\%$

Portfolio 1

Investment	Beta	Invested	
		£m	
	X	Y	X × Y
a	1.4	3.8	5.3
b	0.0	5.2	0.0
c	0.7	6.1	4.3
d	1.1	2.9	3.2
		18.0	12.8

Portfolio beta = 12.8/18.0 = 0.71

$E(r_j) = 5.5 + (12.5 - 5.5) \times 0.71 = 10.47\%$

Portfolio 2

Investment	Beta	Invested £m	
	X	Y	X × Y
a	1.2	7.1	8.5
b	0.8	2.7	2.2
c	0.2	5.4	1.1
d	1.5	2.8	4.2
		18.0	16.0

Portfolio beta = 16.0/18.0 = 0.89

$E(r_j) = 5.5 + (12.5 - 5.5) \times 0.89 = 11.73\%$

In both cases the expected return from the portfolio is above the required return as calculated using the CAPM. However, the differential is slightly greater in respect of **Portfolio 2** and this is therefore the **recommended choice** on financial grounds. The company must also take into account its **attitude towards risk** in making this decision, and it may be that in practice it will prefer Portfolio 1 since this has a lower beta factor and therefore a lower risk level. This could be important since the investment is only to be held for a short period of time.

Alternative answer 2: Portfolio theory

If the company uses portfolio theory, and assuming all investments are uncorrelated, total risk can be estimated from:

$$\sigma_p = \sqrt{\sigma_a^2 x_a^2 + \sigma_b^2 x_b^2 + \sigma_c^2 x_c^2 + \sigma_d^2 x_d^2}$$

Where $x_a^2, x_b^2, x_c^2, x_d^2$, are the proportions of the total invested in each individual security

$\sigma_a, \sigma_b, \sigma_c, \sigma_d$ are the standard deviations of the expected returns of the individual investments in the portfolios.

Portfolio 1

$$\sigma_p = \sqrt{7^2 \times (0.211)^2 + 2^2 \times (0.289)^2 + 5^2 \times (0.339)^2 + 13^2 \times (0.161)^2} = 3.13\%$$

Portfolio 2

$$\sigma_p = \sqrt{9^2 \times (0.394)^2 + 4^2 \times (0.150)^2 + 3^2 \times (0.300)^2 + 14^2 \times (0.156)^2} = 4.30\%$$

Using portfolio theory, it is not clear which portfolio is to be preferred: the portfolio with the higher risk also has the higher return.

21 PHANTOM

(a) The method that should be used is to measure the **risk** (as represented by the **standard deviation**) and **expected return** of each of the possible **two asset portfolios**. The **formula** to be used to calculate the standard deviation is:

$$\sigma_p = \sqrt{\sigma_a^2 x^2 + \sigma_b^2 (1-x)^2 + 2x(1-x)p_{ab}\sigma_a\sigma_b}$$

where σ_p = standard deviation of a portfolio of two investments, A and B
  σ_a = standard deviation of the returns from investment A
  σ_b = standard deviation of the returns from investment B
  x = the proportion of investment A in the portfolio
  p_{ab} = the correlation coefficient of returns from investment A and B

The expected return of each portfolio can be calculated using:

$$\bar{r}_p p = x\bar{r}_a + (1-x)\bar{r}_b$$

where $\bar{r}_p$ = Expected return of the portfolio

  $\bar{r}_a$ = Expected return from investment A

  $\bar{r}_b$ = Expected return from investment B

  x = the proportion of investment A in the portfolio

The risk and return for each portfolio can now be calculated.

Mangeit Foods and Altalk Communications

$$\sigma_p = \sqrt{(17^2 \times 0.5^2) + (29^2 \times 0.5^2) + (2 \times 0.5 \times 0.5 \times 0.0 \times 17 \times 29)}$$

$\sigma_p = 16.81$

$\bar{r}_p = (0.5 \times 11) + (0.5 \times 20) = 15.5\%$

Mangeit Foods and Legi Printers

$$\sigma_p = \sqrt{(17^2 \times 0.5^2) + (21^2 \times 0.5^2) + (2 \times 0.5 \times 0.5 \times 0.62 \times 17 \times 21)}$$

$\sigma_p = 17.12$

$\bar{r}_p = (0.5 \times 11) + (0.5 \times 14) = 12.5\%$

Altalk Communications and Legi Printers

$$\sigma_p = \sqrt{(29^2 \times 0.5^2) + (21^2 \times 0.5^2) + (2 \times 0.5 \times 0.5 \times 0.40 \times 29 \times 21)}$$

$$\sigma_p = 21.03$$

$$\bar{r}_p = (0.5 \times 20) + (0.5 \times 14) = 17.0\%$$

The portfolio containing Altalk Communications and Legi Printers is more efficient than that containing Mangeit Foods and Altalk Communications since it has both a higher expected return and a lower level of risk. However, it is not possible to say which of the other two portfolios is the most efficient since the Mangeit and Legi portfolio has both a lower risk and a lower return than the Altalk and Legi portfolio. The differences between the levels of risk and return for the two portfolios are broadly similar, and hence it is not possible even to guess at which may be the most efficient.

(b) As with all investment decisions, the criteria to be used will be dependent upon the purpose for which the investments are being made. In this case, Phantom is buying the shares with a view to making a **future acquisition,** and therefore the criteria to be used must be those of best strategic fit with those of Phantom's existing businesses. Obviously, **financial performance** will be relevant to this decision, but the normal rules that are used for constructing a portfolio of investments are not of primary importance in this situation.

Even if Phantom was buying the shares with a view to investment performance rather than making future acquisitions, it would not be correct to base the decision on the relative efficiency of the two asset portfolios. Phantom would need to consider the effect of the share purchases on its overall portfolio of investments and activities, and not to view the new investments in isolation.

A further problem is that portfolio theory measures the total risk of the possible portfolios. However, if Phantom is well diversified it will already have minimised the level of unsystematic risk to which it is exposed, and it should only be concerned with the systematic risk of the new investments.

(c) The decision on the investment in bonds can be made in the same manner as any investment decision, that is by **trading off expected return against risk.**

The appropriate return for bonds is the **yield to redemption,** while risk is measured by **credit rating** and also influenced by the **period to redemption.**

	Magnacorp	Suprafirm	Grandit
Redemption yield	7.0%	7.5%	6.0%
Credit rating	A–	BBB+	A–
Period to redemption	10 years	10 years	4 years

By examining the given figures, it appears that:

(i) Magnacorp bonds have a **higher return** than **Grandit bonds** and the **same credit rating**. There is no obvious case for changing to Grandit if the intention is to hold the investment for ten years. However, if the investment needs to be **realised within four years**, and if interest rates are predicted to rise, there may be **less risk** associated with **holding** Grandit bonds to **redemption** than with selling Magnacorp bonds before their redemption date.

(ii) Magnacorp bonds have a lower return than Suprafirm bonds but a slightly higher credit rating. Both bonds have the same period to redemption. A change to Suprafirm may be considered worthwhile, depending on **attitude to risk** and assuming that **transaction costs** do **not outweigh** the gains.

129

(d) The value of Grandit bonds is estimated by discounting its cash flows to redemption at 6%:

Year		£	6% discount factor	PV £
1 - 4	Interest	7.8	3.465	27.03
4	Redemption	100	0.792	79.20
				106.23

The bond is actually selling at £105.83, which is 40 pence below the calculated figure. This indicates that the redemption yield is slightly higher than 6%.

22   BARTOO

> **Tutor's hint.** In (a) you should discuss not only the nature of the alternative portfolios, but also the different investment opportunities available in the context of the purpose for which the cash is being held. A question like (b) may be asked in the exam without referring to the excess return of a share over its CAPM required return as the 'alpha value'.
>
> **Examiner's comment**. In (a) many answers displayed poor understanding of the nature of systematic and unsystematic risk. Few candidates suggested that equity investment, which involves significant price risk, is not the best form of investment when a company does not wish to experience capital loss. Many candidates who attempted (b) did not earn any marks at all. Some thought that alphas were the same as betas, others thought that alpha is one minus beta. Many computed the betas wrongly.

(a) Any decision regarding the investment of surplus funds must be based on the **purpose** for which the investment is being made and the intended eventual use of those funds. In this case the funds are to be used in 18 months' time to finance the building of a factory extension. It is therefore important that the element of downside risk is low, ie that at least £500,000 will be available at that time in order that Bartoo can undertake the project as planned.

In view of this, a relatively low risk investment strategy is required. **Equities**, even in stable blue chip companies, are a relatively high risk form of investment, dependent not only on the performance of the individual companies but also on wider stock market fluctuations. It is therefore suggested that if it has not already done so, the company should consider some of the other **lower risk investments** available, including the following.

(i)   Government securities of an appropriate term
(ii)   Bank deposits
(iii)   Money market deposits
(iv)   Local authority deposits
(v)   Finance house deposits
(vi)   Sterling certificates of deposit
(vii)   Foreign currency investments, with appropriate hedging

If Bartoo is prepared to accept the risk of an equity portfolio, then it is most important that the portfolio should contain shares from companies in a wide range of market sectors in order to maximise the amount of diversification. The proposed list does appear to offer a good spread, although there is no obvious manufacturing company included. **Diversification** is important because this is the principal means of eliminating unsystematic risk from the portfolio, leaving only **systematic risk** ie the inherent risk attaching to a specific investment that cannot be eliminated by diversification. Bartoo needs to consider diversification because it is a private company, and thus has a small number of shareholders who are unlikely to be personally diversified.

In general, it is recommended that an equity portfolio should contain at least 15 or 20 securities from a spread of different sectors in order to minimise the **unsystematic risk** element. Since Bartoo is currently only considering eight companies, it is suggested that they should all be included in the portfolio rather than reducing the number still further to five. Ideally, additional securities should be considered, or perhaps a **mix of equities** and some of the **lower risk investments** discussed above. Including all eight securities would result in a portfolio beta of 0.98 (average betas) reducing the level of risk to below that of the market. Including only the five lowest betas would reduce the portfolio beta to 0.86, but some of the benefits of diversification would be lost and the overall level of risk would consequently be higher.

In conclusion, it is recommended that the directors should give careful consideration to the **overall level of risk** that they are prepared to accept and to structure the portfolio accordingly. If low risk is important, then at least a part of the investment should be made in fixed interest securities. If an equity investment at some level is selected, then the portfolio should be large enough to eliminate a substantial part of the unsystematic risk element.

(b)   The **alpha value** is the difference between:

(i)   The **actual or forecast rate of return** from an investment; and

(ii)   The **required return** as computed from the capital asset pricing model (CAPM) using the beta value of the investment

The **betas** of the given companies' shares are calculated by the formula:

$$\beta_y = \frac{cov(x,y)}{var(x)}$$

where y is the share and x is the stock market as a whole.

The **variance**, var, is the square of the standard deviation. The variance of the market is therefore $5^2 = 25$.

	cov (x,y)	var (x)	Beta
Dedton	32	25	1.28
Paralot	19	25	0.76
Sunout	24	25	0.96
Rangon	43	25	1.72

The required return of each investment is estimated by the CAPM formula:

$$E(r_j) = r_f + (E(r_m) - r_f)\beta_j$$

r_f is 6% and $E(r_m) - r_f$ is: 14.5% – 6% = 8.5%.

CAPM required returns		Forecast returns	Alpha values
Dedton	6% + 8.5% × 1.28 = 16.88%	16%	–0.88%
Paralot	6% + 8.5% × 0.76 = 12.46%	12%	–0.46%
Sunout	6% + 8.5% × 0.96 = 14.16%	14%	–0.16%
Rangon	6% + 8.5% × 1.72 = 20.62%	19%	–1.62%

If a share has a **negative alpha** value based on forecast returns against the CAPM, the implication is that an investor will make an abnormally low return by investing in the share. This in turn implies that the share is currently over-valued by the market.

A financial manager who wants to invest surplus funds would therefore look for shares **with positive alpha values**, whereas a financial manager examining the company's cost of capital would be pleased with a **negative alpha value** because it implies that the cost of equity capital is lower than that predicted by the CAPM for the level of systematic risk.

However, it must be appreciated that estimation of alpha values is subject to a high level of error and that, over time, **most alpha values will have an average value of zero.**

23   WONPAR

> **Tutor's hint.** The main difficulty with this question is answering it at the appropriate level of detail. Diversifying internationally reduces portfolio risk unless the UK is perfectly representative of the world economy. It is very tempting to try to calculate something, but the question specifically excludes calculations.
>
> **Examiner's comment.** In (a) candidates showed a good understanding of portfolio theory, but did not always relate this to international portfolio investment. There was some confusion between systematic, unsystematic risk and total risk. Time was sometimes wasted by undertaking additional calculations despite being advised in the question requirements that these were not required.

(a)   To: The Board of Directors, Wonpar plc
      From: Financial Consultant
      Date: 12 January 20X1
      Subject: Report on investment of £5 million in ordinary shares

This report addresses the general benefits of international portfolio diversification and comments specifically on the suggestions made by two of your directors.

(i)   **Possible benefits of international portfolio investment**

Portfolio theory shows that when two or more risky investments are combined in a portfolio the overall risk of the portfolio is reduced with no equivalent reduction in return. This effect is most pronounced when the correlation between the investments is low, but risk reduction will be possible whenever the correlation coefficient is less than perfectly positive (ie $< +1$).

The risk of an investment can be categorised under two labels: **systematic risk,** which is the sensitivity of the investment to general economic factors, and **unsystematic risk**, which is caused by risk factors specific to the investment. When investments are combined in a portfolio, some of the unsystematic risk factors cancel out (a gain for one investment is a loss for another) but the systematic risk is unchanged.

The theory goes on to suggest a simple two-stage investment strategy for portfolios of quoted securities which optimises the return obtainable at any given level of risk:

(1)   Decide how much of **your available investment** funds to place in risky assets (eg ordinary shares) and how much to invest in risk free assets such as bank deposits or government stock.

(2)   **Spread the funds** to be **invested** in risky assets over as wide a portfolio as possible. This will eliminate virtually all of the unsystematic risk, leaving only systematic risk.

The benefits of **international portfolio diversification** are felt in stage 2 of this process. The logic is simple. You are not spreading your funds as widely as possible if you confine yourself to one country. The theory suggests that the ideal portfolio would contain shares from every country in the world! In practice this means spreading your portfolio across the economies of all major countries.

But how do we know that the UK, for example, is not representative of the whole **world economy**? Is it not just a slice of the world economy? If it were, then surely portfolio diversification within the UK would be sufficient.

We can answer this question by looking at the data attached to this report *(ie the data given in the exam question)*. The first table shows that correlations between different countries' economies are much less than +1. This shows that none of these economies are identical and that risk reduction is possible by combining investments in different countries. In the second table, beta is the **index of systematic risk** in the country's economy. Any country which was representative of the whole world would have a systematic risk of 1. In fact we see that UK has a beta of less than one, which indicates that the UK economy is less volatile in economic cycles than most countries, whereas Hong Kong has a beta much greater than one, indicating an economy which is highly sensitive to economic cycles. America, being the major world economy, has a beta close to 1.

Because no individual countries' economies are representative of the whole world, it is possible to reduce risk by international diversification. The **conclusion** from portfolio theory is therefore that the new £5 million investment should be spread across *all* major countries.

Tutor's hint. Assuming that such a diversified world portfolio is held, returns in individual countries can then be evaluated by the capital asset pricing model, which suggests that the average rate of return shown by each country *should* depend on its systematic risk (ie its beta factor) not its total risk. The best investments are therefore found by looking for countries exhibiting *higher* returns than would be expected for the level of systematic risk. From the data given, the best investments appear to be in UK and Hong Kong. However, all the figures given are based on historical data. Caution must be exercised in interpreting these figures because the future might offer different results, especially as the world economy is currently exhibiting turbulent changes.

(ii)   **Comments on the directors' suggestions**

Director 1. In the data given, France shows a relatively **high return** and a **low total risk**. However these facts are only relevant for investors who wish to invest in France alone. Since Wonpar already has investments in the UK, an investment in France may not be particularly beneficial because the correlation with UK is high.

If, as we suggest, you spread your investment across a world portfolio, then France's return is no more attractive than any other country: its return is only what should be expected from its relatively high systematic risk.

Director 2. When added to a UK portfolio, an investment in Singapore offers good risk reduction potential because of its low correlation with UK. However, better results can be obtained by diversifying worldwide. The returns offered by Singapore then appear quite disappointing compared with what is expected from its systematic risk.

Conclusion. Our recommendation is to invest the £5 million in a broad portfolio of shares spread across all the major world economies.

(b)   We can use the CAPM formula:

$$E(r_j) = r_f + (E(r_m) - r_f)\beta_j$$

to estimate the returns.

	CAPM expected returns	*Actual returns*	*Alpha values*
Jan-Mar X8	7.50% + (8.5% × 1.25) = 18.125%	20.0%	+1.875%
Apr-Jun X8	7.50% + (8.5% × 1.25) = 18.125%	18.2%	+0.075%
Jul-Sep X8	7.00% + (8.5% × 1.25) = 17.625%	17.6%	−0.025%
Oct-Dec X8	6.75% + (8.5% × 1.25) = 17.375%	17.2%	−0.175%
Jan-Mar X9	6.75% + (8.5% × 1.25) = 17.375%	19.0%	+1.625%
Apr-Jun X9	6.25% + (8.5% × 1.25) = 16.875%	17.0%	+0.125%
Jul-Sep X9	6.25% + (8.5% × 1.25) = 16.875%	17.0%	+0.125%
Oct-Nov X9	6.00% + (8.5% × 1.25) = 16.625%	16.6%	−0.025%

In both years the **alpha values** (the difference between actual and expected returns) is significant in January to March, and negligible for the rest of the year. The reason for this may be a commonly observed stock market effect, that **returns** in the **first few months of the year** are often higher than expected.

24   MUNXAY

> **Tutor's hint.** The key in (b) is that the overall beta and the overall historical return can be measured by weighted averages of the four projects. If you remember the formula for beta and the problems which apply to CAPM, you should score well on this question.
>
> **Examiner's comment.** In part (b) reasons must be given for why the share is thought to be over or under valued. Answers to (c) were often confined to the assumptions underlying the CAPM, and did not focus on its limitations and market efficiency.

(a)   Because share prices fluctuate, shares will show temporary positive or negative alpha values most of the time. However, if the CAPM is a valid model, positive alpha values should be eroded by investors buying the shares, causing a price increase and hence reducing the expected future returns for investors who follow them. Similarly, negative alphas will be eroded by investors selling the shares. The same alpha values would not therefore be expected to exist in one year's time.

Estimation of alpha values is subject to **high statistical error** resulting from both the forecast of a company's return and the estimates input to the CAPM. For example the margins of error on beta factors are quite high and R_m is difficult to estimate. At any point in time it is therefore difficult to say whether an alpha value is significant information or just a statistical error.

However, research on the CAPM has shown that some companies do seem to have alpha values that persist for longer than would be statistically expected. This signals that the CAPM is not a perfect model. For example the CAPM tends to overstate the required return of high beta shares and to understate the required return of low beta shares. The returns of **small companies** may be understated and returns on certain days of the week or months of the year are different from those predicted.

Much research has been devoted to finding a better model than the CAPM, for example **arbitrage pricing theory** (APT) which uses several factors to predict returns. Despite this, the CAPM remains a useful model because of its **simplicity**.

(b)   The expected return of Munxay plc shares can be computed from the **capital asset pricing model**. The company's overall beta factor can be computed from the weighted average of its investment betas, as follows:

Project	Beta	% of company value
1	$15 \times 0.55/13 = 0.635$	28%
2	$20 \times 0.75/13 = 1.154$	17%
3	$14 \times 0.84/13 = 0.905$	31%
4	$18 \times 0.62/13 = 0.858$	24%

$$\text{Overall beta} = 0.635 \times 28\% + 1.154 \times 17\% + 0.905 \times 31\% + 0.858 \times 24\%$$
$$= 0.860$$

Assuming the company has no debt, using the CAPM

$$\text{Required return} = 5\% + (14\% - 5\%)\,0.860$$
$$= 12.74\%$$

The historical return over the last 5 years has been:

Weighted average of project returns
$$= 10\% \times 28\% + 18\% \times 17\% + 15\% \times 31\% + 13\% \times 24\%$$
$$= 13.63\%$$

The actual return is expected to continue in future and, because it is higher than the required return, the share must have a cheaper price than expected, that is its shares are undervalued.

(c) The above calculations are subject to errors because:

(i) The **historical data** is **unlikely** to be **repeated** in future. Forecasts should be used, but are subject to forecasting errors.

e **subject** to **statistical error** and should be ence limits.

t be **efficient** and may not reflect the available

s **semi-strong efficient**, investors may not have lent to that given in the data.

ble single factor single period model and does ts, for example for low or high beta shares, for h low P/E ratios and at certain times of the year els, such as arbitrage pricing theory may produce

rket over the risk free rate varies and may be

wings, which affects its equity beta and share

he ex div share price to calculate the market value. vidend payment instead of the full payment for the ax cost of debt when estimating the cost of the

of which are distributed as dividends, the **cost**

$$Ke = \frac{D}{P_0}$$

where D = annual dividend

P₀ = ex-div market value

Earnings available to be paid as dividends are as follows.

	£'000
Earnings before interest and tax	15,000
Interest (£23,697,000 × 16%)	3,792
	11,208
Tax at 31%	(3,474)
	7,734

$$Ke = \frac{7,734,000}{12,500,000 \times 4 \times 0.80} = 19.34\%$$

The **cost of debt** can be estimated by comparing the current market value of the debt with the discounted payments due to be made by the company up to the redemption date.

Year	Cash flow	8% discount factor	PV	10% discount factor	PV
	£'000		£'000		£'000
0	(105.50)	1.000	(105.50)	1.000	(105.50)
1-3	16(1 − 0.31)	2.577	28.45	2.487	27.46
3	100	0.794	79.40	0.751	75.10
			2.35		(2.94)

Interpolating:

$$\text{Post-tax cost of debt, Kd (1 − t)} = 8\% + \frac{2.35}{2.35 + 2.94} \times (10 - 8) = 8.88\%$$

$$\text{WACC} = Ke_g \frac{E}{E+D} + Kd(1-t)\frac{D}{E+D}$$

$$= 19.34 \times \frac{40}{40+25} + 8.88 \times \frac{25}{40+25} = 15.32\%$$

(b) (i) Using **Modigliani and Miller's theory**, the market value will equal the market value of the company if it were wholly equity financed, plus the present value of tax relief on any debt interest:

$$MV_g = MV_u + Dt$$

where: MV_g = total market value (D + E)

MV_u = market value if equity financed

D = debt

t = tax rate

In this case:

MV_g = £32.5m + (£5m × 0.31)

= £34.05m

and: D = £5m

∴ E = £29.05m

The market value will increase by £1.55m = (£34.05m − £32.5m).

(ii) Using answer to (b)(iii) below:

$$\text{WACC} = Ke_g \left(\frac{E}{E+D}\right) + Kd(1-t)\left(\frac{D}{E+D}\right)$$

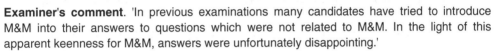

$$17.18 = Ke_g \times \frac{29.05}{34.05} + 13 \times (1 - 0.31) \times \frac{5}{34.05}$$

$$15.86 = Ke_g \times \frac{29.05}{34.05}$$

$$Ke_g = 18.59\%$$

The cost of equity has therefore risen by 0.59% due to the presence of financial risk.

(iii)   The weighted average cost of capital (WACC) can be found as follows.

$$WACC = Ke_u \left[1 - \frac{Dt}{E + D} \right]$$

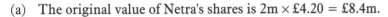

$$= 0.18 \left[1 - \frac{5 \times 0.31}{34.05} \right] = 17.18\%$$

The weighted average cost of capital has fallen by 0.82% due to the benefit of tax relief on debt interest payments.

26   NETRA

> **Tutor's hint.** Part (a) is one of those delightful questions where there are at least three ways of arriving at the correct answer. Our answer shows the quickest. Part (b) is a variant on the standard question 'What's wrong with M&M's theory?' Note that part (c) is asking for a critique of the weaknesses of the traditional theory, not an explanation of the theory itself.
>
> **Examiner's comment**. 'In previous examinations many candidates have tried to introduce M&M into their answers to questions which were not related to M&M. In the light of this apparent keenness for M&M, answers were unfortunately disappointing.'
>
> *Other points.* The examiner's comment is ironic. M&M: love 'em or loathe 'em, you just can't ignore 'em!

(a)   The original value of Netra's shares is 2m × £4.20 = £8.4m.

If the company borrows £2m and redeems £2m of shares, the value of shares will be reduced by £2m but increased by the value of the tax shield Dt = £2m × 33% = £0.66m. The capital structure in market values will therefore be:

	£m
Ordinary shares (E) (8.4 – 2 + 0.66)	7.06
Debt (D)	2.00
E + D	9.06

Similarly, if £4m is borrowed, the tax shield will be 4 × 33% = £1.32m and the capital structure in market values will be:

	£m
Ordinary shares (E) (8.4 – 4 + 1.32)	5.72
Debt (D)	4.00
E + D	9.72

The company's earnings before interest and tax are £2.5m. When the company is ungeared there is no interest cost, so tax is 33% × £2.5m = £0.825m and earnings after tax (available for ordinary shareholders) are £2.5m – £0.825m = £1.675m.

Assuming no growth in earnings, and that all earnings are paid out as dividends, the company's cost of equity capital is £1.675m/£8.4m = 19.94%.

Using Modigliani and Miller's model (with corporate tax) the company's weighted average cost of capital (WACC) at any other gearing ratio can be estimated from the formula:

$$WACC_g = Ke_u \left(1 - \frac{Dt}{E+D}\right)$$

When £2m is borrowed, $WACC_g = 19.94\% \ (1 - 0.66/9.06) = 18.49\%$.

When £4m is borrowed, $WACC_g = 19.94\% \ (1 - 1.32/9.72) = 17.23\%$.

This illustrates the Miller/Modigliani theory that WACC decreases with increased gearing.

> *Other points.* The same conclusion can be reached by examining equity earnings at each gearing level and hence computing Ke. Combining this with the after tax cost of debt (6.7%) gives the same WACC figures as above.

Alternative solution to part (a)

The current Ke_u is after tax earnings/market capitalisation = 2.5m(1 – 0.33)/(2m × 4.20) = 19.94%

If £2m of debt is introduced:

The new market value will be: $MV_g = MV_u + Dt = 8.4m + 2m \times 0.33 = 9.06m$

The new WACC will be $WACC = Ke_u\left(1 - \frac{Dt}{E+D}\right) = 19.94\% \ (1 - 2 \times 0.33/9.06)$

$= 18.49\%$

If £4m of debt is introduced:

The new market value will be: $MV_g = MV_u + Dt = 8.4m + 4m \times 0.33 = 9.72m$

The new WACC will be $WACC = Ke_u\left(1 - \frac{Dt}{E+D}\right) = 19.94\% \ (1 - 4 \times 0.33/9.72)$

$= 17.23\%$

(b) Although it is likely that WACC will fall as gearing is increased (provided gearing does not get too high), the estimates of WACC made in the above computations are subject to a high degree of error because of restrictive assumptions made by the Miller/Modigliani model and factors which it ignores.

These assumptions include a **perfect capital market** with **no transactions costs**, **information** which is **costless** and readily available, risk free debt and rational investors who all make the same forecasts of companies' results.

The two most important omissions from the theory are:

(i) **Personal taxation**: the theory allows for corporate tax relief on debt interest but ignores the fact that investors' equity returns are not taxed in exactly the same way as interest. Introduction of personal taxation into the theory is difficult (and different for every country) but clearly has a material effect on the predicted cost of capital.

(ii) **Insolvency risk**: in MM's theory, risk is measured entirely by volatility of earnings. The fact that earnings may be so bad that the company goes bust is ignored, yet this undoubtedly works to increase the cost of both equity and debt at high levels of gearing, causing WACC to rise.

Other problems with the theory at high gearing levels are agency costs (eg lenders impose restrictive covenants, causing a rise in the cost of equity) and **'tax shield exhaustion'** (if taxable profits are zero, interest paid cannot produce any further reduction in tax).

(c) The traditional theory of capital structure contends that there is an **optimal mix of debt and equity** in a company's financial structure. It is based on the assumption that the introduction of debt into the capital structure initially causes the WACC to fall due to the lower after tax cost of debt; however as the gearing increases, the **cost of equity will increase** to reflect the rising level of financial risk to the shareholders. Beyond a certain optimal point, the cost of equity will increase at a faster rate and will more than offset the benefits of using debt.

The theory therefore assumes that the **cost of equity changes** in a **non-linear** way as gearing rises; it is basically an intuitive theory. It does have attractions since it is clear that at very high levels of gearing the Modigliani and Miller model breaks down and share prices fall with a rapidly increasing cost of equity. It suggests that there will be at least an **optimal range of gearing levels** which a company should seek to attain, and this may be useful when making financing decisions. However, it does not provide a precise method of determining what this range is in practice.

27   DARON

> **Tutor's hint**. For (a), it is inappropriate to calculate expected values since the two scenarios are mutually exclusive. In your discussion it is important to identify the strategic implications as well as the technical limitations of the calculations. In part (b), when discussing the implications of the call and put options, you should also take into account the likely reasons why the share price might move in the manner shown, and the effect of this on the financing options.
>
> **Examiner's comment**. Discussion for part (a), about which alternative should be selected was often very brief, and many candidates failed to earn marks as they did not comment upon the weaknesses/limitations of the data analysis. For part (b), complex calculations to investigate the implications of the convertible debenture for Daron were not required by the question, were almost always incorrect and resulted in time being wasted.

(a)   REPORT

To:	Managers of Daron
From:	Company Accountant
Date:	14 December 20X6
Subject:	Long-term strategic options

The purpose of this report is to evaluate the **strategic options** available to the company, namely an immediate sale of the company, continuation of existing operations, and diversification in the event of party A winning the forthcoming election.

Sale of the company. This option can be evaluated in terms of the value of the offer to the shareholders. The informal offer of $20m from the competitor compares with the current market value of the equity of $18.4m (20m × $0.92), a premium of 8.7%. However, it is perhaps more helpful to attempt a valuation of the company based on future cash flows, and figures illustrating this are included in Appendix 1 of this report. These suggest that if party A wins the election, the NPV of the future cash flows will amount to $30.3m, whereas if party B wins, the NPV will be $21.1m. Both of these are in excess of the competitor's offer, suggesting that if the shareholders do wish to sell they should seek a higher price for the company. However, these estimates are subject to a number of uncertainties which will be considered further in the next section of the report.

The shareholders will also need to consider some of the other implications of selling, such as the effect on the other stakeholders in the firm. For example, will many jobs be lost in redundancies? How will customers and the local community be affected by such a decision?

Continue existing operations. The figures contained in Appendix 1 represent a projection of performance for the ten year period up to 20Y6. However, when forecasting over such a long timescale the likelihood of inaccuracy increases, particular areas of potential error being as follows.

(i)   The assumption that the **cost of capital** will remain **constant** throughout the period

(ii)   The assumptions made about the **inflation rate**

(iii)   The **effect on economic conditions** of possible further elections beyond the one in the immediate future

(iv)   The assumption that the **tax rate** will remain constant at 30%

(v)   Errors in the projections of sales revenues and costs

A further major assumption built into the figures is that there will be no significant additional capital investment throughout this period. This raises a number of questions, including the following.

(i)   Will **other opportunities** be **forgone** during this period if the company starts to lag behind its competitors in technology?

(ii)   Will significant major new investment be required beyond 20Y1 to allow the company to continue operations?

(iii)   What is the realisable value of the company in 20Y1?

This final factor could also have a significant impact on the calculations in Appendix 1, and could mean that the true value of the future cash flows for the period in question is even higher than the figures suggest.

In view of the uncertainties described, it is proposed that further work needs to be done, particularly in investigating the sensitivities of the NPVs to changes in assumptions concerning the key variables.

Diversification into hotel industry. The figures relating to the diversification are contained in Appendix 2. These suggest that the project should yield a NPV of $0.56m. However, a major element in this forecast is the **terminal value** of $10m **on disposal** in 20Y1, and any variation in the amount realised is likely to have a significant effect on the projections. Again it is suggested that sensitivity analysis be undertaken to establish the impact of changes in this variable.

In addition to making the financial evaluation, Daron needs to consider the **investment** in the light of its **strategic objectives**. If the investment is essentially opportunistic with the diversification being for the benefit of the shareholders in terms of reducing their level of risk, this may be a mistaken goal. The shareholders can achieve diversification of their portfolios by themselves in their choice of other investments, and are unlikely to look to Daron to achieve this for them.

The key question is what the **company strategy** is to be in the face of the declining market for its core business. It may well be appropriate to seek **diversification** as a means for survival and growth, but the markets into which Daron seeks to diversify should be carefully chosen and should ideally be related in some way, be it **technological basis** or customer spread, to those in which it currently operates. The greater the departure from its existing experience, the greater the risk that the diversification will be less successful than anticipated.

Conclusions. Daron needs to consider its **long-term strategic objectives** and the **desires** of its **shareholders** before making any choices between the options facing it. If sale is perceived to be the best option, then the directors should seek to present the company to the market in the best possible light so as to **maximise the disposal proceeds**, and not just take the offer from the competitor because it is there. If continuing the existing business is desired, careful attention should be given to **long-term market conditions** and to the effect of alternative investment policies. If diversification is to be pursued then products and markets should be properly evaluated to obtain the best fit with the existing business.

APPENDIX 1: ESTIMATES OF THE PRESENT VALUE OF DARON

Scenario 1: Party A wins the election

	20X7 $m	20X8 $m	20X9 $m	20Y0 $m	20Y1 $m
Sales	28.0	29.0	26.0	22.0	19.0
Variable costs	(17.0)	(18.0)	(16.0)	(14.0)	(12.0)
Fixed costs	(3.0)	(3.0)	(3.0)	(3.0)	(3.0)
Depreciation	(4.0)	(3.0)	(3.0)	(2.0)	(1.0)
Taxable income	4.0	5.0	4.0	3.0	3.0
Tax at 30%★	(1.2)	(1.5)	(1.2)	(0.9)	(0.9)
Post tax income	2.8	3.5	2.8	2.1	2.1
Add back non-cash depreciation★	4.0	3.0	3.0	2.0	1.0
Working capital movement		1.0	2.0	3.0	3.0
Net cash flow	6.8	7.5	7.8	7.1	6.1
13% discount factors (see Note 1)	0.885	0.783	0.693	0.613	0.543
PV cash flow	6.0	5.9	5.4	4.4	3.3

> **Tutor's hint.** Alternatively, depreciation can be excluded from the calculation, and two figures calculated: firstly, the tax on sales less variable and fixed costs (in 20X7: 30% × (28 − 17 − 3) = $2.4m); secondly, the tax saving on depreciation is added back (in 20X7: 30% × $4m =1.2m). The overall effect is the same.

Total PV = $25.0 million (20X7 - 20Y1)

To these figures must be added the PV cash flow for the period 20Y2-20Y6. This can be found by applying the 13% annuity value for periods 6 to 10 (5.426 –3.517=1.909) to the annual cash flows. These cash flows will be similar to those for 20Y1 excluding depreciation and working capital movements.

	$m
Sales	19.0
Variable costs	(12.0)
Fixed costs	(3.0)
Taxable income	4.0
Tax at 30%	(1.2)
Annual cash flow	2.8
Annuity value	1.909
PV cash flow	5.3

The NPV of the cash flows for the period 20X7 to 20Y6 is therefore $25.0m + $5.3m = $30.3m.

Note 1. The discount rate to be used is the cost of capital. This can be estimated by finding the cost of equity using the CAPM, and then weighting the relative costs of debt and equity on the basis of market values.

The current market value of equity is 20m × $0.92 = $18.4m. It is assumed that the balance sheet value of the debt approximates to its market value ie $14m. Its cost (Kd)

is taken as the current bank rate of 10%. The risk free rate of return including inflation is $(1.05 \times 1.04) - 1 = 9.2\%$. The market rate of return including inflation is $(1.10 \times 1.05) - 1 = 15.5\%$.

Using the CAPM: $\quad E(r_j) = r_f + [E(r_m) - r_f]\, \beta_j$

$$= 9.2\% + [15.5\% - 9.2\%] \times 1.25\% = 17.075\%$$

The WACC can now be estimated.

$$\mathrm{WACC} \;=\; Ke\!\left(\frac{E}{E+D}\right) + Kd\,(1-t)\!\left(\frac{D}{E+D}\right)$$

$$= 17.075\% \times 18.4/(18.4 + 14) + 10\% \times (1 - 0.3) \times 14/(18.4 + 14)$$

$$= 12.72\% \;(\text{approx } 13\%)$$

Scenario 2: Party B wins the election

	20X7	20X8	20X9	20Y0	20Y1
	$m	$m	$m	$m	$m
Sales	30.0	26.0	24.0	20.0	16.0
Variable costs	(18.0)	(16.0)	(15.0)	(12.0)	(11.0)
Fixed costs	(3.0)	(3.0)	(4.0)	(4.0)	(4.0)
Depreciation	(4.0)	(3.0)	(3.0)	(2.0)	(1.0)
Taxable income	5.0	4.0	2.0	2.0	0
Tax at 30% ★	(1.5)	(1.2)	(0.6)	(0.6)	0
Post tax income	3.5	2.8	1.4	1.4	0
Add back non-cash depreciation★	4.0	3.0	3.0	2.0	1.0
Working capital movement	(1.0)	2.0	2.0	3.0	3.0
Net cash flow	6.5	7.8	6.4	6.4	4.0
18% discount factors (see Note 2)	0.847	0.718	0.609	0.516	0.437
PV cash flow	5.6	5.6	3.9	3.3	1.7

Tutorial note. See *Tutorial note* on Scenario 1 earlier.

Total PV = $20.1 million (20X7-20Y1)

The PV cash flow for the period 20Y2-20Y6 can be found by applying the 18% annuity value for periods 6 to 10 (4.494 − 3.127=1.367) to the annual cash flows. These cash flows will be as for 20Y1 excluding depreciation and working capital movements.

	$m
Sales	16.0
Variable costs	(11.0)
Fixed costs	(4.0)
Taxable income	1.0
Tax at 30%	(0.3)
Annual cash flow	0.7
Annuity value	1.367
PV cash flow	1.0

The NPV of the cash flows for the period 20X7 to 20Y6 is therefore $20.1m + $1.0m = $21.1m.

Note 2. The discount rate to be used is the cost of capital, which can be estimated by the same method as in Scenario 1.

The current market value of equity is again $18.4m. It is assumed that the balance sheet value of the debt approximates to its market value ie $14m, with its cost taken at the bank rate of 15.5%. The risk free rate of return including inflation is $1 - 1.04 \times 1.1 = 14.4\%$. The market rate of return including inflation is $1 - 1.10 \times 1.1 = 21.0\%$.

Using the CAPM: $K_e = r_f + [E(r_m) - r_f] \beta_j$
$= 14.4\% + (21.0\% - 14.4\%) \times 1.25 = 22.65\%$

The WACC can now be estimated.

$$\text{WACC} = K_e\left(\frac{E}{E+D}\right) + K_d(1-t)\left(\frac{D}{E+D}\right)$$
$$= 22.65\% \times 18.4/(18.4 + 14) + 15.5\% \times (1 - 0.3) \times 14/(18.4 + 14)$$
$$= 17.55\% \text{ (approx 18\%)}$$

APPENDIX 2: CASH FLOW EVALUATION OF DIVERSIFICATION PROJECT

To estimate the **APV**, it is first necessary to find the **base case NPV**. This is calculated using the ungeared cost of equity. This can be found using the expression:

$$\beta_a = \beta_e \frac{E}{E + D(1-t)}$$

where: β_a = ungeared beta
β_e = geared beta (1.25)
E = market value of equity ($18.4m)
D = market value of debt ($14.0m)
t = tax rate (30%)

$$\beta_a = 1.25 \times \frac{18.4}{18.4 + 14(1 - 0.3)} = 0.82$$

The ungeared cost of equity can now be estimated using the CAPM:

$$K_u = r_f + [E(r_m) - r_f]\beta$$
$$= 9.2\% + (15.5\% - 9.2\%) \times 0.82 = 14.4\% \text{ (say, approximately 14\%)}$$

This can be used to calculate the NPV of the project as if it were all equity financed.

	20X6 $m	20X7 $m	20X8 $m	20X9 $m	20Y0 $m	20Y1 $m
Turnover		9.0	10.0	11.0	12.0	13.0
Variable costs		(6.0)	(6.0)	(7.0)	(7.0)	(8.0)
Fixed costs		(2.0)	(2.0)	(2.0)	(2.0)	(2.0)
Taxable income		1.0	2.0	2.0	3.0	3.0
Tax at 30%		(0.3)	(0.6)	(0.6)	(0.9)	(0.9)
Post tax income		0.7	1.4	1.4	2.1	2.1
Purchase cost	(9.0)					
Working capital movement		(1.0)			(1.0)	
Realisable value						10.0
Cash flow	(9.0)	(0.3)	1.4	1.4	1.1	12.1
14% discount factors (see below)	1.000	0.877	0.769	0.675	0.592	0.519
PV cash flow	(9.0)	(0.3)	1.1	0.9	0.7	6.3

Total PV (base case NPV)= –$300,000

The next stage is to use the **Modigliani and Miller formula** for the relationship between the value of geared and ungeared companies to establish the effect of gearing on the value of the project. The amount to be financed by debt will be the purchase cost of the hotel plus the issue costs: $9m/98% = $9.184m.

The present value of the tax shield on the debt interest can now be found.

Annual interest charge: $9.184m × 10%	$918,400
Tax saving: 30%	$275,520
Cost of debt (pre tax)	10%
PV of tax savings at 10% for 5 years: $275,520 × 3.791 (in round $'000)	$1,044,000

143

The APV is the base case NPV plus the financing side effects (including issue costs):

	$'000
Base case NPV	(300)
Issue costs	(184)
PV of tax savings	1,044
APV	560

This assumes firstly that all the funds required can be raised in the form of debt ie that Daron will have sufficient debt capacity, and secondly that the coupon rate of 10% is an accurate reflection of the risk of the convertible debentures.

(b) A number of factors must be taken into account when evaluating the financing of the diversification by means of the convertible debenture issue, as follows.

(i) **Gearing.** The current gearing (debt:equity) based on book values is 63.6% ($14m/22m). The immediate effect of an issue of $9m debt would increase this to 104.5% (23/22), although on conversion there would be a substantial fall in the ratio. However, it would still be high for a significant period, especially for a company in a declining industry. The level of financial risk is therefore high with the company having to meet annual interest costs of nearly $1m during the period prior to conversion.

(ii) **Cost.** The coupon rate of the debentures is 10%. This is the same as the current rate at which Daron can borrow from the bank. Since one of the benefits of convertibles is that they can usually carry a lower coupon rate due to the attractiveness of conversion, this rate seems to be high. Presumably this is due to the effect on the gearing described above.

(iii) **Conversion price.** The effective conversion price is $100/60 = $1.67 per share. This is a premium of $0.75 over the current market price of $0.92, a percentage increase of 81.5% over five years or $\sqrt[5]{1.815} - 1 = 12.7\%$ annually. While this may be possible if the market as a whole goes up, it is certainly not guaranteed.

(iv) **Call option.** This allows Daron to restrict the potential gains made by the debenture holders. If the share price rises to $2 between 1 January 20Y2 and 31 December 20Y4, then the company can force the debenture holders to convert, thus restricting their capital gain on conversion to $0.33 per share. Such an option may be unpopular with potential investors since it both restricts their possible gains and could force them to convert at a time that is inappropriate from the point of view of their personal tax position.

(v) **Put option.** If the share price only rises to $1, the company can be forced to redeem the debentures at par. This is a risky position for the company to be in, since if the share price is performing that badly in five years' time, it is likely that it will not be generating the level of revenues anticipated in the forecasts. The implication of this is that it could be very difficult for the company to raise the funds required to repay the debenture holders, either from reserves or through its restricted ability to raise and to service additional debt.

28   KULPAR

Tutor's hint. This question is a step up in difficulty from the usual capital structure analysis. For part (a), the best approach is: (i) estimate the company's existing value and WACC; (ii) estimate the changes to cost of capital under both cases of gearing change; (iii) estimate the growth rate implied by existing valuation; and (iv) estimate the company value under changed gearing by using the costs of capital.

The discussion in part (b) can be answered largely by considering standard criticisms of capital structure theory (simplifying assumptions and problems at high gearing) but additional discussions on free cash flow and credit rating would also be useful.

Examiner's comment. This question appeared to differentiate weak and strong candidates very clearly in that strong candidates appreciated the impact of changes in the capital structure on the cost of equity, weak candidates used the same cost whatever the capital structure was. Few candidates made use of the credit rating information to calculate the cost of debt. Some candidates incorrectly believed that the cost of debt was zero because the beta of debt was zero. Another common error was to assume that growth was zero rather than constant.

Answers to (b) were generally too brief. Some candidates focused solely on Modigliani and Miller.

(a)   **Existing position**

The company's existing gearing and value are:

	£m	%
Equity	458	60%
Debt	305	40%
Company value	763	100%

$\beta_e = 1.4$

$Ke = r_f + [E(r_m) - r_f]\beta_e$

$\quad = 5.5 + [14 - 5.5]\,1.4$

$\quad = 17.4\%$

Credit rating is A and so pre-tax cost of debt is 9%.

After tax cost of debt $\quad = 9\%\,(1 - 0.3)$

$\qquad\qquad\qquad\qquad = 6.3\%$

WACC $\; = $ (Equity proportion $\times$ Ke) + (Debt proportion $\times$ (Kd $(1 - t)$))

$\qquad\quad = (0.6 \times 17.4) + (0.4 \times 6.3)$

$\qquad\quad = 13.0\%$

Effect of changes of gearing on cost of capital

$$\beta_a = \beta_e \frac{E}{E + D(1 - E)} + \beta_d \frac{D(1 - t)}{E + D(1 - t)}$$

Assume β_d is zero

$$\beta_a = 1.4 \frac{458}{458 + 305\,(1 - 0.3)}$$

$\qquad = 0.955$

We can use this ungeared beta to assess the effect of different capital structures.

80% equity 20% debt

$$\beta_e = \beta_a \frac{E + D(1-t)}{E}$$

$$= 0.955 \left(\frac{0.8 + (0.2(1-0.3))}{0.8} \right)$$

$$= 1.122$$

$$Ke = 5.5 + (14 - 5.5)\,1.122$$

$$= 15\%$$

Cost of debt depends on interest cover. Assuming value of company is unchanged,

$$Debt = 20\% \times \pounds763m$$

$$= \pounds152.6m$$

If credit rating improves to AA, annual interest would be at maximum $8\% \times \pounds152.6m = \pounds12.21m$.

Earnings before interest and tax $= \pounds90m$

$$\text{Interest cover} = \frac{90}{12.21}$$

$$= 7.37$$

This confirms credit rating AA and interest cost of 8%.

$$WACC = (0.8 \times 15) + (0.2(8(1-0.3)))$$

$$= 13.1\%$$

40% equity 60% debt

$$\beta_e = 0.955 \left(\frac{0.4 + (0.6(1.03))}{0.4} \right)$$

$$= 1.958$$

$$Ke = 5.5 + (14 - 5.5)\,1.958$$

$$= 22.1\%$$

Assuming value of company is unchanged:

$$Debt = 60\% \times \pounds763m$$

$$= \pounds457.8m$$

If credit rating worsens to BB, annual interest would be at maximum $11\% \times \pounds457.8m = \pounds50.36m$

Earnings before interest and tax $= \pounds90m$

$$\text{Interest cover} = \frac{90}{50.36}$$

$$= 1.79$$

This confirms credit rating BB and interest cost of 11%.

$$WACC = (0.4 \times 22.1) + (0.6\,(11(1-0.3)))$$

$$= 13.5\%$$

Effect of gearing changes on WACC

The existing capital structure gives the lowest WACC, 13%. If gearing is decreased, some of the benefit of the tax shield on debt is lost. If gearing is increased, the increased financial risks causes an increase in the cost of debt.

Effect of gearing changes on company valuation

$$\text{Free cash flow this year, } CF_0 = \text{EBIT} (1 - t) + \text{depreciation} - \text{capital spending}$$

$$= 90 (1 - 0.3) + 20 - 20$$

$$= \pounds 63m$$

Free cash flow next year, $CF_1 = 63 (1 + g)$

$$\text{Current valuation, } 763 = \frac{CF_1}{(k - g)}$$

$$= \frac{63(1+g)}{(k - g)}$$

$$= \frac{63(1+g)}{(0.13 - g)}$$

Therefore

$$763 (0.13 - g) = 63 (1 + g)$$

Rearranging

$$36.19 = 826g$$

$$g = 4.38\%$$

Capital structure 80% equity 20% debt

WACC is 13.1%

$$\text{Valuation} = \frac{63 \times 1.0438}{0.131 - 0.0438}$$

$$= \pounds 754m$$

Capital structure 40% equity 60% debt

WACC is 13.5%

$$\text{Valuation} = \frac{63 \times 1.0438}{0.135 - 0.438}$$

$$= \pounds 721m$$

The existing capital structure therefore gives the highest valuation.

(b) The estimates of corporate value based on the formulae used depend on a number of simplifying assumptions which are not true in practice and may cause significant valuation errors. For example:

    (i)   **Assumptions**

         Various factors which are **assumed** to be **constant** are likely to vary: these include the **growth rate** g, **capital expenditure**, and the **tax rate**, t. The formulae also assume that changes in capital structure can be achieved at **current market values, without transaction costs** and **without changing assets** or earnings. In practice, this is not possible.

(ii) **Formula for free cash flows**

The formula for free cash flow could be improved by **charging tax on earnings after interest** rather than before interest, and by including estimates of **changes in working capital,** which have been omitted.

(iii) **Credit rating**

The company's credit rating will depend on more factors than just interest cover, for example assets available for **security, cash flow volatility** and perceived **management ability.** Also a change in credit rating may **affect** the company's **operating income,** by altering its attractiveness to customers and suppliers.

(iv) **Risk of debt**

The company's debt has been assumed to be risk free. In practice this risk, which can be measured by the debt beta, is likely to **increase with gearing** and will affect the cost of capital.

(v) **Effect of high gearing**

Other factors affect the cost of capital at high gearing: for example direct and indirect **bankruptcy costs,** and 'tax exhaustion' (insufficient profitability to get the full benefit of tax relief on interest).

29 YOUR COMPANY

> **Tutor's hint.** In (a) the revised manual and illustrations should be presented as a whole, even if some of the instructions do not change.
>
> In (b) computations on convertibles are not common, but the main thing to remember here is how to value a convertible as (i) debt and (ii) converted to equity. Make sure you provide adequate words to explain your computations.
>
> **Examiner's comment.** The question examines understanding of the issues influencing the determination of the discount rate in a capital investment, and requires the modification of the incorrect cost of capital estimates. Common problems in illustration 1 included not adjusting for the growth rate in the dividend valuation model, using earnings growth rather than dividend growth, failure to adjust the asset beta correctly, using the wrong cost of debt figures, using book rather than market values and adding in inflation to the WACC. Errors in illustration 2 were ungearing the beta (it was already ungeared) and use of the comparator company's capital structure rather than the company's own capital structure.
>
> Some candidates failed entirely to revise the guidance notes despite there being 14 marks available for doing so; others only commented on one or two. Candidates also failed to highlight the links between investment risk and the discount rate.
>
> In (b) whilst candidates showed a good understanding of the cost of capital, only a minority managed to value debt and equity correctly.

(a) **Revised guidance manual**

(i) The discount rate for a project should reflect the **cost of finance** for that project, taking into account its risk. There are two main ways of doing this.

(1) The discount rate for a project should reflect the weighted average cost of capital for the company **only** if both the **business risk** and **financial risk** of the project are the same as the company's.

(2) If the project finance will change the company's gearing, the **adjusted present value method** should be used.

(ii)   The cost of equity and cost of debt should always be estimated using **market values (no change from the original)**.

(iii) If project cash flows include estimates for expected inflation, the **discount rate** should also **allow for inflation**. Discount rates calculated by the normal methods described in this manual will automatically contain this inflation allowance. If project cash flows are estimated in real terms (at today's prices), the discount rate will also need to be **adjusted** to real terms, by removing the expected inflation rate.

(iv)   To estimate the cost of equity capital for a project we recommend the **Capital Asset Pricing Model** (CAPM), which relates the cost of capital to the project's systematic risk. The cost of equity capital for the whole company can also be estimated from the CAPM or from the **dividend valuation model** which relates the cost of capital to the company's share price and expected future dividend payments. Both models contain theoretical simplifications and require estimates which are subject to inaccuracies.

(v)   The company's cost of debt should be estimated from the **current market rate** it is paying. For some types of loan the market rate is quoted transparently. For others it is necessary to **compute** the **redemption yield**, taking into account **interest** and **capital payments** compared with current market value. In each case, the cost to the company is after allowing for **corporate tax relief** on interest. Where there are several forms of company debt, the weighted average can be taken.

(vi)   There is **no need** to **round** the cost of capital to the nearest whole percentage, although it must be appreciated that the estimate is usually subject to a high margin of error. The practice of rounding *up* to be more prudent is wrong, as this may cause **potentially profitable projects** to be **incorrectly rejected**. It is good practice, however, to use sensitivity analysis to gauge the risk of accepting the project.

Revised illustrative examples

Illustration 1 – when the company is expanding existing activities

Cost of equity

Dividend valuation model

The model should be based on next year's dividend D_1. g should be estimated dividend growth, not earnings growth.

$$
\begin{aligned}
D_1 &= D_0\,(1 + g) \\
    &= 24 \times 1.06 \\
    &= 25.44 \text{ pence}
\end{aligned}
$$

$$
\begin{aligned}
\text{Market price per share} &= \text{£214m/50m} \\
&= 428 \text{ pence}
\end{aligned}
$$

$$
\begin{aligned}
\text{Cost of equity} &= \frac{D_1}{P} + g \\
&= 25.44/428 + 0.06 \\
&= 0.119 \\
&= 11.9\%
\end{aligned}
$$

Capital Asset Pricing Model

The company's equity beta, not asset beta, should be used to estimate the cost of equity shares. Assuming that debt is risk free (and beta of debt is therefore zero):

$$\beta_a \quad = \beta_e \frac{E}{E+D(1-t)}$$

$$\therefore 1.1 = \beta_e \times 214/[214 + 85(1 - 0.3)]$$
$$= \beta_e \times 214/273.5$$

and $\beta_e = 1.1 \times 273.5/214$
$$= 1.41$$

The cost of equity, Ke = 6% + (14% – 6%) 1.41 = 17.3%.

The two estimates of cost of equity are now very different. The CAPM estimate is used in the computation of WACC.

Cost of debt

The debenture is used to estimate the current cost of debt because no direct estimate of future borrowing cost is available. The debenture has a book value of £40m and a market value of £85m – £40m = £45m. Annual interest payments are 10% of £40m = £4m and result in tax savings of 30%, for which the timing difference is ignored, giving a net interest cost of £4m × 0.7 = £2.8m. Assuming the debt is redeemed at par of £40m,

Rough cost = 2.8/45 + (40 – 45)/(4 × 45)
= 6.2% – 2.8%
= 3.4%

For a more accurate answer, find the cost by estimating the IRR of the cash flows at 3% and 4% and interpolate:

Year	£m	3%	PV £m	4%	PV £m
0	–45.0	1.000	–45.00	1.000	–45.00
1-4	2.8	3.717	10.41	3.630	10.16
4	40.0	0.888	35.52	0.855	34.20
			0.93		–0.64

By interpolation, cost of debt = 3% + 0.93/(0.93 + 0.64)
= 3.59%, say 3.6%

Weighted Average Cost of Capital (WACC)

$$WACC \quad = Ke_g \left(\frac{E}{E+D}\right) + Kd\,(1-t)\left(\frac{D}{E+D}\right)$$

$$= 17.3\left(\frac{214}{214+85}\right) + 3.6\left(\frac{85}{214+85}\right)$$

$$= 13.4\%$$

The discount rate for the project is 13.4%. No further adjustment is needed because the market costs of equity and debt already allow for expected inflation.

Illustration 2 – when the company is diversifying its activities

Cost of equity

The asset beta of a similar sized company in the industry in which the company proposes to diversify is 0.90. This can be used as the asset beta of the new project.

(**This does not need to be 'ungeared' as in the original example, as it is an asset beta not an equity beta**).

To estimate the equity beta for our company for the new project, we use the formula:

$$\beta_a = \beta_e \frac{E}{E + D(1-t)}$$

$$\therefore \beta_e = 0.90 \times 273.5/214$$

$$= 1.15 \text{ (\textbf{same computation as in illustration 1 with a different asset beta})}$$

Using the CAPM, Ke = 6% + 8% × 1.15
= 15.2%

Cost of debt

This is unchanged at 3.6%.

WACC = 15.2% × 214/299 + 3.6% × 85/299
= 11.9%

(b) (i) **No conversion: share price is 470 pence**

If no conversion takes place, the value of the convertible will be as debt with 4 years to maturity. Its value is found by **discounting interest** and **redemption** value at 9%, which is the company's pre-tax cost of debt.

Year		£	9% factors	PV £
1-4	Interest	8	3.240	25.92
4	Redemption	100	0.708	70.80
				96.72

(Note that the value per share for conversion to take place would need to be at least £96.72/20 = 484 pence).

Total market value of the debentures = 96.72/100 × £20 million
= £19.34 million

Other debt has a market value of £23m, giving total debt value of £42.34m and a cost of 9%(1 – 0.3) = 6.3% after tax.

If the share price falls to 470 pence

Total market value of shares = 470/520 × £180m
= £162.69 million

The cost of equity is 15% because its systematic risk is the same as that of the market.

Total value of debt plus equity = £42.34m + £162.69m
= £205.03 million

Weighted average cost of capital = 15% × 162.69/205.03 + 6.3% × 42.34/205.03
= 13.2%

(ii) **Conversion: share price is 570 pence**

Number of new shares issued = 20 × £20m/£100
= 4 million

Value of new shares issued = 4m × 570p
= £22.8 million

Value of existing shares = 570/520 × £180m
= £197.31 million

Value of all shares = £220.11 million

Debt remaining = £23 million

Total value of equity and debt = £243.11 million

Assuming the cost of equity and debt are unchanged

Weighted average cost of capital = $15\% \times 220.11/243.11 + 6.3\% \times 23/243.11$
= 14.2%

The cost of capital is higher if conversion takes place because **cheaper debt** has been **replaced** with **more expensive equity shares.**

This calculation is unlikely to be correct because the **assumption** that the costs of equity and debt are unchanged by the conversion is probably **wrong.** When debt is reduced, the **financial risk** to shareholders **decreases**, causing a reduction in the cost of equity. However, it is unlikely that the cheaper equity will compensate for the loss of cheap debt in the capital structure because **debt interest** is **tax allowable** whereas dividends to shareholders are not.

Marking guide		Marks	
(a)	*Guidance manual*		
	(i) Criteria for use, and relating discount rate to investment risk	3-4	
	(ii) Unchanged	1	
	(iii) Discussion of nominal v real	2-3	
	(iv) Problems of models	3-4	
	(v) Comments including tax	2-3	
	(vi) Disagreement, plus comments	1-2	
			14
	Illustration 1		
	Cost of equity		
	Dividend valuation model	2	
	CAPM	3	
	Cost of debt		
	Correct market value	2	
	Cash flows and redemption yield	3	
	No adjustment for inflation	1	
	WACC	1	
	Illustration 2		
	Cost of equity		
	Ungearing and regearing	1	
	CAPM	2	
	WACC	1	
			16
(b)	Value of convertible as straight debt	1	
	Conversion prices	1	
	WACC assuming fall in share prices	3	
	WACC assuming rise in share prices	3	
	Discussion	2	
			10
			40

30   PROGROW

> **Tutor's hint**. The industry beta for garden tool production can be used to calculate the appropriate equity beta for this part of the business, and hence the discount rate to be used in the appraisal. Once this has been found it is possible to calculate similar figures for the jack production. In your report it is helpful to consider what information is missing from that provided for the financial analysis and to mention possible market reactions and changes that should be considered.
>
> **Examiner's comment**. Many candidates attempted to calculate the NPV of total jack production rather than the NPV of incremental production.

REPORT

To: Board of Directors, Progrow plc
From: Accountant
Date: 17 December 20X5
Subject: Evaluation of the opportunities for jacks production cost reduction and garden tools expansion

This report contains a **financial evaluation** of the alternative uses of surplus factory space for investing in equipment to reduce the production cost of jacks, or expanding the garden tools operation. Detailed numerical analysis is included in the Appendix to the report.

Financial evaluation

The investments have been evaluated on the basis of the **net present value of their incremental cash flows**. A different discount rate has been used for each investment to reflect the different levels of risk. Expansion of the garden tools division shows a NPV of £281,500, compared with a NPV of £56,500 from increasing the capital intensity of the jacks production. On the basis of the information provided this is therefore the preferred option.

However, the financial analysis ignores the following factors.

(a) No allowance has been made for **additional working capital requirements** in the garden tools expansion. Similarly, there may be additional overheads to be incurred as a result of the expansion.

(b) Although the discount factors have been adjusted to take account of the different levels of risk, it would be helpful to establish the **sensitivity** of the returns to changes in the actual sales volumes and prices achieved. Progrow must be confident that it will be able to sell all the additional output without affecting the level of market prices.

Non-financial factors

There are a number of **other issues** which should be addressed before a final decision is taken.

(a) The **managing director's fears** as to the **result of not undertaking the investment** in jack automation should be investigated further. The cost of **not investing** in terms of **lost market share or margin** should be quantified and taken into account.

(b) The **effect of the redundancies** associated with the jacks investment on the morale of the remaining workforce and on employee relations should be considered.

(c) The **long-term competitive** structure and **growth prospects** of the two markets should also be considered and the investment decision set in the strategic context.

(d) Progrow could consider the **space demands** of the existing operations to ensure that all production space is being used as effectively as possible. It may be possible to **free up space** so as to allow both projects to be undertaken, since they both deliver a positive NPV. Alternatively, if there are funds available it could consider taking on additional factory space in order to undertake both of the projects.

APPENDIX

The incremental cash flows from the two options must be discounted to find the net present values of the alternatives. Progrow's current weighted average cost of capital (WACC) should not be used due to the differences in the systematic risk levels of the two projects.

The average equity beta of other garden tool manufacturers can be **ungeared** to estimate the asset beta, and then **regeared** to reflect the financial structure of Progrow. Since corporate debt can be assumed to be risk free ($B_d = 0$), the asset beta can be estimated as follows.

$$\beta_a = \beta_e \frac{E}{E + D(1-t)} + \beta_d \frac{D(1-t)}{E + D(1-t)}$$

$$\beta_a = 1.4 \times \frac{50}{50 + 50(1 - 0.25)} + 0 = 0.8$$

In the case of Progrow, the market values of debt and equity are:

E = £2,800,000 × £1.62 = £4,536,000

D = £1,250,000 + £400,000 = £1,650,000

$$0.8 = \beta_e \times \frac{4,536}{4,536 + 1,650(1 - 0.25)}$$

$$\beta_e = 1.018$$

The CAPM can now be used to find the cost of Progrow's equity.

$$Ke = r_f + [E(r_m) - r_f] \beta_e$$

$$Ke = 7\% + (14 - 7) \times 1.018\% = 14.13\%$$

Since the corporate debt can be assumed to be risk free, we will assume that the cost of the debt is 7% (the risk-free rate of return).

The WACC for the manufacture of garden tools can now be found.

$$WACC = Ke_g \times \frac{E}{E + D} + Kd(1 - t) \times \frac{D}{E + D}$$

$$= 14.13 \times \frac{4,536}{4,536 + 1,650} + 7.0(1 - 0.25) \times \frac{1,650}{4,536 + 1,650} = 11.76\%$$

The garden tools expansion project will, for ease of calculation, be discounted at 12%.

Since the equity beta of garden tools is now known, and it is known that garden tools represent 60% of the company's total market value, it is possible to estimate the **beta** of the jacks division (β_j):

$$1.3 = 1.018 \times 0.6 + \beta_j \times 0.4$$

$$\beta_j = 1.723$$

Substituting into the **CAPM**:

$$Ke = r_f + [E(r_m) - r_f] \beta_j$$

$$Ke = 7\% + (14 - 7) \times 1.723 = 19.06\%$$

$$WACC = Ke \times \frac{E}{E + D} + Kd(1 - t) \times \frac{D}{E + D}$$

$$= 19.06 \times \frac{4{,}536}{4{,}536+1{,}650} + 7.0(1-0.25) \times \frac{1{,}650}{4{,}536+1{,}650} = 15.38\%$$

The jacks project will therefore be discounted at 15%.

(i) *Evaluation of jacks production*

(Monetary figures are in £'000)

Calculation of incremental tax:

Year	0	1	2	3	4	5	6
Direct labour saved		271.6	287.9	305.2	323.5	342.9	
Redundancy cost	(354.0)						
Retraining	(15.0)						
Maintenance		(46.8)	(48.7)	(50.6)	(52.6)	(54.7)	
Depreciation	(267.5)	(66.9)	(50.2)	(37.6)	(28.2)	(44.6)	
Taxable income	(636.5)	157.9	189.0	217.0	242.7	243.6	
Tax at 25%		159.1	(39.5)	(47.3)	(54.3)	(60.7)	(60.9)

Calculation of incremental cash flow:

Year	0	1	2	3	4	5	6
Cost of m/cs	(535.0)						
Sale proceeds		125.0				40.0	
Direct labour saved		271.6	287.9	305.2	323.5	342.9	
Redundancy cost	(354.0)						
Retraining	(15.0)						
Maintenance		(46.8)	(48.7)	(50.6)	(52.6)	(54.7)	
Tax		159.1	(39.5)	(47.3)	(54.3)	(60.7)	(60.9)
Net cash flow	(904.0)	508.9	199.7	207.3	216.6	267.5	(60.9)
Disc @ 15%	1.000	0.870	0.756	0.658	0.572	0.497	0.432
PV cash flow	(904.0)	442.7	151.0	136.4	123.9	132.9	(26.3)

The expected NPV of the jacks project is £56,600.

Notes

(1) Direct labour savings have been inflated at 6% per annum.

(2) Maintenance costs have been inflated at 4% per annum.

(3) Depreciation is calculated as follows:

Year	0	1	2	3	4	5
Capital cost	535.0					(40.0)
Depreciation	267.5	66.9	50.2	37.6	28.2	44.6
Closing balance	267.5	200.6	150.4	112.8	84.6	0.0

(4) It is assumed that Progrow is able to utilise all the additional tax allowances in year 1.

(ii) *Evaluation of garden tools production*

(Monetary figures are in £'000)

Calculation of incremental tax:

Year	0	1	2	3	4	5	6
New sales		573.3	602.0	632.1	663.7	696.8	
Direct costs		(422.9)	(448.3)	(475.2)	(503.7)	(534.0)	
Depreciation	(100.0)	(25.0)	(18.8)	(14.1)	(10.5)	(17.6)	
Taxable income	(100.0)	125.4	134.9	142.8	149.5	145.2	
Tax at 25%		25.0	(31.4)	(33.7)	(35.7)	(37.4)	(36.3)

Calculation of incremental cash flow:

Year	0	1	2	3	4	5	6
Cost of m/cs	(200.0)						
Sale proceeds						14.0	
New sales		573.3	602.0	632.1	663.7	696.8	
Direct costs		(422.9)	(448.3)	(475.2)	(503.7)	(534.0)	
Tax	0.0	25.0	(31.4)	(33.7)	(35.7)	(37.4)	(36.3)
Net cash flow	(200.0)	175.4	122.3	123.2	124.3	139.4	(36.3)
Disc @ 12%	1.000	0.893	0.797	0.712	0.636	0.567	0.507
PV cash flow	(200.0)	156.6	97.5	87.7	79.1	79.0	(18.4)

The expected NPV of the garden tools operation is £281,500.

Notes

(1) Sales have been inflated by 5% per annum

(2) Direct costs have been inflated by 6% per annum

(3) Depreciation is calculated as follows:

Year	0	1	2	3	4	5
Capital cost	200.0					(14.0)
Depreciation	100.0	25.0	18.8	14.1	10.5	17.6
Closing balance	100.0	75.0	56.2	42.1	31.6	0.0

31 HUSOC

> **Tutor's hint**. The answer brings in various strategies, abandon, continue and postpone and discusses use of options in general terms. The costs of abandonment may be significant here.

(a) (i) As we are at the end of year 2, years 2-5 have to be treated as years 0-3 in this calculation.

Year		£'000	10% discount factor	Present value £'000
0	Further production costs	(30)	1.000	(30)
1	Net loss	(50)	0.909	(45)
2	Net profit	300	0.826	248
3	Net profit	640	0.751	481
				654

(ii)

Year				
1	Net profit	240	0.909	218
2	Net profit	300	0.826	248
3	Net profit	310	0.751	233
				699

(b) As it stands, the net present value calculation suggests that Husoc should **abandon** plans to produce for the two higher levels and concentrate on producing material for the lowest level of the qualification. In addition the revised figures have only taken account of the feedthrough effects on higher level sales of fewer students than expected enrolling during the first year. Expectations of numbers enrolling may not be fulfilled in subsequent years and this should have a bigger impact on the present value of the option to proceed.

However the calculations show much higher profit levels in the last year for the continuation option than for the abandonment option. If the calculation was carried on for an **extra year**, it might well suggest that Husoc should publish books for all levels.

There are a number of other factors that Husoc should consider:

(i) A continued presence at all levels may give Husoc the chance to publish **different types of material**. We are told that assessment procedures are flexible, and Husoc may be able to publish further assessment-orientated material, or even become involved in the assessment process.

(ii) If Husoc is the only publisher producing material for this qualification, and it decides to abandon plans to produce material for the higher levels, **fewer students** than predicted may enrol at the lowest level because there is no tailored material to help them later in their studies.

(iii) Publication of the textbooks at all levels appears ultimately to be a profitable opportunity. If Husoc decides not to publish at the higher levels, **Isecon may** take the decision to **publish** after all. This would clearly threaten Husoc's sales at the lowest levels, as colleges may well prefer to buy material at all levels from a single publisher. It may also threaten Husoc's other sales if schools and colleges are no longer able to buy all the books they need from Husoc, use Isecon's material, and are favourably impressed by Isecon.

(iv) It may be unrealistic to assume that Husoc has **just two possible strategies**. The extra costs of £30,000 are not that material in the context of total project revenues, and year 3 sales of the second level material may give Husoc information about likely sales at the higher levels which it can use to make a further decision in a year's time.

(v) Husoc may be able to use some of the material written for this qualification in **other titles**.

These factors can be incorporated formally into the DCF analysis by means of option theory. The decision to continue would be a **call option**, the decision to abandon the project would be a **put option**. The options calculations will take account of the present value of **future benefits and costs,** the **timescale** within which decisions should be made, the **variability of expected returns** and the **risk-free rate of interest**.

32   PREPARATION QUESTION: BID CALCULATIONS

(a) The first step is to calculate the **theoretical market capitalisation** of the two companies once the reorganisation has taken place.

National plc

	£'000
Existing market capitalisation (45m × 166p)	74,700.0

P/E ratio 74,700 / 9,337.5 = 8.0

Existing equity earnings	9,337.5
Less: earnings lost on sale of division	(1,500.0)
	7,837.5
Add: 20% efficiency savings	1,567.5
New annual equity earnings	9,405.0

	£'000
Theoretical new capitalisation assuming P/E of 8.0 (× 9,405)	75,240.0
Add: proceeds from sale of division	10,200.0
Total capitalisation	85,440.0

Provincial plc

	£'000
Existing market capitalisation (14m × 840p)	117,600.0
Add: proceeds from property sale	16,000.0
Less: reorganisation costs	(4,500.0)
Total capitalisation	129,100.0

The total combined market capitalisation after reorganisation is:

£85,440,000 + £129,100,000 = £214,540,000

The total number of shares in issue in National plc is 45 million. A two for nine offer means that Provincial plc will need to issue a further 10 million shares, bringing the total number of Provincial shares in issue to 24 million.

The theoretical price of a Provincial share is therefore 214,540,000 / 24,000,000 = 894 pence.

The theoretical price of a National share is 2/9 times the Provincial share price = 198.7 pence.

(b) The shares in National plc will not only be valued on the basis of market estimates of the potential merger synergy. **In practice**, the price will depend on the **expectations** of **buyers and sellers** of the **likely success** and **ultimate format** of the bid, as well as the amount of competition for the company from other bidders. If **competition** for the acquisition is **strong**, then it is likely that the shares in National plc will rise to a higher level as the market anticipates a premium having to be paid by the final buyer in order to secure the company. On the other hand, if there is **little interest** in the company from other bidders, Provincial may not need to offer much above the current market price of the shares in order to secure the acquisition, and National's shares will therefore be valued at a lower figure.

(c) Since investors are **risk-averse**, a **cash alternative** will normally be more attractive than a share offer. This is supported by the fact that many mergers fail to achieve the forecast synergies as quickly as expected, and therefore earnings in the early years post-merger are often lower than anticipated. Thus a cash alternative is likely to be lower than the current value of the share exchange.

However, Provincial plc must also take into account the **tax situation** of the **National shareholders** and the reason why they are holding National shares. Thus although a cash offer will avoid the investors incurring transaction costs when they wish to sell their new shares, they will immediately become liable to **capital gains tax** and this may make a cash offer less attractive. Provincial should ascertain the ownership structure of the National equity, for example the proportion of institutional investors, and seek to ascertain the preferences of the major shareholders.

(d) The existing price of a National share is 166p. For the shareholders in National to achieve a 10% gain in the value of their shares, the price would have to be 166 × 1.1 = 182.6p.

A share price of 182.6 pence implies a market capitalisation for National of 45m × 182.6p = £82,170,000. The total market capitalisation of the new group is £214,540,000 (as calculated above). With a share price of 182.6 pence, the National shareholders would therefore hold 38.3% of the group.

The number of new shares to be issued by Provincial plc to achieve this can be calculated as follows.

Let n = additional number of shares to be issued.

$$\frac{n}{14m + n} = \frac{38.3}{100}$$

$$100n = 38.3n + 536.2m$$

$$61.7n = 536.2m$$

$$n = 8.69m$$

Thus Provincial plc will have to offer 8.69 million shares in exchange for the 45 million existing National plc shares. This represents an offer of one for 5.18.

33   PEDEN AND TULEN

> **Tutor's hint.** (a) illustrates how shareholders gain from creditors in a bankruptcy scenario because of their limited liability. The key is that when Peden is a stand-alone company, the minimum value of its equity is zero, causing a drop in the value of debt, but when combined with a low-geared company the debt recovers its value at the expense of equity.
>
> (b) is not asking for a description of synergy, but an analysis of the ways in which it may arise.
>
> **Examiner's comment.** Many candidates aggregated equity and debt without considering their individual values, and produced implausible solutions. Candidates also ignored the narrative in the question that stated that operational synergy did not occur.

(a) To find the value of Peden's equity shares, subtract debt of £45m from the total value:

Peden	*Recession*	*Slow growth*	*Rapid growth*
	£m	£m	£m
Equity	(3)	10	30
Debt	45	45	45
Total	42	55	75

This gives a **negative value to equity** in the recession scenario, which cannot happen because the shares have limited liability. Assume the shares are zero value and the debt has declined to £42m because of bankruptcy risk. The expected value of equity of debt can then be computed:

Peden	*Recession*	*Slow growth*	*Rapid growth*	*Expected value*
Equity	0	10	30	12.50
Debt	42	45	45	44.55
Total	42	55	75	57.05

To find the value of Tulen's equity shares, subtract debt of £10m from the total value:

Tulen	*Recession*	*Slow growth*	*Rapid growth*	*Expected value*
Equity	53	70	110	75.45
Debt	10	10	10	10.00
Total	63	80	120	85.45

When the companies merge, **add** the **economic values** of **equity** and **debt** together. This means using the negative £3 million value for Peden's equity in the recession scenario. Its debt will be restored to £45 million because the bankruptcy risk will have disappeared by combination with a low geared company. This is known as the coinsurance effect.

Combined	*Recession*	*Slow growth*	*Rapid growth*	*Expected value*
Equity	50	80	140	87.50
Debt	55	55	55	55.00
Total	105	135	195	142.50

Summary

Expected equity values

	£m
Peden	12.50
Tulen	75.45
Total	87.95
Combined company	87.50
Loss in equity value after combination	0.45

Expected debt values

	£m
Peden	44.55
Tulen	10.00
Total	54.55
Combined company	55.00
Gain in debt value after combination	0.45

After the combination, in the absence of synergy, the total economic value of the businesses remains at £142.5 million, but the total expected value of debt has increased by £0.45m at the expense of equity. This is because, under the recession scenario, there is **no longer** a **bankruptcy risk** for the debt holders of Peden. The previous advantage conferred on Peden equity by limited liability has now disappeared.

Furthermore, the cash flows of the combined company may **reduce in volatility** because of the portfolio effect and this may further reduce the cost of debt, increasing its value.

(b) Synergy can be described as the '2 + 2 = 5' effect, whereby a group after a takeover achieves combined results that reflect a better rate of return than was being achieved by the same resources used in two separate operations before the takeover. The main reasons why synergy might exist are as follows.

(i) **Operating economies**

(1) **Economies of scale** arise when fixed operating costs can be spread over a larger production volume, eg larger machines can be used to produce at a lower cost per unit than smaller machines. Similarly, there may be opportunities to purchase in bulk and thereby reduce the unit cost of the raw materials.

(2) **Economies of scope** may arise when companies have complementary resources in areas such as advertising and distribution.

(3) **Management** levels may be rationalised allowing a flatter organisation structure that will reduce the overall cost of management. The bidding company may have a more efficient management team that allows other costs to be saved.

(4) **Control over resources** may be improved in a vertical integration. For example, the purchase of a supplier by its main customer may improve the quality and timeliness of the supply of raw materials and reduce administration and distribution costs.

(ii) **Financial synergies**

(1) **Earnings stability** is likely to improve as a result of there being a wider spread of activities within the business. Even though the systematic risk is not reduced, the reduction in earnings volatility is likely to make it easier and cheaper to obtain additional sources of loan finance.

(2) **Liquidity** may be improved by the acquisition of a more financially stable company.

(3) **Tax factors** may be relevant where the new group is able to use tax shields or tax losses that were previously unavailable.

(iii) **Market position**

(1) The formation of a larger entity may mean that the new group is able to exert more **control over prices** charged to its customers, and thereby improve its profitability.

(2) The company's **profile** may become **higher**.

34 OAKTON

Tutor's hint. Read the question in section (a) carefully – you are required to provide critical comment on each of the valuation methods used, not just that in part (iii), and you must also make a reasoned recommendation as to whether Oakton should make the bid for Mallard.

The calculations in (a)(iii) can appear confusing. You must work out which figures and discount rates are real rates excluding inflation, and which are money rates including inflation. You must be particularly careful with the consultancy fees to the directors; firstly, you will need to adjust for tax. We have used the nominal rate to discount these fees, rather than the real rate used to discount the ongoing cash flows. If however you choose to apply the real rate to the directors' fees, you need to remember that the fixed amounts that the directors receive each year will be decreasing in real terms due to the effects of inflation. Therefore, before applying the real rate to the directors' fees you would need to deflate the fees in line with inflation.

In part (b), remember that the form of the bid has yet to be agreed with Mallard, and that the views of the Mallard shareholders are just as relevant as the financial position of Oakton.

Examiner's comment. The standard of calculations in part (a) was varied. A disappointing number of candidates were unable to calculate correctly the earnings per share of Mallard, which was surprising at the professional stage of examinations.

In part (b), few candidates discussed the possible tax implications of a cash offer, or stressed the importance of the existing shareholders' views in determining the form of the offer.

(a) (i) Since Mallard operates in a different industry, the comparative P/E ratio valuation must be based upon the average P/E ratios in that industry. The P/E ratio of 7:1 will therefore be used.

Current share price	370 pence
Earnings yield	19.2%
Earnings per share	71.04 pence ($370 \times 19.2\%$)
Price per share	497.28 pence (71.04×7)
Value of Mallard £24.857m	(7×3.551m)

The problem with this approach is that P/E ratios are based on historic performance, and take no account either of the likely impact of the takeover on the performance of the company, or of its current earnings projections. In this case, there is a further problem in that it is not known whether the recently taken over companies on which the ratio is based were sufficiently similar to Mallard in terms of size, rate of growth, type of activities and overall level of risk. It may well be that the average should be adjusted to take into account the particular situation of Mallard.

(ii) The dividend valuation method (including growth) for share valuation is:

$$P_0 = \frac{D_0(1+g)}{(r-g)}$$

where   P   = current market value ex div

D_0 = current level of dividends

g   = expected annual rate of growth in dividends

r   = required return

In the case of Mallard:

D_0 = £842,000

g   = 8%, assuming that this rate of dividend growth will continue

r   = can be estimated using the Capital Asset Pricing Model (CAPM):

$Ke = r_f + [E(r_m) - r_f]\beta_j$

where Ke = cost of equity

r_f = risk free rate of return (6%)

β_j = beta factor (0.8)

$E(r_m)$ = market rate of return (14%)

$$Ke = 6\% + 0.8(14\% - 6\%) = 12.4\%$$

$$P = \frac{£842,000(1 + 0.08)}{(0.124 - 0.08)} = £20.667\text{m}$$

The main weakness of this approach is the **method used** to **estimate the growth rate**. This assumes that the historic rate of dividend growth will continue at a constant rate into the future, but the current rate of dividend growth is different from that of Oakton, and could well change following the acquisition. However, the model does attempt to relate the share price to the future stream of earnings from the business, and in this sense is more realistic than the comparative P/E ratio basis of valuation.

(iii)   The first stage is to estimate what the operating cash flows will be following the acquisition.

	£'000
Current pre-tax operating cash flow	5,300
Post acquisition adjustments:	
Annual wage savings	750
Advertising/distribution savings	150
	6,200
Taxation (33%)	2,046
Annual post tax cash flow	4,154

The other cash flows to be taken into account are:

		£'000
Year 0:	Redundancy costs (after tax)	(1,200)
	Sale of land and buildings (after tax)	800

Years 1-3:   Consultancy payments of £201,000 (£300,000 × 0.67) per year after tax

The **discount rate used** will be the **existing weighted average cost of capital** (WACC) for Mallard, although it must be recognised that this could be different after the acquisition since Oakton is a much larger company and its shares are quoted on the main market rather than the AIM. The cost of equity has already been calculated above as 12.4%, and the cost of debt is 11% as per the balance sheet. The following expression will be used.

$$\text{WACC} = Ke\frac{E}{(E + D)} + Kd(1 - t)\frac{E}{(E + D)}$$

where: Ke = cost of equity

Kd = cost of debt

t = tax rate (33%)

E = market value of equity (5m × £3.70 = £18.5m)

D = market value of debt (£3.5m)

$$WACC = 12.4\% \frac{18.5}{(18.5+3.5)} + 11\%(1-0.33)\frac{3.5}{(18.5+3.5)}$$

WACC = 11.60%

This nominal discount rate has been calculated on the basis of **market values**, and therefore will incorporate inflation. The cash flows (with the exception of the consultancy fees) all exclude inflation, and therefore either the nominal discount rate that has been calculated must be adjusted to the real rate, or the cash flows must be adjusted to include inflation. If we adjust the nominal rate to exclude the 2.4% rate of inflation, 1.116 ÷ 1.024 = 1.0898, the real discount rate is 8.98%, say 9%.

The present value of the cash flows can now be found.

	Year 1 £'000	Year 2 £'000	Year 3 £'000	Total £'000
Gross payment to directors (after tax)	201	201	201	
11.6%, say 12% discount factors	0.893	0.797	0.712	
PV cash flow	179	160	143	(482)
Ongoing cash flows for 10 years at 9% (4,154 × 6.418)				26,660
Income from land and buildings				800
Redundancy costs				(1,200)
Total PV of relevant operating cash flows				25,778

Although this is theoretically the best method of valuation to use, the calculations are in reality quite crude. Any **likely changes** in the **pattern of the cash flows** following the acquisition are **ignored**, as are any strategic plans that the company may have for such a long time frame. Ten years is a long period over which to estimate cash flows, inflation rates and discount rates, and there will inevitably be a large margin for error in the figures. In addition, the question of what happens at the end of the ten year period is not addressed – Is there an appropriate terminal value that could be used in the calculations to reflect the ongoing value of Mallard as a business?

Two of the valuation methods used, including the present value of the operating cash flows (which is possibly the best of the three approaches) give a valuation greater than the proposed offer price of £22m. If Oakton can successfully complete negotiations at this price, and if the acquisition of Mallard would be in line with Oakton's long-term strategic objectives, then it is recommended that the offer should go ahead.

(b) Factors that will influence the form of the payment include the following.

(i)   A cash offer would effectively **use up all** of Oakton's **cash deposits**. Oakton must therefore consider its overall cash flow projections when deciding the form of the bid, so as to avoid possible liquidity problems.

(ii) Oakton must also consider what its **desired long-term capital structure** should be in terms of gearing level, type of debt used etc, and try to structure the bid to fit these requirements.

(iii) Both the **long-term costs** of the **different sources of finance**, and the transaction cost of raising the finance in relation to the size of the bid must be taken into account.

(iv) The **requirements of the Mallard shareholders** must also be considered. Since three individuals own 50% of the shares, it is unlikely that they would be happy with a 100% cash offer since this would mean that they would incur a large capital gains tax liability.

(c) Financial post-audits following a merger or takeover are important because:

(i) The knowledge that a post-audit will take place will **discourage growth** by acquisition **without** proper strategic **analysis** and **planning**.

(ii) They **identify problems** which have occurred since the merger or acquisition, identify whether these were unexpected or whether contingency plans had been made, and ensure that management confront the problems.

(iii) By **analysing results** against **forecasts** made before the merger or takeover, they provide valuable feedback on the **reliability** of the **forecasting** and **planning** methods used.

(iv) They identify **factors** which may have been **overlooked** and which need to be incorporated into future merger and takeover proposals.

Marking guide	Marks
For high marks there must be discussion in some depth.	
(a) Comparative P/Es:	
Mallard's EPS	1
Value (per share or total)	1
Comments	2
Dividend valuation model:	
Cost of equity	1
Next dividend	1
Value (per share or total)	1
Comments	2
PV of cash flows:	
Adjusted cash flows	1
Discount rate	3
Use of real with real or nominal with nominal	1
Present values	2
Value (per share or total)	1
Comments	2
Conclusion	1
	20
(b) Oakton's preferences	2-3
Shareholders' preferences	2-3
	5
(c) Each important factor 1-2 marks each	5
	30

35 DEMAST

Tutor's hint. In part (b) it is helpful to make an evaluation of the likely purpose of the two bidders in making their offers for Demast. On the basis of this, it is possible to suggest appropriate valuation techniques to estimate a fair price for the company. The full value of the various offers can then be calculated and compared with the valuations to determine whether the bids are appropriate under the circumstances.

(a)   A company planning to grow must decide on whether it will try to achieve this through organic growth alone or through some combination of **organic growth** and **acquisition**. The advantages of growth by acquisition include the following.

(i)   The company may be able to **grow much faster** than would be possible through purely organic development. This is particularly true if the company is seeking to **expand into a new product or market** area when acquisition will allow the company to gain technical skills, goodwill and customer contracts which would take it a long time to develop by itself.

(ii)   If the acquisition is financed through a share exchange, then the company will **not face the pressures on cash** that often result during a time of organic growth. However, it must take account of the likely affect of such an acquisition on the share price, earnings per share and gearing. If the target company is financially more stable it may be able to improve its liquidity and ability to raise further finance.

(iii)   In some markets it is argued that a company **requires 'critical mass'** in order to operate effectively. This is particularly true in industries where a high level of capital investment is required. Acquisition may allow a company to reach an efficient size much more quickly than if it were to try to get there through organic growth.

(iv)   A larger company with a better spread of products, customers and markets faces a **lower level of operating risk** than a small company which may be more dependent on a small number of customers and suppliers. Acquisition will therefore allow the company to reduce its operating risk more quickly. This effect is enhanced if the company is using acquisition as a means of diversification into new product/market areas.

(v)   Acquisition may permit the company to make **operating economies** through the rationalisation and elimination of duplication in areas such as research and development, debt collection and corporate relations.

(vi)   Acquisition may allow the company to achieve a **better level of asset backing** if it has a high ratio of sales to assets.

(vii)   The acquisition may be to some **extent opportunistic** if the bidding company identifies a firm where the assets are undervalued.

Evidence in the UK shows that many acquisitions are financially unsuccessful. **Disadvantages associated with takeovers** include the following.

(i)   **Failure to integrate the management and operations effectively** and thus to achieve the planned economies. A recent report also highlighted the failure to achieve a good adaptation of corporate cultures post-merger, and it was the realisation of the inherent difficulties of this process that caused the proposed merger of the Leeds and the National Provincial building societies to be called off fairly recently.

(ii)   If an acquisition is being made for strong strategic reasons there may be **competition between bidding companies** which forces the price up to a level beyond that which can be justified on financial grounds. If too high a price is paid then the post-merger financial performance is likely to be disappointing. The costs of mounting the bid and of the subsequent reorganisations may also mean that earnings are depressed, at least in the short term.

(iii)   The acquisition may lead to **inequalities in returns** between the shareholders of the bidding and the target companies. It is often the case that the shareholders in the target company do disproportionately well when compared with the shareholders in the bidding company. This is likely to be the case when the price paid for the acquisition is towards the top of the projected range.

(b)   The appropriate valuation technique will depend on the plans which the bidding company has for Demast post-merger. Demast is an unlisted company and therefore there is no market price available. It is assumed that Nadion would intend to continue the operations as a going concern and therefore an earnings based valuation is appropriate in this case. BZO might also plan to continue to operate the business in its present form, or alternatively it might be planning to asset strip if it believes the assets are significantly undervalued. If this is the case, then the company should be valued on a net assets basis.

(i)   **Asset basis valuation.** Demast's net assets currently amount to £6.5m at book values. However, the stock must be written down by 10% to its realisable value, giving a revised net assets figure of £5.95m or £1.49 per share. This valuation does not take into account a number of factors including:

(1)   The **land and buildings** have **not been revalued** since 20W9. Property prices have fallen since then during the recession and therefore they may be overvalued.

(2)   The **patents are excluded** from the balance sheet and may have a significant value if there are a number of years left to run.

(3)   There is no information to suggest whether the **other components** of the asset base are realistically valued, in particular any plant and equipment.

(ii)   **Earnings basis valuations**

(1)   **P/E ratio.** If it is reasonable to assume that Demast should operate on a similar P/E ratio to Nadion since they are both in the same sector, then Nadion's P/E ratio can be used in calculations. This should be approximately correct since although Nadion is much bigger and is a listed company, Demast is showing a much higher rate of growth.

Nadion's P/E ratio is $320/58 = 5.517$

If applied to Demast's earnings, this would suggest a valuation of £4.44 per share (80.5×5.517).

(2)   **Dividend valuation model.** This approach allows the calculation of the theoretical share price based on the projected dividend stream and the cost of capital:

$$P_0 = \frac{D_0(1+g)}{(r-g)}$$

where P_0 = theoretical share price
D_0 = dividend in year 0 (37.5p per share)
g = expected rate of growth in dividends
r = cost of equity capital

$$P_0 = \frac{37.5\,(1+0.09)}{(0.16-0.09)} = £5.84 \text{ per share}$$

The value of the various bids can now be calculated.

(i)   *7 September*

BZO bids 2 for 3 at a price of 710p = £4.73/share

(ii) *2 October*
Nadion bids:

	£
Cash per share	1.70
Debentures: £100 for (6.25/0.25 =) 25 shares equates to cash per share	4.00
Total value at date of merger	5.70

In addition the shareholders gain the opportunity to purchase new shares in 5 years' time at £3.85 (£100/26). This is 15% above Nadion's current share price and therefore if the current rates of growth continue should provide the opportunity to acquire new shares at a significant discount to the prevailing market price.

(iii) *19 October*

BZO bids in cash £6.00 per share.

Considering firstly the bid by Nadion, it is assumed that the company intends to continue to operate Demast as a **going concern**. The bid of £5.70 per share is 14 pence below the most optimistic theoretical share price calculated on the basis of the dividend growth model. This would appear to be a **realistic but prudent bid** from the point of view of Nadion's shareholders. The 5% rise in the price of Nadion's shares following the announcement of the bid suggests that the market also believes that the acquisition would be financially beneficial.

BZO's initial bid of £4.73 per share is **well above** the **net assets valuation** of £1.49 per share. However it is in **line** with the **P/E ratio valuation** of £4.44 per share. Thus if BZO were intending to continue to operate Demast as a going concern, the bid appears to be prudent. However, if BZO's purpose in acquiring Demast is to dispose of all or part of the assets and to change fundamentally the structure of the company, then the bid does not appear sensible. This view is confirmed by the markets which down-valued BZO's shares 9% on the announcement of the offer.

BZO's final cash offer of £6.00 per share is **above** the **most optimistic valuation based** on the dividend growth model. In view of BZO's previous deals, it must be assumed that the management perceive Demast to be in possession of significantly undervalued and under-used assets. Additionally, the use of the term loan to finance the offer will increase BZO's level of debt from £65m to £89m. The current level of gearing is:

$$\frac{£30m + £35m}{£123m + £72m - £91m - £35m} = 94\%$$

Therefore, a further significant increase in this level would not appear to be a prudent move from the point of view of the shareholders in BZO. This view is confirmed by the further slide in the share price to 680 pence.

(c)   **Corporate governance** was defined in the Cadbury Report as 'the **system** by which **companies are directed** and **controlled**'. The directors are responsible for the corporate governance of the company and should act in the best interests of shareholders, taking account of the needs of other groups such as employees, creditors and customers.

During the conduct of a takeover bid the directors are additionally bound by the rules of the **City Code** concerning the way in which the bid is conducted. The directors of both companies are required to disregard their own interests when advising their shareholders.

As has been outlined above, it is doubtful whether the directors of BZO are acting in the best interests of their shareholders by bidding such a high price and by taking on a further £24m of debt. They appear to be following a strategy of **growth at any price** which may not be in the best long-term interests of the group.

When the final bids of Nadion and Demast are compared, they appear to be very close, particularly when the likely capital gain on conversion in the Nadion offer is taken into account. It therefore seems surprising that the directors of Demast should advise acceptance of the BZO offer in preference to the Nadion offer, particularly since **continuity of the current operations** is more likely if Nadion gained ownership. It appears that they may have been swayed by the offer of directorships by BZO and the prospect of continued well paid employment in advising acceptance of the offer. If this is the case then they were acting in their own best interests and not fully taking into account the needs of the owners of the remaining 75% of the shares.

The bid by BZO is also less likely to be to the benefit of **other interested parties** such as employees and customers since the prospects of at least a partial breakup and asset disposal are more likely if BZO gains ownership.

36   AIRGO

> **Tutor's hint.** This question on the financing of a leveraged buyout can be regarded as typical of the type of question that can be expected on management buyouts. It is similar to one which was set some years ago by the same examiner. The question was not answered well by candidates: the examiner's comments explain why.
>
> **Examiner's comment.** This question was very poorly answered by candidates. Part (a) does *not* require the advantages and disadvantages of buy-outs! It requires the advantages and disadvantages of the specific finance mix which is suggested. Common errors included:
>
> - Using the full available finance of £40m, instead of scaling it down to £35m
> - Taking ASTER's share as 20% of total capital instead of 20% of equity
> - Confusing warrants with convertibles
> - Not calculating the new level of interest payments when estimating future earnings
>
> Even if candidates had not finished the computations they could have commented on the possible gearing restriction in 4 years' time, but they lost marks by not doing so. Part (b) was better done.

(a)   To: The Managers of the proposed Airgo plc
      From: Management Consultant
      Date: 12 January 20X2
      Subject: Report on the financing mix for the proposed leveraged buy-out of the regional airport

If the airport can be purchased for £35 million, **the financing mix** is proposed as:

	£m
Equity: 50 pence ordinary shares	
8 million purchased by managers and employees	4
2 million purchased by ASTER plc	1
Debt	
EPP Bank: secured floating rate loan at LIBOR + 3%	20
Allvent plc: mezzanine debt with warrants (balancing figure)	10
Total finance	35

Up to £15 million of the mezzanine debt is available, which could be used to replace some of the floating rate loan. However, this possibility has been rejected because its cost is 18% compared with 13% and the warrants, if exercised, could dilute the manager/employee shareholding.

A **leveraged buyout** of the type proposed allows managers and employees to own 80% of the equity while only contributing £4m out of £35m capital (11%). However, it is important that the managers and employees agree on the company's strategy at the outset. If the shareholders break into rival factions, control over the company might be difficult to exercise. It would be useful to know the disposition of shareholdings among managers and employees in more detail.

The initial **gearing** of the company will be extremely high: the debt to equity ratio is 600% (£30 million debt to £5 million equity). Clearly one of the main medium-term goals following a leveraged buyout is to reduce gearing as rapidly as possible, sacrificing high dividend payouts in order to repay loans. For this reason EPP Bank, the major creditor, has imposed a covenant that capital gearing (debt/equity) must be reduced to 100% within four years or the loan will be called in.

The gearing will be reduced substantially by **steady repayment** of the unsecured mezzanine finance. This carries such a high interest rate because it is a very risky investment by the venture capital company Allvent plc. A premium of 5% over secured debt is quite normal. The debt must be repaid in five equal annual instalments, that is £2 million each year. If profits dip in any particular year, Airgo might experience cash flow problems, necessitating some debt refinancing.

If the **warrants** attached to the mezzanine debt are exercised, Allvent plc will be able to purchase 1 million new shares in Airgo plc for £1 each. This is a cheap price considering that the book value per share at the date of buyout is £3.50 (£35m/10 million shares). The ownership by managers and staff will be diluted from 80% to approximately 73%, with ASTER plc holding 18% and Allvent plc holding 9%. This should not affect management control provided that managers and staff remain as a unified group.

The forecast profit and loss accounts for the first four years of the company's operations are shown in the appendix to this report, together with estimates of gearing for each year, measured as total book value of debt divided by book value of shareholders' funds. A key assumption behind these predictions is that **no dividends are paid** over this period. This may not be acceptable to managers or employees. It is also assumed that cash generated from operations is sufficient to repay £2 million of mezzanine debt each year, which is by no means obvious from the figures provided.

Using these assumptions and ignoring the possible issue of new shares when warrants are exercised, the **gearing at the end of four years** is predicted to be 132%, which is significantly above the target of 100% needed to meet the condition on EPP's loan. If warrants are exercised, £1 million of new share capital will be raised, reducing the year 4 gearing to 125%, still significantly above the target.

Results will be worse if LIBOR rises above 10%, over the period. However the purchase of the cap will stop interest payments on EPP's loan rising above 15%. Conversely if LIBOR falls, the increase in profit could be considerable, but it is still very unlikely that the loan condition will be met by year 4.

There will therefore definitely be a **problem in meeting** the EPP's loan condition. However, if the company is still showing steady growth by year four, and there have been no problems in meeting interest payments, EPP bank will probably not exercise its right to recall the loan.

If the loan condition is predicted to be a problem, the directors of Airgo could consider:

(i)   Aiming for **continuous improvement** in **cost effectiveness**

(ii)   **Renegotiating the central services contract** with ASTER, or providing central services in-house, in order to save costs

(iii)   **Renegotiating the allowed gearing ratio** to a more realistic figure

(iv)   Going for **further expansion after**, say, one or two years (eg extension of a runway in order to handle long-haul flights); financing this expansion with an issue of equity funds. However, this may affect control of the company

(v)   **Looking for possible alternative sources of debt or equity finance** if the EPP loan is recalled, including the possibility of flotation on the stock market

APPENDIX

Airgo plc: forecast profit and loss accounts for the first four years and computation of debt/equity gearing ratios

	Estimates from Year 0 £'000	Year 1 £'000	Year 2 £'000	Year 3 £'000	Year 4 £'000
Landing fees	14,000				
Other turnover	8,600				
	22,600				
Labour	5,200				
Consumables	3,800				
Other expenses	3,500				
	12,500				
Direct operating profit growing at 5% pa	10,100	10,605	11,135	11,692	12,277
Central services from ASTER		(3,000)	(3,150)	(3,308)	(3,473)
EPP loan interest at 13% on £20m		(2,600)	(2,600)	(2,600)	(2,600)
Mezzanine debt interest at 18%					
on £10m		(1,800)			
on £8m			(1,440)		
on £6m				(1,080)	
on £4m					(720)
Profit before tax		3,205	3,945	4,704	5,484
Tax at 33%		1,058	1,302	1,552	1,810
Profit after tax		2,147	2,643	3,152	3,674
Reserves b/f		0	2,147	4,790	7,942
Reserves c/f		2,147	4,790	7,942	11,616
Share capital + reserves		7,147	9,790	12,942	16,616
Total debt at end of year		28,000	26,000	24,000	22,000
Gearing: debt/equity		392%	266%	185%	132%

If warrants are exercised, £1 million of new share capital is issued, reducing the gearing at year 4 to 22,000/17,617 = 125%.

Assumptions

The central services will be provided by ASTER for the full 4-year period.

No dividend will be paid during the first four years.

Sufficient cash will be generated to repay £2 million of mezzanine finance each year and to fund increased working capital requirements.

LIBOR is assumed to remain at 10%.

(b)   In order to decide whether the management buy-out can be considered for a £10 million loan, the venture capital company would need the following information:

(i)   The **purpose** of the buy-out

(ii)   Full **details of the management team,** in order to evaluate expertise and experience and to check that there are no 'gaps' in the team

(iii)   The company's **business plan,** based on a realistic set of strategies (apparently most approaches to venture capital companies fail on this criterion)

(iv)   **Detailed cash flow forecasts** under different scenarios for economic factors such as growth, and interest rates. Forecasts of profit and balance sheets

(v)   Details of the **management team's investment** in the buy-out. Venture capital companies like to ensure that the team is prepared to back their idea with their own money

(vi)   Availability of **security** for the loan, including personal guarantees from the management team. Any other **'sweeteners'** that could be offered to the lender, such as warrants

(vii)   The possibility of **appointing a representative of the venture capital company as a director** of Airgo

Marking guide	Marks	
(a) Format report	1	
Data on financing mix	2	
Advantages and disadvantages of the financing mix		
Key points are form of finance, gearing and control	5	
Warrants	1	
Interest cap	1	
Projected profit and loss accounts		
For maximum marks assumptions must be given	4	
Other comments, (dividend level and working capital)	2	
Future gearing estimates	2	
Suggestions about the covenant	4	
	22	
(b) Two marks for each good point including discussion	8	
	30	

37   DRICOM

Tutor's hint. Once you have seen a structured approach to a question on financial reconstruction schemes, you are well equipped to handle others which might occur. There is no need to produce pages of 'waffle' provided you structure your answer in a logical sequence. Half the battle is knowing which calculations to do and how to interpret the results.

Other points. You are advised to treat this question as 'definitive' for the area of financial reconstructions and then to compare it with previous questions on the same topic.

Examiner's comment. Candidates who addressed the basic principles of success for a reconstruction scheme scored very highly – in some cases they scored nearly full marks. Other answers were poorly structured. In particular, net present values and T accounts were not required for this question! Common errors/omissions were (i) incorrect estimation of liquidation value; (ii) insufficient discussion of the effect on all investors; (iii) no attempt to compute share issue prices; (iv) no discussion of risks faced by investors and why some would not be happy; (iv) no conclusion.

To: Board of Directors of Dricom
From: Consultant

Report on the proposed scheme of reconstruction of Dricom plc

1   **The basic requirements for success**

If a **financial reconstruction** is to be successful, it should exhibit the following characteristics:

(a)   Creditors must be as least as well off as under a liquidation. Otherwise they will force the company into receivership or petition for a liquidation.

(b)   The scheme must raise enough finance to action the proposed plans.

(c)   The reconstructed company must have a financially viable future.

(d)   All parties involved must be treated fairly. This is because any class of shareholder or creditor can veto the scheme if they do not vote in favour of it.

2   **Reasons for the proposed reconstruction**

Reliability problems and **increased competition** have caused large accumulated losses over the last two years. The company is now **technically insolvent** (see Appendix 1) and there is no chance of an improvement to cash flow unless new capital is raised to finance the proposed technical improvement programme. If the directors knowingly allow the company to trade in an insolvent condition they are guilty of an offence. In addition, the convertible debenture must be redeemed within two years and there are no funds available for this.

This report proceeds by firstly discussing the relevant calculations and then by considering the position of each relevant category of shareholder and creditor.

3   **The position if the company were to be wound up today**

Appendix 1 shows the position if the company were to **wound up,** based on asset values at 30 September 20X7. The **net asset position** might have become worse since then but, based on these values:

(a)   Secured creditors could be repaid in full.
(b)   The redundancy payment would be made.
(c)   Unsecured creditors would receive only 63 pence for every pound of debt.
(d)   There would be nothing left to give to ordinary shareholders.

4   **Net cash raised to finance the technical improvement programme**

Appendix 2 shows that the immediate **cash flows** associated with the reconstruction scheme improve the company's cash balance from £35,000 to £255,000. Provided that all the parties agree to the scheme, there are sufficient funds to invest in the new machinery. However, no account has been taken of the **increased working capital requirement** which will be necessary to underpin increased sales activity. This should be investigated.

5   **Position of creditors immediately after the scheme has been implemented**

As a theoretical exercise, Appendix 3 shows the **position of the creditors** if the company were to liquidate immediately after the scheme had been set up. This shows that there would be sufficient cash to pay all creditors, secured and unsecured, in full and there would be some money for distribution to shareholders. Of course, this computation ignores the position of the existing convertible debenture holders, who have exchanged secured debt for risky equity shares. This matter is dealt with later.

6   **Disposition of shareholdings if the scheme is operational**

Appendix 4 shows that:

(a)   The venture capital company becomes the largest shareholder (39%) buying its shares at the cheapest price (£1.43).

(b)   Directors and employees buy 28% of the shares at £1.50 each.

(c)   Based on existing market value of the convertibles, these investors will receive 33% of the new shares at the relatively expensive effective price of £1.57.

7   **Viability of the company's operations after the investment is made**

Appendix 5 shows the **projected profitability** of the company if the scheme is operational. Total interest is expected to be £417,000, giving interest cover of 1.8 times, which may not be enough to satisfy the unsecured lenders, particularly those who are unsecured.

The projected equity earnings give **a P/E ratio** (based on a subscription price of 150 pence) of 8.1 for the first two years, when the company is not expected to pay tax, but 12.1 when tax is paid from year 3 onwards. Given that the average P/E ratio in Dricom's industry is 12, these results are acceptable but not exciting. However, the projected earnings figures are considered prudent and growth may turn out to be better than expected.

8   **Position of the company's existing creditors and shareholders**

The **existing creditors and shareholders** will have to vote on the scheme and will wish to ensure that they are being treated fairly.

Secured creditors

(a)   **9% debenture holders**. The 9% debenture holders are safe if a liquidation were to take place either today or in the future. They are unlikely to oppose the scheme but may try to negotiate an **extra reward** for supporting it, such as a free issue of warrants on the company's shares.

(b)   **BXT Bank.** BXT is to play a major part in the proposals by contributing an additional £1.2 million of loan finance. The bank will **improve its position** by supporting the proposals, even if the scheme is tried and fails, because the interest rate will be increased and the overdraft will be converted into a secured loan. (I assume the overdraft is with BXT.) If there were to be a liquidation now, the overdraft would only be 63% repaid.

The bank will therefore probably support the scheme. It will, however keep a very close watch on the company's cash flow, calling in the **receiver** if the position deteriorates, because **interest cover** is low.

(c)   **8% convertible stock.** The holders of the 8% convertible stock will certainly not be happy with what they are offered. They are being asked to **exchange a secured loan,** which would be fully repaid on a liquidation, for an **investment in risky shares** at a higher price than any other category of new shareholder! Unless the offer to these creditors is drastically improved, the scheme will undoubtedly fail.

Unsecured creditors

The position of the overdraft has already been discussed. **Other unsecured creditors,** including the 10% loan stock holders, are **likely to agree** to the scheme because they stand a much better chance of full repayment if the scheme is agreed. However, if the scheme takes too long to arrange, they may prefer the certainty of cash from the liquidation.

Existing shareholders

The cash offer of 28 pence per share is far too generous and is very likely to be **accepted by shareholders**, given that their alternative is zero if a liquidation takes place. Other classes of investor may, however, take issue with the terms offered to shareholders.

The current market price of the shares, 23 pence, is not really relevant once the scheme is announced. At that point the shareholders' future wealth depends on the decisions of other key parties, especially the bank, the convertible holders and the venture capital company. If the shareholders all attempt to sell their shares at that point, they will certainly not get 23 pence per share.

For tax reasons, some of these investors may wish to remain as shareholders, in which case suitable tax-efficient arrangements should be made and a suitable subscription price negotiated.

9 **Position of the new investors in the reconstructed company**

The venture capital company

The venture capital company is **unlikely to approve** of the suggested terms, for the following two main reasons.

(a)   It is **unlikely to want** the **major shareholding** (39%) in the reconstructed company, given that its objective will be to find a suitable 'exit route' after, say, five years.

(b)   The **projected profitability and growth** are **not good enough** for the risk involved and the price suggested.

If it does agree to the scheme, it will certainly want board representation and will probably negotiate for further benefits, such as options on further share issues.

Directors and employees

Presumably the directors have already agreed to **subscribe the necessary cash** but have assumed that the company's employees will be able to provide the necessary balance. This is an uncertainty that needs further investigation.

10 **Conclusion**

As it stands, the scheme is **unlikely to be successful** because, in particular, the **convertible debenture holders** are being **unfairly penalised**, and the offer is too generous to existing shareholders and not attractive enough to the venture capital company.

In any revision of the scheme it is unlikely that gearing can be significantly increased. This puts the burden onto directors and employees to contribute more cash.

BPP PUBLISHING

Appendix 1: Distribution of assets if Dricom plc were to be wound up today

	£'000	£'000
Estimated net realisable value of fixed assets		
Land and buildings (80% × book value)		1,200
Plant and machinery (book value less £500,000)		1,600
		2,800
Less: Creditors secured on fixed assets		
9% debenture (secured on factory building)	500	
8% Convertible debenture (floating charge)	1,000	
Term loan BXT Bank (floating charge)	800	
		2,300
Balance available for other parties to the liquidation		500
Estimated net realisable value of current assets		
Stocks (50% × book value)	670	
Debtors	1,090	
Cash	35	
		1,795
Balance of total assets available for distribution		2,295
Distribution of assets		
Preferential creditor		
Redundancy payments		1,000
Balance available for unsecured creditors		1,295
Unsecured creditors		
10% Loan stock	500	
Overdraft	620	
Other creditors	940	
		2,060

The unsecured creditors would receive 1,295/2,060 = 63%, or 63 pence per pound of debt.

Appendix 2: Cash flows associated with the reconstruction scheme

Ref to notes in question		£'000	£'000
	Current cash at bank and in hand		35
	Receipts		
1 (v)	Sale of obsolete machinery		300
	New share capital:		
2 (ii)	Venture capital company		1,000
2 (iii)	Directors and employees (500,000 × £1.50)		750
2 (v)	Increase in BXT term loan (£2m – £0.8m)		1,200
			3,285
	Payments		
1 (iv)	Redundancy	500	
2 (i)	Distribution to ordinary shareholders (1m × 28p)	280	
			780
	Balance available for investment in machinery		2,505
	Estimated investment cost		2,250
	Cash balance after scheme is implemented		255

Appendix 3: Position of the parties if there were a liquidation immediately after the reconstruction scheme

	£'000	£'000
Net realisable value of fixed assets		
Land and buildings		1,200
Original plant and machinery (1,600 – 300)		1,300
New plant and machinery ★		2,250
		4,750
Secured creditors		
9% debenture	500	
Term loan BXT bank	2,000	
Overdraft	620	
		3,120
Balance for other parties		1,630
Current assets		
Stock	670	
Debtors	1,090	
Cash	255	
		2,015
Balance of total assets available for distribution		3,645
Distribution of assets:		
Preferential creditor		
Redundancy payments (1,000 – 500) ★★		500
Balance available for unsecured creditors		3,145
Unsecured creditors		
10% Loan stock	500	
Other creditors	940	
		1,440
Available for ordinary shareholders		1,705

★ New plant and machinery would actually be worth less than £2.25 million if sold, but this factor has been ignored in the calculation.

★★ It is assumed that, if the company were to liquidate *after* the scheme has been implemented, the remainder of the redundancy money would have to be paid.

Appendix 4: Disposition of shareholdings if the scheme is operational

	'000	%		Price per share £
Venture capital organisation	700	39	1,000/700	1.43
Directors and employees	500	28		1.50
Convertible holders (£1m × 60/£100)	600	33	1,000× 94%/600	1.57
	1,800	100		

Appendix 5: Projected profitability of the company if the scheme is operational

	£'000
Interest payable	
9% debenture: 9% × £500,000	45
Term loan: estimated 13% × £2m	260
Overdraft: estimated 10% × £620,000	62
10% loan stock: 10% × £500,000	50
	417
Projected profitability	£'000
Expected earnings before interest and tax	750
Interest	417
Profit before tax	333
Tax (from year 3 at 33%)	110
Profit after tax	223

Ratios

Interest cover (750/417)   1.80 times

Earnings per share and P/E ratio   EPS   *P/E (based on price of 150p)*
   Years 1 and 2 - no tax (333/1,800)   18.5 pence   (150/18.5)   8.1
   Years 3 to 5 - after 33% tax (223/1,800)   12.4 pence   (150/12.4)   12.1

Marking guide	Marks
Criteria for the success of a reconstruction	2
Implications for the company if no reconstruction takes place	1
Valuation in receivership/liquidation	3
Implications of corporate failure for the providers of finance	2
Estimate of finance provided from the reconstruction (for full marks, working capital comment required)	4
Individual finance providers	
Shareholders	2
BXT Bank	3
Straight debentureholders	1
Loan stock holders	1
Convertible debentureholders (discuss validity of share price and valuation)	4
Venture capital organisation (discuss validity of share price and valuation)	3
Other creditors	1
Directors and employees	1
Conclusion	2
	30

38   PLANETSPAN

Tutor's hint. Unlike many long questions, this question is not split into defined sections. However, to answer it effectively and to ensure that nothing is missed out, you will need to construct your own breakdown. You may find it helpful not just to split the discussion into two sections related to each press release, but to approach it statement by statement within each press release.

This is a very wide-ranging question that covers a number of different areas of the syllabus. It is easy to start on a section, identify the main topic being examined, and become blinkered to the other issues that are relevant and on which comment should be made.

There are numerous potential pitfalls relating to the calculations required in the evaluation of the second press release. These include using LSER's cost of capital rather than Planetspan's, omitting to ungear the cost of equity, including the marketable securities with the operating cash flows (instead of the financing side effects), omitting the cost of the debt being taken over from the consideration and omitting the tax shield on the additional debt capacity from the financing side effects.

Examiner's comment. Many candidates were unable to correctly calculate the existing earnings per share of the two companies, which was surprising at the professional stage of examinations. Even where good attempts were made at this calculation, candidates were often unaware of how these earnings per share should be weighted in order to estimate the expected earnings per share of the new combined entity.

Where APV was estimated, candidates often failed correctly to identify the financing side effects, or the total amount payable for the acquisition of LSER. A common error was for an APV to be estimated without deducting the purchase cost of LSER. Not surprisingly a very favourable APV resulted.

The statements contained in the two press releases will be considered one by one.

Press release one

1   **The proposed acquisition is likely to lead to an *immediate* increase in earnings per share for the new company.**

(a)   The first step is to **calculate the number of shares** that will be in issue following the acquisition. Planetspan will have to pay a 25% premium over the current LSER share price. The price per share will therefore be 387p × 1.25 = 483.75pence.

(b)   The acquisition would be financed wholly by an **issue of new shares**. Since the existing share price of Planetspan is 220 pence, this means that each shareholder in LSER could expect to receive 2.2 (483.75 ÷ 220) Planetspan shares for every LSER share held.

(c)   LSER currently has 19.44m shares in issue. Planetspan will therefore have to **issue an additional 42.768m shares** (19.44m × 2.2) to make the acquisition.

(d)   The **total number of shares** that will be in issue in the new company immediately following the acquisition will therefore be 125m + 42.768m = **167.768m**.

(e)   The next step is to **calculate the earnings** of the new company. It is assumed that the acquisition will make no difference to the earnings performance *immediately* following the acquisition.

(f)   **Existing earnings after tax** can be calculated by multiplying the earnings per share for each company by the number of shares in issue.

	EPS	Shares	Total earnings (£)
Planetspan	14 pence	125m	17.5000m
LSER	36 pence	19.44m	6.9984m
Total			24.4984m

(g)   The expected EPS for the new company is £24.4984m ÷ 167.768m = **14.60 pence.**

The proposed acquisition will therefore lead to a small increase in the level of EPS for existing shareholders in Planetspan.

2   **...and a potential post acquisition market price of 230 pence per share.**

The **post acquisition share price** can be estimated by **calculating the market capitalisation** of the new company and **dividing by the number** of shares in issue. The market capitalisation can be estimated as the sum of the existing market capitalisations of the two companies, less the purchase costs, plus an adjustment to reflect the savings in operating costs. It is assumed that the value of the marketable securities is fully reflected in the current share price, and therefore no adjustment will be made for this item.

		£
Planetspan	125m shares × 220 pence	275.0000m
LSER	19.44m shares × 387 pence	75.2328m
Less costs of acquisition		(6.0000m)
Operating costs saved in perpetuity (using cost of capital of 13% calculated below)		7.6923m
Market capitalisation of new company		351.9251m
Number of shares in issue (see above)		167.7680m
Post acquisition share price		210 pence

The **expected post acquisition market price** is therefore **lower** than that **predicted in the press release**. This is because Planetspan is paying a 25% premium to acquire the shares of LSER, which does not reflect the additional value that immediately arises from the acquisition. However, it may be that the acquisition gives rise to synergies that have not been quantified in the information provided. If operating income is expected to rise following the acquisition, this would mean that the share price would be higher to reflect the expected increases in the NPV of the earnings stream that would accrue to the shareholders.

It seems likely that the share price of 230 pence was calculated by applying Planetspan's existing P/E ratio of 15.71 (220/14) to the new EPS of 14.6 pence. The problems with this approach are as follows.

(a) The **P/E ratio** would be **unlikely to remain at 15.71**, unless there were large synergies, because LSER's P/E ratio is much lower at 10.75.

(b) The fact that Planetspan is paying a **premium** to acquire LSER is ignored.

(c) The **costs of the acquisition** are ignored.

To summarise, although the existing shareholders of Planetspan would gain a small increase in the level of EPS, they would experience a larger drop in the value of their shares due to the expected fall in the share price.

3 **The new company will be less risky for bondholders as the volatility of cash flows will be reduced, which should lead to a reduction in the company's cost of finance.**

Earnings stability is likely to improve as a result of there being a **wider spread of activities** within the business. Even though the systematic risk is not reduced, the reduction in earnings volatility is likely to make it easier and cheaper to obtain additional sources of loan finance.

Liquidity may be improved by the coming together of the two companies.

Tax factors may be relevant where the new group is able to use tax shields or tax losses that were previously unavailable.

4 **Synergies from the acquisition will increase cash flows which should eventually increase the share price even further.**

Since the companies operate in the same industry, it is likely that there are **potential synergies** and that will increase the **operating cash flows**. However, if these synergies can be reasonably predicted, then if it is assumed that the capital markets are efficient, these synergies will be recognised by the market and the share price will adjust to reflect them immediately.

Press release two

1 **The key factor determining the success or failure of an acquisition is the effect of the acquisition on the group's future cash flows.**

This statement is correct in identifying the expected level of future cash flows as being the key to the financial success of the acquisition. If success is being measured in terms of the share price, then the degree to which share price is correlated with expected cash flows will depend on the level of efficiency in the market. In particular, it is the present value of the cash flows that is more important than the gross cash flows themselves.

2 **Based upon Planetspan's assessment of future discounted cash flows, using the widely accepted adjusted present value techniques, the acquisition is likely to result in an adjusted present value of approximately £10 million, and significantly to increase shareholder wealth.**

Although the theoretical validity of the **adjusted present value (APV) approach** is widely accepted, it is not yet widely used by companies, and in this sense it cannot be said to be *generally* widely accepted.

The APV method involves two stages:

(a) **Evaluate the project** first of all as if it were **all equity financed** to find the 'base case NPV'

(b) **Make adjustments** to this to allow for the effects of the method of financing that has been used

In this case, the incremental cash flows arising from the acquisition will be discounted at the ungeared cost of equity for Planetspan. The ungeared beta can be found using the following expression:

$$\beta_a = \beta_e \frac{E}{E + D(1-t)} + \beta_d \frac{D(1-t)}{E + D(1-t)}$$

where:

β_a	= ungeared beta	
β_e	= geared beta	= 1.25
β_d	= debt beta	= 0
E	= market value of equity in geared company	= 60%
D	= market value of debt in the geared company	= 40%
t	= corporation tax rate	= 33%

$$\beta_a = 1.25 \times \frac{60}{60 + 40(1 - 0.33)} = 0.864$$

This can now be substituted into the CAPM to find the cost of capital:

$$Ke = r_f + [E(r_m) - r_f]\beta_j$$

where:

Ke	= cost of equity	
r_f	= risk free rate of return	= 6%
$E(r_m)$	= market rate of return	= 14%
β_j	= equity beta	= 0.864
Ke	= 6% + 0.864(14% – 6%)	
Ke	= 12.91%, say 13%	

This **cost of capital** can now be used to **discount the expected cash flows** that will arise from the acquisition. It is assumed that the marketable securities will be realised immediately on acquisition since the cash flows provided exclude any income from these assets. It is also assumed that the costs of acquisition will be payable immediately. These two elements will be included with the financing side effects and will not form part of the base case NPV.

	Year 1 £million	Year 2 £million	Year 3 £million	Year 4 £million	Year 5 £million	Yrs 6-10 £million	Total £million
LSER cash flows	8	9	10	11	12	14	
Acquisition effects:							
Cost savings	1	1	1	1	1	1	
Net cash flow	9	10	11	12	13	15	
13% disc factors	0.885	0.783	0.693	0.613	0.543	1.909*	
Present values	7.965	7.830	7.623	7.356	7.059	28.635	66.468

* Ten year annuity value at 13% less five year annuity value at 13%.

The acquisition therefore generates operating cash flows of £66.468m. From this must be deducted the price that is to be paid for the company. This has two components.

(a) **Equity**. Planetspan is purchasing the 19.44 million ordinary shares at a price that is at a premium of 25% to the market price. This part of the consideration therefore amounts to 19.44m × £3.87 × 1.25 = £94.041m.

(b) **Debt**. The debt obligation being taken over by Planetspan also forms part of the cost of the acquisition. The liability comprises the annual interest payment of £1.628m (£20.35m × 8%) that must be paid for five years, and the repayment of principal in five years time. The present value cost of this will be found using the cost of debt to Planetspan, which is 10%:

		£million
Interest:	£1.628 × 3.791	6.172
Principal:	£20.35m × 0.621	12.637
Total cost		18.809

The total consideration is therefore £94.041m + £18.809m = £112.85m. The cash flows generated amount to £66.468m. The base case NPV is therefore **negative** at **£46.382m.**

The financing side effects include the following.

(a) **Tax relief on the debt acquired**: £20.35m × 8% × 33% = £537,240 per year. This is available for five years and will be discounted at Planetspan's cost of borrowing of 10%. The present value is therefore £537,240 × 3.791 = £2.037m.

(b) **Tax relief on the additional debt capacity**: £20m × 10% × 33% = £660,000 per year. Since the operating cash flows are being evaluated over a ten year timescale, the same period will be applied in calculating the present value (again at 10%): £660,000 × 6.145 = £4.056m.

(c) The cash **realised immediately** on the sale of the marketable securities = £3m.

(d) The **purchase expenses** = £6m.

The total of these is therefore £2.037m + £4.056m + £3m − £6m = **£3.093m.**

The APV is therefore £3.093m − £46.382m = £43.289 negative.

The press release claims that the APV will be around £10m positive, and there is thus a major discrepancy in the calculations. On the basis of the reworked figures, the APV is negative, and this means that the proposed acquisition is **not financially viable**. However, the calculations do not include any estimate of a terminal value for the investment, and it must be presumed that the executive who prepared the press release assumed a **significant terminal value** in his figures. In view of the lack of any such figures provided in the information, the best that can be done is to make the following adjustments:

(a) Discount the £15m per year operating cash flows from year ten to infinity:

£15m × 0.295 ÷ 13% = £34.04m

(b) Discount the tax relief on the additional debt capacity from year ten to infinity:

£660,000 × 0.386 ÷ 10% = £2.55m

The total of these adjustments is £36.59m. This is still insufficient to make the APV become positive, and therefore the acquisition must still be regarded as being of bad value to the shareholders.

39 GROCAS

(a)

REPORT

To: Board of Directors, Grocas plc
From: Accountant
Date: 15 February 20X6
Subject: Strategic review of operating subsidiaries

Introduction

This report forms part of the strategic review of the operating subsidiaries and is particularly concerned with the **financial implications of possible divestment.** Detailed numerical analysis is contained in the Appendix to this report.

General considerations

Grocas currently operates in four separate and very different market areas. There may be sound strategic reasons for continuing to operate in a diversified way and for remaining in or pulling out of specific market sectors. These should be given serious consideration but are beyond the scope of this report which is concerned with the financial dimension of the decision making process.

Financial considerations

Grocas currently has in issue 20 million shares with a market value of 360p. The market value of the company is therefore £72m (£82m if the long-term debt is included). The current estimate of the after tax realisable value of the subsidiaries is £92.2m which is in excess of the market value of the company, and this could reflect a market perception that some subsidiaries are being held back by subsidising less profitable areas. The implication of this conglomerate discount is that the market value of four separate divested companies would be above that of the Grocas group in its present form. It therefore appears that it would be **in the interests of the shareholders to undertake some level of divestment.**

The question as to which areas are most appropriate for disposal can be approached in a number of ways. One argument is that Grocas should **dispose of its businesses** in the **weaker areas,** ie textiles and engineering, which on the basis of the industry P/E ratios have lower growth prospects than food processing and printing. However it may be that Grocas occupies a strategic niche in these areas which would argue against their divestment.

If **divestment** is a **serious option** this could be undertaken either **now** or at the **end of 20X9.** The calculations in the Appendix seek to estimate the PV of the likely realisable values at the end of 20X9, taking account of the **projected cash flows** in the intervening period, and to compare these with the estimates of current realisable values. With the exception of the low estimate for the textiles subsidiary, it appears that in all cases the realisable value at the end of 20X9 is likely to be better than the current value. However, there is a higher degree of uncertainty attaching to the longer timescale projections, and the timing of disposal must also depend on there being an appropriate opportunity to find a willing purchaser.

Effect of reducing diversification

Financial theory holds that investors will achieve their own desired level of **diversification,** and therefore the degree of diversification within Grocas is irrelevant to them. However in practice this is rarely true for 100% of the shareholders, and therefore some of them would be likely to find their level of risk affected by the reduction in the diversification of the group.

The industry sectors within which Grocas operates are **unrelated,** and even possibly **negatively correlated** with regard to the business cycle. A reduction in the level of diversification could therefore result in a **less stable pattern of cash flows,** which could in turn **increase the level of financial risk** to the company. This is likely to be to the disadvantage of the employees whose prospects for continuing stable income and employment may be reduced as a result of the divestment.

Conclusions

The figures suggest that **some level of divestment** is likely to be appropriate for Grocas, although other strategic factors must be taken into account in determining what, if any, form the divestment takes. Projected realisable values appear to be higher at the end of 20X9 than at present, although the inaccuracies and risks of long-term projections must be taken into account, as must the practicalities of divestment opportunities. The negative implications for some of the shareholders and for the employees should also be taken into account when making the divestment decision.

APPENDIX: FINANCIAL CALCULATIONS

This appendix contains calculations to establish the estimated PV of the realisable values of the different subsidiaries at the end of 20X9. The **discount rates** used to establish the PVs are those which are specific to the industries concerned and are estimated using the **capital asset pricing model (CAPM).** The weighted average cost of capital of Grocas is not appropriate for this purpose.

Calculation of discount rates using the CAPM:

$$K = r_f + [E(r_m) - r_f]\beta_j$$

where

K	=	Cost of capital
r_f	=	Risk free rate of return (6%)
$E(r_m)$	=	Market rate of return (13%)
β_j	=	Beta value of given industry

Industry sector	β	K(%)
Textiles	0.86	12.0
Engineering	1.29	15.0
Food processing	0.57	10.0
Printing	1.43	16.0

These discount rates can now be used to estimate the PV of the cash flows. It is assumed that the forecasts of profits and overheads provided include the effects of inflation. Only the part of the group charges which represents directly attributable overhead is relevant to the calculations. Corporation tax is charged on the same year's profits.

Using **asset betas** will give an estimate of the 'base case' NPV for each division. The gearing capacity will probably vary by division, so we'll ignore the tax shield effect, to give a minimum NPV. To this should be added the value of the tax shield associated with the borrowing capacity of each division for an accurate assessment of the APV of each division. This complexity is ignored in the rest of this solution.

All monetary figures below are in £m.

183

Textile subsidiary

	20X6	20X7	20X8	20X9
Operating profit	1.00	1.00	1.00	1.00
Overhead	(0.50)	(0.50)	(0.50)	(0.50)
Profit before tax	0.50	0.50	0.50	0.50
Tax at 30%	(0.15)	(0.15)	(0.15)	(0.15)
Net cash flow	0.35	0.35	0.35	0.35
Discount at 12%	0.893	0.797	0.712	0.636
PV of cash flow	0.31	0.28	0.25	0.22

Total cash flow PV = £1.06 million.

Comparison of PV of realisable values:

	Current	20X9 low	20X9 high
Net realisable value	5.20	6.50	7.00
Discount factor	1.00	0.636	0.636
PV of realisable value	5.20	4.13	4.45
Add PV of additional cash flows		1.06	1.06
Total realisable value	5.20	5.19	5.51

Engineering subsidiary

	20X6	20X7	20X8	20X9
Operating profit	2.21	2.32	2.43	2.55
Overhead	(0.50)	(0.50)	(0.50)	(0.50)
Profit before tax	1.71	1.82	1.93	2.05
Tax at 30%	(0.51)	(0.55)	(0.58)	(0.62)
Net cash flow	1.20	1.27	1.35	1.43
Discount at 15%	0.870	0.756	0.658	0.572
PV of cash flow	1.04	0.96	0.89	0.82

Total cash flow PV = £3.71 million.

Comparison of PV of realisable values:

	Current	20X9 low	20X9 high
Net realisable value	14.00	18.00	20.00
Discount factor	1.00	0.572	0.572
PV of realisable value	14.00	10.30	11.44
Add PV of additional cash flows		3.71	3.71
Total realisable value	14.00	14.01	15.15

Food processing subsidiary

	20X6	20X7	20X8	20X9
Operating profit	7.55	7.70	7.85	8.01
Overhead	(1.00)	(1.00)	(1.00)	(1.00)
Profit before tax	6.55	6.70	6.85	7.01
Tax at 30%	(1.97)	(2.01)	(2.06)	(2.10)
Net cash flow	4.58	4.69	4.79	4.91
Discount at 9%	0.909	0.826	0.751	0.683
PV of cash flow	4.16	3.87	3.60	3.35

Total cash flow PV = £14.98 million.

Comparison of PV of realisable values:

	Current	20X9 low	20X9 high
Net realisable value	28.00	30.00	33.00
Discount factor	1.00	0.683	0.683
PV of realisable value	28.00	20.49	22.54
Add PV of additional cash flows		14.98	14.98
Total realisable value	28.00	35.47	37.52

Printing subsidiary

	20X6	20X7	20X8	20X9
Operating profit	13.53	14.88	16.37	18.01
Overhead	(1.00)	(1.00)	(1.00)	(1.00)
Profit before tax	12.53	13.88	15.37	17.01
Tax at 30%	(3.76)	(4.16)	(4.61)	(5.10)
Net cash flow	8.77	9.72	10.76	11.91
Discount at 16%	0.862	0.743	0.641	0.552
PV of cash flow	7.56	7.22	6.90	6.57

Total cash flow PV = £28.25 million.

Comparison of PV of realisable values:

	Current	*20X9 low*	*20X9 high*
Net realisable value	45.00	45.00	50.00
Discount factor	1.00	0.552	0.552
PV of realisable value	45.00	24.84	27.60
Add PV of additional cash flows		28.25	28.25
Total realisable value	45.00	53.09	55.85

Summary of estimated PV realisable values

Subsidiary	*Current*	*20X9 low*	*20X9 high*
Textiles	5.20	5.20	5.52
Engineering	14.00	14.01	15.15
Food processing	28.00	35.47	37.52
Printing	45.00	53.09	55.85

(b) The printing subsidiary is the largest within the group in **terms of operating profits**, accounting for 54% of profits in 20X5. It also has much the highest level of return on sales at 24%. The benefit of a **partial demerger** is that the **quality of its performance** within the group would be **highlighted** without any significant loss of control. As a result it is possible that the conglomerate discount discussed in the report (in part (a)), whereby the market price of the company is below the value of its component parts, might be reduced or eliminated.

Assuming that the realisable value of £45m is reasonable, Grocas might expect to raise £11.25m from a partial demerger, although in practice this could well be lower since the investor would not be gaining control of the subsidiary. This would provide finance for investment either in the printing company itself, or in one of the other subsidiaries, which would hopefully enhance the returns to shareholders.

40   PREPARATION QUESTION: HERLER

> **Tutor's hint.** The problems in this question lie in the high inflation rate and the use of a six monthly time interval. The suggested solution demonstrates the correct way to calculate a six monthly discount factor, but if raising numbers to unusual powers is beyond the ability of your calculator, you could estimate the factor from the discount tables. You will also need to think quite carefully about how to calculate the variable costs.
>
> Part (b) requires you to think creatively about how the exchange risk could have been reduced **before** the contract was agreed. Techniques used to hedge exchange rate exposure are therefore not particularly relevant in this case.

(a) The first step is to estimate the exchange rates at the six monthly payment intervals, using purchasing power parity.

$$\text{'old' exchange rate} \times \frac{(1+\text{inflation rate}) \text{ in country A}}{(1+\text{inflation rate}) \text{ in country B}}$$

BPP
PUBLISHING

In six months' time: $\qquad 2{,}400 \times \dfrac{(1+2.5)^{0.5}}{(1+0.05)^{0.5}} = 4{,}382$

In one year's time: $\qquad 2{,}400 \times \dfrac{(1+2.5)}{(1+0.05)} = 8{,}000$

In eighteen months' time: $\qquad 2{,}400 \times \dfrac{(1+2.5)^{1.5}}{(1+0.05)^{1.5}} = 14{,}606$

In two years' time: $\qquad 2{,}400 \times \dfrac{(1+2.5)^{2}}{(1+0.05)^{2}} = 26{,}667$

Since the cash flows arise at six monthly intervals, it is also necessary to calculate the 12% discount factors at six months and eighteen months:

At six months: $\qquad \dfrac{1}{(1+0.12)^{0.5}} = 0.945$

At eighteen months: $\qquad \dfrac{1}{(1+0.12)^{1.5}} = 0.844$

The sterling receipts can be calculated as follows.

	Now	6 months	12 months	18 months
Percentage of contract sum	25%	25%	15%	35%
Receipts in Surkayan francs (m)	2,000	2,000	1,200	2,800
Exchange rate (S francs/£)	2,400	4,382	8,000	14,606
Receipts in sterling	833,333	456,413	150,000	191,702

The variable costs can all be calculated in relation to the initial receipt, since this is the exchange rate that is to be applied to these costs, and it is known that 25% of the variable costs will be incurred at this stage. It is then possible to calculate the sterling cash flow at each stage, and this can then be discounted at 12% to find the NPV of the project.

	Now	6 months	12 months	18 months
Percentage of contract sum	25%	25%	15%	35%
Receipts in sterling	833,333	456,413	150,000	191,702
Variable costs	416,667	416,667	250,000	583,333
Sterling cash flow	416,666	39,746	(100,000)	(391,631)
12% discount factors	1.000	0.945	0.893	0.844
Present values	416,666	37,560	(89,300)	(330,537)

The project therefore has a **positive NPV of £34,389**. The project will therefore be financially viable if inflation in Surkaya continues at the present levels.

(b) Assuming that there are no derivative product hedges available to Herler plc, the options that the company could have used to reduce the exchange risk prior to agreeing the contract include the following.

(i)   The company could negotiate cash flows with a **greater proportion** of the **contract price** being paid in the early stages of the project.

(ii)   At present virtually all the **variable costs** are **incurred in sterling**. If Herler could source materials and labour locally it would be able to match costs and revenues, and thereby mitigate some of the effects of the high inflation rate.

(iii) **Payment** could be in the form of a **countertrade agreement** whereby payment is made in a commodity that could be easily resold outside the country and which would retain its value better than the Surkayan currency.

(iv)   If, as appears likely, Surkaya is a struggling third world country, and if the construction project was for the long-term benefit of the people, **international aid** might be available to help finance the project.

(v)   If Herler could negotiate a **currency swap** with a Surkayan company that requires sterling now, it would at least be able to fix the exchange rate for the reversal of the swap and thereby fix its commitments.

(vi)   Herler could **negotiate** a **back-to-back loan arrangement** (a loan in Surkayan francs to match the expected receipts).

41   PREPARATION QUESTION: FINANCIAL FUTURES

REPORT

To: Board of Directors
From: Accountant
Date: 15 June 20X6
Subject: Use of financial futures within the company

The purpose of this report is to deal with three main areas: the benefits of futures; the risks of futures; strategies for the minimisation of futures risks.

(a)   **The benefits of futures**

Futures are a form of **forward contract**, which give a fixed rate for a financial instrument, such as security prices, exchange rates or interest rates, at a future date. Financial futures can be used to hedge against risks of movements in:

(i)   Gilt prices
(ii)   Interest rates
(iii)   Foreign currency exchange rates
(iv)   Share prices
(v)   Bond prices

For a manufacturing company, the principal advantage of futures is in the **hedging** of interest rates, and possibly share prices where the company holds an equity portfolio. Other products such as forward contracts are available for the reduction of exchange rate exposure. A company with a large amount of borrowings that is concerned about a possible rise in the level of interest rates could sell interest rate futures in the expectation that if interest rates rise the same type and amount of futures contracts may be bought at a cheaper price to close out the futures commitment, and the profit made on the futures deals will compensate for any extra interest that the company must pay.

(b)   **The risks of futures**

Futures hedges are unlikely to be perfect for the following reasons.

(i)   The movement in futures prices may **not** be an **exact reflection** of the movement in interest rates.

(ii)   Futures contracts are of a **standard size**, and it may not be possible to match exactly the amount of the borrowings.

The example described involves the use of futures to hedge against a **known financial** position. This is quite different from the Barings situation, where futures were being used to speculate on movements in derivative prices - a quite different and much more risky operation. Futures continue to provide a valuable means of hedging against known specific financial risks.

(c) **Strategies for the minimisation of futures risk**

Internal rules should be formulated to allow the use of futures to hedge against known specific financial risks, but to restrict the use of futures in open speculation. Principles to be used include the following.

(i) There should be **strict limits** on the **size of contracts** that may be used.

(ii) The **responsibility** for **reporting** on futures activity should be **separate** from the **responsibility for decision making** on futures trading.

(iii) The **use of derivatives** should be **centralised,** with local management not being allowed to trade in derivatives.

(iv) Futures activity should be subject to **regular detailed scrutiny** by an independent department such as internal or external audit, reporting to the audit committee.

42 VERTID

> **Tutor's hint**. Part (b) is asking for an evaluation of all the different types of risk in foreign trade, not just foreign exchange risk. Note that the Thodia deal can be hedged via the US$, although the risks of a change in the relationship between the two currencies should be highlighted.
>
> In part (c), your proposals should take into account the size of the company. Options that are only available to large exporters should not be included.
>
> **Examiner's comment.** Marks were lost by poor hedging calculations. In general, candidates displayed knowledge of 'what to do', but not of 'how to do it', though there were some excellent answers. Incorrect exchange rates were frequently used, as were one year interest rates rather than three month.

(a) **Werland franc**

Vertid must make a payment of 3 million Werland francs (Wf) in three months time. At the current spot rate of Wf290 this equates to £10,345. Vertid runs the risk that the Wf could strengthen against the pound, thus increasing the liability when it falls due. **Purchasing power parity theory** provides a method of estimating the likely level of future exchange rates on the basis of the relative rates of inflation in the countries concerned, as follows.

$$\text{Annual change in value} = \frac{i_f - i_{uk}}{1 + i_{uk}}$$

where: i_f = inflation rate of foreign country

i_{uk} = inflation rate of UK

In this case: $\dfrac{0.12 - 0.03}{1.03}$ = 8.74% pa devaluation of Wf against the pound.

This represents a 2.18% devaluation in three months, giving a predicted exchange rate of 296.32 Wf/£. At this rate, the amount of sterling required to settle the debt would be £10,124. Thus contrary to the Sales Manager's predictions, the movement in exchange rates is likely to be **small and favourable** to Vertid. However, it must be appreciated that **purchasing power parity theory** is only a **partial predictor** of exchange rate movements, and the actual rate in three months time could differ significantly from that predicted due to other factors.

Thodian peso

Vertid is anticipating a receipt in six months time of 3.5m Thodian pesos (Tp). The Sales Manager predicts that there is little risk associated with the transaction because the Tp is directly linked to the dollar. However, although the risk is small, purchasing parity theory suggests that there is some risk of a negative movement in the rates because the rate of inflation in the USA is higher than that in the UK.

$$\frac{0.06 - 0.03}{1.03} = 2.9\% \text{ pa depreciation in the dollar against the pound}$$

This equates to a 1.45% devaluation in six months which would result in sterling receipts being slightly lower than anticipated.

However, a greater risk arises from the fact that there is a large difference in inflation rates between Thodia and the USA, with Thodian rates being well above US rates. In these circumstances, it would be surprising if the Tp could maintain its direct linkage with the dollar without there being some significant devaluation. If this happened it would have a substantial negative impact on Vertid's expected receipts. Thus the sales manager is incorrect and Vertid does face quite significant **foreign exchange risk** in its dealings with Thodia.

(b) REPORT

To: Managing Director, Vertid Ltd
From: Consultant
Date: 15 June 20X5
Subject: Protection against the risks of overseas trade

Introduction

The purpose of this report is to set out the options that are available to protect the company from the following principal **risks arising from overseas trade**: foreign exchange risk, commercial risk and political risk.

Foreign exchange risk

(i)   **Werland deal.** The two main options available are a money market hedge and the use of currency options.

(1)   A **money market hedge** would involve borrowing the required amount to settle the debt now in sterling, converting it into Werland francs on the spot market, investing the Werland francs for three months and using the balance, including the interest to settle the debt in three months' time.

The problem with this is that it may be difficult to negotiate a further loan from the bank given the current position with regard to the overdraft. The sterling amount that would need to be raised now can be found as follows.

Amount required in three months' time	Wf3,000,000
Wf investment interest rate for 3 months	3.125%
Wf amount required to yield Wf3m	Wf2,909,091
Current spot rate	290Wf/£
Sterling loan required	£10,032

Interest on the sterling loan would be payable at 10% for three months and would amount to £251. The total cost of this method is therefore £10,283, which is less than the current spot price of £10,345 (Wf3m/290).

(2)   A **currency option** is similar to a share option in that it is an agreement involving an option, but not an obligation, to buy or sell a given amount of currency at a stated rate at a certain time in the future. It therefore provides protection against downside movements, but would allow Vertid to take advantage of any favourable movements in the rate. The price of this is the payment of an upfront premium.

The OTC option available has an exercise price of 300Wf/£ and therefore will only be exercised if the spot rate in three months' time is below this rate. The costs of an option for Wf3m at different spot rates in three months' time are tabulated below. The premium cost is (Wf25 × Wf3m/300)/290 = £862.

Spot rate	Exercise? Y/N	Premium cost £	Currency cost £	Total cost £
280	Y	862	10,000	10,862
290	Y	862	10,000	10,862
300	Y	862	10,000	10,862
310	N	862	9,678	10,540
320	N	862	9,375	10,237
330	N	862	9,091	9,953

The calculations suggest that **hedging using options** would be **significantly more expensive** than a money market hedge. The spot rate would have to rise close to 320Wf/£ for the option to become attractive, and since estimates based on the purchasing power parity theory suggest that the rate is likely to stay below 300 Wf/£, the money market hedge is recommended.

(ii) **Thodia deal.** There is no **fully efficient hedge** available for this deal because there is no forward market for the Thodian peso and Vertid is unable to borrow in this currency. However, since the peso is currently linked to the US dollar, a partial hedge is available through the US currency. To do this, Vertid would need to sell US$ six months forward - at the current spot rate of Tp228/$ this would yield $15,350. The six month $/£ forward rate is 1.4876 ($1.4690 + 1.86cents). The sterling receipt would therefore be $15,350/1.4876 = £10,319.

Although this hedge appears attractive, it must be stressed that it will only be **effective** if the **peso maintains its relationship** to the US dollar. Since the link is under strain due to the disparity in inflation rates in the two countries, there is a significant risk that the connection could be severed or the peso devalued. If this occurs, then the hedge would be ineffective.

Commercial risk relates to the risk that arises through the customer being located in a country other than the UK. There are two main types of commercial risk, as follows.

(1) **Physical** is the risk that the goods could be lost in transit. Insurance cover is available for this type of risk which can be arranged on a deal by deal basis, or using a blanket policy if the company engages in a large number of relatively small export transactions.

(2) **Credit risk** is significant because it is harder to force repayment against a debtor who is a slow payer or who goes into liquidation in a foreign country. Vertid should make **careful checks** on the **creditworthiness** of potential export customers, and could consider the use of irrevocable letter of credit to minimise the risk of non-payment. Alternatively, credit insurance is available through organisations such as NCM.

Political risk arises through the actions of the government of the country in which the trading partner is located. For example, the government could place a freeze on the movement of funds out of the country and this could jeopardize payments to Vertid. There is little that can be done to hedge against this form of risk.

(c) The export deal is being partially financed by the three months credit that has been negotiated for the Werland deal. However, although Vertid is only a small exporter, additional finance could be raised from the following sources.

(i)   **Short-term bank finance.** Although it appears unlikely that the overdraft can be extended, Vertid might be able to raise a further short term bank loan fixed in term and amount, possibly with a different bank. It is likely that this would be an expensive option.

(ii)   **Bill of exchange.** If the export deal can be linked to a bill of exchange which is accepted by the bank, then this could be discounted to provide immediate finance now rather than in six months time.

(iii) **Use of an agent.** The Thodia deal could be routed through an agent rather than directly with the customer. In this situation Vertid should be able to receive payment upon shipment of the goods and the agent will bear the credit risk, generally in return for payment of a commission.

43   LANVERT

> **Tutor's hint.** Be aware that the question is directing you to use different types of hedge for the two transactions, even though this is not explicit in the instructions. It is possible just to calculate the worst case scenario (the option being exercised) but the question appears to warrant a more detailed discussion.
>
> In part (a) most candidates produced good answers relating to forward market and money market hedges. Where errors existed, they normally involved incorrect choice of forward exchange rates, or interest rates.

(a)   **Dollar transactions**

Since the receipt and payment are expected to arise at the same time, it is only necessary to hedge the net payment that will be required of $2.8m ($7.6m – $4.8m) in three months time. The methods available are the forward market and currency options.

Using the forward market

Lanvert should buy $2.8m three months forward at 1.0715/$.
The cost of this is $2.8m × 1.0715 = **€3,000,200**.

Using currency options

Set up

(a)   Date September

(b)   Type of contract put as wish to buy $/sell € with option contract in €.

(c)   Exercise price, use current spot rate €1.0661/$ ie $0.9380/€

(d)   Number of contracts

$$\frac{2,800,000 \div 0.938}{62,500} = 47.8 \text{ contracts, say } 48$$

(e)   Tick size = 0.0001 × 62,500
                     = $6.25

(f)   Premium cost
       = 6.25 × 157 ticks × 48
       = $47,100 @ 1.0661
       = €50,213

Cost of financing must be included. Cost of overdraft is currently 7% per year, and cost for three months is 1.75%.

Total cost of premium = €50,213 × 1.0175

= €51,092

(Normally the time value of money is ignored)

Closing spot rate

The overall dollar cost of using this hedge is not known since it will depend on the spot rate in three months time and whether or not the option is exercised. Options allow Lanvert to protect itself against adverse exchange rate movements (dollar per euro becomes less) at a cost. However, they also allow Lanvert to benefit from favourable exchange rate movements, unlike forward contracts.

Choose one closing spot price above option strike price, say 0.9500, and one below, say 0.9000.

Outcome

(a)   Spot market

	0.9000	0.95000
At opening spot rate	€	€
$2.8 million ÷ 0.9380	2,985,075	2,985,075
At closing spot rate		
$2.8 million ÷ closing spot	3,111,111	2,947,368
Profit/(loss)	(126,036)	37,707

(b)   Options

	0.9000	0.9500
Strike price	0.9000	0.9500
Closing futures price	0.9380	0.9380
Exercise	Yes	No
If exercised, tick movement	380	
Outcome of options position	380 × $6.25	
	× 48 = $114,000	

(c)   Net outcome

Spot market payment	3,111,111	2,947,368
Option profit ÷ closing rate	(126,667)	
Option premium	51,092	51,092
Net outcome	3,035,536	2,998,460

These calculations ignore any hedge inefficiency. Hedge inefficiency derives from two factors:

1   **Basis risk** – the fact that option may be closed out at a rate that differs from the underlying spot. This will be the case if the option is not taken to delivery.

2   A **difference** between the **number of contracts** taken out and the **underlying exposure**, as in this case. Such differences might be covered by a forward contract.

Alternative hedge strike prices may offer more protection (at a higher premium) or less protection (at a lower premium). They might also offer a better 'match' between the hedge amount and the number of contracts.

Swiss franc transactions

As in the case of the dollar transactions, only the net amount of receipts and payments should be hedged, ie a net receipt of SF1.7m in six months' time. The methods available are the forward market and the money market.

Using the forward market

Lanvert should sell SF1.7m six months forward at €0.6197/SF.

The cost of this is SF1.7m × 0.6197 = **€1,053,490**

Using the money market

Borrow sufficient Swiss francs now for six months at 9.8% per year in order to have a balance of SF1.7m in six months time. The net trading receipts will then be used to repay this loan. The interest rate for six months will be 4.9%.

The amount to be borrowed is SF1,620,591 (1.7m ÷ 1.049).

The Swiss francs will be converted into Euros at spot: SF1,620,591 × 0.625 = €1,012,869

These Euros can then be invested in France for six months at 5.25% per year (2.625% for six months) to yield at the end of six months €1,012,869 × 1.02625 = **€1,039,456**.

A better use of the funds would be to pay off a part of the overdraft. If it is assumed that the overdraft is at six months interest rates, this would save 3.625% for six months. The yield in this case would be €1,012,869 × 1.03625 = **€1,049,585**.

However, this would still yield less than would the use of the forward market hedge, and it is therefore recommended that Lanvert should use the latter approach.

(b) If the Swiss customer defaults on its payment, Lanvert will still have to **fulfil any obligations** that it has in connection with foreign exchange transactions. If it has used the forward market hedge, it will still have to sell SF1.7m, and it will probably need to purchase Swiss francs on the spot market and accept any foreign exchange loss that results. Similarly, if a money market hedge is used, Lanvert will have to purchase sufficient Swiss francs on the spot market to pay off the loan.

If Lanvert believes that there is a significant risk of default, then it should consider other means of minimising this, such as restructuring the payments, or taking out credit insurance.

44 KYT

> **Tutor's hint.** This question is a good one to work as revision of the basic futures hedging contract and the nature of basis risk. Make sure you understand the relationship between the dollar-yen and yen-dollar exchange rates – one is the reciprocal of the other.
>
> **Examiner's comment.** There was considerable confusion in part (a) about the nature of transaction exposure. Candidates often considered this to be commercial risk in its broadest sense, especially relating to the possibility of default by customers. Transaction exposure was also confused with translation exposure. Other common errors were use of the incorrect number of futures contracts and incorrect calculation of basis risk, a topic that has been frequently examined.

(a) **Transaction exposure** is the risk of **adverse exchange rate movements** occurring in the course of normal international trading transactions. This arises when export prices are fixed in foreign currency terms, or imports are invoiced in foreign currencies. This form of exposure can give rise to real cash flow gains and losses, and therefore an important function of treasury management is the assessment and management of this risk using various hedging techniques.

Translation exposure arises from **differences in the currencies** in which **assets and liabilities are denominated**. If a company has different proportions of its assets and liabilities denominated in particular currencies, then exchange rate movements are likely to have varying effects on the value of these assets and liabilities. These effects become most obvious when consolidated group accounts are prepared and the values of assets denominated in a foreign currency are translated into the home currency. The importance of this form of exposure to the financial manager stems from the fact that this could influence investors' and lenders' attitudes to the financial worth and creditworthiness of the company. Such risk can be reduced if assets and liabilities denominated in particular currencies can be held in balanced amounts. Unlike transaction exposure, translation exposure is effectively an accounting measure and is not reflected in actual cash flows. This means that hedging techniques are not normally relevant.

(b) (i)   KYT can hedge using futures as follows:

- Use September futures, since these expire soon after 1 September, price of $1/0.007985 = 125.23$ ¥/$.

- **Buy** futures, since it wishes to acquire yen to pay the supplier, and the futures contracts are in Yen.

- Number of contracts 140m / 12.5m = 11.2 contracts ~ 11 contracts.

- Tick size

  $0.000001 \times 12.5m = \$12.50$

(ii)   Basis risk is the difference between the spot and futures prices.

Spot price $= 1/128.15$
$= 0.007803$

Basis $= 0.007803 - 0.007985$
$= 182$ ticks with 3 months to expiry

Basis with one month to expiry, assuming uniform reduction $= 1/3 \times 182$
$= 61$ ticks

Spot price on 1 Sept $= 1/120 = 0.008333$

Therefore predicted futures price $= 0.008333 + 0.000061$
$= 0.008394$

(iii) **Outcome**

Spot market

	$
At opening spot rate (¥140m ÷ 128.15)	1,092,470
At closing spot rate (¥140m ÷ 120)	1,166,667
Loss	74,197

Futures market

Opening futures price	0.007985
Closing futures price	0.008394
Movement in ticks	409 ticks

Futures market profit $409 \times 11 \times \$12.50 = \$56,238$

Net outcome

	$
Spot market payment	(1,166,667)
Futures market profit	56,238
	(1,110,429)

Hedge efficiency

$$\frac{56,238}{74,197} = 76\%$$

This hedge is not perfect because there is **not** an **exact match** between the exposure and the number of contracts, and because the **spot price** has moved more than the futures price due to the reduction in basis. The actual outcome is likely to differ since basis risk does not decline uniformly in the real world.

45   USA OPTIONS

Tutor's hint. To compare the participating option with the traded option, it is best to look at the same exercise price for both (£1 = $1.65). Since you need to look at the outcomes for a range of possible exchange rate movements, it is convenient to use the range from $1.55 to $1.70 given in the traded option table. Discussion on collars is optional.

Examiner's comment. Poorer candidates confused futures and options, showed a lack of understanding of option premia or the possibility of options lapsing.

(a)   **Current spot rate**

At the current exchange rate of £1 = $1.6100, the receipt of $1,800,000 will produce £1,118,012.

Participating option

Using the **participating option**, there is no premium. An examination of possible receipts under 4 possible exchange rates in 6 months time shows the following.

	$1.55 £	$1.60 £	$1.65 £	$1.70 £
Spot market				
At opening spot rate $1.8 million/$1.61	1,118,012	1,118,012	1,118,012	1,118,012
At closing spot rate $1.8 million/closing rate	1,161,290	1,125,000	1,090,909	1,058,824
Gain/(loss)	43,278	6,988	(27,103)	(59,188)
Options market				
Buy at	1.65	1.65	1.65	1.65
Sell at	1.55	1.60	1.65	1.70
Exercise?	No	No	Yes/No	Yes
Outcome of option position			As for $1.65 on spot market	As for $1.65 on spot market
Net outcome	£	£	£	£
Gain/(loss)	43,278	6,988	(27,103)	(27,103)
Half gain to bank	(21,639)	(3,494)		
Net gain/(loss)	21,639	3,494		

Traded option

Set up option

(i)   Contract date June

(ii)   Option type call

(iii)   Strike price $1.65 and $1.70 have premium costs less than £10,000. Choose $1.65 for comparison

(iv) Number of contracts

$$\frac{1,800,000 \div 1.65}{31,250} \approx 34.9 \text{ contracts, say } 35$$

(v) Tick size $= 31,250 \times 0.0001$
$$= \$3.125$$

(vi) Premium $= \dfrac{1.1}{100} \times 31,250 \times 35$
$$= \$12,031 @ 1.605$$
$$= £7,494$$

Closing prices

As for participating option.

Outcome

		$1.55	$1.60	$1.65	$1.70
(i)	Spot market				

As for participating option

(ii)	Options market					
	Strike price call	$1.65	$1.65	$1.65		$1.65
	Closing price	$1.55	$1.60	$1.65		$1.65
	Exercise ?	No	No	Yes/no		Yes
	Tick movement			500		
	Options outcome			$500 \times 35 \times 3.125 = \$54,688$		

(iii)	Net outcome	£	£	£	£
	Spot market gain/(loss)	43,278	6,988	(27,103)	(59,188)
	Options market gain ÷ spot rate				32,169
	Options premium	(7,494)	(7,494)	(7,494)	(7,494)
		35,784	(506)	(34,597)	(34,513)

Comparison of the two pay-off schedules shows that using the participating option is probably preferable, as the resulting cash receipt is less sensitive to exchange rate fluctuations and, in particular, shows a lower maximum loss.

Creation of collar

As a more advanced use of traded options, the company could consider creating a 'collar'. In order to hedge the purchase of pounds with dollars, the company should buy call options and sell put options.

For example, the cost of purchasing $1.60 options (5.3 cents) can be offset by selling $1.60 put options (4.0 cents). The net premium cost per £ is 1.3 cents.

Receipt $= 1,800,000/1.60$

$= £1,125,000$

Premium $= \$1.3/100 \times 1,125,000$

$= \$14,625$, which at today's spot rate of $1.6055 would be £9,109, which is within the £10,000 limit.

Effect of collar

The combination of two options on the same exercise price *fixes* the exchange rate to £1 = \$1.60. When the net premium cost is added, the effective exchange rate for buying pounds with dollars is £1 = \$1.613. This is an alternative to using forward or futures contracts.

Use of collars with calls and puts on different exercise prices gives a **pay off schedule** with a **risk profile intermediate** between a fixed return and the call option pay off shown above.

(b) If the foreign subsidiary is selling predominantly in its own country, the principle of **matching assets and liabilities** says that the subsidiary should be financed as far as possible in the currency of that country. Ideally the subsidiary will be highly geared with loans and overdrafts in the developing country's currency. If local finance has not been used and the sales invoice which is about to be sent is large, then an overdraft in the same currency should be taken out and the receipt converted to sterling immediately.

If it is impossible to borrow in the local currency, the company should attempt to find a hard currency which is highly positively correlated with the local currency. For example, some countries have a policy of pegging their currency to the US dollar. The receipt can then be hedged by selling the US dollar forward.

This technique is, however, open to the risk that the local currency suddenly devalues against the dollar, as happened in 1997 with a number of Asian currencies. The likelihood of this happening is high if there is high inflation in the country and it has low reserves.

If the company is fairly certain that the local currency is going to devalue and that it cannot borrow in that currency, the **remaining alternatives** are:

(i) **Increase the sales price** by the amount of the expected devaluation and bear the risk

(ii) **Invoice in a hard currency**, for example US dollars, which can then be sold forward

(iii) **Arrange a 'countertrade' agreement** (ie barter) in which the sale of the company's textiles is paid for by the purchase of local raw materials or other products

46   RCB

> **Tutor's hint.** Part (a) of this question is very easy compared with some of its predecessors, with full marks being relatively easy to obtain if you remembered to sell March futures now and buy them back at the end of February. If interest rates rise, the futures price will fall, enabling the company to make a futures gain offsetting the additional interest suffered. The 'sting' was in part (b). Basis risk is the risk that the futures contract does not move by the same number of basis points (or 'ticks') as the underlying interest rate. The key is that, at the date of expiry, the futures contract and the underlying interest rate must have the same value.

(a) **Set up**

(i) Use March contracts; December contracts don't cover full period

(ii) Sell March futures

    (iii) Number of contracts

$$\frac{3{,}000{,}000}{500{,}000} \times \frac{4}{3} = 8 \text{ contracts}$$

Summary

Today (end of September): sell 8 LIFFE sterling three month March contracts at 91.80.

End of February: buy 8 LIFFE sterling three month March contracts.

(b) When a futures contract expires, its price should be identical with the spot price of the underlying commodity. At any time before expiry, its price will be different. For interest rate futures the difference can be measured in basis points, otherwise known as '**ticks**'.

Here the tick size is $0.01\% \times \dfrac{3}{12} \times £500{,}000 = £12.50$

At the end of September, the March sterling 3 month future is trading at 91.80, which represents a sterling interest rate of $100\% - 91.80\% = 8.20\%$. The spot rate for LIBOR is 7.50%. The **basis difference** for the March futures contract is therefore 0.70%, or 70 basis points.

This basis difference will close to zero by the end of March, in six months time. Assuming it closes at an even rate over time (which it probably will not) the basis difference at the end of February (in five months time) will be one-sixth of 70 basis points, that is approximately 12 basis points.

In practice the basis difference in February could be higher or lower than 12 points, depending on movements in yield curves.

If LIBOR rises by 2% to 9.5% by the end of February, the futures contract will be 12 basis points different from this at 9.62%, represented by a futures price of 90.38.

Outcome in spot market

	£
At opening spot rate (£3 million × 9.5% × 4/12)	95,000
At closing spot rate (£3 million × 11.5% × 4/12)	115,000
(Loss)	(20,000)

Outcome in futures market

Opening futures price	91.80 sell
Closing futures price	90.38 Buy
Movement in ticks	142

Futures market profit $142 \times 8 \times £12.50 = £14{,}200$

Net outcome

	£
Spot market payment	115,000
Futures market profit	(14,200)
	100,800

Hedge efficiency

$$\frac{14{,}200}{20{,}000} = 71\%$$

(c) The main importance of the Greeks is that they indicate the **risks** to which an option position is exposed, and hence help determine how best to hedge the risk. The main Greeks are as follows.

(i) **Delta** measures the change in the option price compared with the change in the value of the underlying asset. Delta values are often used when deciding which options to sell or buy, their trend being particularly significant

(ii) **Gamma** measures the amount by which the delta value changes as the share price changes. The gamma value indicates how difficult an option writer will find maintaining a delta hedge; a high gamma value will indicate a greater need for portfolio changes if the value of the underlying security changes.

(iii) **Theta** measures how much the value of the option diminishes over time. Theta increases as the date of option expiry approaches.

(iv) **Rho** measures the sensitivity of the value of the option to interest rate changes.

(v) **Vega** measures the sensitivity of an option's value to a change in its implied volatility. Long-term options tend to have larger Vegas because of the greater uncertainty about the exercise price.

If the value of all the Greeks is at or near zero, it indicates that the position will be unaffected by changes in any of the main risks. Generally hedging strategies will try and keep the total values of Greeks below set levels, to limit the exposures to the underlying risks.

47 **CATHLYN**

> **Tutor's hint.** If you can work your way through the formula and are able to use the discount table, this question is actually not that bad. In (i), we need the standard deviation, σ, so therefore we need to take the square root of the variance which we are given in the question. We have used interpolation to find the values in (ii).

(a) (i) Find (d_1) and (d_2)

$$d_1 = \frac{\ln(3.50/3.30) + (0.08 \times 0.25)}{\sqrt{0.12}\sqrt{0.25}} + (0.5 \times (\sqrt{0.12} \times \sqrt{0.25}))$$
$$= 0.4552 + 0.0866$$
$$= 0.5418$$

$$d_2 = 0.5418 - (\sqrt{0.12}\sqrt{0.25})$$
$$= 0.5418 - 0.1732$$
$$= 0.3686$$

(ii) Find N (d_1) and N (d_2) using normal distribution tables

N (0.5418) $= 0.5 + 0.2060 = 0.7060$
N (0.3686) $= 0.5 + 0.1438 = 0.6438$

(iii) Using the Black-Scholes formula

$$C_0 = (3.50 \times 0.7060) - ((3.30e^{-0.08 \times 0.25}) \times 0.6438)$$
$$= 2.4710 - 2.0825$$
$$= 38.85p$$

(b) The main limitations of the Black-Scholes model are:

(i) The model is **only designed** for the valuation of **European call options**.

(ii) The basic model is based on the assumption that **shares pay no dividends**.

(iii) The model assumes that there will be **no transaction costs**.

(iv) The model assumes knowledge of the **risk-free rate of interest,** and also assumes the risk-free rate will be constant throughout the option's life.

(v)   Likewise the model also assumes accurate knowledge of the **standard deviation of returns,** which is also assumed to be constant throughout the option's life.

48   SARHALL

> **Tutor's hint**. This question illustrates how the data that you need to use in the Black-Scholes formula may be given in an exam question. Remember in (a) that increases in time and volatility are to the benefit of the option holder as they increase the chances of the option holder benefiting from an increase in the security price. If the security price falls to below the exercise price, the option holder will not exercise the option. The data given in the question indicates you can use simple discounting to adjust the value of future dividends. In a more complex scenario, you may have to adjust future dividends by e^{-rT}.

(a)   The value of the option depends on the following variables.

(i)   **The price of the security**

An increase in the price of the security will mean that a call option becomes **more valuable.** Exercising the option will mean purchasing a security that has a higher value.

(ii)   **The exercise price of the option**

An increase in the exercise price will mean that a call option becomes **less valuable;** the profit that can be made from exercising the option will have decreased.

(iii)   **Risk free rate of return**

An increase in the risk free rate will mean that a call option becomes **more valuable.** The purchase of an option rather than the underlying security will mean that the option holder has spare cash available which can be invested at the risk free rate of return. An increase in that rate will mean that it becomes more worthwhile to have spare cash available, and hence to have an option rather than having to buy the underlying security.

(iv)   **Time to expiry of the option**

An increase in the time of expiry will mean that a call option becomes **more valuable,** as the time premium element of the option price has been increased.

(v)   **Volatility of the security price**

An increase in volatility will mean that a call option becomes **more valuable.** An increase in volatility will increase the chance that the security price will be above the exercise price when the option expires.

(b)   To the shareholders the main advantage of any employee incentive scheme should be that employees are highly **motivated** to improve their own wealth and that in doing so they also increase shareholder returns.

Basic salary plus bonus related to the pre-tax profit of the employee's department

To the employees the advantages are as follows.

(i)   **Increased profits** are **rewarded immediately** by the equivalent of a dividend pay-out. The **cash benefit** is **received sooner** than for many share option schemes where employees have to wait for the scheme to come to maturity.

(ii)   The bonus is **based** on the **performance** of the employee's **own department.** Poor performance of other parts of the organisation can be ignored.

The disadvantages are as follows.

(i)   The **basic salary** element is likely to be **lower** than for a 'straight salary' employment. This can cause hardship in years of poor performance.

(ii)   **Poor performance** of a department may **not** be the **fault of the employee**. Some employees may be rewarded more than others simply because they are fortunate enough to work in an already successful department.

To the shareholders the main advantage is that **salary costs** will automatically be **lower** in **years of poor performance**. In other words, the conversion of a fixed salary cost to a variable one lowers the company's operating risk.

There are, however, numerous disadvantages to shareholders of this type of scheme.

(i)   **Departmental profits** will need **auditing**. This is an added expense.

(ii)   Employees can be encouraged to take a **short-term view of profits** (eg a cost-cutting approach, minimising new investment). This may cause the share price to drop.

(iii)   Employees may make **decisions** which **benefit their own department** at the expense of the company as a whole, again causing a drop in share price.

A basic salary plus a share option scheme

A share option scheme gives employees the potential opportunity of **acquiring shares** in the company for a **cheap price**. They can either **retain** the **shares** to **supplement future income with dividends** or sell them to make a capital gain.

The main disadvantage of this type of scheme to employees is seen when the stock market declines and, despite a relatively good performance by the company, the company's **share price** does **not improve**. In this situation, employees may receive **no reward** for their efforts. A good incentive scheme should reward effort, not luck. The Black-Scholes model assumes that the historic volatility of the share price will continue in the future. This may well not be true, and **different volatility** will have a significant impact upon the value of the option when it is due to expire.

Further problems include:

(i)   Employees may have to wait to **receive cash benefits** from the scheme.

(ii)   There is no easy way of **basing rewards** on **departmental performance**.

To shareholders, advantages of the share option scheme are as follows.

(i)   Employees are **motivated** to work towards the **same goal** as **shareholders**, i.e. maximising share values.

(ii)   There are **no subjective estimates** to be audited.

(iii)   The scheme will **not motivate a short-term outlook** unless the time to maturity is too short. From a shareholder's point of view the longer the time horizon the better, but there must be a trade-off with the employee's reduction in motivation if the time horizon is too long. A typical compromise period would be two to three years.

To shareholders, the main disadvantage of share option schemes is the **dilution in earnings** that results when the options are exercised.

(c)   The Black Scholes Formula is:

Call price = Ps N (d$_1$) – Xe^{-rT} N (d$_2$)

The **share price** must be adjusted by the dividends expected to be paid during the option period discounted at the risk-free rate.

$$Ps = 650 - \frac{35}{(1.07)} - \frac{35}{(1.07)^2}$$

$$= 586.72$$

$$d_1 = \frac{\ln(Ps/X) + rT}{\sigma\sqrt{T}} + 0.5\,\sigma\,\sqrt{T}$$

$$= \frac{\ln(586.72/450) + 0.07(2)}{0.35 \times \sqrt{2}} + (0.5 \times 0.35 \times \sqrt{2})$$

$$= 1.0663$$

$$d_2 = 1.0663 - (0.35 \times \sqrt{2})$$

$$= 0.5713$$

$$N(d_1) = 0.5 + 0.3570$$

$$= 0.8570, \text{ using interpolation}$$

$$N(d_2) = 0.5 + 0.2161$$

$$= 0.7161, \text{ using interpolation}$$

$$\text{Call price} = (586.72\,(0.8570)) -$$
$$(450\,e^{-0.07 \times 2}\,(0.7161))$$
$$= 222.67$$

The expected option call price is 222.67p per share, giving a current option value of $6,000 \times 222.67 = £13,360$.

This is some way above the bonuses that would have been paid over the last few years. The options are in the money and will be more attractive to employees.

(d) Put price $= \text{Call price} - Ps + Xe^{-rT}$

$$= 222.67 - 586.72 + 391.21$$

$$= 27.16p$$

Call options are thus more valuable in this situation.

49   MURWALD

> **Tutor's hint.** In part (b), relate the nature of the products to Murwald's specific situation - do not just provide a simple description of the products available.
>
> **Examiner's comment.** Although candidates often showed some knowledge of the principles of hedging, the application of those principles using actual data (part (a)) was very poor, especially with respect to options hedges. Few candidates commented upon whether or not the financial constraint could be met, or discussed the best hedging strategy to be adopted.

The first step is to calculate the amount of interest that Murwald would be liable to pay at the end of six months if interest rates remain at their current levels.

Cash deficit to be financed	£12m
Interest rate (base + 1.5%)	7.5% pa
Proportion of year	50%
Interest	£450,000

The requirement of the Treasury team is that interest charges should not exceed £460,000 (£450,000 + £10,000). Hedges will be based on the assumption that interest rates will rise.

(a) (i)   **Hedge using futures**

Set up

- Either March or June contracts can be used. In this solution use June contracts

- Sell June futures

- Number of contracts

$$\frac{£12\,\text{million}}{£500,000} \times \frac{6}{3} = 48 \text{ contracts}$$

- Tick size

$$(0.01\% \times \frac{3}{12} \times 500,000) = £12.50$$

Closing futures price

93.10 − 1.8 = 91.30 or 93.10 + 0.9 = 94.00

Outcome

- Spot market

	9.5%	6.5%
	£	£
At opening rate (£12m × 7.5% × 6/12)	450,000	450,000
At closing rate (£12m × 9.5%/6.5% × 6/12)	570,000	390,000
(Loss)/Profit	(120,000)	60,000

- Futures outcome

		9.5%	6.5%
At opening rate:	sell 48 @	93.10	93.10
At closing rate:	buy 48 @	91.30	94.00
Tick movement:	$\frac{\text{opening rate} - \text{closing rate}}{0.01}$	180	(90)
Futures Profit/(Loss):	48 × £12.50 × tick movement	108,000	(54,000)

- Net outcome

	£	£
Payment in spot market	(570,000)	(390,000)
Profit/(Loss) in futures market	108,000	(54,000)
Net cost of loan	(462,000)	(444,000)

(ii)   **Hedge using options**

Set-up

- June contracts
- Buy put options
- Strike price 93.50
- 48 contracts
- Tick size £12.50
- Premium 125 ticks
- Total premium 48 × 125 × 12.50 = £75,000

Closing prices

Option 1 Interest rates rise	91.30
Option 2 Interest rates fall	94.00

Outcome

	Option 1	Option 2
	Option 1	*Option 2*
• Spot market outcome	£570,000	£390,000
• Options market outcome		
Strike price right to sell put	93.50	93.50
Closing futures price buy at	91.30	94.00
Exercise?	Yes	No
Tick movement $\dfrac{93.50-91.30}{0.01}$	220	-
Outcome of options positions		
$220 \times 12.50 \times 48$	£132,000	-

• Net position

	£	£
Spot	570,000	390,000
Option	(132,000)	-
Option premium	75,000	75,000
Net outcome	513,000	465,000

The results of the various hedges can be summarised as follows.

The figures represent the saving/(deficit) on the £460,000 interest cost target.

	Futures	Options (9350)
	£	£
2% rise in rates	(2,000)	(53,000)
1% fall in rates	16,000	(5,000)

The calculations show that Murwald will not be able to meet its target with certainty using either futures or options. If a simple choice between the two approaches is to be made, futures provide the best hedge since gains are maximised and losses minimised.

However, an alternative approach would be for Murwald to use a **collar option**. While protecting the company against the cost of increases in interest rates, it would at the same time restrict its ability to profit from favourable movements, thereby effectively fixing its interest rate and reducing its premiums.

For example, it could buy 48 put options at 9400 and sell 48 call options at 9400. This gives a net premium cost of 0.10% (1.84 − 1.74). This effectively fixes costs at the current interest rate for a cost of £12.50 × 10 × 48 = £6,000 and would therefore allow the Treasury team to meet its targets. 9400 equates to the current base rate (100 − 94 = 6%), and gives the company an effective interest rate of 6% + 1.5% + 0.1% = 7.6%.

> **Tutor's hint**. The interest rates the examiner gives are not consistent with an efficient market, since put and call options with the same strike price can be combined to give an artificial futures contract at a lower rate than that quoted for futures. Therefore a number of collar combinations could be designed which would reduce the effective interest rate.

Alternative solution

Since the team is hedging a payment of interest, a **put option** is required.

A put option is the right, but not the obligation, to sell a future in a risk free three month government deposit any time up to the date of expiry of the future (same as option expiry date). What is important is that the value of this right will increase as short term interest rates rise, and this compensates for the rise in interest costs on the underlying loan.

Level at which 'insurance' is available (ignoring Murwald's risk premium), if the option is held to delivery.

Price	Exercise rate	Premium	Total rate
9300	7.0%	0.92%	7.92%
9350	6.5%	1.25%	7.75%
9400	6.0%	1.84%	7.84%
9450	5.5%	2.90%	8.40%
9500	5.0%	3.46%	8.46%

The corporate treasury team 'does not want interest payments during the six month period to increase by more than £10,000 from the amounts that would be paid at current interest rates'.

The £10,000 premium represents a movement of 10,000/12m = 0.0833%/6 months = 0.167% pa, ie 6.167% + risk premium. The available rates are substantially above this, even allowing for the slight adjustments necessary because the futures market does not exactly follow the underlying spot.

Conclusion: **options alone** cannot be used to hedge the exposure within the requisite limits.

An **artificial futures contract** can be **created by buying a put option** and simultaneously writing a call at the same exercise price. (This can be thought of as a tight collar.) If rates fell below the exercise price the company would lose on the call, and if rates rose above the exercise price they would gain on the put. This is what happens with a futures contract.

Arbitrage says that in the real world, the value of an artificial futures contract should be very close to a real future: otherwise an arbitrage opportunity exists. However, in this example, the net cost of buying a put option and selling a call is as follows.

Price	Exercise rate	Put premium	Call premium	Net
9300	7.0%	0.92%	2.55%	5.37%
9350	6.5%	1.25%	2.20%	5.55%
9400	6.0%	1.84%	1.74%	6.10%
9450	5.5%	2.90%	1.32%	7.08%
9500	5.0%	3.46%	0.87%	7.59%

(ie, in the real world, 5.37 = 5.55 = 6.1 = 7.08 = 7.59 = futures price for a June future at the same date.)

However, in this question there is obviously the opportunity to construct an artificial future at 6.1% (at 9400), ie a 0.1% premium on the market – less than £10,000 above the market 6% rate. There are even better opportunities at 9300 and 9350!

(b) Alternative derivative products that could be considered include the following.

(i) **Forward rate agreements (FRAs)** are agreements, usually with a bank, that fix the rate of interest on future borrowings (or deposits). Murwald could enter into an agreement to **fix the interest rate** at 7.5% (for example). If rates rose to a higher level the bank would compensate the company for the difference in interest incurred. If rates fell, then Murwald would have to make a similar payment to the bank.

A likely disadvantage of this product is that the **rate negotiated** by the bank will **reflect the bank's own expectations** of interest rate movements. If the bank also expects a significant rise in rates, Murwald is unlikely to be able to negotiate a FRA at the rate it would need to achieve its targets.

    (ii) **Interest rate swaps** are transactions that exploit different interest rates in different markets for borrowing. Two companies, or a company and a bank, swap interest rate commitments with each other. Thus Murwald might be able to convert its floating rate interest into a fixed rate liability thereby fixing its interest costs at somewhere near to present levels. Swaps are **cheap and easy** to arrange, but it may be **difficult to restrict the period** to six months.

    (iii) **Over the counter (OTC) options** are similar in form to the traded options considered above, but instead of being purchased on the exchange, they are obtained from a bank and tailored to suit the company's specific requirements. Murwald would be able to buy some form of collar that might be appropriate, but the **cost could be higher** than using LIFFE.

    (iv) **Swaptions**. This is a **traded option** to **buy an interest rate swap**. Thus Murwald could buy an option to enter into a swap within a prescribed period. The **cost** of a swaption is likely to be relatively **high** if there is a general expectation of a rise in rates and it may not achieve the financial targets that Murwald has set.

50 HYK

> **Tutor's hint**. In part (a) the question does not give a suggested figure for the movement in the price of the futures contract. It is better to assume that basis risk narrows evenly over the life of the contract. Alternatively you may assume that there is no change in basis risk. In either case, state your assumption, but see examiner's comment.
>
> **Examiner's comment.** Common problems in (a) were using the wrong number of contracts in the hedge, use of the wrong month, buying rather than selling (remember selling will mean a profit is made if interest rates rise and futures are bought back at a lower price), or buying and selling futures contracts. The company aims to protect against the most significant risk. Candidates also failed to consider basis risk.
>
> In (b) many candidates confused exchange traded options with foreign exchange linked options; even where the correct options were discussed, there was little consideration of their advantages. In (c) many relevant factors, including exercise price, maturity date, and whether a call or put option was being purchased were only rarely discussed.

(a) The cost for HYK plc of borrowing £18 million for 4 months at today's rate of LIBOR + 0.75% (6.5% + 0.75% = 7.25%) is £18m × 4/12 × 7.25% = £435,000.

$$\text{Maximum interest desirable} = £18\text{m} \times 4/12 \times 7.5\%$$
$$= £450,000$$

Hedging the borrowing rate using futures

Setup

(i) Either March or June contracts; use March

(ii) Sell March futures

(iii) Number of contracts

$$\frac{£18 \text{ million}}{£500,000} \times \frac{4}{3} = 48 \text{ contracts}$$

(iv) Tick size

$$(0.01\% \times \frac{3}{12} \times 500,000) = £12.50$$

Estimate closing futures price

March contract expires in 4 months
LIBOR is 6.5% (93.50)

March contract basis risk 93.50 – 93.10 = 40 ticks

1 February $40 \times \dfrac{2}{4} = 20$ ticks

$\Rightarrow$ If LIBOR rises to 8% (92.00) future will be 91.80.

If LIBOR falls to 6% (94.00) future will be 93.80.

Outcome

The results of the hedge under cases (i) and (ii) are shown below.

(i) **Spot market**

	(i)	(ii)
LIBOR	8.0%	6.0%
Spot market	£	£
At opening rate (as above)	435,000	435,000
At closing rate (LIBOR + 0.75%) × £18m × 4/12	525,000	405,000
Profit/(Loss)	(90,000)	30,000

(ii) **Futures market**

	Rises	*Falls*
1 Dec: Sell 48 @	93.10	93.10
1 Feb: Buy 48 @	91.80	93.80
Tick movement: $\dfrac{\text{opening rate} - \text{closing rate}}{0.01}$	130	(70)
Profit / (Loss) 48 contracts × £12.50 × tick movement	78,000	(42,000)

(iii) **Net outcome**

	£	£
Payment in spot market	(525,000)	(405,000)
Profit/(Loss) in futures market	78,000	(42,000)
Net cost of loan	(447,000)	(447,000)
As annual % (Cost/£18m × 12/4)	7.45%	7.45%

In both cases the net interest cost after hedging is below the target maximum of £450,000 (or 7.50%).

In practice **basis risk** may **not move evenly**. Potential futures gains or losses between December and February may be large if interest rates are volatile, because they are computed on a daily basis.

Hedging the borrowing rate using traded options

Setup

(i) March or June contracts can be used. Assume March, since this will have a lower time premium at close out on 1 March.

(ii) Buy put options

(iii) A strike price of 93.50 will be used since this is closest to today's LIBOR. (100 – 6.5 = 93.50)

(iv) Number of contracts 48

(v) Tick size £12.50

(vi) Option premium March Put 0.60, 60 ticks

Total premium = 48 × 60 × 12.50 = £36,000

Closing prices

	(i)	(ii)
Spot	8.75%	6.75%
Futures	91.80	93.80

Outcome

		(i)	(ii)
(i)	**Spot market outcome**	£525,000	£405,000

(ii)   **Option market outcome**

On 1 February, the possibilities are:

	(i)	(ii)
	Rises	Falls
LIBOR	Rises	Falls
Put option strike price (right to sell)	93.50	93.50
March futures price	91.80	93.80
Exercise option? (prefer to sell at highest price)	Yes	No
Gain (ticks)	170	nil
Option outcome (170 × 12.50 × 48)	£102,000	nil

(iii)   Net position

	£	£
Actual interest cost	(525,000)	(405,000)
Value of option gain	102,000	nil
Premium	(36,000)	(36,000)
Net cost of loan	(459,000)	(441,000)
Effective interest cost (cost/18m × 12/4)	7.65%	7.35%

Similarly, the results of using options with the other two strike prices are shown below

Strike price	94.00		93.00	
Premium on setup	135 ticks × 48 × 12.50 = 81,000		20 ticks × 48 × 12.50 = 12,	
	(i)	(ii)	(i)	(ii)
	Rises	Falls	Rises	Falls
LIBOR	Rises	Falls	Rises	Falls
Put option exercise price	94.00	94.00	93.00	93.00
March futures price	91.80	93.80	91.80	93.80
Exercise option?	Yes	Yes	Yes	No
Buy 48 @	91.80	93.80	91.80	No action
Sell 48 @	94.00	94.00	93.00	No action
Gain (ticks)	220	20	120	-
Option outcome	132,000	12,000	72,000	-
	£	£	£	£
Actual interest cost	(525,000)	(405,000)	(525,000)	(405,000)
Value of option gain	132,000	12,000	72,000	-
Premium	(81,000)	(81,000)	(12,000)	(12,000)
Net cost of loan	(474,000)	(474,000)	(465,000)	(417,000)
Effective interest cost	7.90%	7.90%	7.75%	6.95%

If LIBOR rises, none of the options **allow** the **required maximum** of 7.50%. If LIBOR falls, the cheapest option (the 93.50 option) is the best, but this is, of course the situation where no hedge is needed. The futures hedge appears to be better.

However, the time value of the options sold, which still have 2 months to expiry, has been ignored in these calculations. This is likely to have a significant impact on the calculations.

(b) Advantages of traded interest rate options are:

    (i)   The **prices** are **clearly visible** and no negotiation is required.

    (ii)   The market place gives **quick access** to buyers and sellers.

    (iii)   The **options** can be **sold** if not required and there is still time to expiry.

    (iv)   **Gains or losses** are **computed** ('marked to market') on a **daily basis** and ability of counterparties to meet obligations is monitored.

    (v)   **Traded options** are **normally American-style** (ie can be exercised at any time). They are more flexible than many OTC options which are European-style (i.e. can only be exercised on maturity date).

    (vi)   The market is **more highly regulated** than the OTC market.

The main advantage of **OTC options** is that they can be **tailored more exactly** to the **needs** of the purchaser, in terms of maturity date, contract size, currency and nature of interest. **Contract sizes** are **larger** than on the traded markets and longer times to expiry are available.

(c) Interest rate option prices are affected by:

    (i)   The **underlying interest rate** and the **price of** the specific interest bearing security which the option gives the right to buy or sell

    (ii)   The **exercise price**

    (iii)   Time to **expiry**

    (iv)   **Volatility** of the underlying interest bearing security

Options can seem expensive, but this is because they act like an **insurance policy**, providing protection against increased interest costs but allowing the purchaser to take advantage of interest rate falls. OTC option prices are not as transparent as market traded options, but there is a competitive market of banks and other sellers. As a safeguard, prices can be **checked** against **option pricing models** and inexperienced purchasers are advised to seek advice in this respect.

Marking guide		Marks	
(a)	Interest rate costs	1-2	
	Number of contracts	1	
	Sell March futures	1	
	Hedge calculation interest rates rise	2	
	Hedge calculation interest rates fall	2	
	Overall interest costs	1	
	Options (need at least 2 exercise prices for full marks)		
	March put options rise	1	
	Interest rates		
	Option premiums and gains from hedge	2	
	Interest costs	2	
	Interest rates fall		
	Correct exercise/don't exercise decision	1	
	Interest costs	2	
	Conclusion	1-2	
			18
(b)	Points with comment 1 mark each		6
(c)	Option price determinants	3-4	
	Expense of options	2-3	
			6
			30

51   TAYQUER

> **Tutor's hint**. The question asks for a recommendation of the exercise prices to be used. In the case of the put option this can only be done with reference to the expected movements in interest rates. There is no absolute 'right' answer. When calculating the premium costs, remember that the rates quoted are *annual* rates for *three month* contracts. Follow the answer carefully if you are unsure about how such a collar works.
>
> **Examiner's comment**. Some candidates with little knowledge of collars unwisely attempted this question.

(a)   **Interest rate exposure** arises when a company's borrowing is such that a change in interest rates might expose it to interest charges that are unacceptably high. For example, if a company has a large tranche of debt at a fixed rate of interest that is due for repayment in the near future, and the loan is to be replaced or renegotiated, the company would be vulnerable to a sudden increase in market interest rates.

Risk management in this context involves using **hedging techniques** to reduce or 'cover' an exposure. However, hedging has a cost, which will either take the form of a fee to a financial institution or a reduction in profit, and this must be weighed against the reduction in financial risks that the hedge achieves. The extent to which the exposure is covered is known as the 'hedge efficiency'. A perfect hedge has an efficiency of 100%.

Methods of managing interest rate risk include the following.

Forward interest rate agreements (FRAs)

A FRA is an agreement, usually between a company and a bank, about the **interest rate** on a future loan or deposit. The agreement will **fix the rate of interest for borrowing** for a certain time in the future. If the actual rate of interest at that time is above that agreed, the bank pays the company the difference, and vice versa. Thus the company benefits from effectively fixing the rate of interest on a loan for a given period, but it may miss the opportunity to benefit from any favourable movements in rates during that time. A FRA is simply an agreement about rates – it does not involve the movement of the principal sum – the actual borrowing must be arranged separately.

Futures

A **financial future** is an **agreement** on the future price of a financial variable. Interest rate futures are similar in all respects to FRAs, except that the terms, sums involved, and periods are standardised. They are traded on the London International Futures and Options Exchange (LIFFE). Their standardised nature makes them less attractive to corporate borrowers because it is not always possible to match them exactly to specific rate exposures. Each contract will require the payment of a small initial deposit.

Interest rate options

An interest rate guarantee (or option) provides the **right to borrow a specified amount** at a guaranteed rate of interest. The option guarantees that the interest rate will not rise above a specified level during a specified period. On the date of expiry of the option the buyer must decide **whether or not to exercise his right to borrow**. He will only exercise the option if actual interest rates have risen above the option rate. The advantage of options is that the buyer cannot lose on the interest rate and can take advantage of any favourable rate movements. However, a premium must be paid regardless of whether or not the option is exercised. Options can be negotiated directly with the bank or traded in a standardised form on the LIFFE.

(b) **Collars** make use of **interest rate options** to limit exposure to the risk of movement in rates. The company would arrange both a **ceiling** or **cap** (an upper limit) and a **floor** (a lower limit) on its interest yield. The use of the cap means that the cost is lower than for a floor alone.

Since Tayquer requires protection for the next eight months, it will need to use March options in order to cover the full period. It is assumed that the floor will be fixed at the current yield of 7.5%. This implies that it will buy call options at 9250. At the same time, Tayquer will limit its ability to benefit from rises in rates by selling a put option at a higher rate, for example 8.5% (or 9150).

If Tayquer does take out the options as described above, the effect will be as follows.

(i)   If interest rates fall below 7.5%, Tayquer will **exercise the call option** and effectively fix its interest rate at 7.5%. The loss on the interest rate will be borne by the seller of the call option.

(ii)   If interest rates remain between the 7.5% floor and the 8.5% ceiling, Tayquer will **do nothing** but will benefit from the effect of any increase in rates above 7.5% within this band.

(iii)   If interest rates rise above 8.5%, the **buyer of the put option** will **exercise their option** once the futures price rises above 9150. Tayquer will effectively achieve an interest rate of 8.5%, but the benefit of any premium on rates above 8.5% will accrue to the buyer of the put option.

The level of premiums payable will depend on the different sizes of collar. The number of three-month contracts required for eight months' cover will be:

$$\frac{£9.75m}{£0.5m} \times \frac{8}{3} = 52 \text{ contracts } (£26m)$$

The premiums payable at different sizes of collar (in annual percentage terms) will be:

Call	Premium	Put	Premium	Net premium	£ cost*
9250	0.68	9200	0.13	0.55	35,750
9250	0.68	9150	0.06	0.62	40,300
9250	0.68	9100	0.02	0.66	42,900

(* eg £26m × 0.55% × ¼ = £35,750)

The potential gross interest rate gain, and the net gain/(loss) taking premiums into account if rates do rise to the various exercise prices, are as follows. The interest rate gain is calculated on £9.75m for eight months.

Put price	Interest rate % rise	Interest gain £	Premium £ cost (above)	Net gain £
9200	0.50	32,500	(35,750)	(3,250)
9150	1.00	65,000	(40,300)	24,700
9100	1.50	97,500	(42,900)	54,600

This suggests that Tayquer could make the greatest potential gain by selling put options at 9100.

In practice, costs will be higher due to the transaction costs that will be incurred.

52 PROJECTIONS

> **Tutor's hint**. This question requires an understanding of how interest rate options can be used to manage short-term interest rate risk, including appropriate calculations. The only slightly confusing part is the fact that the company does not require an exact number of contracts to match the size of the cash flow deficit. In this situation, you should round up the number of contracts to ensure that the risk is fully hedged. In (b) only the final four years of the loan are relevant to the calculations which should incorporate the premium into the effective annual interest rate of the fixed rate loan being offered.
>
> **Examiner's comment**. Weaknesses in (b) were confusion of swaps and swaptions, and incorrect illustration of the circumstances when the swaption would be of value.

(a) It appears that although interest rates are likely to rise over the next five months, it is possible that they could fall instead. In this type of situation, options are useful in that they allow the company to be protected against adverse rate movements but at the same time to benefit if the rate does move in the company's favour. The drawback to the use of interest rate options is that the premium costs tend to be quite high. However, the company could restrict the premium costs by using a collar.

The outcomes on the spot market, and if the company used options, are as follows.

Setup

(i) June contract

(ii) Buy put options

(iii) Exercise price 93.00 (100.00 − 7.00)

(iv) Number of contracts $\dfrac{\text{£2 million}}{\text{£0.5 million}} \times \dfrac{5}{3} = 6.67$, say 7 contracts

(v) Tick size
£0.5 million $\times$ 0.01% $\times$ 3/12 = £12.50

(vi) Premium at 93.00 June puts = 0.59 = 59 ticks

Contracts $\times$ Premium in ticks $\times$ Tick value = $7 \times 59 \times$ £12.50 = £5,162

Closing prices

	Interest rates rise by 1%	*Interest rates fall by 0.75%*
Spot price (LIBOR + 1.5%)	9.5%	7.75%
Futures price (assume basis zero)	92.00	93.75

Outcome

(i)	Spot market outcome	*Interest rates rise by 1%*	*Interest rates fall by 0.75%*
	At period end	£2m $\times$ 9.5% $\times$ 5/12 = £79,167	£2m $\times$ 7.75% $\times$ 5/12 = £64,583
(ii)	Options market outcome	93.00	93.00
	Closing futures price	92.00	93.75
	Exercise?	Yes	No
	Tick movement	100	-
	Outcome	100 $\times$ 12.50 $\times$ 7 = £8,750	-

(iii)   Net position

	£	£
Actual interest cost	(79,167)	(64,583)
Option	8,750	-
Premium	(5,162)	(5,162)
Net outcome	(75,579)	(69,745)
Position if interest rates unchanged		
£2m × 8.5% × 5/12	70,833	70,833
Net position	75,579	69,745
Net profit/(loss)	(4,746)	1,088

(b)   A **swaption** is a derivative product which combines the features of different financial hedging instruments. It is an instrument which is traded on the OTC market and is effectively an option to buy an interest rate (or currency) swap during a specified time period and at a specified rate. A swaption would therefore offer Noswis protection against rises in interest rates and at the same time allow it to take advantage of falls in rates. A '**European-style**' swaption is exercisable only on the maturity date while an '**American-style**' swaption is exercisable on any business day during the exercise period.

The swaption would be likely to be exercised if interest rates rose above 9.5%.

To evaluate the benefit of the swaption, ignoring the time value of money, it is first necessary to evaluate its cost over the remaining four year period of the loan.

	SFr
Interest: SFr3million × 9.5% × 4	1,140,000
Premium	100,000
Total cost	1,240,000

This represents an effective annual rate of interest of 10.33% $\left(\dfrac{1,240,000}{\text{SFr3m} \times 4} \right)$. The average rate of interest payable by Noswis without the swap would therefore have to exceed 10.33% for the swaption to be beneficial.

If interest rates fall, the swaption will not be exercised and the company will be able to take advantage of lower interest payments.

The company should also take into account the fact that if it does enter into the agreement, the **premium** will be payable whether or not the swaption is exercised. The premium is effectively the price paid for the possibility of taking advantage of lower interest rates.

53   SOMAX

> **Tutor's hint**. In part (a), you should take into account the absolute size of the loan and the Euromarket alternatives, ie a direct issue by the company as compared with a Euroloan.
>
> The question states both that 'the systematic risk of debt may be assumed to be zero' and 'Somax can borrow in Swiss Francs at a floating rate of between 5.75% and 6%... Swiss Franc Libor is currently 5%'. These statements appear to be contradictory.
>
> In part (c), the cost of the bond can be estimated by comparison with the existing five year bond. This can then be used in the marginal rate calculations to evaluate the swap.
>
> **Examiner's comment**. In part (a), many focused on foreign exchange risk, which is largely irrelevant as the loan could be arranged in the same currency in most domestic banking systems and the euromarkets.

(a) (i) At current exchange rates of around SFr2.4/£, the **size of the deal** equates to approximately £93m. This is an unusually large amount to borrow from a single bank, although it is possible that the loan could be arranged through one of the largest Swiss banks. However, for a loan of this size it would be more likely to spread the arrangement across a number of banks which would also have the advantage of spreading the risk of default. Long-term loans of this size could be of either fixed or floating rate, and therefore obtaining floating rate finance would not be a problem.

Advantages of using the banking system are that once arranged such a loan would be very secure, and that the very size of the arrangement with a reputable bank would enhance the credit rating of the company should it wish to raise further finance from other sources.

The principal **disadvantage** is that due to the **level of regulation and reserve requirements**, the cost of the loan is likely to be higher than if it were to be raised from other sources. This is because the spread between the rates at which the banks lend and borrow is higher to finance their additional costs. It is also likely that the banks will require **security** in the form of a charge over the assets of the company.

(ii) If Somax elects to use the Euromarkets it could either issue securities such as **Eurobonds** directly, or it could raise a **Euroloan** through the international banking system. The length of term required would make this probably too long-term for a loan on the Eurocurrency market, but a **Eurocredit** arranged through the international banks would be a possibility. Such loans are normally floating rate so this would not be a problem. Advantages include the fact that security is less likely to be required and arrangement costs are relatively low.

The alternative is for Somax to issue **Euronotes or some other form of paper**, and these may be tailored to make them more attractive to investors eg with warrants attached. A further advantage is that the cost of the finance is likely to be lower than if it is arranged through the banks, and no security will be required. Disadvantages include the length of time it will take to arrange the issue and the costs of the issue itself, which will be higher than the arrangement fee for a loan.

(b) The discount rate that should be used is the **weighted average cost of capital (WACC)**, with weightings based on market values. The cost of capital should take into account the **systematic risk** of the new investment, and therefore it will not be appropriate to use Somax's existing equity beta. Instead, the estimated equity beta of the main Swiss competitor in the same industry as the new proposed plant will be ungeared, and then the capital structure of Somax applied to find the WACC to be used for the discount rate.

Since the systematic risk of debt can be assumed to be zero, the Swiss equity beta can be **ungeared** using the following expression.

$$\beta_a = \beta_e \frac{E}{E + D(1-t)}$$

where: β_a = asset beta

         β_e = equity beta

         E   = proportion of equity in capital structure

         D   = proportion of debt in capital structure

         t   = tax rate

For the Swiss company:

$$\beta_a = 1.5 \times \frac{60}{60 + 40(1 - 0.33)}$$

$$= 1.037$$

The next step is to calculate the debt and equity of Somax based on market values.

			£m
Equity:	2 × 225m = 450m shares at 376p		1,692.00
Debt:	Bank loans		135.00
	Bonds (75m × 1.195)		89.63
	Total debt		224.63

This can now be substituted into the **capital asset pricing model (CAPM)** to find the cost of equity.

$$Ke = r_f + [E(r_m) - r_f]\,\beta_a$$

where: Ke = cost of equity
r_f = risk free rate of return
$E(r_m)$ = market rate of return
Ke = 7.75% + (14.5% – 7.75%) × 1.037 ≐ 14.75%

Then, re-gear at the company's gearing ratio, using MM:

$$WACC_g = Ke_u\left[1 - \frac{Dt}{E + D}\right]$$

$$= 14.75 \times (1 - (224.63 \times 0.33)/(1{,}692 + 224.63)) = 14.18\%$$

(c) (i) The **annual interest cost** to Somax of issuing a five year sterling fixed rate bond is not known. It can probably best be estimated by comparison with the existing 14% fixed rate bonds due to mature in five years time and redeemable at £100. The effective interest rate on this bond is that at which the cost of the remaining interest payments and redemption equals the current market price of £119.50. This can be calculated as follows:

	£14 × 5 year annuity at n%
plus	£100 discounted at n% in five years time
equals	£119.50

This can be estimated by trial and error from present value and annuity tables. (Alternatively, the internal rate of return of the cash flows relating to the bond can be calculated.)

		£
At 9%:	£14 × 3.890	54.46
	£100 × 0.650	65.00
		119.46

This is very close to £119.50, and therefore the cost of the five year fixed rate bond is approximately 9%.

Summary of swap transactions

	Somax	*Swiss co*
Borrowing (actual)	(9.0%)	(SFr LIBOR + 1.5%)
Payments		
Somax to Swiss co.	(SFr LIBOR + 1.0%)	SFr LIBOR + 1.0%
Swiss co. to Somax	9.5%	(9.5%)
Net payment after swap	(SFr LIBOR + 0.5%)	(10%)

If Somax were to enter into the **swap**, it would receive a fixed rate of interest from the Swiss company of 9.5% per year, which represents a net benefit of 0.5% (9.5% – 9%). At the same time it would pay the Swiss company at SFr LIBOR +

1.0% per year, making a net cost of SFr LIBOR + 0.5% per year. The alternative would be to borrow directly at SFr LIBOR + 0.75% per year (5.75% − 5.0%). Thus the swap offers Somax a gain over direct borrowing of 0.25% per year. Against this must be offset the annual fee to the bank of 0.20%, giving Somax a net gain of 0.05% per year.

From the point of view of the Swiss company, it can borrow directly at SFr LIBOR + 1.5%. Against this can be offset the annual interest payments from Somax of SFr LIBOR + 1.0%, making a net cost of 0.5% per year in addition to the 9.5% interest payment to Somax. This equates to an annual cost of 10.5%, to which must be added the bank fee of 0.2% giving a total cost of 10.2%. This compares with the cost to the Swiss company of borrowing fixed rate sterling at 10.5% per annum - a net annual benefit of 0.30%.

Thus both parties will benefit from the swap, although the Swiss company stands to gain more than Somax. However, if the SFr strengthens against the pound, then the benefits to Somax could be further reduced since the value of the sterling interest payments will fall relative to those denominated in SFr.

(ii)   The **benefits of swaps** include the following.

(1)   The companies may be able to **structure** the **timing of payments** so as to improve the matching of cash outflows with revenues.

(2)   The companies gain **access to debt finance** in another country and currency where it is little known, and consequently has a poorer credit rating, than in its own country.

(3)   The swap provides a **hedge against currency risk** for the full five year period.

(4)   Swaps give the companies the opportunity to **restructure their interest rate liabilities** in terms of the relative proportions of fixed rate and floating rate debt, without the need to restructure the debt base itself.

(5)   The bank **benefits from the fees** from the swap; it may also gain the opportunity to undertake further business with the two parties if it is not already their first line bank.

The **disadvantages of swaps** include the following.

(1)   There is the **risk** of one of the parties **defaulting**.

(2)   There is the **risk** that **interest rates** and **exchange rates** could **move** in such a way that the net payments arising as a result of the swap are higher than they would have been had the swap not been undertaken.

(3)   If the bank takes on a temporary role in the financing during the arrangement of the swap, it runs the risk that rates could **move during the delay** involved in completing the transactions.

54   PZP

> **Tutor's hint.** Part (a) is a standard computation to test the viability of an interest rate swap. Part (b) is a variation from the normal question asked but the requirements are clear enough. The only unusual point is the use of the floating rate as discount rate.

(a) Compare the rates at which the two companies can borrow from the market:

	Fixed	*Floating*
PZP plc	11.35%	LIBOR + 0.60%
Foreten plc	12.80%	LIBOR + 1.35%
Differential	1.45%	0.75%

	%
Difference between the differentials (1.45% – 0.75%)	0.70
Less bank commission	0.25
Available arbitrage gain	0.45
Gain required by PZP	0.40
Gain available for Foreten	0.05

PZP has comparative advantage borrowing fixed rate, so it will gain if it borrows at fixed and swaps into floating rate. The reverse is true for Foreten. The **arbitrage gain** figures show that a swap can be arranged which will benefit all parties, but PZP gains much more than Foreten, who may not agree to the deal.

(b) (i) Amount borrowed = £15m.

If PZP borrows at fixed rate of 11.35%, annual interest is £1.7025m.

If it uses the swap, its rate will be LIBOR + 0.6% – 0.4% gain = LIBOR + 0.2%, that is 10.7% in year 1 and 12% in years 2 to 5. These swap rates are also the discount rates.

Year	*Fixed interest* £m	*Floating rate interest* %	£m	*Interest difference* £m	*Discount factor*	*PV* £m
1	1.7025	10.70	1.605	0.0975	0.903	0.0880
2 - 5	1.7025	12.00	1.800	(0.0975)	2.712	(0.2644)
						(0.1764)

Discount factor year 1 = 1/1.107.
Discount factor years 2 – 5 = 12% annuity years 1 – 4 /1.12 = 3.037/1.12.

In situation (i), the swap leaves PZP worse off by £176,400.

(ii)

Year	*Fixed interest* £m	*Floating rate interest* %	£m	*Interest difference* £m	*Discount factor*	*PV* £m
1	1.7025	10.70	1.605	0.0975	0.903	0.0880
2	1.7025	10.70	1.605	0.0975	0.816	0.0796
3	1.7025	10.70	1.605	0.0975	0.737	0.0719
4	1.7025	9.00	1.350	0.3525	0.708	0.2496
5	1.7025	9.00	1.350	0.3525	0.650	0.2291
						0.7182

In situation (ii), PZP is better off by £718,200 if it uses the swap.

The figures reflect the risk of borrowing at floating rate. If interest rates rise the company loses out but if they fall it gains. PZP will be aware of this risk and will not enter into the swap if it believes interest rates are going to rise significantly. These calculations are unlikely to affect PZP's decision to use the swap because the 0.4% gain will give it a significant advantage in expected value terms.

(c) The main purpose of a delta hedge is to ascertain what securities need to be added to a position to make it **delta-neutral**, that is to reduce delta to zero and thus eliminate the risk of the option position. If the hedge is carried out correctly, any change in the value of the underlying security will be exactly offset by changes in the values of options.

BPP
PUBLISHING

Original number of shares held to be delta-neutral can be calculated as:

Number of shares = Number of contracts × Delta × Size of contract

$$= 200 \times 0.8 \times 1,000$$
$$= 160,000 \text{ shares}$$

If the delta changes to 0.5 then

Number of shares = $200 \times 0.5 \times 1,000$
$$= 100,000 \text{ shares}$$

Thus 60,000 shares must be sold to maintain the hedge.

55 PREPARATION QUESTION: EXCHANGE RATE SYSTEMS

> **Tutor's hint**. You should have illustrated exchange rate systems with actual examples.

The foreign exchange rate systems of countries fall into a number of different categories, ranging along a spectrum from 'fixed' to 'independent float'.

Fixed

The objective of fixed exchange rates between two or more countries is that the rate should not change. There are a number of different examples:

(a) The **Eurozone currencies** of Europe are now exchanged at a fixed rate against the euro. There is a central European bank. In effect, the euro is the only currency in this zone. The original currencies will disappear according to a planned timetable.

(b) Many currencies of smaller countries are '**pegged**', that is fixed, against a stronger currency such as the US dollar. These countries all have their own central banks and can determine their own monetary policy. Inevitably, divergence of economic fundamentals necessitates periodic revaluations of some of these currencies.

(c) In the same way, a currency may be pegged against a **basket of currencies**, often of countries with which there are strong trading links. The objective is to create a more stable base for the exchange rate than is possible with just one currency.

Independent float

At the other extreme are approximately 50 countries allowing their currency exchange rates to be determined, in theory, entirely by market forces. This system is known as an independent float. In practice, however, there is sometimes intervention by governments, for example if an exchange rate is thought to be suffering a temporary decline because of speculative forces. This implies that many independent floats are in fact managed floats (see below).

Limited variations in exchange rate

Many countries allow their currency exchange rate to float within predefined boundaries. Examples include:

(a) **Managed float** (sometimes called a 'dirty float'). The aim is to keep the currency within an unofficial **upper and lower range** against a 'strong' currency. The central bank will buy or sell the currency in an attempt to keep within the pre-defined range (which is usually not publicised). Recently, for example, financial resources of several countries were mobilised in an attempt to maintain the value of the euro against the dollar.

(b) A **fixed exchange rate** within published **tolerance limits**. This is an example of a managed float where the range between upper and lower limits is very small and is officially acknowledged. It was used during the **Exchange Rate Mechanism (ERM)** period in Europe (before the creation of the euro) in which the participating countries allowed small variations against each other but, as a group, floated freely against external currencies such as the US dollar.

(c) The exchange rate against a **hard currency** is adjusted in response to changes in economic **indicators** (eg inflation). This has the advantage of allowing for longer term trends while avoiding the short term speculative fluctuations of independent float.

56 AXELOT

> **Tutor's hint**. This question requires an analysis of the effect of the projections on financial performance under the different financing options. State clearly how any ratios are calculated, and assumptions used in making projections. The question also provides the opportunity to demonstrate an understanding of the purchasing power parity theory of exchange rates.

(a) In order to assess to feasibility of Mr Axelot's proposal it is necessary to calculate the effect of 100% debt finance on some of the key financial performance indicators. In particular, attention should be directed to **earnings per share**, **interest cover** and **gearing** since these represent the effect on the financial risk of the company, and therefore the likely effect on the ordinary shareholders and the market valuation of the shares.

The effect on these indicators of financing expansion using a 13% debenture is calculated below. It can be seen that the growth in earnings is sufficient to support 100% debt financing and still produce an **improvement in interest cover** and earnings per share, as well as a reduction in the level of gearing. Thus, contrary to expectations, the policy does appear to be feasible.

Year	0	1	2	3	4	5
	£'000	£'000	£'000	£'000	£'000	£'000
EBIT (+20% pa)	13,750	16,500	19,800	23,760	28,512	34,214
Interest	(3,000)	(3,650)	(4,300)	(4,950)	(5,600)	(6,250)
	10,750	12,850	15,500	18,810	22,912	27,964
Tax (Note 1)	(3,762)	(4,497)	(5,425)	(6,583)	(8,019)	(9,787)
	6,988	8,353	10,075	12,227	14,893	18,177
Dividend (@ 40%)	(2,795)	(3,341)	(4,030)	(4,891)	(5,957)	(7,271)
Retained profit	4,193	5,012	6,045	7,336	8,936	10,906
EPS (p) (Note 2)	43.7	52.2	63.0	76.4	93.1	113.6
Interest cover (Note 3)	4.6	4.5	4.6	4.8	5.1	5.5
Total debt	24,000	29,000	34,000	39,000	44,000	49,000
Equity	24,600	29,612	35,657	42,993	51,929	62,835
Gearing (Note 4)	97.6%	97.9%	95.4%	90.7%	84.7%	78.0%

Notes

1 Taxation is assumed to be at the same rate as in the year ending 31 March 20X1 (35%).

2 Earnings per share is calculated as earnings available to equity ie profit after tax but before dividend, divided by the number of shares in issue (4,000 / 0.25 = 16,000).

3 Interest cover is calculated as earnings before interest and tax divided by interest.

4   Gearing is calculated as total debt over equity. Included in the total debt figure are short-term loans, overdrafts, debentures and loan stock and unsecured bank loans.

When assessing these figures however, it should be borne in mind that they are likely to be **sensitive** both to **earnings growth** being **lower than predicted**, and to the actual interest rate being higher than predicted. Either of these circumstances could produce an outcome significantly worse than the scenario evaluated, and a consequent increase in the level of risk borne by the ordinary shareholders.

(b) The effect on performance of financing using the 13% debenture has been calculated in (a) above. For the debenture to be attractive to investors there needs to be an expectation that the share price will have increased to at least 450p per share in year 5 so that it will be worth exercising the warrants and achieving some capital gain. Assuming that the rate of return required by investors does not change over the period, it is possible to calculate the theoretical share price in year 5 using the **dividend valuation model**, as follows:

$$P_0 = D_1 / r$$

where: P_0 = market price of shares
       D_1 = dividend per share
       r = rate of return required by investors

Currently: 250 $= 17.47 / r$
            r $= 7\%$

At the end of year 5:

$$P_0 = 45.44 / 7\% = 650p$$

On this basis, the warrants priced at 450p should be very attractive to investors with a potential capital gain of 200p per share at the exercise date. In practice, the gain may be less than this since exercise of the warrants may cause some dilution of earnings, and hence dividends, per share.

The effect of financing using the Swiss Franc bond will depend on the effective interest rate incurred. This in turn will depend on the relative rates of interest and inflation in the UK and Switzerland, and the movements in the exchange rate over the period.

The likely movement in the exchange rate can be calculated using the **purchasing power parity theory** which relates movements in exchange rates to inflation. Since inflation in the UK is higher than in Switzerland, the pound is likely to fall in value against the Swiss franc. By the end of the first year, the pound is likely to have fallen as follows.

$$\% \text{ fall} = \frac{i_{uk} - i_f}{1 + i_{uk}} = \frac{\text{UK inflation rate} - \text{Swiss inflation rate}}{1 + \text{UK inflation rate}}$$

$$\% \text{ fall} = \frac{0.08 - 0.02}{1.08} \times 100 = 5.56\%$$

$$\frac{100 - 5.56}{100} \times 2.445 = 2.3091$$

$$\frac{100 - 5.56}{100} \times 2.450 = 2.3138$$

The exchange rate should therefore be SF2.3091 - 2.3138/£.

The actual amount of interest payable at the end of year 1 will be:

$$\frac{12.25m \times 8\%}{2.3091} = £424,408$$

This represents an effective rate of interest of 8.5%. The amount to be repaid at the end of the period will also increase if the pound continues to fall by 5.56% per year. This means that although the annual interest cost of the Swiss Franc bond is less, it could actually prove to be a more expensive financing option than the 13% debenture. The precise effect will depend on the relative **movements in exchange rates** over the ten year period. A further factor which should be considered is the currency structure of IXT's receipts and payments. If IXT earns revenues denominated in Swiss Francs, then it may be able to match these receipts with the payments of interest and capital due under the bond, and in this situation the bond is likely to be more attractive than the debenture since losses on exchange can be avoided.

The effect of using a **placing** can be calculated in a similar manner to the effect of using a debenture. It can be seen that due to dilution, the effect on earnings per share is not quite as good as that achieved through using the debenture. However, there is a significant improvement in both interest cover and the level of gearing, the latter being reduced from 97.6% to 33.5% by year 5. Thus the placing would provide a less risky offer than using debt finance. It is also likely however that the use of a placing, possibly with institutional investors, would significantly alter the ownership structure of IXT, and this may not be popular with existing shareholders, including Mr Axelot who currently has the controlling interest.

To summarise, provided that the financial sensitivities are acceptable, the use of debt finance is likely to prove more attractive to the existing shareholders. This also has the benefit of providing the best improvement in **earnings per share**.

57 PREPARATION QUESTION: RISK DATA

> **Tutor's hint**. This question deals with the assessment of political risk and the way in which such information should be included in the decision making process. It is not testing any particular area of the syllabus in depth, but it does require you to think broadly about the issues involved and to use your knowledge to make a reasoned discussion of the issues involved.
>
> **Examiner's comment**. Part (a) was quite well answered, with many candidates correctly stressing that the table contained details of only a limited number of factors that might measure political risk, and that many other important factors exist. Good candidates also stressed the subjective nature of the data. Answers to part (b) were weaker. Good answers stressed the difference between macro and micro measures of political risk, and the fact that investments should be made on the basis of strategic fit, and expected cash flow, rather than be based on just political risk.

To: Board of directors
From: Accountant
Date: 17 December 20X8
Subject: The evaluation of political risk in investment decisions

The measurement of political risk

Political risk in foreign investment could be defined as the threat that a foreign government will change the rules of the game after the investment has been made. There are various agencies that can provide risk scores for different countries, but the key problem for all such approaches is that the scores that they use will always be subjective. The best example of the limitations of this approach is the case of Iran. Most commentators believed the regime under the Shah to be inherently stable, but as it turned out, this belief was completely wrong.

Considering the data that is being used in this case in more detail, there are a number of weaknesses that should be recognised.

(a) **Economic performance** is one of the most heavily weighted factors. However it can be argued that this is not really a component of political risk.

(b) There is **no information** as to how the **weightings have been arrived** at.

(c) A number of factors that could have been included have been ignored. These include:

    (i)   Cultural homogeneity

    (ii)   Quality of infrastructure

    (iii) Legal system

    (iv) Record on nationalisation

    (v)   Currency stability

The directors should also consider some of the other approaches to the evaluation of political risk. These include:

(a) Seeking the **views of individuals** with direct experience of the countries in question, such as academics, diplomats and journalists

(b) **Social** as well as **economic analysis**

The decision about which country to invest in

The evaluation of political risk must obviously form some part of the decision about which country to invest in. However, the use of this type of data to evaluate political risk in this context can be misleading for the following reasons:

(a) These scores are valid at the macro level, but they do not **measure the risk** that is faced at the **micro level** by the industry or firm. Certain industries, such as mining and agriculture are more prone to political risk than are others. Some activities will be welcomed by countries due to the perceived benefits that their presence can bring. Examples of this can be seen in the UK economy where the activities of the multinational biotechnology companies are being severely restricted, while investment by Japanese microchip companies is welcomed and assisted.

(b) It can lead to an **over-emphasis** on the **political features** of the host country while neglecting other **vital considerations** such as the **strategic fit** of the new investment with the company's other operations.

This type of data therefore has relevance to the investment decision, but should not form the sole basis on which the decision is made. Although Forland comes out best in the overall scores, it has the **worst level** of **economic performance**. If the subsidiary is being developed with a view to serving primarily the local market, then this factor should receive a higher weighting in the overall decision making process since it will have a significant impact on the expected cash flow that will be generated.

58   RIPPENTOFF

> **Tutor's hint**. In (a) it is important to distinguish which costs and revenues are relevant in the technical sense to each party. Part (b) requires an assessment of the various risks of overseas investments by multinationals in the context of the example given.

(a) The **proposed investment** will be worthwhile to either party if the return on the investment **equals or exceeds the cost of capital to the company**. It is assumed that since the subsidiary is paying a dividend and has its own cost of equity, it also has local shareholders and is not wholly owned by Rippentoff. The element of borrowing in the investment is therefore considered to be irrelevant to Rippentoff.

The situation from the point of view of Rippentoff must be evaluated in US dollars. It is assumed that the exchange rate is expected to remain stable throughout the life of the project.

Rippentoff's initial investment can be calculated as follows.

	Gross cash payment		Offset	Net cash
	LCU m	$m	$m	$m
Capital funds supplied	30	6	0	6
Plant: due for scrap	(10)	(2)	0.1	(1.9)
due for replacement	(10)	(2)	1.5	(0.5)
new machine	(10)	(2)	1.9	(0.1)
Stock	(5)	(1)	0.75	(0.25)
Total	(5)	(1)	4.25	3.25

In the case of the plant, the **opportunity cost** has been offset to calculate the net cash inflow to Rippentoff. For the first machine this is the amount that would have been received had the item been scrapped. For the second two machines this is the amount that will have to be spent on replacement and purchase.

In the case of the stock, the effective net cash inflow is the contribution on the cost of materials.

In return for its investment, Rippentoff will receive each year a management fee of $1m, together with a contribution of 25% on materials supplied amounting to $0.5m $(20 \times 0.5 \times 0.25 \times 0.2)$.

Thus Rippentoff will earn an annual return of $1.5m on its initial investment of $3.25m which amounts to 46.15%. This exceeds 15% which is the cost of capital, and therefore the investment is worthwhile.

(b) Rippentoff would also have to take into account the following factors.

(i) **Exchange rate risk**

The calculations assume that the **exchange rate remains constant** throughout the life of the project. It would be useful to calculate the sensitivity of the return to movements in the exchange rate, and to form a view of the likelihood of such movements occurring. Exchange rate movements could impact on the project in two main ways.

(1) The **value of the assets employed** may **go down** due to a fall in the value of the local currency against the dollar.

(2) **Payments received for materials** and the **management fee** may be affected by the **exchange rate ruling** at the date of the transaction. This risk can be averted to some extent by hedging through timing the payments judiciously, and through the use of the option and currency markets. However these methods will not avert the consequences of a long term downward movement in the local currency, or of a deterioration in the local economy. An example is Peru where inflation has been spiralling out of control and the currency has become almost worthless.

(ii) **Political risk**

Rippentoff must assess the political situation and take account of the likelihood of the government taking action that would jeopardise its ability to extract cash from Penuria, and even its ownership of the assets. Possible government actions include the following.

(1) **Import quotas** which might restrict the volume of materials being purchased from Rippentoff and the contribution earned from them

(2) **Import tariffs** on the materials supplied

(3) **Exchange control regulations** which might restrict the ability of Rippentoff to obtain regular payments of the management fee

(4) **Nationalisation of assets**

(5) **Legislation** restricting the granting of work permits to foreigners might cause Rippentoff a problem in the management of the investment

Alternatively, it is possible that the government might look favourably on **foreign investment** as a means of developing the local economy. If this is thought to be likely, then Rippentoff should aim to time its investment to take maximum advantage of any government support that will be available.

(iii) **Geographical separation**

Management and control are likely to be more difficult due to the **geographical separation** of parent and subsidary, and communication problems may be enhanced by language barriers. This may mean that the actual return achieved on the investment is less than the potential performance assumed in the calculations.

59   FDI

Tutor's hint. This is not an easy question to answer. Stick to sound economic arguments and avoid being overtly political. Read (b) carefully. It is asking for the effects of the investment on the host country, and not the multinational.

Examiner's comment. Good answers to (a) included discussions of competitive advantage, market imperfections, economies of scale, acquisitions, organic growth and internalised skills. Some answers were too general and did not focus sufficiently on multinational companies. The main advantages for the overseas host country of foreign direct investment (FDI) by multinational companies are as follows. In (b) any candidates did not carefully read what was required. Candidates frequently discussed the advantages and disadvantages of foreign direct investment from the viewpoint of a multinational company, rather than the viewpoint of the host government. Few or even no marks were then earned, which for some candidates made the difference between success or failure in the examination.

(a)   The enormous size of some multinationals creates **economies of scale** in purchasing (by bargaining for lower prices), **production** (by optimal size and location of facilities), **marketing** (by efficient distribution systems, and common brand image) and **finance** (by bargaining power in financial markets). These economies of scale help to create a significant competitive advantage over smaller companies. However, multinationals are also able to use **market imperfections** and the **comparative advantage** of countries in order to lower costs further, set favourable selling prices and increase profitability.

Operational and sales issues

The combination of one country's technical and management expertise with another country's low labour costs creates world class products at a low cost. Alternatively an investment may be made in one country to secure the supply of raw materials, which are then shipped to another country for further processing. As they grow larger, multinationals can more easily switch some forms of production from one country to another in order to take advantage of **labour costs** and **conditions, local tax rates** or political situations.

Country or **regional assembly and distribution centres** are often set up in order to circumvent trade barriers, in the form of tariffs or quotas. **Sales prices** are set at **different levels** in **different countries** in order to exploit differences in market price, in some cases taking advantage of monopolistic or oligopolistic situations. **Transfer prices** of components, services, and inter-company fees can be manipulated in order to minimise global tax liability.

Finance

Finance can be raised in the country where it can be **most cheaply obtained**. Alternatively it can be raised on **international markets** in a variety of currencies, in order to take advantage of cost differentials and expected exchange rate movements.

Competition

The large size of successful multinationals also creates **high barriers to entry** by competitors, for example through **cheap production costs**, **brand image** and **high promotion expenditure**. This in turn facilitates **growth by acquisition**. Multinationals, with their efficient distribution systems, regularly acquire young innovative companies which cannot afford to exploit their products in world markets.

Various other tactics are adopted to inhibit competition from smaller local companies. For example, a major factor in maintaining competitive advantage is to keep control of the **key technology**. This will be protected by international patents. Commonly, a production process is split between various countries in order to make **technology transfer more difficult**.

Those multinational companies which can offer world class products and which have established high quality management have been able to **exploit successfully** the progressive reduction in international trade barriers and strengthening of international property rights which has taken place in the second half of the twentieth century. However, for every successful multinational company, there are many that have failed because of inferior products or management. This shows that competition remains high.

(b) The main advantages for the overseas country of **Foreign Direct Investment (FDI)** by multinational companies are as follows.

(i)   There will be an **initial boost to the balance** of payments as the multinational imports capital to establish the operation.

(ii) If the host country is less developed, there is also likely to be the **introduction of new technology** into the economy.

(iii) The introduction of new technology will be accompanied by the **development** of the **skills** of the indigenous workforce as they are trained in the new methods.

(iv) The economy will be **stimulated** by the creation of additional employment.

(v)   The investment by the multinational may **improve international perceptions** of the host country and lead to further investment by other companies.

(vi) The **introduction of new management practices** may spin off improvements in performance in the local industries.

Disadvantages of FDI include the following.

(i) Over time, the **impact on the balance of trade** may be **negative** as the multinational seeks to remit funds earned out of the country to other operations.

(ii) In the long term, the **economy** may be more **unstable**, since in times of economic pressure it is the operations that are furthest from the head office that tend to be closed first. This could magnify the problems of world recession for the host country.

(iii) **Loss of control over key resources** may occur if a multinational comes to own strategic resources in the country, such as mineral deposits.

(iv) The multinational may try to **evade local taxation** through the clever management of funds eg through transfer pricing. If this occurs, then the economic benefits to the host country will be less than originally anticipated.

(v) If the multinational sends a large number of overseas staff to run the subsidiary, this may result in the introduction of **different value systems** and lifestyles that undermine the traditional culture.

(vi) If the multinational is taking advantage of lax local regulations, there is the risk of **environmental degradation** through pollution or excess exploitation of natural resources.

60 DIALTOUS

> **Tutor's hint.** In part (a) the effect of issuing additional debt on the gearing and interest cover should be calculated. You should also explain whether it is the group or the subsidiary figures that are relevant in this context. All three options in part (b) (of which only *two* need to be analysed) require the calculation of the cost of redeemable debt using interpolation to estimate the effective interest rate. Other factors to be considered include the term of the loans, the nature of the exchange risk faced by Dialtous, and in the case of the eurobond, the likelihood of conversion.
>
> **Examiner's comment.** In part (b), candidates discussed all three financing sources rather than the two required in the question. Marks are not earned for discussing an extra financing source, but valuable time is wasted. [*BPP note.* Our answer deliberately covers all three.]

(a) In general terms there are three main advantages in the use of debt to finance foreign subsidiaries.

(i) **Flexibility.** Debt finance is more easily arranged than equity and it is easier to make changes to its form in the future. For example, swaps can be arranged to take advantage of changes in interest rates, and the currency in which the debt is denominated can be selected to optimise the foreign currency exposure of the group as a whole.

(ii) **Cost.** In most countries, interest payments are allowable against tax, and this means that debt is often cheaper than equity. In addition some governments may offer subsidised loans to attract foreign investment.

(iii) **Ease of remittance.** While some countries may place restrictions on the level of dividends that can be remitted to the parent company, it is rare for restrictions to be placed on interest payments.

Against these advantages must be set the increased risks that may be associated with the increase in the level of debt. Raising the gearing will generally result in an increase in the level of financial risk faced by the company, and the **cash demands** will be higher as the company has to make regular interest payments.

Although Itdial currently has a high level of gearing at 120% (short and long-term debt:equity plus reserves, 170/142) and low interest cover at 2.11 times (38/18), this is not necessarily of much significance in the context of the financing decision. If the financing is to be undertaken and underwritten by the group, then the **financial position of the group** is the most important factor. The capital structure of the individual subsidiary should be arranged to maximise the benefit to the group as a whole, and not judged in the same way as a stand-alone enterprise.

Dialtous currently has a gearing level of 73% (125/171) and interest cover of 5.42 times (76/14). The additional debt would amount to approximately £41.6m (Won100 billion / 2,404) which would increase the gearing to 97% (166.6/171) and, assuming an interest rate of 8.5%, reduce the interest cover to 4.3 times (excluding additional operating profit from Itdial). Although this gearing level is quite high, the prospective **interest cover** appears reasonably good and should permit Dialtous to raise and support the additional finance in the form of debt. However, it would be interesting to evaluate the costs of raising the money in the form of equity, and also to have some information on the views of the market on the performance of the company.

(b) Given the small level of initial charge, and the long length of each source of finance, a simple estimate of the IRR for each source of finance can be made. In each case it is unnecessary to convert currencies, since any interest rate calculated would be sensitive to the currency in which the interest is paid. We should therefore work in that underlying currency.

It is also unnecessary to use the full value of each loan. A simple £100 or FR100 or Won100 base can be used. (Two of the three sources to be discussed.)

(i) The UK bank loan would have an initial cost of 8.5% per annum (7% + 1.5%). However, this is a floating rate loan and it is not possible to comment on the likely cost over the life of the project since interest rates cannot be predicted that far into the future. The overall cost can be estimated if it is assumed that interest rates do remain stable.

Net cost:

8.5%/0.995 + 0.5%/7 = 8.61%

Alternatively, calculate an IRR:

Year	Cashflow £	Disc factor 8%	Present value £	Disc factor 9%	Present value £
0	(99.5)	1.000	(99.5)	1.000	(99.5)
1-7	8.5	5.206	44.251	5.033	42.781
7	100	0.583	58.3	0.547	54.700
			3.051		(2.019)

Net cost:

$$8\% + (9-8) \times \frac{3.051}{3.051 + 2.019} = 8.6\%$$

The main risks associated with the loan are:

(1) Interest rate movements

(2) Exchange rate movements, as revenues are denominated in lire but interest and capital payments must be made in sterling

(3) Dialtous must provide security to the bank

(4) Greater cost than for the convertible

The main benefit of this loan is that the term matches the length of the project.

(ii)   The first stage in evaluating the convertible eurobond is to establish the likelihood of the bond being converted. The **effective share value on conversion** is $1,000/50 = $20 per share.

At current spot price: $20/1.5456 = £12.94 per share

Since the current share price is £7.60 this represents a premium on conversion of 70.3%. Under current circumstances it is therefore unlikely that investors would choose to convert unless there is a substantial rise in the share price in the intervening period, or unless there are significant changes in interest rates and exchange rates.

The amount to be raised excluding issue costs is Won100bn/1,552 = $64,432,990 (or approximately $64,433,000).

The total sum including the issue costs is $64,432,990/0.98 = $65,747,949, say $65.748m.

Assuming the conversion is not exercised:

7%/0.98 + 2%/10 = 7.34%

Alternatively, calculate an IRR:

Year	Cashflow $	Disc factor 7%	Present value $	Disc factor 8%	Present value $
0	(98)	1.000	(98)	1.000	(98)
1-10	7	7.024	49.168	6.710	46.97
10	100	0.508	50.80	0.463	46.3
			1.968		(4.73)

Net cost:

$$7\% + (8 - 7) \times \frac{1.968}{1.968 + 4.73} = 7.294\%$$

Other factors to be taken into account are as follows.

(1)   The **dilution effect on EPS** if investors do convert. An additional 3.29 million (65,748 × 50) shares would need to be issued. Since there are currently 40 million shares (20m/0.50) in issue the dilution effect should be small.

(2)   If as currently appears likely the majority of investors choose not to convert, then the **loan must be redeemed** in ten years' time. In this event Dialtous faces the risk of adverse movements in exchange rates in the intervening period making the cost of redemption higher than predicted.

(3)   Since the loan is fixed rate at below the current level of UK interest rates, it appears to be **cheap**, given that it is unlikely that interest rates in the UK will fall significantly at least in the short term. However, if the won falls against the dollar then the interest costs will effectively increase.

(iii)   Swapping the Swiss franc bond into a South Korean won loan provides the benefit of **completely hedging the interest payments** since these will be matched against lire revenues. At the end of ten years the principal will be swapped back into the original currencies at the original rates for repayment. The bond can be evaluated as follows.

11.75%/0.97 + 3%/10 = 12.41%

Alternatively, calculate an IRR:

Year	Cashflow Won	Disc factor 12%	Present value Won	Disc factor 13%	Present value Won
0	(97)	1.000	(97)	1.000	(97)
1-10	11.75	5.650	66.388	5.426	63.756
10	100	0.322	32.200	0.295	29.500
			1.588		(3.744)

Net cost:

$$12\% + (13 - 12) \times \frac{1.588}{1.588 + 3.744} = 12.30\%$$

Although the interest payments are hedged, since the principal will be swapped back into Swiss francs at the end of the term, Dialtous still runs the risk of a fall in the value of the won against the Swiss franc making the costs of repayment relatively more expensive. Risks of default by the other party to the swap must be also considered.

Conclusions

The forward rates suggest that sterling, US dollars and Swiss francs are all likely to strengthen against the won, although it must be taken into account that the periods of time being considered are so long as to make this only a very approximate guide. Similarly, all three loans are exposed to **exchange risk** on repayment of the principal.

Although the third option is the only option which hedges the currency risk of interest payments, it appears to be significantly **more expensive** than the other two options. The choice therefore lies between the sterling bank loan and the eurobond.

Based on mid-rates, the relative sizes of the expected depreciation in the won against sterling and the dollar can be estimated as follows.

Sterling: $(2,465 - 2,412)/2,412 = 2.2\%$
US dollar: $(1,613 - 1,559)/1,559 = 3.5\%$

The **currency risk** attaching to the eurobond is therefore **higher,** and the term does not match the life of the project as it does for the UK loan. In addition, there is the possibility that Dialtous could have to issue further equity which it wishes to avoid. On the basis of the information provided it is therefore recommended that the project be financed by means of the UK bank loan. However, it must be stressed that since this is a floating rate loan, there is a significant risk that the cost could turn out to be higher than the estimates suggest.

(c) Dialtous could alternatively issue a **sterling bond**. A fixed or floating rate could be used, the choice being made according to which produced a better rate in the swap market. The bond could be swapped into fixed rate won for the period of seven years. Interest would be payable on the bond in wons from the won cash flows of Itdial. Using a sterling loan would avoid currency risk exposure for Dialtous when the loan is redeemed.

61 OMNIKIT

> **Tutor's hint**. Two foreign investment appraisals in one question! For this sort of question, which is relatively common and contains many computational techniques, you need to develop a standard approach and practice it hard, because a look at the marking scheme shows that not many marks are awarded for each computational element. Never miss out the discussion parts of a question like this: they are far better value for time than the computational parts. Our answer shows you the best sequence in which to tackle the problem.

> **Examiner's comment.** The discussion in part (a) was well answered. Answers to (b) varied greatly. The best answers showed a clear structure to the computations, whereas others presented figures in a way that was difficult to follow and hence difficult to mark. Some candidates did not realise that the foreign currency figures needed to be converted to sterling for the investment appraisal.

(a) Compared with growth by acquisition, the main advantages of **organic growth** are:

    (i)   It can be carefully planned to fulfil strategic objectives.

    (ii)   It is more likely to involve existing front-line managers than growth by acquisition and hence can be more motivating.

However, the costs of **entering new lines of business** can be high and the lead times involved might be too long to enable the business to gain competitive advantage. The new business has to researched, developed and planned, production facilities have to be acquired and suitable staff hired. The organisation then goes through a learning curve, often repeating the mistakes made by competitors.

Growth by acquisition, on the other hand:

    (i)   Provides a **quicker method of entering new markets** or acquiring new technology or patents, sometimes enabling very rapid growth

    (ii)   **Enables increased market power** by eliminating competitors

    (iii) **Provides economies of scale** by elimination of duplicated resources, combining complementary resources, etc

By its nature, however, growth by acquisition cannot be **planned** in as much detail as organic growth. Quick decisions sometimes have to be made in response to acquisition opportunities, often without as much information as the acquiring company would like. Major acquisitions may change the company's strategic direction. Staff problems are more likely to arise as attempts are made to integrate or change the cultures of merged organisations.

(b) The evaluation of each of the two alternatives is made in terms of how well each one contributes to the **achievement of organisational objectives** and strategies. The information given enables a financial appraisal of each alternative to be made. This will only be part of the input to the final decision, albeit an important part. Many non-financial factors will also have to be taken into account.

The financial appraisal is shown below. The basic approach is to estimate cash flows in the foreign currency, convert them to the home currency and discount them at a rate based on home country cost of capital.

> **Tutor's hint.** These questions are usually very long: you need to adopt a disciplined approach and practice it several times before the exam. Firstly establish the time horizon for your appraisals, then try scoring some easy marks first, such as prediction of exchange rates and computation of the discount rate.

Financial appraisal of the two alternative investments

The time horizon for appraisal of both investments is 7 years: six years of operation plus one further year to allow for the tax delay.

Working 1: Computation of exchange rates for the next 7 years

For ease of computation, the spot rate will be taken as the mid-market exchange rate.

Spot rate for SFr = (2.3140 + 2.3210)/2 = 2.3175

Spot rate for $ = (1.5160 + 1.5210)/2 = 1.5185

Using purchasing power parity theory, each year the SFr/£ exchange rate is multiplied by 1.05/1.03 and the $/£ rate is multiplied by 1.06/1.03.

Tutor's hint. Using the 'constant' factor on a scientific calculator can produce these figures very quickly: it is well worth while learning this technique.

Year	SFr/£	$/£
0	2.3175	1.5185
1	2.3625	1.5627
2	2.4084	1.6082
3	2.4551	1.6551
4	2.5028	1.7033
5	2.5514	1.7529
6	2.6010	1.8040
7	2.6515	1.8565

Working 2: Discount rate for the investments

Because both investment alternatives represent an expansion of the existing business, the company's existing weighted average cost of capital can be used as a discount rate.

The debt is borrowed in the UK where interest will save tax at the rate of 33%. Its after tax cost is 10%(1 − 0.33) = 6.7%

Tutor's hint. Arguably, to reduce foreign exchange risk, the company should attempt to borrow locally, in which case the tax saving on debt would be 40% for Swiss debt, or 33% (not 30%! – see later) for US debt. However, the question clearly states that the borrowing is in the UK, where tax saved will be 33%.

Market values should be used as weights.

WACC = $0.7 \times 15\% + 0.3 \times 6.7\% = 12.51\%$

Tutor's hint. Now start workings for the Swiss investment. Standard workings which can be prepared are tax depreciation, adjustment of working capital for inflation and contribution figures (if they help to reduce detailed computations).

Swiss investment

Working 3: Tax saved by tax-allowable depreciation (machinery only) in Switzerland

(Figures in SFr'000)

Year	1	2	3	4	5	6	7
Asset value at start of year	6,400	4,800	3,600	2,700	2,025	1,519	
25% depreciation	1,600	1,200	900	675	506	380	
Tax saved at 40%			1,120	360	270	202	152

It is assumed that, because the Swiss subsidiary earns no profits in year 1, the tax depreciation in year 1 cannot be claimed until year 2. The allowance in year 2 will therefore be 2,800, giving rise to a tax saving of 1,120 in year 3.

No **balancing allowance** has been shown, as the asset will still be in use after year 6 and its value is included in the after-tax realisable value of the investment, SFr16.2m.

Notes **Answers**

Working 4: Investment in working capital - Switzerland

It is assumed that total working capital requirement increases with inflation at 5% per year and is returned at the end of year 7. It is assumed that the amount of working capital at year 6 is *not* included in the value of the investment at that stage.

> **Tutor's hint.** In the absence of clear instructions, reasonable assumptions have to be made, but clearly alternatives are possible.

(Figures in SFr'000)

Year	1	2	3	4	5	6	7
Total working capital	11,500	12,075	12,679	13,313	13,979	14,678	
Investment in WC	(11,500)	(575)	(604)	(634)	(666)	(699)	14,678

Working 5: Contribution per unit - Switzerland

At current prices (year 0):	SFr
Sales price	20,000
Variable costs	11,000
Contribution	9,000

This will increase by 5% per year. Contribution per unit in year 2 will be $9,000 \times 1.05^2$ = SFr 9,923.

Appraisal of Swiss investment

Year	0	1	2	3	4	5	6	7
Production/sales units			2,000	2,500	2,500	2,500	2,500	
Cont. per unit, SFr (W5)			9,923	10,419	10,940	11,487	12,061	
	SFr '000	SFr '000	SFr '000	SFr '000	SFr '000	SFr '000	SFr '000	SFr '000
Total contribution			19,846	26,048	27,350	28,718	30,153	
Royalty(£750,000 ÷ exch.rate)			(1,806)	(1,841)	(1,877)	(1,914)	(1,951)	
Operating cash flow			18,040	24,207	25,473	26,804	28,202	
Tax at 40%				(7,216)	(9,683)	(10,189)	(10,722)	(11,281)
Tax saved by dep'n all. (W3)				1,120	360	270	202	152
Land	(2,300)							
Building	(1,600)	(6,200)						
Machinery		(6,400)						
After tax realisable value							16,200	
Working capital (W4)		(11,500)	(575)	(604)	(634)	(666)	(699)	14,678
Cash remitted to UK	(3,900)	(24,100)	17,465	17,507	15,516	16,219	33,183	3,549
Exchange rate SFr/£ (W2)	2.3175	2.3625	2.4084	2.4551	2.5028	2.5514	2.6010	2.6515
	£'000	£'000	£'000	£'000	£'000	£'000	£'000	£'000
Cash remitted from Switzerland	(1,683)	(10,201)	7,252	7,131	6,199	6,357	12,758	1,338
Royalty received			750	750	750	750	750	
Tax at 33% on royalty				(248)	(248)	(248)	(248)	(248)
Net cash	(1,683)	(10,201)	8,002	7,633	6,701	6,859	13,260	1,090
12.51% d.f. (W2)	1.000	0.889	0.790	0.702	0.624	0.555	0.493	0.438
Present value	(1,683)	(9,069)	6,322	5,358	4,181	3,807	6,537	477

The Swiss investment has a positive net present value of **£15.93 million**.

> **Tutor's hint.** Appraisal of the US investment follows the same lines but is easier.

Working 6: Working capital

Year	0	1	2	3	4	5	6	7
	$'000	$'000	$'000	$'000	$'000	$'000	$'000	$'000
Total working capital	4,000	4,240	4,494	4,764	5,050	5,353	5,674	
Investment in WC	(4,000)	(240)	(254)	(270)	(286)	(303)	(321)	5,674

Appraisal of US investment

Year	0	1	2	3	4	5	6	7
	$'000	$'000	$'000	$'000	$'000	$'000	$'000	$'000
Pre-tax cash flow		2,120	3,371	3,573	3,787	4,014	4,255	
Tax at 30%			(636)	(1,011)	(1,072)	(1,136)	(1,204)	(1,277)
Cost of acquisition (assume maximum)	(10,000)							
Machinery	(2,000)							
After tax realisable value							14,500	
Working capital (W6)	(4,000)	(240)	(254)	(270)	(286)	(303)	(321)	5,674
Cash remitted to/from USA	(16,000)	1,880	2,481	2,292	2,429	2,575	17,230	4,397
Exchange rate (W1)	1.5185	1.5627	1.6082	1.6551	1.7033	1.7529	1.8040	1.8565
Cash remitted to/from USA	(10,537)	1,203	1,543	1,385	1,426	1,469	9,551	2,368
Additional UK tax (3%) (See Note below)			(41)	(63)	(65)	(67)	(69)	(71)
Net cash	(10,537)	1,203	1,502	1,322	1,361	1,402	9,482	2,297
12.51% d.f.	1.000	0.889	0.790	0.702	0.624	0.555	0.493	0.438
Present value	(10,537)	1,069	1,187	928	849	778	4,675	1,006

Net present value = (£45,000)

Note: Additional tax of 3% (33% – 30%) is suffered in the UK on US taxable profits. This is computed by converting the pre-tax cash flow at the exchange rate for the year and then multiplying by 3%. e.g. Year 1: 2,120 ÷ 1.5627 × 3% = 40.69, rounded to 41.

The net present value of the US investment is **negative £45,000** if the investment cost is the maximum $10 million.

If the cost is only $8m, the NPV is increased by $2m / 1.5185 = £1.317m, giving a **positive NPV of £1.272m.**

Conclusion

From the financial appraisal, the Swiss investment is the better alternative. If the US investment is thought to have a positive NPV, then both investments could be undertaken (they are not mutually exclusive) provided adequate funds and management resources were available.

The financial appraisals are based on several assumptions, which are stated during the course of the computation.

Most of the estimates are subject to considerable uncertainty, for example:

(i) **Estimates of future exchange rates** are based upon **forecast inflation levels** and purchasing power parity theory.

(ii) **Inflation is unlikely to remain** at the **levels given** and may affect different types of costs and revenues in different ways.

(iii) **Tax rates** may change.

(iv) As in most financial appraisals, the most difficult figure to estimate is the **residual value** at the end of the time horizon of six years.

(v)   Estimates for the **Swiss sales figures** are **more difficult to make** than for the US investment, because it is a start-up business.

(vi)   The **systematic risk** of both investments is assumed to be the same as Omnikit's existing business. If this is not the case then project specific discount rates should be used.

(vii) _Sensitivity analysis could be used to provide more information on which of the above uncertainties cause the most problems.

Marking guide		Marks
(a)	Organic growth	3
	Growth by acquisition	3
		6
(b)	Exchange rates forecasts	2
	(Allow mid rates or bid/offer rates)	
	Swiss investment	
	Taxable cash flows	1
	Tax, lagged 1 year	1
	Tax saved from allowance	2
	Working capital	2
	(1 if no increase for inflation is mentioned)	
	Fixed assets	1
	Remittable cash flows (£)	1
	Royalty and tax on royalty	2
	Discount factors and NPV	2
	US investment	
	Remittable cash flows ($)	2
	UK tax	1
	Discussion of non-financial factors	2
	Commentary of the limitations of estimates	4
	Conclusion	1
		24
		30

62   VALTICK

> **Tutor's hint.** In (a) you will need to justify briefly why companies invest in foreign operations, but then concentrate on the specific advantages and disadvantages of joint ventures.
>
> The main calculation, like most on foreign investments, is very long. A neat layout with headings for workings will assist the marker, even if you do not complete it. Resist the temptation to ignore the discussion aspect, which is worth 10 marks.
>
> **Examiner's comment.** This question required understanding of international joint ventures and the evaluation of whether or not a joint venture is viable, taking into account relevant financial and non-financial factors. (a) was generally well answered. Problems in (b) included incorrect capital allowances, failure to consider relevant sterling cash flows and ignoring UK taxation. Another common failing was only considering one or two years' cash flows, rather than cash flows of the entire period. Candidates also failed to provide deep enough analysis in the written section; in particular the various contributions that Valtick could make.

(a)   The aims of establishing foreign operations include development of new markets, international diversification, creation of economies of scale, profiting from the comparative advantage of different countries, and circumventing trade barriers.

A joint venture with a local partner is one way of achieving these aims, with the following specific advantages:

(i)   **Costs** and **risks** are **shared** by more than one party.

(ii)   A good local partner will have **specific knowledge** of the environment, including culture, market analysis, competition, distribution methods, availability of skills, preferred methods of doing business and associated constraints.

(iii)   Each party to the joint venture can use their **specific expertise** and **experience**. A local partner should have expertise in the parts of the operation to which they will contribute.

(iv)   **Access** to **local capital markets** may be made cheaper and easier by using a joint venturer.

(v)   **Availability** of **government incentives** (eg tax or grants) may be **greater**.

(vi)   Some governments insist that foreign direct investment is conducted by way of joint venture with a **local firm.**

Difficulties and disadvantages include the following:

(i)   A company may have **difficulty** in **finding** a **local partner** with suitable expertise or experience. This may need to be rectified by **appropriate training**.

(ii)   **Divergence** of **objectives** may mean that the terms of the joint venture are difficult to negotiate. For example, on the financial side, international transfer pricing policy and local dividend policy can create conflicts.

(iii)   The difficulty of valuing the **inputs** of the joint venturers (especially the intangible inputs) may lead to difficulties in **negotiating profit sharing arrangements** and/or representation on the board of directors.

(iv)   There is the risk of **technology transfer** to the local partner, enabling them to set up independently. Patent agreements may not be enforceable locally.

(v)   Governments pursuing a policy of **nationalisation** or expropriation of foreign investments may find it easier to take over joint ventures than wholly owned subsidiaries.

(b)   Assuming that its share of profits is remitted to UK annually, the method used will be to **convert** Valtick's foreign cash flows to sterling and to discount these cash flows using a **suitable cost of capital**. It is first necessary to compute predicted exchange rates, total peso sales and joint venture taxable profits. Time horizon is 5 years (4 years project plus one year for tax delay).

W1 Exchange rates

Assuming purchasing power parity holds, predicted future exchange rates are:

Year	Peso/£	Peso/$
0	32.78	18.32
1	38.19	20.94
2	44.49	23.93
3	49.68	26.21
4	55.46	28.70
5	61.93	31.44

For example, year one rate for peso/£ is $32.78 \times 1.2/1.03 = 32.78$, and for peso/$ is $18.32 \times 1.2/1.05 = 20.94$.

Peso sales	0	1	2	3	4	5
Unit price		480	576	662	762	
Units sold		40,000	44,000	48,400	53,240	
Total m pesos		19.20	25.34	32.04	40.57	
Dollar sales						
10,000 units at $30		300	300	300	300	
Total m pesos		6.28	7.18	7.86	8.61	
Direct costs		50,000	54,000	58,400	63,240	
Direct costs / Unit		200	240	276	317	
Total m pesos		10.00	12.96	16.12	20.05	

Cash flows in m pesos	0	1	2	3	4	5
Peso sales		19.20	25.34	32.04	40.57	
Dollar sales		6.28	7.18	7.86	8.61	
Direct costs		(10.00)	(12.96)	(16.12)	(20.05)	
Fixed costs		(4.00)	(4.80)	(5.52)	(6.35)	
Depreciation		(20.00)	(10.00)	(5.00)	(2.50)	
Taxable profit		(8.52)	4.76	13.26	20.28	
20% Tax, 1 yr lag					(1.91)	(4.06)
Add back depreciation		20.00	10.00	5.00	2.50	
Capital expenditure	(40.00)					
Working capital	(5.00)					
	(45.00)	11.48	14.76	18.26	20.87	(4.06)
Valtick's share	(13.50)	5.74	7.38	9.13	10.43	(2.03)
Terminal value					30.00	
Valtick cash flows	(13.50)	5.74	7.38	9.13	40.43	(2.03)

Sterling cash flows	0	1	2	3	4	5	6	7
Valtick's Peso cash flows	(412)	150	166	184	729	(33)		
UK tax thereon at 10%					(10)	(18)		
Technical assistance	(105)							
Ongoing technical aid		(52)	(53)	(55)	(56)			
Lost exports		(33)	(34)	(35)	(36)	(37)	(37)	
Patent income lost		(40)	(40)	(40)	(40)	(40)	(40)	
Total additional UK costs		(125)	(127)	(130)	(132)	(77)	(77)	
Tax thereon			37	38	39	40	23	23
	(517)	25	76	92	626	(88)	(54)	23
DF at 1%	1.000	0.847	0.718	0.609	0.516	0.437	0.370	0.314
PV	(517)	21	55	56	323	(38)	(20)	7
NPV	(113)							

Workings

Additional UK tax on peso profits:	1	2	3	4	5
Valtick's 50% share of Taxable peso profits	0.00	0.00	4.76	10.12	
in sterling			96	183	
10% thereon, 1 yr lag				10	18

Assumptions

Beyond the life of the patent, the impact of the project on Valtick's cash flows is minimal.

Conclusion

From the estimates made, the net present value over a 7 year time horizon (the life of the patent) is £113,000 negative, indicating that the investment is not worthwhile. The net present value would be made worse by considering any lost income or costs beyond year 7.

However the following factors must be considered.

(i) **Financial contributions of Valtick and the Marantintan company**

Although Valtick contributes only 30% of the start up cost, the total investment in the joint venture, taking into account technical assistance, ongoing aid and the value of the royalty is more like £1.9 million, of which Valtick contributes approximately 50% (see below). Although the Marantinian company contributes local knowledge and expertise, Valtick also suffers lost exports from its home company. There may possibly be scope to increase Valtick's profit share from 50%, which might make the project viable.

Investment costs

	Total £'000	Valtick's share	£'000
Initial capital	1,373	30%	412
Initial technical assistance	105	100%	105
After tax TV of ongoing aid: 50,000/(0.18 – 0.03) × 0.7	233	100%	233
After tax PV of royalty value: 40,000/0.18 × 0.7	156	100%	156
	1,867		906

(ii) **Other factors affecting the decision**

The discount rate has been increased arbitrarily by 4% to allow for the risk of operating in Marantinta. This may not be appropriate to Valtick's shareholders who are concerned with the project's impact on systematic (market) risk. The investment might actually **lower systematic risk** if the investors are not already exposed to the Marantintan economy, and other risk aspects (e.g. political, cultural, foreign exchange risk) are to a large extent unsystematic or reduceable by hedging.

The cash flows therefore need to be **evaluated** at **various possible discount rates**. This would be part of a larger exercise on **sensitivity analysis** because the cash flow estimates themselves are subject to high margins of error. The variability of the NPV to estimates of all key variables should be tested.

Besides South and North America, the joint venture may be able to **supply other markets** such as Asia or Europe. The effect on the Welsh facility would need to be evaluated, however. The joint venture needs to be evaluated in the context of a strategic analysis of Valtick's opportunities and threats.

Marking guide		Marks
(a)	Advantages and disadvantages, 1-2 marks each	10
(b)	Criterion for decision	1
	Expected exchange rates	3
	Peso cash flows	
	Sales	3
	Costs	2
	Tax allowable depreciation	1
	Marantintan taxation	1
	Cash flows - Valtick	1
	UK cash flows	
	Exports foregone	2
	Aid	1
	Patent's opportunity cost	2
	Additional UK taxation	1
	Correct discount rate	1
	NPV and conclusion	1
		20
(c)	Joint ventures terms	4-5
	Non-financial factors	2-3
	Other aspects (strategic importance, sensitivity)	3-4
		10
		40

63   FORUN

> **Tutor's hint.** In part (a) take into account the wider economic and political factors that affect foreign investment strategy as well as the more obvious movements in exchange rates.
>
> In part (b) the first stage is to net receipts and payments to calculate the amounts to be hedged. Calculations of the receipts and payments under the different hedging options can then be made.
>
> **Examiner's comment.** Answers to part (a)(i) were disappointing, with limited use made of the data provided. Many candidates did little more than discuss the implications of the inflation rates for future foreign exchange rates, ignoring the other data. For part (a)(ii), candidates ignored the fact that the director was trying to reduce translation exposure, and discuss the three hedges in general terms. Some candidates failed to gain marks for part (b)(i) by incorrectly stating that netting reduced foreign exchange risk, rather than the transactions costs associated with foreign exchange payments.

(a) (i)   The managing director's information relates to the relative sizes and strengths of the economies under consideration and should be capable of being used as an input to the strategic decision making process.

Following **interest rate parity theory**, the currency in countries where the interest rate is higher than that in the UK can be expected to depreciate against the pound and *vice versa*.

On the basis of the information shown, all the currencies should be expected to depreciate against sterling, with the smallest movement being seen in countries 1 and 4. However, in the short term, there may be significant movements in exchange rates which differ from those predicted by the theory. The impact of the other factors can be scored from 1 to 4 (4 being highest) as follows.

	Country			
	1	*2*	*3*	*4*
Inflation	3	1	2	4
GDP growth	1	4	3	3
Balance of payments	3	1	4	2
Base rate	3	1	3	4
Unemployment rate	3	1	4	2
Population	3	4	2	1
Currency reserves per capita	3	1	4	2
IMF loans per capita	4	3	2	1
Total 'score'	23	16	24	19

Population has been ranked on size as reflecting potential size of market.

On the basis of the table, the countries with the strongest economies are 1 and 3 which perform significantly better than country 4. It is assumed that the managing director was placing a disproportionate weight on the importance of interest rates in determining exchange rates in selecting country 4 for concentration of activities.

While ranking tables such as that shown above are commonly used, their **shortcomings** must be **noted**. Each of the factors will probably vary in importance, both absolutely and for the particular company. For instance, high unemployment may be an indicator of low demand and high instability for some corporates, or an indicator of a cheap labour source for another. Broadly, a multinational will wish to invest in a high growth, stable country with cheap factors of production.

When making strategic decisions, it is not only the **valuation of assets denominated in foreign currencies** which is important. **Other factors** include the **potential for economic growth** and therefore the size of periodic remittances to the UK, political and economic stability, and the ease of moving funds in and out of the country. It is too simplistic to use relative rate movements alone as a basis for investment decisions. In fact, the effect of a depreciating currency may be to make the product increasingly attractive when compared with foreign imports and therefore increase the profitability of the foreign subsidiary.

Although the use of a wide range of **macro-economic data** is helpful in supporting the strategic process, even this is not sufficient. **Other information** is also important, for example if the company has the opportunity to exploit a particularly fast growing business sector in the country in question where there is little local competition.

A further impact of the proposed policy is to reduce the extent of Forun's **diversification** and therefore to increase its level of risk. Rather than trying to concentrate activities in the strongest two economies, it may be more appropriate to look for additional countries into which to expand rather than to reduce the range of existing operations.

(ii)   The non-executive director is concerned with the foreign exchange exposure which arises on the **translation** of assets denominated in foreign currencies on consolidation. The most effective way to reduce this when the foreign currency is depreciating is to minimise the value of the net assets denominated in the currencies in question. The **effects of the hedging proposals** are likely to be as follows.

(1) The effect of **early collection of foreign currency receivables** will depend on the relationship between the currency in which the receivables are denominated and the local currency. If the former is expected to depreciate against the latter, then early collection will assist in reducing translation exposure. If however, it is the local currency which is expected to depreciate, then delaying collection will actually increase the value of the receivable and thus reduce translation exposure; hastening collection would have the opposite effect.

(2) The effect of **early loan repayment** will also depend on the relationship between the loan in which the currency is denominated, the operating currency and sterling. If the loan currency is depreciating, then holding the loan as a liability in the balance sheet will help to reduce the net asset position and therefore reduce translation exposure. If however the loan is denominated in a relatively strong currency, then early repayment is advised, providing that funds are available to do this without detriment to ongoing operations.

(3) A **reduction in the stock level** will reduce the risk of translation exposure since it will reduce the level of net assets. However, such a reduction should not be at the expense of operating efficiency and competitive position in the subsidiary.

Although the advice to reduce translation exposure will improve the appearance of the group's accounts, it must be appreciated that such a loss is different from transaction exposure since it is not a **realised loss**. Indeed it may be effectively offset if high interest rates are linked to high inflation rates which are increasing the market price of the assets. Therefore in reality, hedging these losses may by unnecessary and expensive. In terms of the share price, if the stock market is efficient and shares are priced on the basis of the earning potential of the assets, a historic loss on translation should have little effect on the market position of the shares.

However, sometimes translation losses have real economic consequences if they lead to the breach of a contract such as a loan agreement. Hedging of translation exposure in the real world is common either because of this or a lack of faith in the efficient market hypothesis.

(b) (i) **Multilateral netting** is a procedure whereby the debts of the different group companies denominated in a given currency are netted off against each other. The principal benefit is that foreign exchange purchase costs, including commission, the buy/sell spread and money transmission costs are reduced. Additionally there is less interest lost since money spends less time in transit. Forun would be able to net as shown in the table below.

	Paying company						Net rec'd/
	UK	1	2	3	4	Total rec'd	(paid)
	$'000	$'000	$'000	$'000	$'000	$'000	$'000
UK		300	450	210	270	1,230	(470)
1	700		420		180	1,300	220
2	140	340		410	700	1,590	380
3	300	140	230		350	1,020	(110)
4	560	300	110	510		1,480	(20)
Total paid	1,700	1,080	1,210	1,130	1,500	6,620	0

Although dollar payments amounting to $600,000 will still need to be made by the UK and countries 3 and 4 to countries 1 and 2, these amounts are small in comparison with the total value of transactions which amounts to $6.62m.

(ii) Since Forun is risk-averse with respect to short-term foreign exchange risk it is recommended that it should hedge its short-term exchange exposure. As was calculated above, no net exposure arises on the inter-company transactions denominated in dollars, and therefore there is no need for hedging in this area. However, it is likely to be necessary to hedge transactions with third parties, and the first step is to calculate what the net transactions denominated in foreign currency will be:

	Receipts	*Payments*	*Net*
Australia ($)	3m	3m	0
USA ($)	12m	0	12m
Switzerland (SFr)		13m	(13m)
South Korea (Won)	32bn	0	32bn

There are three alternative methods of hedging available to Forun: using the forward market, using the futures market or using currency options. These will be evaluated below.

(1) **Forward markets**

Forun can use the market to buy and sell currencies forward to match known future payments and receipts. It is known that the dollar and Swiss Franc transactions will take place in six months time and therefore the six months rates will be used. In the case of the won the exact timing of the receipt is uncertain, and therefore the currency will be bought at the rate which is the least favourable to Forun, ie the six month rate. The specific transactions are as follows.

Forun sells $12m at 1.46	£8,219,178
Forun buys SFr13m at 2.383	£5,455,308
Forun sells Won32bn at 2232	£14,336,918

(2) **Futures market**

These can only be used to hedge exposure to the dollar and the Swiss Franc. They are similar to forward exchange contracts, but are traded on a formal exchange and can only be taken out in fixed units of currency. It is assumed that the futures price will move by the same amount as the spot price.

US dollars

Setup

- December contract

- Buy £ futures

- Number of contracts $= \dfrac{\$12\,\text{million} \div 1.48}{62,500}$

    $= 129.7$, say 130 contracts

- Tick size £62,500 × 0.0001 = $6.25

Closing futures price

Assume futures price has moved by 3.9 cents to 1.441, the same as the spot rate.

241   BPP
PUBLISHING

Hedge outcome

- Spot market

	£
At opening spot rate $12m ÷ 1.499	8,005,337
At closing spot rate $12m ÷ 1.46	8,219,178
Gain on spot market	213,841

- Futures market

Opening futures price   1.480 buy
Closing futures price   1.441 sell
Movement in ticks   390 loss
Futures loss 390 × $6.25 × 130 = $316,875

- Net outcome

	£
Spot market receipt	8,219,178
Futures loss (316,875 ÷ 1.46)	(217,038)
	8,002,140

Swiss Francs

Setup

- December contract

- Sell £ futures

- Number of contracts $= \dfrac{\text{SFr13 million} \div 2.448}{62,500}$

  = 84.96, say 85 contracts

- Tick size £62,500 × 0.0001 = SFr6.25

Closing futures price

Assume futures price has moved by SFr0.073 to SFr2.375

Hedge outcome

- Spot market

	£
At opening spot rate SFr13 million ÷ 2.456	5,293,160
At closing spot rate SFr13 million ÷ 2.383	5,455,308
Loss on spot market	(162,148)

- Futures market

Opening futures price   2.448 sell
Closing futures price   2.375 buy

Movement in ticks   730

Futures profit 730 × SFr6.25 × 85 = SFr387,812

- Net outcome

	£
Spot market payment	(5,455,308)
Futures profit (387,812 ÷ 2.383)	162,741
	(5,292,567)

Use of the futures market when compared with the forward contracts is therefore beneficial from the point of view of the Swiss Franc payment, but more costly in terms of the dollar receipt. The cost of basis risk and the need for a margin deposit have been ignored and could affect the relative performance of the two types of hedge.

(3) **Currency options**

These are available in respect of the $12m receipt due in six months time. The benefit of options is that while protecting against downside risk they also allow advantage to be taken of any favourable movements in exchange rates. Forun will probably select December options (since these cover the full period of exposure, and call options are required since the dollars will be used to purchase sterling.)

The **choice of exercise price** depends on the level of risk protection Forun requires. If it only wishes to hedge against movement in the current spot rate then an exercise price of $1.50 will be adequate for a relatively low premium. However, the forward contract provides a rate of $1.46, and if Forun wishes to improve on this it will need to select an exercise price of $1.45 which carries a much higher premium.

The costs of the alternatives are as follows.

Exercise price $1.45

Buy $\dfrac{\$12m/1.45}{31{,}250}$ = 264.8, ie 265 contracts

Premium cost: 265 × £31,250 × $0.0575 = $476,172, at spot rate of $1.496 = £318,297

Exercise price $1.50

Buy $\dfrac{\$12m/1.50}{31{,}250}$ = 256 contracts

Premium cost: 256 × £31,250 × $0.0195 = $156,000, at spot rate of $1.496 = £104,278

Summarised results at various exchange rates

Option price $1.45

- Spot rate $1.40

  Option not exercised

		£
Receipt $\dfrac{\$12{,}000{,}000}{1.40}$		8,571,429
Less: Premium		(318,297)
		8,253,132

- Spot rate $1.45

		£
Receipt $\dfrac{\$12{,}000{,}000}{1.45}$		8,275,862
Less: Premium		(318,297)
		7,957,565

- Spot rate $1.50

  Option exercised; result as for 1.45.

Option price $1.50

- Spot rate $1.40

  Option not exercised

	£
Receipt	8,571,429
Less: Premium	(104,278)
	8,467,151

- Spot rate $1.45

  Option not exercised

	£
Receipt	8,275,862
Less: Premium	(104,278)
	8,171,584

- Spot rate $1.50

	£
Receipt $\dfrac{\$12,000,000}{1.50}$	8,000,000
Less: Premium	(104,278)
	7,895,722

The choice of hedge will depend on expectations of movement in the dollar against the pound during the next six months. The result against a range of possible spot rates can be summarised as follows.

	Sterling December receipts (£'000)		
Exchange rate	*1.40*	*1.45*	*1.50*
Forward contracts	8,219	8,219	8,219
Futures	8,002	8,002	8,002
Options:			
Exercise price 1.45	8,253	7,958	7,958
1.50	8,467	8,172	7,896

If Forun is confident of the dollar strengthening to $1.40/£ by the end of the six months, then a currency option at an exercise price of $1.50 provides the most benefit. However, this does not appear very likely since the forward rate is only $1.46. Forun is known to be risk averse and therefore the safest approach would be to use a forward contract.

64   AXMINE

> **Tutor's hint**. For parts (b) and (c) it is helpful to establish clear steps in the process of analysing the financial implications of the project.
>
> (i)   Realise that since the project is to be undertaken in the foreign country the actual cash flows will be denominated in pesos even though they may be calculated on the basis of sterling figures.
>
> (ii) Once the project cash flows have been established these can be used to calculate the tax liability in the foreign country.
>
> (iii) When tax has been deducted, the net cash flows can be translated into sterling at the appropriate year end rate which is calculated on the basis of the relative inflation rates of the two countries for the year.
>
> (iv) The incremental UK tax payable can then be found, but take care to base this on the taxable income, and not the translated figure including WDAs. The net sterling cash flow can then be discounted to find the NPV of the project. In the report, take into account non-financial factors.

In (d) and (e) avoid the temptation to launch into too much discussion of the political rights or wrongs of writing off LDC debt! Concentrate on what the question asks for, outlines of methods suggested to reduce the problem.

Examiner's comment. Answers to (d) tended to focus on macroeconomic solutions and ignored other methods of resolving the problem (restructuring, forgiveness.) Most candidates failed to appreciate the opportunities the debt problem gave multinationals as well as the problems.

(a) **Non-tariff barriers** of the following types might be imposed.

(i) **Complex bureaucratic procedures**, for example in passing exports through customs, or licensing requirements which must be met before trading. Such measures will delay the trading process for overseas buyers of copper and increase their costs.

(ii) Regulations which **prohibit trade** with particular countries.

(iii) A **quota system on copper exports**, which would maintain higher prices if the country is a major copper supplier or if quotas are also agreed by other copper-exporting countries. Quotas on quantities exported might also help to prevent overexploitation of copper reserves.

(iv) **Setting of minimum or raised prices** for copper through regulations fixing exchange rates for copper sales at non-market levels.

Trade protection measures are often imposed in order to create a favourable balance of trade position and are therefore more often imposed on imports than on exports. If the South American country has a need for foreign exchange to finance imports, for example of oil and machinery, it may in fact wish to encourage exports.

The **General Agreement on Tariffs and Trade (GATT)** has been successful in reducing the general level of tariffs over the past 30 years, but many non-tariff barriers to trade remain. Non-tariff barriers are more difficult to identify than tariffs, for example where they appear as health and safety regulations. However, the reduction of non-tariff barriers was an important aim of the Uruguay round of GATT negotiations. GATT has been re-named the **World Trade Organisation** (WTO).

It may be that the WTO has no effect on the South American country, if it is not a WTO member. If the country does belong to the WTO, it may be able to impose non-tariff barriers of some of the types for which examples are given above, either covertly or more overtly evading WTO requirements.

(b)   REPORT

To: Board of Directors
From: Accountant
Date: 14 December 20X2
Subject: Proposed joint venture with Traces SA

Introduction

This report addresses the **financial implications** of the proposed joint venture with Traces SA. A detailed financial analysis can be found in the Appendix to this report.

Financial implications

On the basis of the assumptions made about **market conditions, likely costs and revenues** and macroeconomic forecasts, the joint venture should produce a positive net present value of £4,722,000 at the lower discount rate of 14%. However, it is likely that this result will be sensitive to changes in the key variables, notably the price of copper over the period, to the relative rates of inflation in the two countries and to other factors influencing the exchange rate. It would be useful to investigate these sensitivities further.

Other considerations

Axmine plc should also consider some of the **wider issues** surrounding the proposed joint venture. These include the nature of the relationship with Traces SA. Can Traces be trusted to fulfil all their obligations with regard to the project? It is assumed that they will be managing the operation and selling the copper - do they have the expertise to do this efficiently and successfully?

A further area of risk concerns the **political stability** of the **country**. Axmine should consider what its position might be and whether it would be able to extract cash from the operation in the event of a change of government.

It would be useful to make **some evaluation** of Axmine's position at the end of the four year period. If it is likely that the joint venture could be extended on favourable terms, then this could further enhance the attractiveness of the project.

Conclusions

On financial grounds, the project appears to be well worth undertaking since it yields a **large positive NPV**. However the sensitivities should be calculated and some of the wider issues surrounding the joint venture addressed before Axmine finally commits itself to the project.

APPENDIX

Annual cash flows (pesos, million)

Year	0	1	2	3	4	5
Sales		1,925	3,215	4,952	7,109	
Costs:						
Machinery	800					
WDA		200	200	200	200	
Supervisors		101	165	250	352	
Local expenses		900	1,476	2,232	3,146	
Taxable	(800)	724	1,374	2,270	3,411	
SA tax (20%)			(145)	(275)	(454)	(682)
Add back WDA		200	200	200	200	
Net cash	(800)	924	1,429	2,195	3,157	(682)

Annual sterling cash flows (£'000)

Year	0	1	2	3	4	5
	£'000	£'000	£'000	£'000	£'000	£'000
Net cash	(5,714)	3,960	4,033	4,425	4,876	(857)
UK tax (15%)			(465)	(582)	(686)	(790)
	(5,714)	3,960	3,568	3,843	4,190	(1,647)
Discount (14%)	1.000	0.877	0.769	0.675	0.592	0.519
Present value	(5,714)	3,473	2,744	2,594	2,480	(855)

Total expected NPV = £4,722,000

Notes

1   The WDAs are added back to the cash flow after the tax has been calculated and deducted because they do not involve any movement in cash terms.

2   UK tax is calculated on the taxable revenue arising in the previous year, translated at the exchange rate ruling at the end of that year ie tax in year 2 is

calculated on the total of 724 million pesos, translated at 233.33 pesos/£. The tax rate used is the incremental rate of 15% (35% − 20%), since tax has already been paid in the country where the income arises and, because of the tax treaty, all foreign tax paid is allowable against UK tax. No adjustment has to be made to the WDAs since the rate is the same in both countries.

Workings

The exchange rate at the end of each year can be calculated using the **purchasing power parity theory** (P'm = millions of pesos).

$$\text{Rate after one year} = \text{spot rate} \times 1 + \left(\frac{i_f - i_{UK}}{1 + i_{UK}} \right)$$

For example, rate at year $1 = 140 \times \left(1 + \dfrac{0.80 - 0.08}{1 + 0.08} \right) = 233.33$

Year	SA infl'n	UK infl'n	Forecast exchange rate
	%	%	P/£
0	100.00	8.00	140.00
1	80.00	8.00	233.33
2	64.00	8.00	354.32
3	51.20	8.00	496.05
4	40.96	8.00	647.44
5	32.77	8.00	795.92

Supervisors' salaries payable in pesos will be:

Year	Infl'n		
	%	£'000	P'm
0	8.00	400.00	
1	8.00	432.00	101
2	8.00	466.56	165
3	8.00	503.88	250
4	8.00	544.20	352

Copper revenues in pesos will be:

Year	Prod'n '000 kg	Infl'n %	Price £/1000kg	Revenue £'000	Revenue P'm
0			1,500.00		
1	5,000	10.00	1,650.00	8,250.00	1,925
2	5,000	10.00	1,815.00	9,075.00	3,215
3	5,000	10.00	1,996.50	9,982.50	4,952
4	5,000	10.00	2,196.15	10,980.75	7,109

Local labour costs and expenses will be:

Year	Infl'n %	P'm
0	100.00	500
1	80.00	900
2	64.00	1,476
3	51.20	2,232
4	40.96	3,146

(c) If **inflation** increases rapidly during the life of the project, provided that the purchasing power parity theory holds good, the exchange rate should move in such a way that local costs (when translated into sterling) effectively only increase at the rate of inflation in the UK (8%). Since it is predicted that copper prices (fixed in sterling) will increase at 10% per year, the project should continue to be attractive.

One adverse effect would be that the value of the **writing down allowances** would be diminished since they are fixed at 200m pesos per year. However, this should be more than offset by the fact that tax is payable a year in arrears. The net effect of this should be to increase the expected NPV of the joint venture.

(d) **Nature of debt crisis**

The 'debt crisis' of Less Developed Countries (LDCs) appeared in the early 1980s when developed counties allowed interest rates to rise sharply following the OPEC oil price increase of 1979. Whereas some counties experienced severe debt problems but recovered, others remained in a severely indebted state.

Reduction of debt problem

Methods to reduce the problem have included **internal measures** by LDCs to restore economic prosperity and **external action** by lenders and the international community to reduce the debt burden. Internal measures to restore prosperity include **investment** in physical and social **infrastructure**, including **education, removal of trade** and other **regulatory restrictions, reduction of tariffs** and **adoption of floating exchange rates**. External action by lenders, especially the IMF, is frequently dependent on these reforms taking place.

Alleviation of debt burden

Methods for relieving the debt burden have included the following.

(i) **Rescheduling of debt**. This includes **postponement** of repayment, **replacement with low interest debt** from international organisations (eg World Bank, IMF) on conditions of economic restructuring such as **control over the money supply** and **reduction in government expenditure.**

(ii) **Moratorium on service payments.** Lenders have permitted postponement of interest payments for a period, in the hope that the economy recovers sufficiently to resume payments later.

(iii) **Writing off debt.** Lenders have cancelled some of the debts of heavily indebted countries on **strict conditions** of **economic, social** and **structural reform**.

(iv) **Securitisation of debt.** Some debt has been sold on secondary markets at heavily discounted prices because of the high probability of default. This has enabled indebted countries to **buy the debt back** or to **swap it** for **equity** in local companies, thus reducing indebtedness.

From time to time, various combinations of these methods have been organised into international plans (eg the Baker Plan and Brady Plan of the 1980s and the Heavily Indebted Poor Countries Initiative of the 1990s).

(e) **Problems for multinational companies**

High national debt is often associated with **political instability, high inflation** and **rapid currency devaluation,** all of which act as deterrents to foreign direct investment. A multinational will not wish to invest in a country where it **cannot guarantee ownership** and/or **control** over its assets, and the **value of its business** is progressively **devalued** by currency shifts. The work of the international community (e.g. IMF, World Bank and other donors) to improve political, legal and economic stability in these countries is therefore vital. Some of the conditions imposed (money supply or government expenditure controls) may, at least in the short-term, be **deflationary** and thus limit demand for investing companies' products.

Opportunities for multinational companies

The advantage of a heavily indebted country to a multinational is the country's desperate need for **foreign capital, technology and expertise.** This may allow negotiation of **advantageous concessions** on **licensing, reduced compliance costs** and **taxation,** and few **formalities** involved in setting up operations.

65 VTW

> **Tutor's hint.** If you read the first part of this question too quickly, it may deceive you. At first sight it looks as if, among other things, it is testing your knowledge of interest rate parity theory. In fact this is totally irrelevant. You need to be able to calculate an exchange rate over three years as one currency depreciates against another, to make PV calculations, and to be able to formulate the problem in the form of an equation so that you can estimate the interest rate.
>
> **Examiner's comment.** For part (a), few candidates produced estimates of the present value of cash flows that would be needed for the investment to be viable, and interest rate estimates varied from negative interest to more than 200% per annum. Unrealistic solutions create a poor impression on the examiner. If answers are obviously unrealistic a comment to that effect might reassure the examiner. Part (b) was well answered by almost all candidates who attempted it.

(a)   The first step is to **calculate the present value in sterling** from the expected dividend stream over the next three years, assuming that the remittance of dividends is not blocked. The cash flows will be discounted at 20%, since this was the rate used in the appraisal of the investment.

	Year 1	Year 2	Year 3	Total
Dividend in pesos (millions)	180	180	180	
Exchange rate (peso/£)	22.00	24.20	26.62	
Dividend in £m	8.182	7.438	6.762	
20% discount factors	0.833	0.694	0.579	
Present value (£m)	6.816	5.162	3.915	15.893

For the investment to remain financially viable, the expected **NPV must remain positive.** The maximum by which the PV cash flows can fall is therefore £2m. Therefore the PV of the cash flows from the remittances must not fall below £13.893m (£15.893m – £2m). If 'x' is the South American country's interest rate, the situation can be summarised as follows. It is assumed that no remittance of interest will be possible until the end of year 3.

	Year 1	Year 2	Year 3
Funds available to invest (pesos)	180	180	180
Funds accumulated at end of year 3	$180(1+x)^2$	$180(1+x)$	180
Exchange rate at which funds will be remitted (peso/£)			26.62
Discount factor			0.579

The following expression can therefore be used to find the minimum rate of interest that will make the investment worthwhile.

$$£13.894\text{m} = \frac{0.579\,(180\,(1+x)^2 + 180\,(1+x) + 180)}{26.62}$$

This can be solved by trial and error, substituting different interest rates until one is found that approximates to a return of £13.893m.

At 15%

$$£13.595m = \frac{0.579\,(180\,(1.15)^2 + 180\,(1.15) + 180)}{26.62}$$

At 17%

$$£13.855m = \frac{0.579\,(180\,(1.17)^2 + 180\,(1.17) + 180)}{26.62}$$

At 18%

$$£13.986m = \frac{0.579\,(180\,(1.18)^2 + 180\,(1.18) + 180)}{26.62}$$

The interest rate at which the NPV falls to zero therefore lies somewhere between 17% and 18%. For the project to remain variable, the interest rate therefore needs to be at 18% or above.

(b) VTW might try to avoid the block on dividend remittances by some of the following methods.

    (i)   If the foreign subsidiary purchases materials or services from the parent company, the **transfer price** could be **raised**. Similarly, if it sells goods to the parent company, the transfer price for these goods could be lowered.

    (ii)   If VTW could make a part of the funding in the form of a **loan**, it might be able to recover some of the funds in the form of interest payments.

    (iii)   The subsidiary could make a **loan to the parent company** that is equivalent in amount to the dividend payments.

    (iv)   Other **forms of cash transfer** could include:

        (1) Patent fees
        (2) Royalties
        (3) Management fees
        (4) Head office overhead charges

    Unfortunately, it is likely that the government of the South American country is likely to block many of these measures as well.

(c) **Multilateral netting** is a procedure whereby the **debts** of the different group companies denominated in a given currency are **netted off** against each other. The principal benefit is that foreign exchange purchase costs, including commission, the buy/sell spread and money transmission costs are reduced. Additionally there is less interest lost since money spends less time in transit.

Tandem would be able to net as shown in the table below.

Receiving company	UK	A	Paying company B	C	D	Total received	Net rec'd /(paid)
	$'000	$'000	$'000	$'000	$'000	$'000	$'000
UK	-	621	751	147	-	1,519	(376)
A	1,024	-	682	329	-	2,035	667
B	671	518	-	568	56	1,813	12
C	-	229	247	-	-	476	(568)
D	200	-	121	-	-	321	265
Total paid	1,895	1,368	1,801	1,044	56	6,164	

Although dollar payments amounting to $944,000 will still need to be made by the UK and country C to countries A, B and D, the amounts are small in comparison with the total value of transactions, which amounts to $6,164,000.

66   CENTRALISATION

> **Tutor's hint.** This question provides an excellent summary of the advantages of a centralised treasury department. To complete the picture you should also study the risks involved.
>
> **Examiner's comment.** (a) was well answered. Some candidates scored full marks. The main weakness was in simply describing possible problems rather than suggesting how the company could minimise these problems. In (b) most candidate did not emphasise correctly the standard deviation of the new combined account.

MEMORANDUM

(a)   To: Directors of all foreign subsidiaries
      From: Group Finance Director

Centralisation of treasury management operations

At its last meeting, the board of directors of Touten plc made the decision to centralise group treasury management operations. A further memo giving detailed plans will be circulated shortly, but my objective in this memo is to outline the potential benefits of treasury centralisation and how any potential problems arising at subsidiaries can be minimised. Most of you will be familiar with the basic arguments, which we have been discussing informally for some time.

What it means

Centralisation of treasury management means that most decisions on borrowing, investment of cash surpluses, currency management and financial risk management will be taken by an enhanced central treasury team, based at head office, instead of by subsidiaries directly. In addition we propose to set most transfer prices for inter-company goods and services centrally.

The potential benefits

The main benefits are:

(i)   **Cost savings** resulting from reduction of unnecessary banking charges
(ii)   **Reduction of the group's total taxation charge**
(iii) **Enhanced control over financial risk**

Reduction in banking charges will result from:

(i)   **Netting off inter-company debts before settlement**. At the moment we are spending too much on foreign exchange commission by settling inter-company debts in a wide range of currencies through the banking system.

(ii) **Knowledge of total group currency exposure from transactions**. Debtors in one subsidiary can hedge creditors in another, eliminating unnecessary hedging by subsidiaries.

(iii) **Knowledge of the group's total cash resources and borrowing requirement**. This will reduce the incidence of one company lending cash while a fellow subsidiary borrows at a higher interest rate and will also eliminate unnecessary interest rate hedging. It will also facilitate higher deposit rates and lower borrowing rates.

Reduction in the group's tax charge will be possible by a comprehensive centrally-set **transfer pricing policy**.

Enhanced control over financial risks will be possible because we will be able to develop a central team of specialists who will have a clear-cut strategy on hedging and risk management. Many of you have requested help in this area.

This team will be able to ensure that decisions are taken in line with **group strategy** and will also be able to provide you with enhanced financial information to assist you with your own decision making.

Potential problems for subsidiaries and their solution

Our group culture is one of **decentralisation** and **enablement of management at individual subsidiary level**. There is no intention to change this culture. Rather, it is hoped that releasing you from specialist treasury decisions will enable you to devote more time to developing your own business units.

The system can only work properly, however, if **information exchange** between head office and subsidiaries is swift and efficient. Enhanced computer systems are to be provided at all centres to assist you with daily reports. It is also important that you keep head office informed of all local conditions that could be beneficial to the treasury function, such as the availability of local subsidised loans, as well as potential local risks such as the threat of exchange control restrictions.

You will find that movements in your cash balances will be affected by **group policy**, as will reported profitability. Any adjustments made by head office will be eliminated when preparing the performance reports for your own business units and we will ensure that joint venture partners are not penalised by group policy.

Please contact me with any further comments that you may have on our new treasury policy.

(b) The current level of cash balances that will be held, allowing three standard deviations from the mean, will be as follows (all figures in millions):

	Average need (local)	3 standard deviations	Total (local)	Exchange rate	Total £m
Gotop plc (UK)	5.5	1.5	7.0	1.00	7.000
Malaysia	8.0	3.0	11.0	3.95	2.785
Hong Kong	18.0	8.1	26.1	11.98	2.179
Total held					11.964

If the accounts are combined into a single account held in the UK, the standard deviation of the new account can be calculated as follows.

	Standard deviation: local	Exchange rate	Standard deviation £m
Gotop plc (UK)	0.5	1.00	0.500
Malaysia	1.0	3.95	0.253
Hong Kong	2.7	11.98	0.225

New standard deviation $= \sqrt{(0.5)^2 + (0.253)^2 + (0.225)^2}$ = £603,850

The average sterling cash need is as follows.

	Average need (local)	Exchange rate	Total £m
Gotop plc (UK)	5.5	1.00	5.500
Malaysia	8.0	3.95	2.025
Hong Kong	18.0	11.98	1.503
Total need			9.028

To this must be added three standard deviations ie $3 \times £603,850$:

£9.028m + £1.812m = £10.840m

The **overall reduction in the level of cash balances** as a result of combining the accounts will therefore be £11.964m – £10.840m = £1.124 million.

67   DEBOIS

> **Tutor's hint**. This is an unusual question, since it is intended by the examiner to deal entirely with **cash** rather than the more commonly discussed **funds**. It is the type of question that encourages you to draw on your practical experience of the international payments system, rather than on theoretical knowledge.
>
> **Examiner's comment**. Many answers to part (a) concentrated too heavily on the influence of governments and political risk, rather than factors such as cost, security, speed and reliability.

(a)   One of the key factors in the management of cash is the need to keep the 'float' to a minimum. The float is the amount of money tied up between the time when a payment is initiated and the time when the funds become available for use in the recipient's bank account. The detailed arrangements that a company uses for the international transfer of cash may therefore vary depending on whether the cash is being transferred within the group, or to a third party. Factors that are relevant include:

(i)   **Cost** – a lower cost transfer will be preferred, all other things being equal

(ii)   **Security** – the risk of fraud or theft must be minimised as far as possible

(iii)   **Reliability** – the mechanism used must be capable of making the transfer at the agreed time

(iv)   **Accuracy** – the correct amount must be transmitted from the correct account to the correct party

(v)   **Speed** – the need for speed will depend on the nature of the transaction, as discussed above

In general, faster more secure means of payment will cost more. The company must therefore decide what is appropriate in any given circumstances, taking into account the size and nature of the transaction.

(b)   (i)   The current position is as follows.

	UK company DKr'000	German company DKr'000	Total DKr'000
Revenues and taxes in the local country			
Sales	18,000	43,750	61,750
Production expenses	(14,400)	(35,000)	(49,400)
Taxable profit	3,600	8,750	12,350
Tax (1)	(900)	(3,500)	(4,400)
Dividend to Denmark	2,700	5,250	7,950
Withholding tax (2)	0	420	420
Revenues and taxes in Denmark			
Dividend	2,700	5,250	7,950
Add back foreign tax paid	900	3,500	4,400
Taxable income	3,600	8,750	12,350
Danish tax due (33.3%)	1,199	2,914	4,113
Foreign tax credit	(900)	(2,914)	(3,814)
Tax paid in Denmark (3)	299	0	299
Total tax (1) + (2) + (3)	1,199	3,920	5,119

PUBLISHING

An increase of 20% in the transfer price would have the following effect.

	UK company DKr '000	German company DKr '000	Total DKr '000
Revenues and taxes in the local country			
Sales	21,600	43,750	65,350
Production expenses	(14,400)	(38,600)	(53,000)
Taxable profit	7,200	5,150	12,350
Tax (1)	(1,800)	(2,060)	(3,860)
Dividend to Denmark	5,400	3,090	8,490
Withholding tax (2)	0	247	247
Revenues and taxes in Denmark			
Dividend	5,400	3,090	8,490
Add back foreign tax paid	1,800	2,060	3,860
Taxable income	7,200	5,150	12,350
Danish tax due	2,398	1,715	4,113
Foreign tax credit	(1,800)	(1,715)	(3,515)
Tax paid in Denmark (3)	598	0	598
Total tax (1) + (2) + (3)	2,398	2,307	4,705

The total tax payable by Debois is therefore reduced by DKr414,000 to DKr4.705million.

(ii)   In practice, governments usually seek to prevent multinationals reducing their tax liability through the **manipulation of transfer prices**. For tax purposes, governments will normally demand that an 'arm's length' price is used in the computation of the taxable profit and not an artificial transfer price. If no such 'arm's length' price is available then there may be some scope for tax minimisation through the choice of the transfer price.

If it is possible to manipulate the transfer price in this way there are **further factors** that the company must take into consideration before making a final decision.

(1)   The **level of transfer prices** will affect the **movement of funds** within the group. If inter company sales involve the use of different currencies the level of the transfer price will also affect the group's foreign exchange exposure. These factors must be taken into account as well as the tax situation.

(2)   The level of profit reported by the subsidiary could affect its **local credit rating** and this could be important if the company wishes to raise funds locally. It could also affect the ease with which credit can be obtained from suppliers.

(3)   The reported profit is likely to have an effect on the **motivation of managers** and staff in the subsidiary. If reported profits are high then they may become complacent and cost control may become weak. If on the other hand profits are continually low, they may become demotivated.

(4)   Transfer prices that do not reflect market levels may lead to subsidiaries making '**make or buy' decisions** that do not optimise the performance of the group as a whole.

68   TAX HAVEN

> **Tutor's hint.** The tax advantages of a tax haven must be weighed against any legal or regulatory restrictions and possible difficulties of operation from that country. The computation in part (b) is easy if set out in tabular format.
>
> **Examiner's comment.** Some candidates failed to gross up the dividends.

(a) For multinational companies, the main factors to consider when deciding whether or not to use a tax haven are as follows.

The amount of tax that can be saved

The amount of tax that can be saved will depend on the **taxes imposed** and **tax rates** in the tax haven compared with those in the existing location, taking into account any **tax treaties** with other countries. If the home country imposes **restrictions** when a tax haven is in use, the advantages may be diminished.

The legal and regulatory framework

This includes laws of ownership, company law, accounting, banking and secrecy rules. **Exchange control regulations** could make a location unattractive.

The ease of operation from the tax haven

The ease of operation depends on many factors including **set-up and operating costs**, the effectiveness of the communications infrastructure, and general **political and economic stability**.

Advantages of specific locations

These may include **proximity** to a **large customer base** or the **organisation's main production location**.

(b) If no tax haven is used:

£'000	Mopia	Blueland	Saddonia	Total
Net dividend	600	800	1,500	
Tax rate	40%	35%	20%	
Grossed up dividend	1,000	1,231	1,875	4,106
Local tax paid	400	431	375	1,206
UK tax liability @30%	300	369	563	
UK tax credit	(300)	(369)	(375)	
Net UK tax paid	-	-	188	188
Total tax charge				1,394

If a tax haven is used, the total grossed up dividend is £4,106,000 on which UK tax at 30% is £1,232,000. Local tax already paid is £1,206,000 leaving a tax liability in the UK of only £26,000. This gives a saving of £162,000.

(c) The factors which are relevant to choosing between borrowing on the euromarkets or the domestic markets are as follows.

(i)   **The currency that the borrower wants to obtain**. Multinational companies often want to borrow in a foreign currency (to reduce their foreign exchange exposure) and it might be more convenient to borrow on the **euromarkets** than in a foreign domestic market. Where foreign exchange exposure can be reduced by **matching income** in a **foreign currency** against interest and capital repayments on borrowing, a further advantage of euromarket borrowing might be that **interest rates** on a foreign currency borrowing might be **lower** than domestic interest rates. For a UK company, interest rates on euros might be a lot less than interest rates on sterling.

(ii) **Cost**. There is often a **small difference** in **interest rates** between eurocurrency and domestic markets. On large borrowing, however, even a small difference in rates can result in a large difference in the total interest charge on the loan.

(iii) **Timing and speed**. In the past, it has usually been possible to raise money on the Euromarkets **more quickly** than on the domestic markets.

(iv) **Security**. **Euromarket loans** are usually **unsecured**, whereas **domestic market loans** are more commonly **secured**. Large borrowers might wish to avoid having to give security and prefer to ask lenders to rely on the borrower's high credit rating.

(v) **Size of loan**. It is often easier for a **large multinational** to raise **very large sums** on the euromarkets rather than in a domestic financial market.

69 PREPARATION QUESTION: ELECTRONICS

> **Tutor's hint.** (a) requires a general discussion on dividend policy but in part (b) you must comment on the figures given. The company's pay-out ratio is falling but the money is being reinvested for profit growth which allows high dividend growth.

(a) In perfect markets a company's dividend policy is not as important as its ability to invest wisely in profitable business projects. If shareholders' funds are invested profitably, they will generate **increased future cash flows**, the expectations of which will cause an **enhanced share price** which more than compensates for a reduced dividend, provided investors receive appropriate information about cash flow prospects.

In reality however, markets are not perfect. In particular:

(i) **Information** to shareholders is **not perfect** and dividends may act as a cheap and valuable method of signalling longer term growth prospects. Many companies aim to pay a steady stream of dividends which smooths out profit fluctuations and which grows at least as fast as inflation.

(ii) **Share issue costs** are **significant**. This gives companies an **incentive** to **use retained earnings** as their main source of equity finance and encourages lower dividend payouts.

(iii) Because of **tax rules**, shareholders differ in their attitude to the proportion of their return taken as dividend compared with capital gains. For a company with a broad spread of shareholders this problem is difficult to resolve.

Other factors influencing dividend policy include:

(i) **The company's rate of growth**. In general, fast growth usually results in a higher proportion of earnings retained and hence a lower pay-out ratio.

(ii) **Volatility of cash flows.** If cash flows are highly volatile, this will also motivate a lower payout ratio in case a dip in future profitability prevents the payment of a smooth trend of dividends.

(iii) **Liquidity**. If dividends are not planned far enough in advance, they may be affected by short term liquidity problems.

(iv) **Legal factors**. Sometimes dividend payments are restricted by company law (e.g. payment from reserves) and sometimes by government restraints, for example on the repatriation of profits from local subsidiaries of foreign companies.

(b)   A major institutional shareholder suggests that the company's dividend payout should be substantially increased. From the figures below it can be seen that the dividend payout has declined as a percentage of earnings from 38% in 20X4 to 31% in 20X8. However, because of very strong earnings growth, **dividends** have **increased steadily** each year by between 7% and 13% in real terms. On this basis there appears to be little substance to the investor's complaint.

However, the share price does not appear to have improved as fast as earnings per share and there may be questions concerning the **risk** of the company's investments or the market's **confidence** in **future growth.** Without comparative data for the market as a whole or for similar companies, however, it is impossible to draw any further conclusions.

	20X4	*20X5*	*20X6*	*20X7*	*20X8*
Earnings per share (pence)	25.6	32.5	39.2	42.4	50.8
% increase		27%	21%	8%	20%
% increase in real terms		23%	18%	5%	17%
Dividend per share (pence)	9.75	11.0	12.75	14.0	15.5
% increase		13%	16%	10%	11%
% increase in real terms		8%	13%	7%	7%
Dividend payout (DPS/EPS)	38%	34%	33%	33%	31%

70   DIVS

> **Tutor's hint.** In part (a)(i), the examiner means a scrip *issue*.
>
> **Examiner's comment.** Marks were frequently lost in part (a) through focusing upon the effect on income of the alternatives, without any consideration of the effect on overall wealth. Answers to (b) were good, with the best marks being awarded to candidates who showed good understanding of the assumptions and limitations of the Miller and Modigliani analysis, and practical influences on the choice of dividend level.

(a)   The Companies Act 1985, gives companies rights to buy back shares from shareholders who are willing to sell them, subject to certain conditions. To give an example, a number of the privatised UK electricity companies have made significant share repurchases during recent years.

Share repurchases enable occasional distributions of surplus funds to be made, without raising expectations of a sustained rise in dividend levels. Among the possible **benefits** of a share repurchase scheme are the following.

(i)   **Finding a use for surplus cash,** which may be a 'dead asset'.

(ii)   **Increase** in **earnings per share** through a reduction in the number of shares in issue. This could lead to a higher share price than would otherwise be the case.

(iii)   **Increase in gearing**. Repurchase of a company's own shares allows debt to be substituted for equity, so raising gearing. This will be of interest to a company wanting to increase its gearing without increasing its total long-term funding.

(iv)   **Readjustment** of the company's **equity base** to more appropriate levels, for a company whose business is in decline.

(v)   Share repurchase may also fulfil **special purposes,** such as preventing a takeover or enabling a quoted company to withdraw from the stock market.

There are also possible **disadvantages** of a share buyback.

(i)   It can be hard to arrive at a **price** which will be **fair** both to the vendors and to any shareholders who are not selling shares to the company.

(ii)   A purchase of shares could be seen as an admission that the company cannot **make better use** of the funds than the shareholders.

(iii) Some shareholders may suffer from being **taxed** on a **capital gain** following the repurchase of their shares rather than receiving dividend income.

(b)   The theory developed by Modigliani and Miller (MM) concerning the irrelevance of dividends in the valuation of a company only holds good under a number of restricting assumptions. The strength of the theory in practice is lessened by a number of distortions, as follows.

(i)   **Transaction costs**

The MM theory assumes that there are **no transaction costs**. In practice this is not the case and shareholders must incur costs in realising a part of the capital gain on their shareholding in order to obtain income. Shareholders who require a regular income from their investment may therefore have a preference for dividends.

(ii)   **Personal taxation**

The **rate** of tax on **dividends and capital gains** in some countries is different, generally with capital gains being taxed at a lower rate. This may mean that investors have a preference for a higher level of capital gains to dividends.

(iii)   **Issue costs**

A company that requires funds for additional investment will generally favour the use of retained earnings since these do not incur the **costs** associated with **new issues of debt and equity**.

(iv)   **Imperfect information**

If both directors and shareholders do not possess the same amount of information about future prospects this may mean that shareholders have **different views** to the directors as to the most appropriate dividend policy.

Thus it can be seen that the level of dividends is relevant to the value of a company and hence the share price and the funds that can be attracted for further investment. The key factors that will determine whether an increase in dividends is beneficial to the shareholders are as follows.

(i)   **Opportunities for alternative investment**

If the company has investment opportunities available which yield a **positive NPV** then it will be to the benefit of the shareholders if a proportion of earnings are **retained and invested** in this way since such an investment should increase the net worth of the company. If however such opportunities are not available then it may be more appropriate to return a higher level of funds to the shareholders.

(ii)   **Cash position**

The company must have **sufficient liquid funds** available to **support the increase** in the level of dividend payments. If cash resources fall too low then the operating capability of the company is put at risk, to the disadvantage of the shareholders.

Dividends are often treated as a **signal of the future prospects of a company**. In this case, the company's growth is slowing and so the reason for any dividend increase should be explained to investors to avoid unrealistic expectations of higher future earnings being created.

Strategic Financial Management

BPP Mock Exam 1:

June 2002

Question Paper:	
Time allowed	**3 hours**
This paper is divided into two sections	
Section A	**BOTH questions are compulsory and MUST be attempted**
Section B	**TWO questions ONLY to be answered**

Disclaimer of liability

Please note that we have based our predictions of the content of the June 2002 exam on our long experience of the ACCA exams. We do not claim to have any endorsement of the predictions from either the examiner or the ACCA and we do not guarantee that either the specific questions, or the general areas, that are forecast will necessarily be included in the exams, in part or in whole.

We do not accept any liability or responsibility to any person who takes, or does not take, any action based (either in whole or in part and either directly or indirectly) upon any statement or omission made in this book. We encourage students to study all topics in the ACCA syllabus and the mock exam in this book is intended as an aid to revision only.

paper 3.7

DO NOT OPEN THIS PAPER UNTIL YOU ARE READY TO START

UNDER EXAMINATION CONDITIONS

Section A – ALL questions are compulsory and MUST be attempted

1 Romage plc has two major operating divisions, manufacturing and property sales, with turnovers of £260 million and £620 million respectively

BALANCE SHEET FOR ROMAGE PLC

	£m
Land and buildings	80
Plant and machinery	140
Current assets	250
Current liabilities	180
	290
Financed by:	
Ordinary shares (25 pence par)	50
Reserves	130
Secured term loan	60
13% debentures 2015 (£100 par)	50
	290

Summarised cash flow data for Romage plc:

	£m
Cash turnover	880
Divisional operating expenses	803
Central costs	8
Interest	11
Taxation	14
Dividends	15

The company's current share price is 296 pence, and the market value of a debenture is £131.

Projected real (ie excluding inflation) per tax financial data (£ million) of the two divisions are:

Year	1	2	3	4	5	6 onwards
Manufacturing:						
Operating net cash flows	45	48	50	52	57	60
Allocated central costs	4	4	4	4	4	4
Tax allowable depreciation	10	8	7	8	8	8
Property sales:						
Operating net cash flows	32	40	42	44	46	50
Allocated central costs	4	3	3	3	3	3
Tax allowable depreciation	5	5	5	5	5	5

Corporate taxation is at the rate of 31% per year, payable in the year that the relevant cash flow arises.

Inflation is expected to remain at approximately 3% per year.

The risk free rate is 5.5%, and the market return 14%.

Romage's equity beta is 1.15

The company is considering a demerger whereby the two divisions are floated separately on the stock market. The debenture would be serviced by the property division and the term loan by the manufacturing division. The existing equity would be split evenly between the divisions, although new ordinary shares would be issued to replace existing shares.

The average equity betas in the manufacturing and property sectors are 1.3 and 0.9 respectively, and the gearing levels in manufacturing and property sales by market values are 70% equity 30% debt, and 80% equity 20% debt respectively.

Notes

(1) Allocated central costs reflect actual cash flows. If a demerger occurs these costs would rise to £6 million per year for each company.

(2) A demerger would involve a one-off after tax cost of £16 million in year one which would be split evenly between the two companies. There would be no other significant impact on expected cash flows.

(3) The current cost of the debenture and term loan are almost identical.

(4) The debenture is redeemable at par.

Required:

(a) **Discuss the potential advantages for Romage plc of undertaking the divestment of one of its divisions by means of:**

     (i)   **a sell-off and**
     (ii)   **a demerger**   (8 marks)

(b) **Using real cash flows, evaluate whether or not it is expected to be financially advantageous to the original shareholders Romage plc for the company to separately float the two divisions on the stock market. Your evaluate should use both a 15 year time horizon and an infinite time horizon.**

     In any gearing estimates the manufacturing division may be assumed to comprise 5% of the market value of equity of Romage plc, and the property sale division 45%.

     State clearly any additional assumptions that you make.   (24 marks)

(c) **Discuss what additional information and analysis would assist the decision process.**   (8 marks)

                                                    (40 marks)

2   (a) Assume that you are the financial manager of a UK company which currently trades only with major European countries. Your managing director has strongly advocated that the UK should join the European Monetary Union (EMU) as sterling will then be replaced by the Euro, which will result in significant savings in transactions costs, and will eliminate all foreign exchange exposure for your company.

     Discuss whether or not the managing director is correct in his comments.

                                                         (5 marks)

     (b) Retilon plc is a medium sized UK company that trades with companies in several European countries. Trade deals over the next three months are shown below. Assume that it is now 20 April.

	Two months time		Three months time	
	Receipts	*Payments*	*Receipts*	*Payments*
France	-	€393,265	€491,011	€60,505
Germany	-	-	€890,217	€1,997,651
Denmark	-	-	Kr 8.6m	-

Foreign exchange rates:

	Dkroner/£	Euro €/£
Spot	10.68 – 10.71	1.439 – 1.465
Two months forward	10.74 – 10.77	1.433 – 1.459
Three months forward	10.78 – 10.83	1.431 – 1.456

Annual interest rates (valid for 2 months or 3 months)

	Borrowing %	Investing %
United Kingdom	7.50	5.50
France	5.75	3.50
Germany	5.75	3.50
Denmark	8.00	6.00

Futures market rates:

Three month Euro contracts (125,000 Euro contract size)

Contracts are for buying or selling Euros. Futures prices are in £ per Euro.

June	0.6964
September	0.6983
December	0.7013

Required:

(i) Using the forward market, money market and currency futures market as appropriate devise a foreign exchange hedging strategy that is expected to maximise the cash flows of Retilon plc at the end of the three month period.

Transactions costs and margin requirements may be ignored for this part of the question. Basis risk may be assumed to be zero at the time the contracts are closed out. Futures contracts may be assumed to mature at the month end.   (15 marks)

(ii) Successive daily prices on the futures market for a June contract which you have sold are:

Selling price	0.6916
Day 1	0.6930
Day 2	0.6944
Day 3	0.6940

Initial margins are £1,000 per contract. Variation margin is 100% of the initial margin.

Spot exchange rates may be assumed to not change significantly during these three days.

Required:

For each of the three days, show the effect on your cash flow of the price changes of the contract.   (4 marks)

(c) Discuss the advantages and disadvantages of forward contracts and currency futures for hedging against foreign exchange risk.   (6 marks)

(30 marks)

Section B – TWO questions ONLY to be answered

3   (a) **In finance theory, it is often assumed that stock markets in the UK and the USA are semi-strong form efficient. Explain this assumption and its implications for financial managers.**   **(6 marks)**

(b) Your managing director has just attended a meeting with an investment analyst who has suggested that your company's shares are overvalued by 10%. The data used by the investment analyst in her calculations is shown below.

Year	Total dividends £'000	Number of shares	Total earnings £'000
20X6	5,680	28,560,000	18,260
20X7	6,134	28,600,000	21,320
20X8	8,108	35,000,000	26,710
20X9	10,007	40,000,000	28,620

Your company's current share price is 645 pence and the cost of equity is estimated to be 12.5%.

Required:

Prepare a brief report for the managing director discussing whether or not your company's shares are likely to be overvalued. Relevant calculations should form part of your report.   **(9 marks)**

4   (a) **Briefly discuss the main ways in which companies might achieve the international transfer of cash.**   **(6 marks)**

(b) HGT plc is a UK based multinational company with two overseas subsidiaries. the company wishes to minimise its global tax bill, and part of its tax strategy is to try to take advantage of opportunities provided by transfer pricing.

HGT has subsidiaries in Glinland and Rytora

Taxation	UK	Glinland	Rytora
Corporate tax on profits	30%	40%	25%
Withholding tax on dividends	-	10%	-
Import tariffs on all goods (not tax allowable)	-	-	10%

The subsidiary in Glinland produces 150,000 graphite golf club shafts per year which are then sent to Rytora for the metal heads to be added and the clubs finished off. The shafts have a variable cost in Glinland of £6 each, and annual fixed costs are £140,000. The shafts are sold to the Rytoran subsidiary at variable cost plus 75%.

The Rytoran subsidiary incurs additional unit variable costs of £9, annual fixed costs of £166,000, and sells the finished clubs at £30 each in Rytora.

Bi-lateral tax agreements exist which allow foreign tax paid to be credited against UK tax liability.

All transactions between the companies are in pounds sterling. The Rytoran subsidiary remits all profit after tax to the UK parent company each year, and the Glinland subsidiary remits 50% of its profit after tax.

Required:

The parent company is considering instructing the Glinland subsidiary to sell the shafts to the Rytoran subsidiary at full cost. Evaluate the possible

effect of this on tax and tariff payments, and discuss briefly any possible problems with this strategy. (9 marks)

(15 marks)

5   (a) Discuss whether trade blocs stimulate or impair international trade.

(11 marks)

(b) Discuss how non-tariff barriers to international trade may be overcome.

(4 marks)

(15 marks)

6   (a) Define free cash flow, discuss the possible conflicts that might exist between managers and shareholders over the use of free cash flows, and illustrate actions shareholders might take to reduce such conflicts.

(9 marks)

(b) Discuss how effectively shareholder value analysis indicates the creation of economic value for shareholders. (6 marks)

(15 marks)

ANSWERS

DO NOT TURN THIS PAGE UNTIL YOU
HAVE COMPLETED THE MOCK EXAM

WARNING! APPLYING THE BPP MARKING SCHEME

If you decide to mark your paper using the BPP marking scheme, you should bear in mind the following points.

1   The BPP solutions are not definitive: you will see that we have applied the marking scheme to our solutions to show how good answers should gain marks, but there may be more than one way to answer the question. You must try to judge fairly whether different points made in your answers are correct and relevant and therefore worth marks according to our marking scheme.

2   If you have a friend or colleague who is studying or has studied this paper, you might ask him or her to mark your paper for you, thus gaining a more objective assessment. Remember you and your friend are not trained or objective markers, so try to avoid complacency or pessimism if you appear to have done very well or very badly.

3   You should be aware that BPP's answers are longer than you would be expected to write. Sometimes, therefore, you would gain the same number of marks for making the basic point as we have shown as being available for a slightly more detailed or extensive solution.

It is most important that you analyse your solutions in detail and that you attempt to be as objective as possible.

Professional Examination - Paper 3.7   **Marking Scheme**

Strategic Financial Management

This marking scheme is given as a guide to markers in the context of the suggested answer. Scope is given to markers to award marks for alternative approaches to a question, including relevant comment, and where well-reasoned conclusions are provided. This is particularly the case for essay based questions where there will often be more than one definitive solution.

A PLAN OF ATTACK

We know you've been told to do it at least 100 times and we know if we asked you you'd know that you should do it. So why don't you do it in an exam? 'Do what in an exam?' you're probably thinking. Well, let's tell you for the 101st time. **Take a good look through the paper before diving in to answer questions.**

First things first

What you must do in the first five or ten minutes of the exam is **look through the paper i**n detail, working out **which questions to do** and the **order** in which to attempt them. So turn back to the paper and let's sort out a plan of attack.

The next step

You're probably either thinking that you don't know where to begin or that you could have a very decent go at all the questions.

Option 1 (if you don't know where to begin)

If you are a bit **worried** about the paper, remember you'll need to do the compulsory questions anyway so it's best to get them over and done with.

- As **question 1** is for the most marks, it may be best to get it out of the way first. You should approach the question in stages doing the written parts first, then filling in the easier figures in the DCF proformas you will have to draw up, and lastly doing the more complicated workings. Remember you will get credit for using the right methods so take a deep breath, head for the formula sheet, and have a go at using the gearing formula. Also look for clues in the question; why for example might you need the inflation rate?

- You do not need the results to part (b) of **question 2** to answer parts (a) and (c). So get those out the way first; they offer good opportunities to earn the majority of the marks you need to pass this question. When tackling (b) (i), work through the various strategies in ascending order of difficulty. Don't miss out (b) (ii).

- If you can't see how to value the shares, don't choose **question 3.** If you are happy using the dividend valuation model, bear in mind that you also will need to think about the practical implications of the efficient market hypothesis in semi-strong form.

- You can get the majority of marks in **question 4** through discussion, and provided you set up a proforma, the calculation isn't too bad.

- **Question 5** is quite a general question with a strong economics basis, so if you revised the topic areas covered, it would be a very good choice.

- Do not choose **question 6** unless you know what free cash flows and shareholder value analysis are. Wrong guesses will not get you any marks.

What you mustn't forget is that you have to **answer questions 1 and 2 and then two questions from Section B**.

Option 2 (if you're thinking 'I can do all of these')

It never pays to be over confident but if you're not quaking in your shoes about the exam then **turn straight to the compulsory questions** in Section A. You've got to do them so you might as well get them over and done with.

- **Question 1** offers some complex investment appraisal and plenty of things to work out. However don't spend all you time on the workings, as there are plenty of marks allocated for discussion. Also read the question carefully and think about the reasons why you might have been given the information; why might inflation rates be significant for instance?

- **Question 2** has plenty of written parts that will need enough time to be allocated to them. In (b) (i) don't just plunge in and do all the calculations you can; think whether the information you have been given could help you take a shortcut.

Once you've done the compulsory questions choose two of the questions in Section B.

- Part (a) of **question 3** isn't maybe as easy as it first appears; it requires you to analyse the assumptions behind, and implications of, the semi-strong state. Also for part (b) you need to think about ways of valuing the company other than the method that is implied by the data given in the question.

- Part (a) of question 4 should certainly offer you the chance to score marks quite easily, but you will need to discuss a range of methods. The calculation in part (b) is quite reasonable but don't forget you'll need to analyse the results.

- If you've revised the topic areas covered by **question 5,** you should score highly on this question as there are no real twists.

- If you think you can define free cash flow and shareholder value analysis, then fine, that will earn you some marks when you come to answer **question 6**. However don't forget that you will need to appraise these techniques critically to gain most of the marks.

No matter how many times we remind you...

Always, always **allocate your time** according to the marks for the question in total and for the parts of the questions. And always, always **follow the requirements exactly**.

You've got free time at the end of the exam.....?

If you have allocated your time properly then you **shouldn't have time on your hands** at the end of the exam. If you find yourself with five or ten minutes spare, however, go back to **any parts of questions that you didn't finish** because you ran out of time.

Forget about it!

And don't worry if you found the paper difficult. More than likely other students would too. If this were the real thing you would need to **forget** the exam the minute you leave the exam hall and **think about the next one**. Or, if it's the last one, **celebrate**!

1

(a)   Demergers and sell-offs are both means of **restructuring businesses**.

(i)   A **sell-off** involves the sale of part of a company to another company. A sell-off can act to **protect the rest of a business from a take-over,** by selling off a part that is particularly attractive to a buyer. It can also **provide cash,** enabling the remaining business to invest further without the need for worsening its gearing by obtaining more debt finance. It would also enable Romage to **concentrate** on what it perceives to be its core business, and **dispose of the more peripheral areas**.

(ii) A **demerger** is the splitting up of a corporate body into two or more separate and independent bodies. It is **not** a **sale** of the separate bodies themselves, as the original shareholders have shares in both companies. The split does **enable analysts** to **understand** the two businesses fully, particularly when, as here, the two main divisions are in different fields. The two divisions are likely to have different risk profiles, and splitting them up enables **shareholders** to **adjust** the **proportion of their holdings** between the two different companies.

Both **methods** can lead to improved **management and control,** and can enable management to **focus** on the **competencies** of the individual divisions rather than the varying considerations of both. These improvements may result in **reverse synergy,** where the combined value of the split-off divisions is more than the company would be worth if the divisions were still together.

The choice for Romage's management is therefore whether they wish to **retain control** of both divisions, or to relinquish control of one and just concentrate on the other division.

Mock exam 1: answers

(b) Manufacturing

	1 £m	2 £m	3 £m	4 £m	5 £m	6 £m
Net operating cash flow	45.0	48.0	50.0	52.0	57.0	60.0
Central costs	(6.0)	(6.0)	(6.0)	(6.0)	(6.0)	(6.0)
Depreciation	(10.0)	(8.0)	(7.0)	(8.0)	(8.0)	(8.0)
	29.0	34.0	37.0	38.0	43.0	46.0
Tax at 31%	(9.0)	(10.5)	(11.5)	(11.8)	(13.3)	(14.3)
Post tax income	20.0	23.5	25.5	26.2	29.7	31.7
Add back non-cash depreciation	10.0	8.0	7.0	8.0	8.0	8.0
One-off cost	(8.0)					
Net cash flow	22.0	31.5	32.5	34.2	37.7	39.7
Discount factors (10%) (W1)	0.909	0.826	0.751	0.683	0.621	
PV cash flow	20.0	26.0	24.4	23.4	23.4	

PV to infinity = PV years 1–5 + PV years 6–infinity

$$= 117.2 + \left(\frac{39.7}{0.1} - (39.7 \times 3.791) \right)$$

$$= £363.7 \text{ million}$$

PV years 1 to 15 = $117.2 + (39.7 \times (7.606 - 3.791))$
= 268.7 million

Property

	1 £m	2 £m	3 £m	4 £m	5 £m	6 £m
Net operating cash flow	32.0	40.0	42.0	44.0	46.0	50.0
Central costs	(6.0)	(6.0)	(6.0)	(6.0)	(6.0)	(6.0)
Depreciation	(5.0)	(5.0)	(5.0)	(5.0)	(5.0)	(5.0)
	21.0	29.0	31.0	33.0	35.0	39.0
Tax at 31%	(6.5)	(9.0)	(9.6)	(10.2)	(10.9)	(12.1)
Post tax income	14.5	20.0	21.4	22.8	24.1	26.9
Add back non-cash depreciation	5.0	5.0	5.0	5.0	5.0	5.0
One-off cost	(8.0)					
Net cash flow	11.5	25.0	26.4	27.8	29.1	31.9
Discount factors (8%) (W2)	0.926	0.857	0.794	0.735	0.681	
PV cash flow	10.6	21.4	21.0	20.4	19.8	

PV to infinity = PV years 1–5 + PV years 6–infinity

$$= 93.2 + \left(\frac{31.9}{0.08} - (31.9 \times 3.993) \right)$$

$$= £364.6 \text{ million}$$

PV years 1 to 15 = $93.2 + (31.9 \times (8.559 - 3.993))$
= 238.9 million

Working 1

Discount rate for manufacturing:

Gearing

MV debt = £60 million

MV equity $= \dfrac{50}{0.25} \times 0.55 \times 2.96$

= £325.6 million

MV equity

$$= \frac{325.6}{325 + 60} \text{ equity,} \qquad \frac{60}{325 + 60} \text{ debt}$$

$$= 84.4\% \text{ equity,} \qquad 15.6\% \text{ debt}$$

This differs from the industry beta, and so we must ungear the industry beta and must regear the asset beta to take into account the differing capital structure.

$$\beta_a = \beta_e \left(\frac{E}{E + D\,(1-t)} \right) \text{ (assuming debt is risk-free)}$$

$$= 1.3 \times \left(\frac{70}{70 + 30\,(1 - 0.31)} \right)$$

$$= 1.00$$

Regearing

$$\beta_e = \beta_a \left(\frac{E + D\,(1-t)}{E} \right)$$

$$= 1.00 \times \left(\frac{84.4 + 15.6\,(1 - 0.31)}{84.4} \right)$$

$$= 1.128$$

$$Ke = r_f + [E(r_m) - r_f]\beta$$
$$= 5.5 + [14 - 5.5]1.128$$
$$= 15.09\%$$

For Kd, calculate redemption yield on debenture as we are told that the cost of the term loan is virtually the same.

$$131 = \frac{13\,(1 - 0.31)}{(1 + Kd(1-t))} + \frac{13\,(1 - 0.31)}{(1 + Kd(1-t))^2} + \ldots + \frac{13\,(1 - 0.31)}{(1 + Kd(1-t))^{15}} + \frac{100}{(1 + Kd(1-t))^{15}}$$

Year		Cash flow £	Discount factor 5%	PV £	Discount factor 6%	PV £
0	Market value	(131.00)	1.000	(131.000)	1.000	(131.00)
1–15	Interest	8.97	10.38	93.11	9.712	87.12
15	Capital repayment	100.00	0.481	48.10	0.417	41.70
				10.21		(2.18)

$$Kd\,(1 - t) = 5\% + \left(\frac{10.21}{10.21 + 2.18} \times (6 - 5) \right)$$

$$= 5.82\%$$

WACC for manufacturing division

$$= Ke_g \left(\frac{E}{E + D} \right) + Kd\,(1 - t) \left(\frac{D}{E + D} \right)$$

$$= 15.09 \left(\frac{325.6}{60 + 325.6} \right) + 5.82 \left(\frac{60}{60 + 325.6} \right)$$

$$= 12.74 + 0.91$$

$$= 13.65\%$$

Real rate

$$= \frac{(1 + \text{money rate})}{(1 + \text{inflation rate})} - 1$$

$$= \frac{1.1365}{1.03} - 1$$

$$= 10.34\%, \text{ say } 10\%$$

BPP PUBLISHING

Working 2

Discount rate for property

MV equity

$$= \frac{50}{0.25} \times 0.45 \times 2.96$$

$$= \text{£266.4 million}$$

MV debt

$$= 50 \times 1.31$$

$$= \text{£65.5 million}$$

Gearing level

$$= \frac{266.4}{266.4 + 65.5} \text{ equity} + \frac{65.5}{266.4 + 65.5} \text{ debt}$$

$$= 80.3\% \text{ equity} + 19.7\% \text{ debt}$$

These are near enough industry averages (80 + 20) and thus there is no need to ungear and regear.

$$\text{Ke} = r_f + [E(r_m) - r_f]\beta$$
$$= 5.5 + [14 - 5.5]0.9$$
$$= 13.15\%$$

$$\text{Kd}(1-t) = \text{same as above, } 5.82\%$$

WACC for property division

$$= \text{Ke}_g\left(\frac{E}{E+D}\right) + \text{Kd}(1-t)\left(\frac{D}{E+D}\right)$$

$$= 13.15\left(\frac{266.4}{266.4 + 65.5}\right) + 5.82\left(\frac{65.5}{266.4 + 65.5}\right)$$

$$= 10.55 + 1.15$$

$$= 11.70\%$$

Real rate

$$= \frac{(1 + \text{money rate})}{(1 + \text{inflation rate})} - 1$$

$$= \frac{1.1170}{1.03} - 1$$

$$= 8.44\%, \text{ say } 8\%$$

Conclusion

Total of two divisions to infinity

$$= 363.7 + 364.6$$

$$= \text{£728.3 million}$$

Total of two divisions to year 15

$$= 268.7 + 238.9$$

$$= \text{£507.6 million}$$

Current market value is £592 million (equity) plus £125.5 million (debt), £717.5 million.

The total of the two separate divisions to infinity is just higher than the current market value, but using a 15 year time horizon the total of the two separate divisions is lower.

As no replacement capital investment has been included in the calculation, it does not appear that Romage should float the two divisions separately.

(c)   The following further information would be helpful.

(i)   The **assumptions** underlying the predicted operating cash flows. We need to know on what basis the steady growth in manufacturing is expected, also the significant growth in property cash flows in year 2 and the steadier growth in other years.

(ii)   It would also help our understanding of the operating cash flows if we had **more details** of the individual figures, and in particular the growth rates of different elements.

(iii)   The model uses operating cash flows. A more reliable estimate of value might be **free cash flows**, taking into account the investment needs of both divisions. Free cash flows could then be used to assess **shareholder value added.** Alternatively other methods, such as **economic value added**, could be used.

(iv)   It seems unlikely that the forecasts include the effects of **real options**. Important real options might include the further investments that each division might wish to make.

(v)   The cash flow forecasts as they stand appear to take no account of **uncertainty**. It would be helpful to see best-worst estimates, simulations or other techniques that incorporate uncertainty.

(vi)   The only information we have about **risk** is industry risk details. The risk profile of either or both divisions might differ significantly.

(vii)   The **initial gearing arrangements** might not be sufficient. The debenture or loan might represent insufficient debt finance for the division concerned if it is to achieve predicted levels of growth. However if extra finance is required, it might be less easy for the individual division to raise than if it had the rest of the group behind it.

(viii) We are not told whether either or both divisions might be more vulnerable to **takeovers** because of their smaller size.

(ix)   We are not told about the views of the **shareholders** on the plans. Also the interests of **other stakeholders** might need to be taken into account - what will **employees** feel about the split, will there be fewer **management opportunities available,** and how will **creditors** view their security.

Marking guide		
		Marks
(a)	Advantages of divestments	4-5
	Differences between sell-offs and demergers	2
	Answer specially related to Romage	2
		8
(b)	**Manufacturing and property cash flows**	
	Central costs	1
	Correct treatment of depreciation	2
	Taxation	1
	One-off cost	1
	Present values to infinity	2
	Present values over 15 years	1
	Discount factors:	
	Cost of equity (manufacturing)	5
	Cost of equity (property)	1
	Cost of debt	4
	Nominal WACCs	1
	Real WACCs	2
	Total values and conclusion	3
	(Marks may be awarded for correct technique even though errors exist.)	24
(c)	1 mark for each valid point. Do not reward one word answers	8
		40

2

Tutor's hint. It would have been possible to conduct hedging in deutschmarks and francs, but transaction costs would have been greater, and (more significantly for your exam), you would have had to have carried out more calculations.

It is not necessarily clear how best to tackle the futures part of (b) (i) given the absence of spot rates at the end of the contract. You need to come up with an answer that can be compared with the results on the forward and money markets. Our answer does this by saying that for the amount hedged, the results on the spot and futures market will balance out to give a net payment at the current futures price. This leaves in both instances a certain amount unhedged which can then be hedged on the forward market. We demonstrate this by using an example although this may not be necessary to gain full marks. The caveat about the lack of basis risk is important.

Examiner's comment. Many candidates wasted time by doing superfluous calculations. Foreign exchange exposure should be netted, and only the net amount hedged, rather than all transactions. It was best to hedge using euros, rather than francs and deutschmarks, since these currencies are fixed against the euro.

Answers to (a) should have focused on the effects on the company of joining the euro, and in particular, the economic exposure that the company still faced.

Answers to (b) showed many weaknesses including use of the wrong rates, the wrong number of contracts, the incorrect decision of whether to buy or sell futures, and the wrong month of contract maturity; answers to the futures part of the question were the least convincing.

(a) The managing director is certainly correct in saying that the **foreign exchange exposure** in dealing with other EMU countries will be eliminated. However foreign exchange exposure will still affect trade with countries that are not members of EMU.

Similarly **transaction costs** involved in trade with other EMU members will disappear, and this could represent a considerable saving. However there will still be transaction costs when trading with other countries who are not EMU members.

In addition the company would still face **economic exposure** even if it only traded with other countries within EMU. If the euro is over-valued with respect to non-members' currencies, companies from non-member countries may gain sales at the expense of the UK company because they can charge cheaper prices. The company may also face **indirect economic exposure** if it buys products from other EMU members who buy their raw materials from non-EMU members. Any adverse exchange movements meaning raw material prices increases would be passed on through the value chain.

(b) (i)

Receipts	Payments
Two months	€393,265
Three months Kr8.6m	$491,011 + 890,217 - 60,505 - 1,997,651$
	$= €676,928$

Forward market hedge

Two months

Payment $\dfrac{€393,265}{1.433} = £274,435$

Three months

Payment $\dfrac{€676,928}{1.431} = £473,045$

Receipt $\dfrac{\text{Kr8,600,000}}{10.83} = £794,090$

Money market hedge

- Two months payment

  We need to invest now to match the €393,265 we require.

  Amount to be invested $= \dfrac{\text{€393,265}}{1 + \dfrac{0.035}{6}}$

  $= \text{€390,984}$

  Converting at spot rate $\dfrac{390,984}{1.439} = £271,705$

  To obtain £271,705, we have to borrow £271,705 for three months.

  Amount to be borrowed $= 271,705 \times \left(1 + \dfrac{0.075}{6}\right)$

  $= £275,101$

- Three months payment

  Again we need to invest

  Amount to be invested $= \dfrac{\text{€676,928}}{1 + \dfrac{0.035}{4}}$

  $= \text{€671,056}$

  Converting at spot rate $\dfrac{671,056}{1.439} = £466,335$

  Borrowing £466,335 for three months

  Amount to be borrowed $= 466,335 \times \left(1 + \dfrac{0.075}{4}\right)$

  $= £475,079$

- Three months receipt

  We need to borrow now to match the receipt we shall obtain.

  Amount to be borrowed $= \dfrac{\text{Kr8,600,000}}{1 + \dfrac{0.08}{4}}$

  $= \text{Kr8,431,373}$

  Converting at spot rate $\dfrac{8,431,373}{10.71} = £787,243$

  Amount to be invested $= 787,243 \times \left(1 + \dfrac{0.055}{4}\right)$

  $= £798,068$

Futures market

For the two months payment:

- We shall be buying June contracts as they mature just after payment date

- Buy € futures

- Number of contracts

$$\frac{393,265}{125,000} = 3.15,\ 3 \text{ contracts. This leaves } €18,265\ (393,265 - 375,000) \text{ not}$$

  covered by contracts.

- Tick size $125,000 \times 0.0001 = £12.50$.

  The €375,000 will, assuming zero basis, be at the current futures price of 0.6964 to £261,150.

  To demonstrate, let us assume spot market rate moves to 1.50.

	£
At opening rate 375,000 ÷ 1.439	260,598
At closing rate 375,000 ÷ 1.50	250,000
Profit on spot market	10,598

  On futures market:

Opening futures price	0.6964
Closing futures price	0.6667
Movement in ticks	297 ticks loss
Loss on futures market	$297 \times 12.50 \times 3 = £11,138$ loss

  Net outcome:

	£
Spot market payment	(250,000)
Loss on futures market	(11,138)
	261,138

allowing for rounding errors is the same as at the current futures price.

We still have to deal with the unhedged €18,265.

Hedging at the forward rate: $\dfrac{18,265}{1.433} = £12,746$

and thus Total payment $= 261,150 + 12,746$

$\qquad\qquad\qquad\qquad\quad = 273,896$

We can use a similar argument for the three months payment. This time the number of contracts will be $\dfrac{676,928}{125,000} = 5.42$, say 5 contracts.

Amount hedged on the futures market will be €625,000, leaving €51,928 to be hedged on the forward market.

Total payment $= (625,000 \times 0.6983) + \dfrac{51,928}{1.431}$

$\qquad\qquad\qquad = 436,438 + 36,288$

$\qquad\qquad\qquad = £472,726$

Conclusion

For the three month Kr receipt, the money market will maximise cash flow. For the two Euro payments, the futures market should maximise cash flow assuming basis risk is negligible. If basis risk does have a significant impact, the forward market may be the best choice.

(ii) **Day 1** movement 0.6930 – 0.6916 = 14 ticks loss. Extra payment of £175 (14 × £12.50) is required. If the extra payment is not made, the contract will be closed out.

Day 2 movement 0.6944 – 0.6930 = 14 ticks loss, extra payment of £175.

Day 3 movement 0.6940 – 0.6944 = 4 ticks profit. Profit = 4 × £12.50 = £50; this can be taken in cash.

(c) The advantages of forward contracts are:

(i) The contract can be **tailored** to the user's **exact requirements** with quantity to be delivered, date and price all flexible.

(ii) The trader will **know in advance** how much money will be received or paid.

(iii) **Payment** is **not required** until the contract is settled.

The disadvantages of forward contracts are:

(i) The user may **not** be able to negotiate **good terms**; the price may depend upon the **size** of the **deal** and how the user is rated.

(ii) Users have to **bear** the **spread** of the contract between the buying and selling price.

(iii) Deals can only be **reversed** by going back to the original party and offsetting the original trade.

(iv) The **creditworthiness** of the other party may be a problem.

The advantages of currency futures are:

(i) There is a **single specified price** determined by the market, and not the negotiating strength of the customer.

(ii) **Transactions costs** are generally **lower** than for futures contracts.

(iii) The exact date of **receipt** or **payment** of the currency does not have to be **known**, because the futures contract does not have to be closed out until the actual cash receipt or payment is made.

(iv) **Reversal** can easily take place in the market.

(v) Because of the process of **marking to market**, there is no default risk.

The disadvantages of currency futures are:

(i) The **fixing** of **quantity** and **delivery dates** that is necessary for the future to be traded means that the customer's risk may not be fully covered.

(ii) Futures contracts may **not** be **available** in the **currencies** that the customer requires.

(iii) The procedure for converting between two currencies, neither of which is the US dollar, can be **complex.**

(iv) **Volatile trading conditions** on the futures markets mean that the potential loss can be high.

Marking guide

			Marks	
(a)		Agree savings in transaction costs	1	
		Elimination of FOREX risk	4	
		(Reward understanding and especially mention of economic exposure)		5
(b)	(i)	Use of net receipts and payments	1	
		Forward market	2	
		Money market	5	
		Futures market	5	
		Conclusions	2	
				15
	(ii)	Understanding of variation margin	1	
		Day 1 and 2 loss	2	
		Day 3 gain	1	
				4
(c)		Advantages and disadvantages of forward contracts	3	
		Advantages and disadvantages of futures	3	
				6
				30

3

> **Tutor's hint.** (a) is a thorough discussion on the semi-strong hypothesis.
>
> **Examiner's comment.** The main error in (b) was use of the wrong growth rate within the model. Other weaknesses included failure to consider how reliable the valuation would be, and what the valuation exercise indicated about market efficiency.

(a) The term 'stock market efficiency' refers to the efficiency with which the stock market **processes information** and is described by the **efficient markets hypothesis** (EMH).

The EMH can be described in three forms: the weak form, the semi-strong form and the strong form. The **semi-strong form** is concerned with **new public information** and can be described as follows:

Share prices react very quickly and logically when new information is made public.

The general principle behind this hypothesis is that information is **intelligently analysed** by investors as soon as it is made public. These investors quickly make decisions to buy or sell shares on the basis of the information, causing the share prices to move swiftly and logically.

This hypothesis is most likely to be true if:

(i)   There are **sufficient investors** to create a market.

(ii)   All investors have **access to the same information** (eg inside information does not exist, or trading on the basis of such information is illegal).

(iii) Investors are **well equipped** to analyse information and have the appropriate training to understand technical detail.

(iv)   **Transactions** costs are **small.**

(v)   Investors act **rationally.**

All these assumptions can be challenged but are more likely to be true for developed stock markets than for emerging markets.

Some of the implications for financial managers of this hypothesis include the following.

(i)   The **market price** of a share is the **best estimate** of the share's real value, based on public information.

(ii)   If details of a proposed new investment project are released to the public, share prices should quickly rise by the amount of the project NPV **when the details are announced**. Note, however, that this assumes that the investing public has not already guessed the company's plans and that it believes the information that is released.

(iii)   Announcement of financial results will cause a **movement** in the **share price** to the extent that these results have not yet been anticipated by investors.

(iv)   If directors need to boost the company's share price (for example if subject to an unwelcome takeover bid) they should release some **good previously unpublished information**. During a takeover bid, share prices of both companies should move to reflect fairly all available public information.

(b)   To: Managing director
From: Financial analyst
Date: 14 January 20X2
Subject: Valuation of shares

The **dividend valuation model** can be used to value the shares.

$$P_0 = \frac{D_0(1+g)}{Ke - g}$$

where g = average rate of dividend growth over the last few years

$$\text{Average rate of dividend growth} = \sqrt[3]{\frac{10,007}{40,000} \div \frac{5,680}{28,560}}$$

$$= \sqrt[3]{1.258}$$

$$= 8\%$$

$$P_0 = \frac{\frac{10,007}{40,000}(1.08)}{0.125 - 0.08}$$

$$= 600p$$

Given that the model suggests the shares are over-valued by 7.5%, it seems that the analyst might well have used the dividend growth model (with a slightly different value for g being employed).

Use of the dividend valuation model suggests that past data is a good guide to current share prices if we do not have any better information about dividend growth rates. This implies that the market is only **weak-form efficient**, just taking into account past data.

However, evidence suggests that many stock markets are at least **semi-strong efficient**, reflecting all publicly available information. In addition, the dividend growth rate model is based on the assumptions.

(i)   That **dividend growth** is **constant**.

Though growth appears to have been fairly steady at around 8% over the last three years, there may not be enough projects in the future with sufficient positive NPVs to maintain the dividend stream.

(ii)   That the **proportion of earnings retained** is **constant**. That is not the case here. The proportion retained peaked at 71.2% in 20X7, but since then has declined to 65.0% in 20X9.

In addition, the company may have a stated policy of trying to maintain an 8% growth rate. However, this is not necessarily a good guide to valuation as companies which pay zero dividends do not have zero valuations.

Thus the market price may reflect factors other than the recent dividend growth; the **desire** and **expectation** of **capital gains** on shares and the market's expectation of how **current projects** will translate into future earnings and dividend streams. The best way of measuring the value of these projects is to use **discounted cash flow methods,** and these may suggest a more realistic valuation than that given by the **dividend valuation** model. Evidence from the use of the dividend valuation model is not therefore enough by itself to indicate over-valuation.

Marking guide

		Marks	
(a)	Conditions underpinning hypothesis	3	
	Implications for financial managers	3	
			6
(b)	Estimate of intrinsic value of share	3	
	Report and discussion. Look for critique of the dividend growth model and comment about efficiency	6	
			9
			15

4

Tutor's hint. In part (a) it is not enough just to list and describe the payment methods; you are also required to discuss them.

Examiner's comment. In part (a) a large number of candidates interpreted the question to mean international transfer of funds rather than the international transfer of cash, and discussed factors such as transfer pricing, dividend remittance, royalties and management fees. Answers to (b) were generally good, although some candidates did not consider the tax effects after UK tax credits.

(a) The main methods of international cash transfer are:

(i) **Cheque payment by post**

This method is **low cost** to the sender of the cash, but is relatively slow, risky and unreliable, since the speed of postal services varies from country to country. It may also be **costly** to the recipient, since the level of bank charges to clear a foreign cheque can be quite high. The time taken by the banks to clear such cheques can also be long – a timescale of weeks rather than days is not unusual. Further risks include the risk of default on the cheque, and exchange controls in the country in which the cheque was issued can mean that the money is not received on time.

(ii) **International money order**

These are arranged through post offices or banks. They are **less risky** than the use of cheques, but they are only suitable for the transfer of relatively **small sums.**

(iii) **Bankers' draft**

These are similar in nature to cheques, but are drawn upon the **account of a bank** rather than on the account of the company, and therefore there is a lower risk of default. Once issued, they cannot normally be stopped.

(iv) **International payment order (by mail or telegraphic transfer)**

This involves **issue** by one bank to another of an **instruction** to pay a specified sum to a specified person on a specified date. The use of mail is slower and cheaper than the use of telegraphic transfer.

(v) **Bills of exchange**

A bill of exchange is **written evidence** of a debt, a form of IOU, which must be accepted by the drawee, and often also by a bank. The **term of the debt** will be specified in the bill, which may be either held to maturity by the payee, or may be sold to a bank prior to maturity. Bills can therefore provide a form of trade credit as well as a cash transfer. However, they are **more expensive** to arrange than many of the other forms of international settlement.

(vi) **Electronic transfer**

SWIFT (Society for Worldwide Interbank Financial Telecommunications). This uses electronic messages between banks, which are effectively another method of sending an international payment order (described above). Settlement will be made through the banks' existing payment systems such as CHAPS.

(b)

	Glinland		Rytora	
	£'000	£'000	£'000	£'000
Sales				
External (150 × 30)				4,500
To Rytora (150 × 6 × 1.75)		1,575		
Variable costs				
Shifts from Glinland	–		1,575	
Other variable costs (150 × 6 / 150 × 9)	900		1,350	
		(900)		(2,925)
Fixed costs		(140)		(166)
Profits before corporate tax		535		1,409
Corporate tax (535 × 40% / 1,409 × 25%)		(214)		(352)
Profit after corporate tax		321		1,057
Tariffs (1,575 × 10%)		–		(157)
Profits available for remittance		321		900
Profits remitted to UK (50% × 321)	160		900	
Less: withholding tax	(16)		–	
Profits sent to UK		144		900
UK tax on profits (535 × 30% / 1,409 × 30%)	161		423	
Less: tax relief	(161)		(352)	
Net UK tax on profits		–		71

Total taxes and tariffs   = 214 + 352 + 157 + 16 + 71
                    = £810,000

If new arrangement is adopted

	Glinland		Rytora	
	£'000	£'000	£'000	£'000
Sales				
External (150 × 30)				4,500
To Rytora ((150 × 6) + 140)		1,040		
Variable costs				
Shifts from Glinland	–		1,040	
Other variable costs (150 × 6 / 150 × 9)	900		1,350	
		(900)		(2,390)
Fixed costs		(140)		(166)
Profits before corporate tax		–		1,944
Corporate tax (1,944 × 25%)		–		(486)
Profit after corporate tax		–		1,458
Tariffs (1,040 × 10%)		–		(104)
Profits available for remittance		–		1,354
Profits remitted to UK	–		1,354	
Less: withholding tax	–		–	
Profits sent to UK		–		1,354
UK tax on profits (1,944 × 30%)	–		583	
Less: tax relief	–		(486)	
Net UK tax on profits		–		97

Total taxes and tariffs = 486 + 104 + 97
                         = £687,000

The new arrangement represents a savings in taxes and tariffs of £810,000 – £687,000 = £123,000. However HGT also needs to consider the following potential problems.

(i)   The Glinland subsidiary no longer makes a profit in return for its efforts and the use of its resources. This may **lessen management motivation**.

(ii)   As Glinland can now re-coup all its costs when selling to Rytora, this may lead to a **loss of control** over costs and may thus increase the costs of the Glinland operation.

(iii) The lack of retained profits may limit the **investment opportunities** of Glinland.

(iv)   The **government** of Glinland might **object** to this arrangement, as it is costing them £230,000 in tax. HGT may be forced to use a more realistic **arms-length price**.

Marking guide

			Marks
(a)	1 mark for brief discussion of each possible transfer mechanism.		
	Do not give full marks for bullet points.		6
(b)	Current position		3
	Revised estimates of tax and tariffs		3
	Possible problems with the change in transfer price		3
			9
			15

5

(a) **Nature of trade blocs**

Trade blocs exist when there is no restriction on the movement of goods and services between countries. Trade blocs are also often customs unions where there is free trade between member countries of the bloc, and also common external tariffs applying to imports into any member countries.

Effects of trade bloc

Within members of the bloc, trade is likely to increase for the following reasons:

(i) Some barriers such as **physical barriers** to trade, may have been removed. Other barriers, for example **technical standards** may have been **harmonised**.

(ii) Increased competition is likely to mean better use of resources as more efficient producers within the bloc have greater marketing opportunities at the expense of less efficient rivals. Overall prices for many goods and services should fall and demand rise and **trade creation** occur. This will particularly apply the more similar the economies within the bloc are.

(iii) Bigger potential markets allow opportunities for **increased specialisation** and **economies of scale**.

(iv) As well as market opportunities, trade blocs are likely to involve **free movement of capital,** hence allowing greater availability and encouraging more investment by businesses.

(v) A co-ordinated approach by governments across the bloc on issues such as **competition regulation** is likely to be effective in removing barriers to entry and ending uncompetitive arrangements than actions taken by individual governments.

(vi) Trade blocs may have **long-term effects** that stimulate trade, for example allowing the introduction of **new technologies** or providing incentives for governments to **improve infrastructure** and thus lower transport costs.

Trade blocs have a potentially negative effect on trade with nations outside the bloc. How great this effect is depends on the level of tariffs that are set.

(i) The imposition of tariffs may mean that **less efficient producers** within the bloc benefit at the expense of **more efficient producers outside** (a process known as trade diversion).

(ii) Imposition of tariffs may lead to **retaliation** by countries outside the bloc. This may hit hard countries within the bloc that previously had good relations with outside countries.

(iii) The benefits may only be felt by **certain members** within the bloc, those with the most efficient businesses or those with the best transport links. The depressive effect on the economies of the less successful members may hit overall trade within the bloc.

Conclusion

Thus a trade bloc should be successful in increasing trade within the bloc, but trading relationships with external countries may be damaged if barriers are significant.

(b) Attempts can be made at a variety of levels to overcome non-tariff barriers. These include the following.

   (i)   The GATT (General Agreement on Tariffs and Trade) negotiations, now policed by the successor body called the **WTO (World Trade Organisation),** aims at liberalising world trade (for example, one result of the Uruguay round was the introduction of tighter rules governing the use of subsidies with some types of subsidy being prohibited).

   (ii) **Direct negotiation with foreign governments** can be entered, in order to win concessions in exchange for the use of imports from the country concerned.

   (iii) The company can **lobby its own government,** to bring pressure to bear upon the foreign government to eliminate or reduce specific barriers.

   (iv) A company with a significant export potential could establish a **subsidiary** in the country in question, or enter into a **joint venture** with a local company.

Marking guide		Marks
(a)	Nature of trade blocs	3
	Discussion – look especially for trade creation and diversion	6
	Conclusion	2
		11
(b)	Methods to overcome barriers (1 mark per valid point)	4
		15

6

> **Tutor's hint.** The question asks for actions shareholders can take to reduce conflicts, and our answer indicates what they can actually do in practice. Whilst they are trying to make management pay them the surplus cash, it is not legally correct to say that they can insist on increased dividends or share repurchase.
>
> **Examiner's comment.** Some answers to (a) were too general, discussing the wider concept of agency theory rather than the agency implications of using free cash flow.

(a) The key element of the free cash flow model is the strategic need of companies to reinvest in new plant to maintain or increase current operating cash flows. In the free cash flow model,

$$\text{Operating free cash flow} = \text{Revenues} - \text{Operating costs} + \text{Depreciation} - \text{Investment expenditure}$$

The free cash flow model is a present value model. It thus suggests that companies can maximise their value by undertaking projects with a positive net present value as well as replacing assets. If, when all available projects have been undertaken, there is still surplus cash, management should return the cash to shareholders by **paying large dividends** or by **buying back shares.**

However management-shareholder priorities may differ.

   (i)   Whilst management may wish to invest in projects with a **large net present value,** shareholders may wish for a more **immediate or steadier return** than these maybe long-term projects offer.

(ii)   Management may dislike the **loss of control** implicit in returning possibly large cash balances to shareholders. The **status** of having large amounts of money to exercise control over may be a significant motivation. Status is also linked into company size, and there may also be more tangible rewards arising from increasing company size, such as **remuneration increases.** These may motivate management to grow the company to a size greater than that required to maximise shareholder wealth.

Hence rather than returning monies to investors, managers may undertake investments with **questionable risk-return trade-offs.** If these produce negative returns, then dividends may suffer and the market value of shares decrease.

(iii)   On the other hand in times of recession management may be more concerned about ensuring the company's (and their own) survival rather than maximising shareholder wealth. Again this may lead to increased investment, but investment designed to reduce risk, for example by **diversification**.

Shareholders ultimately have the **right to remove directors** at the annual general meeting, and can indicate their disapproval in other ways at the meeting, for example **voting down the annual report and accounts,** or voting to reject the **report of the remuneration committee.** Legally they cannot however force management to pay more than the dividend they recommend. Nor can they force managers to buy back shares or increase the level of gearing, which will increase interest payments and reduce the cash flows available for management investment. There is a general legal rule that shareholders cannot usurp the power of the directors to manage the company.

(b) **Shareholder value analysis** focuses on the creation of economic value for shareholders, as measured by the share price performance and the flow of dividends. Under shareholder value analysis key decisions with implications for cash flow and risk are specified. These will be decisions that impact upon **value drivers,** factors that have the greatest impact on shareholder value, such as sales growth rate, profit margin, working capital investment and the required rate of return.

Under the model:

Corporate value	=	**PV of free cash flows**	+	**Current value of marketable securities and other non-operating investments**

and Shareholder value = Corporate value – Debt

The model has some limitations.

(i)   The model makes the questionable assumptions that **sales growth rates** are **constant,** that **operating profit rates** are **also constant** and that **tax** is a **constant percentage** of operating profit.

(ii)   Some of the **necessary data** may not be readily available.

(iii) The present values of all the business's activities have theoretically to be taken to **infinity**. This difficulty can be overcome by taking a **terminal value** at some point in the future. However this introduces a further problem; not only do future cash flows have to be estimated, but a decision is needed on when those estimates cease to be realistic, and the terminal value has to be taken. Also the **terminal value** may prove difficult to **estimate.**

(iv)   The **value drivers** that the business is focusing on may not always give the **same message**.

Marking guide

		Marks	
(a)	Definition of free cash flow	2	
	Possible conflicts, look especially for conflicts with respect to the disposal of cash and firm size. Reward understanding and different relevant discussion	5	
	Actions to reduce conflict	2	
			9
(b)	Definition	2	
	Limitations of model	4	
			6
			15

Strategic Financial Management
BPP Mock Exam 2: Pilot Paper

Question Paper:	
Time allowed	**3 hours**
This paper is divided into two sections	
Section A	**BOTH questions are compulsory and MUST be attempted**
Section B	**TWO questions ONLY to be answered**

paper 3.7

DO NOT OPEN THIS PAPER UNTIL YOU ARE READY TO START

UNDER EXAMINATION CONDITIONS

Section A – ALL questions are compulsory and MUST be attempted

1   Novoroast plc manufactures microwave ovens which it exports to several countries, as well as supplying the home market. One of Novoroast's export markets is a South American country, which has recently imposed a 40% tariff on imports of microwaves in order to protect its local 'infant' microwave industry. The imposition of this tariff means that Novoroast's products are no longer competitive in the South American country's market but the government there is, however, willing to assist companies wishing to undertake direct investment locally. The government offers a 10% grant towards the purchase of plant and equipment, and a three-year tax holiday on earnings. Corporate tax after the three-year period would be paid at the rate of 25% in the year that the taxable cash flow arises.

Novoroast wishes to evaluate whether to invest in a manufacturing subsidiary in South America, or to pull out of the market altogether.

The total cost of an investment in South America is 155 million pesos (at current exchange rates), comprising:

-    50 million pesos for land and buildings

-    60 million pesos for plant and machinery (all of which would be required almost immediately)

-    45 million pesos for working capital

20 million pesos of the working capital will be required immediately and 25 million pesos at the end of the first year of operation. Working capital needs are expected to increase in line with local inflation.

The company's planning horizon is five years.

Plant and machinery is expected to be depreciated (tax allowable) on a straight-line basis over five years, and is expected to have negligible realisable value at the end of five years. Land and buildings are expected to appreciate in value in line with the level of inflation in the South American country.

Production and sales of microwaves are expected to be 8,000 units in the first year at an initial price of 1,450 pesos per unit, 60,000 units in the second year, and 120,000 units per year for the remainder of the planning horizon.

In order to control the level of inflation, legislation exists in the South American country to restrict retail price rises of manufactured goods to 10% per year.

Fixed costs and local variable costs, which for the first year of operation are 12 million pesos and 600 pesos per unit respectively, are expected to increase by the previous year's rate of inflation.

All components will be produced or purchased locally except for essential microchips which will be imported from the UK at a cost of £8 per unit, yielding a contribution to the profit of the parent company of £3 per unit. It is hoped to keep this sterling cost constant over the planning horizon.

Corporate tax in the UK is at the rate of 30% per year, payable in the year the liability arises. A bi-lateral tax treaty exists between the UK and the South American country, which permits the offset of overseas tax against any UK tax liability on overseas earnings. In periods of tax holiday assume that no UK tax would be payable on South American cash flows.

Summarised group data:

	£ million
Novoroast plc, summarised balance sheet:	
Fixed assets (net)	440
Current assets	370
Less current liabilities	(200)
	610
Financed by	
£1 ordinary shares	200
Reserves	230
	430
6% Eurodollar bonds, eight years until maturity	180
	610

Novoroast's current share price is 410 pence per share, and current bond price is $800 per bond ($1,000 par and redemption value).

Forecast inflation rates

	UK	South American country
Present	4%	20%
Year 1	3%	20%
Year 2	4%	15%
Year 3	4%	15%
Year 4	4%	15%
Year 5	4%	15%

Foreign exchange rates

	Peso/£
Spot	13.421
1 year forward	15.636

Novoroast plc believes that if the investment is undertaken the overall risk to investors in the company will remain unchanged.

The company's beta coefficients have been estimated as equity 1.25, debt 0.225.

The market return is 14% per annum and the risk free rate is 6% per annum.

Existing UK microwave production currently produces an after tax net cash flow of £30 million per annum. This is expected to be reduced by 10% if the South American investment goes ahead (after allowing for diversion of some production to other EU countries). Production is currently at full capacity in the UK.

Required:

(a) **Prepare a report advising whether or not Novoroast plc should invest in the South American country. Include in your report a discussion of the limitations of your analysis.**

What other information would be useful to assist the decision process?

All relevant calculations must be shown in your report or as an appendix to it.

State clearly any assumptions that you make.

(Approximately 20 marks are available for calculations and 10 for discussion) (30 marks)

(b) **If, once the investment had taken place, the government of the South American country imposed a block on the remittance of dividends to the**

UK, discuss how Novoroast might try to avoid such a block on remittances.
(5 marks)

(c) **Briefly discuss ethical issues that might need to be considered as part of a multinational company's investment decision process.** (5 marks)

(40 marks)

2 The directors of Minprice plc, a food retailer with 20 superstores, are proposing to make a takeover bid for Savealot plc, a company with six superstores in the north of England. Minprice will offer four of its ordinary shares for every three ordinary shares of Savealot. The bid has not yet been made public.

Summarised Accounts
Balance Sheets as at 31 March 20X0

	Minprice plc			Savealot plc		
	£ million	£ million	£ million	£ million	£ million	£ million
Land and buildings (net)			483			42.3
Fixed assets (net)			150			17.0
			633			59.3
Current assets						
Stock	328			51.4		
Debtors	12			6.3		
Cash	44			5.3		
		384			63.0	
Creditors: amounts falling due in less than one year						
Creditors	447			46.1		
Dividend	12			2.0		
Taxation	22			2.0		
		(481)			(50.1)	
			(97)			12.9
Creditors: amounts falling due after more than one year						
14% loan stock			(200)			
Floating rate bank term loans			(114)			(17.5)
			222			54.7
Shareholders' Funds						
Original shares 25 pence per			75	50 pence par		20.0
Reserves			147			34.7
			222			54.7

Profit and loss accounts for the year ending 31 March 20X0

	£ million	£ million
Turnover	1,130	181
Earnings before interest and tax	115	14
Net interest	(40)	(2)
Profit before tax	75	12
Taxation	(25)	(4)
Available to shareholders	50	8
Dividend	(24)	(5)
Retained earnings	26	3

BPP PUBLISHING

The current share price of Minprice plc is 232 pence, and of Savealot plc 295 pence. The current loan stock price of Minprice plc is £125.

Recent annual growth trends:	Minprice plc	Savealot plc
Dividends	7%	8%
EPS	7%	10%

Rationalisation following the acquisition will involve the following transactions (all net of tax effects):

(a) Sale of surplus warehouse facilities for £6.8 million.
(b) Redundancy payments costing £9.0 million.
(c) Wage savings of £2.7 million per year for at least five years.

Minprice's cost of equity is estimated to be 14.5%, and weighted average cost of capital 12%. Savealot's cost of equity is estimated to be 13%.

Required:

(a) **Discuss and evaluate whether or not the bid is likely to be viewed favourably by the shareholders of both Minprice plc and Savealot plc. Include discussion of the factors that are likely to influence the views of the shareholders.**

   All relevant calculations must be shown.   (15 marks)

(b) **Discuss the possible effects on the likely success of the bid if the offer terms were to be amended to a choice of one new Minprice plc 10 year zero coupon debenture redeemable at £100 for every 10 Savealot plc shares, or 325 pence per share cash. Minprice plc could currently issue new 10 year loan stock at an interest rate of 10%.**

   All relevant calculations must be shown.   (7 marks)

(c) The directors of Savealot plc have decided to fight the bid and have proposed the following measures:

   (i)   Announce that their company's profits are likely to be doubled next year.

   (ii)   Alter the Articles of Association to require that at least 75% of shareholders need to approve an acquisition.

   (iii) Persuade, for a fee, a third party investor to buy large quantities of the company's shares.

   (iv)   Introduce an advertising campaign criticising the performance and management ability of Minprice plc.

   (v)   Revalue fixed assets to current values so that shareholders are aware of the company's true market values.

   Acting as a consultant to the company, give reasoned advice on whether or not the company should adopt each of these measures.   (8 marks)

   (30 marks)

Section B – TWO questions ONLY to be answered

3   (a)   Your managing director has received forecasts of Euro exchange rates in two years' time from three leading banks.

Euro/£ two year forecasts
Lottobank   1.452
Kadbank   1.514
Gross bank   1.782

The current spot mid-rate Euro 1.667/£

A non-executive director of your company has suggested that in order to forecast future exchange rates, the interest rate differential between countries should be used. She states that 'as short term interest rates are currently 6% in the UK, and 2.5% in the Euro bloc, the exchange rate in two years' time will be Euro 1.747/£'.

Required:

(i)   **Prepare a brief report discussing the likely validity of the non-executive director's estimate.**   (4 marks)

(ii)   **Explain briefly whether or not forecasts of future exchange rates using current interest rate differentials are likely to be accurate.**
                                                                              (3 marks)

(b)   You have also been asked to give advice to your managing director about a tender by the company's Italian subsidiary for an order in Kuwait. The tender conditions state that payment will be made in Kuwait dinars 18 months from now. The subsidiary is unsure as to what price to tender. The marginal cost of producing the goods at that time is estimated to be Euro 340,000 and a 25% mark-up is normal for the company.

Exchange rates
Euro/Dinar
Spot   0.256 - 0.260

No forward rate exists for 18 months' time.

		Italy	Kuwait
Annual inflation rates		3%	9%
Annual interest rates available to the Italian			
subsidiary:	Borrowing	6%	11%
	Lending	2.5%	8%

Required:

Discuss how the Italian subsidiary might protect itself against foreign exchange rate changes, and recommend what tender price should be used.   (8 marks)

All relevant calculations must be shown.   **(15 marks)**

4   (a)   Panon plc has a commitment to borrow £6 million in five months' time for a period of four months. A General Election is due in four months' time, and the managers of Panon are concerned that interest rates could significantly increase just after the election.

Panon can currently borrow at LIBOR + 1%. Three month split LIBOR is at 7.1%.

Current LIFFE £500,000 Sterling three month interest rate futures prices are:

September 92.50
December 92.10

Assume that it is now the end of June and that futures contracts mature at the end of the relevant month.

Required:

(i)   **Illustrate how Panon plc could use a futures hedge to protect against its potential interest rate risk.**   (4 marks)

(ii) **Estimate the basis for this hedge both now, and at the time the contract is likely to be closed out.**

      Estimate the expected effective interest rate for Panon in four months' time.

      Comment upon whether or not this interest rate is likely to be achieved.   (5 marks)

(b)   Panon borrowed two million Euros in four-year floating rate notes funds nine months ago at an interest rate EURIBOR plus 1%, in an attempt to reduce the level of interest paid on its loans. At that time EURIBOR was 6%. Unfortunately EURIBOR interest rates have increased since that time to 7.2%. The company wishes to protect itself from further interest rate volatility, but does not wish to lose the benefit of possible interest rate reductions that might occur in a few months' time. An adviser has suggested the use of a six-month American style Euro swaption at 8.5% with a premium of Euro 50,000, commencing in three months' time and with a maturity date the same as the floating rate Euro loan.

Required:

Briefly explain what is meant by a 'swaption'.

Illustrate under what circumstances this proposed swaption would benefit Panon.

The time value of money may be ignored.   (6 marks)

                                                                                (15 marks)

5   (a)   **Discuss whether or not an increase in dividends is likely to benefit the shareholders of a plc.**   (8 marks)

    (b)   The board of directors of Serty plc is discussing the level and nature of the company's next dividend payment. Three options are under consideration:

          (i)   A cash dividend of 15 pence per share, or

          (ii)   A 5% scrip dividend, or

          (iii) The company repurchases 10% of the ordinary share capital at the current market price and then pays a cash dividend as in (i) above.

          Summarise financial accounts for Serty are shown below:

Profit and loss account (£ million)

Turnover	150.0
Operating profit	15.0
Net interest earned	4.0
	19.0
Taxation	6.3
Available to shareholders	12.7

Balance Sheet (£ million)

Fixed Assets (net)			60
Current assets	Stock	20	
	Debtors	20	
	Cash and bank	40	80
Less current liabilities			(30)
			110
Shareholders funds			
Issued ordinary shares (50p par)			20
Reserves			90
			110

Serty's current share price is 400 pence cum div.

Required:

Calculate the expected effect of each suggestion on a shareholder in Serty owning 1,000 shares. Explain briefly how accurate your estimates are likely to be.   (7 marks)

Taxation may be ignored.   **(15 marks)**

6   Discuss how a government might try to reduce a large, persistent, current account deficit on the balance of payments, and illustrate what impact such government action might have on a multinational company operating in the country concerned. Explain the possible role and impact of the International Monetary Fund (IMF) in this process.   **(15 marks)**

298

ANSWERS

DO NOT TURN THIS PAGE UNTIL YOU
HAVE COMPLETED THE MOCK EXAM

WARNING! APPLYING THE BPP MARKING SCHEME

If you decide to mark your paper using the BPP marking scheme, you should bear in mind the following points.

1   The BPP solutions are not definitive: you will see that we have applied the marking scheme to our solutions to show how good answers should gain marks, but there may be more than one way to answer the question. You must try to judge fairly whether different points made in your answers are correct and relevant and therefore worth marks according to our marking scheme.

2   If you have a friend or colleague who is studying or has studied this paper, you might ask him or her to mark your paper for you, thus gaining a more objective assessment. Remember you and your friend are not trained or objective markers, so try to avoid complacency or pessimism if you appear to have done very well or very badly.

3   You should be aware that BPP's answers are longer than you would be expected to write. Sometimes, therefore, you would gain the same number of marks for making the basic point as we have shown as being available for a slightly more detailed or extensive solution.

It is most important that you analyse your solutions in detail and that you attempt to be as objective as possible.

Professional Examination - Paper 3.7   **Marking Scheme**

Strategic Financial Management

This marking scheme is given as a guide to markers in the context of the suggested answer. Scope is given to markers to award marks for alternative approaches to a question, including relevant comment, and where well-reasoned conclusions are provided. This is particularly the case for essay based questions where there will often be more than one definitive solution.

A PLAN OF ATTACK

We've already established that you've been told to do it 101 times, so it is of course superfluous to tell you for the 102nd time to **Take a good look at the paper before diving in to answer questions.**

The next step

You may be thinking that this paper is a lot more straightforward than the first mock exam; however, having sailed through the first mock, you may think this paper is actually rather difficult.

Option 1 (Oh dear)

If you are challenged by this paper, it is still best to **do the compulsory questions first.** You will feel better once you've got them out the way. Honest.

- Of the two, it's probably best to do **question 1** first; there are some straightforward marks to be gained on every part of the question. Draw up the report format and set out the proforma for the NPV calculations. Certain figures can be slotted in straightaway but don't at first worry about the figures that need detailed workings. Then answer the written parts of part (a) – limitations and other information, and also parts (b) and (c). You can then tackle the rest of the calculations knowing that you've already got the majority of the question under your belt.

- The easiest marks in **question 2** are in part (c); as you do not need to use your answers to (a) and (b) in (c), it's best to do it first. There are a number of calculations you need to do in parts (a) and (b), but remember you need to spend sufficient time writing pertinent comments.

- Choose **question 3** only if you feel you can use and discuss the international Fisher effect and purchasing power parity theories.

- **Question 4 (a)** is a fairly straightforward question on futures; you don't even have to calculate the outcome. However do not attempt to guess what a swaption is if you do not know; you will get **no credit** for writing about an incorrect guess.

- The mathematics in **question 5** are fairly straightforward. In addition **question 5(a)** isn't just about Modigliani and Miller; discussing the practical aspects of dividend policy will actually gain you more marks.

- If you have revised balance of payments policy and the IMF, **question 6** contains no hidden traps. There are no calculations involved either.

Option 2 (This one's definitely easier)

Are you **sure** it is? If you are then that's encouraging. You'll feel even happier when you've got the compulsory questions out the way, so why not **do Questions 1 and 2 first.**

- The main danger in **question 1** is spending so much time trying to get the calculations right that you neglect the written parts of the question, which are worth about half the marks.

- Similarly in **question 2,** it's not enough just to carry out lots of calculations; you'll need to make relevant comments and discuss the limitations of what you've done.

- **Question 3** is mainly about purchasing power parity and the international Fisher effects; the marks are split between calculations and discussion roughly 50/50.

- If you can write about swaptions, certainly choose **question 4,** as part (a) is a very reasonable question on futures.

- Choose **question 5** if you feel happy about the calculations later in the question, but also have at your fingertips the range of issues (theoretical and practical) that determine dividend policy.

- If you revised the areas covered by **question 6** thoroughly, you should quite easily be able to score close to maximum marks on it.

Once more

You must must must **allocate your time** according to the marks for the question in total, and for the parts of the questions. And you must must must also **follow the requirements exactly.**

Finished with fifteen minutes to spare?

Looks like you slipped up on the time allocation. However if you have, make sure you don't waste the last few minutes; go back to **any parts of questions that you didn't finish** because you ran out of time.

Forget about it!

Forget about what? Excellent, you already have.

1

> **Tutor's hint**. In the report format asked for in part (a), it is probably easier to place your calculations as part of the report than as an appendix at the end. Because the 20 marks for the computation are spread fairly evenly and there is no need to know the final result, you should stop your computations as soon as the allotted time is up (approximately 36 minutes) and concentrate on the 10 discussion marks.

(a) To: Board of Directors of Novoroast plc
From: Strategic Financial Consultant

Proposed Investment in South American Manufacturing Subsidiary

1   **Introduction**

The proposed investment has been triggered by the imposition of a very **high import tariff** (40%) in the South American country. The effect of this tariff is that all sales from the UK to this country will be lost (10% of total UK sales). This loss of UK sales will occur whether or not the proposed investment is made, and has therefore been omitted from the financial evaluation which follows.

2   **Financial evaluation**

A financial evaluation of the investment, based on discounting the sterling value of incremental cash flows at the company's weighted average cost of capital, shows a **negative net present value** of £610,000, indicating that the investment is not expected to show high enough returns over the five year time horizon to compensate for the risk involved. Calculations are followed by workings and assumptions.

Year	0	1	2	3	4	5
Profit and cash flow - peso million						
Total contribution (W1)		5.80	44.20	92.82	97.04	100.92
Fixed costs (per year inflation increases)		(12.00)	(14.40)	(16.56)	(19.04)	(21.90)
Tax allowable depreciation		(12.00)	(12.00)	(12.00)	(12.00)	(12.00)
Taxable profit		(18.20)	17.80	64.26	66.00	67.02
Tax: from year 4 only at 25%					(16.50)	(16.76)
Add back depreciation		12.00	12.00	12.00	12.00	12.00
Net after-tax cash flow from operations		(6.20)	29.80	76.26	61.50	62.26
Investment cash flows						
Land and buildings (W3)	(50)					104.94
Plant and machinery (less 10% govt. grant)	(54)					
Working capital (W4)	(20)	(29.00)	(7.35)	(8.45)	(9.72)	74.52
Cash remittable from/to UK	(124)	(35.20)	22.45	67.81	51.78	241.72
Exchange rate P/£	13.421	15.636	17.290	19.119	21.141	23.377
UK cash flows (£m)						
Cash remittable	(9.24)	(2.25)	1.30	3.55	2.45	10.34
Contribution from sale of chips (£3 per unit)		0.02	0.18	0.36	0.36	0.36
Tax on chips contribution at 30%		(0.01)	(0.05)	(0.11)	(0.11)	(0.11)
Additional UK tax at 5% on S.Am. profits					(0.16)	(0.14)
Net cash flow in £m	(9.24)	(2.24)	1.43	3.80	2.54	10.45
14% (W5) discount factors	1	0.877	0.769	0.675	0.592	0.519
Present value £m	(9.24)	(1.96)	1.10	2.57	1.50	5.42

Net present value	(£610,000)

Workings

1

Year	0	1	2	3	4	5
Contribution per unit						
Sales price (10% increases - pesos)		1450.0	1595.0	1754.5	1930.0	2123.0
Variable cost per unit in pesos (previous year inflation increases)		600.0	720.0	828.0	952.2	1095.0
Chip cost per unit (£8 converted to pesos - W2)		125.1	138.3	153.0	169.1	187.0
Contribution per unit (pesos)		724.9	736.7	773.5	808.7	841.0
Sales volume ('000 units)		8	60	120	120	120

2   **Prediction of future exchange rates**

Future exchange rates have been predicted from expected inflation rates, on the principle of Purchasing Power Parity Theory. eg Year 1 exchange rate = $13.421 \times 1.20/1.03 = 15.636$, etc.

	Inflation		
	UK	SAm	*Exchange rate*
Spot			13.421
Year 1	3%	20%	15.636
Year 2	4%	15%	17.290
Year 3	4%	15%	19.119
Year 4	4%	15%	21.141
Year 5	4%	15%	23.377

3   **Land and buildings**

Value after 5 years = $P50m \times 1.2 \times 1.15^4 = P104.94m$. It is assumed no tax is payable on the capital gain.

4   **Working capital**

Value of working capital increases in line with inflation each year. The relevant cash flow is the difference between the values from year to year. Working capital is assumed to be released at the end of year 5.

End of year	0	1	2	3	4	5
Local inflation		20%	15%	15%	15%	
Value of Year 0 investment	20	24	27.60	31.74	36.50	0.00
Year 1 investment		25	28.75	33.06	38.02	0.00
Cumulative investment	20	49	56.35	64.80	74.52	0.00
Incremental cash flow	(20)	(29)	(7.35)	(8.45)	(9.72)	74.52

5   **Discount rate**

The company's WACC has been used as a discount rate, on the grounds that overall risk to investors is not expected to change as a result of this investment.

From the CAPM, Ke = 6% + (14% – 6%)1.25 = 16%.

Kd = 6% + (14% – 6%)0.225 = 7.8% pre-tax. After-tax rate = 7.8%(1 – 0.3) = 5.46%.

Market values: Equity: 200m × £4.10 = £820m. Debt: £180m × 800/1,000 = £144m.

Total = £964m.

WACC = 16% × 820/964 + 5.46% × 144/964 = 14.42%.

The discount rate will be **rounded** to 14% for the calculation.

3   **Limitations of the analysis**

The calculations are based on many assumptions and estimates concerning future cash flows. For example:

(i)   **Purchasing power parity**, used to estimate exchange rates, is only a 'broad-brush' theory; many other factors are likely to affect exchange rates and could increase the risk of the project.

(ii)   **Estimates** of inflation, used to estimate costs and exchange rates in the calculations, are subject to **high inaccuracies**.

(iii) **Assumptions** about future tax rates and the restrictions on price increases may be **incorrect**.

(iv)   **Cash flows** beyond the five year time horizon may be **crucial** in determining the viability or otherwise of the project; economic values of the operational assets at year 5 may be a lot higher than the residual values included in the calculation.

The calculations show only the medium term financial implications of the project. Non-financial factors and potentially important strategic issues have not been addressed.

4   **Other relevant information**

In order to get a more realistic view of the overall impact of the project, a strategic analysis needs to be carried out assessing the long term plans for the company's products and markets. For example, the **long term potential growth** of the South American market may be of greater significance than the medium term problems of price controls and inflation. On the other hand, it may be of more importance to the company to **increase its product range** to existing customers in Europe. There may also be further opportunities in other countries or regions.

Before deciding whether to invest in the South American country, the company should commission an evaluation of the **economic, political and ethical environment**. **Political risks** include the likelihood of imposition of exchange controls, prohibition of remittances, or confiscation of assets.

The value of this project may be higher than is immediately obvious if it opens up longer term opportunities in South American markets. Option pricing theory can be used to value these opportunities.

As regards the existing financial estimates, the **uncertainties** surrounding the cash flows can be quantified and understood better by carrying out **sensitivity analysis**, which may be used to show how the final result varies with changes in the estimates used.

5   **Conclusion**

On the basis of the evaluation carried out so far, the project is not worthwhile. However other opportunities not yet quantified may influence the final decision.

(b) Restrictions on the transfer of dividends from one country to another can be circumvented by two main methods:

(i)   **Adjusting transfer prices** for inter-company sales of goods or services between the subsidiary and other group companies; and/or

(ii)   **'Dressing up'** equity finance as debt finance.

Under the heading of transfer prices, the following techniques can be used:

(i)   **Increasing prices** for the **subsidiary's purchases** from the parent or other group companies

(ii)   **Reducing** (or abolishing) **prices** for sales by the subsidiary to other group companies

(iii)   Charging the subsidiary for head office **overhead and management charges**

(iv)   Charging the subsidiary for **royalties and patents** on processes used

The government of the South American country would probably attempt to prevent these arrangements from being effective.

If the company had foreseen the possibility of **dividend restriction**, it could have arranged for the subsidiary to be financed mainly by an inter-company loan, with equity investment nominally small. All expected returns could then be paid as inter-company loan interest.

A less obvious way of achieving the same objective is for the parent to **lend the major part** of its **investment** to an independent international bank, which then lends to the South American subsidiary. Returns would be paid as interest to the bank, which would in turn pay interest to the parent company.

If these financing arrangements have not already been made by the time dividend restrictions are imposed, the subsidiary may try to **lend its cash surpluses** to the **parent** (interest free) or, if this is prevented, to **lend** to the **subsidiary** of **another company** needing funds in the South American country, with an arrangement that the parent receives a corresponding loan from the parent of the other company. This device is known as a **parallel loan** and is, in effect, a currency swap.

(c)   All companies have to balance the need to compete against their ethical duty of care to stakeholders. The laws of developed countries have progressively reflected voters' concerns on ethical issues by banning activities considered harmful to society (eg drug dealing) or to the economy (eg corruption) and by developing numerous constraints on companies' behaviour towards employees, the local community and the environment. These are intended to give companies a level playing field on which they can compete vigorously.

Where potentially unethical activities are not banned by law, companies need to make difficult decisions, weighing up increased profitability against the harmful effects of bad publicity, organisational ill-health and the knowledge that some activities are clearly wrong. Whereas in developed countries such decisions might relate to experimentation on animals or sale of arms, the laws of developing countries are far less advanced, forcing companies to make their own decisions on major issues such as the following:

(i)   Provision of proper safety equipment and working conditions for employees
(ii)   Use of child labour
(iii)   Wage rates below subsistence level
(iv)   Discrimination against women, ethnic minorities, etc
(v)   Pollution of the environment
(vi)   'Inducement' payments to local officials to facilitate investment

In addition, multinational companies must decide whether it is right to invest at all in some countries which are regarded as **unethical**, for example because of violation of human rights.

Marking guide

		Marks	
(a)	Report format	1	
	Criterion (a) for the decision	1	
	South American cash flows:		
	Variable costs	1	
	Fixed costs	1	
	UK chips	1	
	Correct treatment of depreciation	2	
	Taxation	1	
	Fixed assets	1	
	Working capital	2	
	UK cash flows:		
	Earnings from chips and tax	2	
	Additional tax on South American cash flow	2	
	Present values	1	
	Discount rate	3	
	NPV and conclusion	1	
	(Reward technique even if calculation errors exist)		
	Comment on lost cash flows	1	
	Comments on accuracy	3-4	
	Other information/analysis that would be useful	5-6	
		Max	30
(b)	1 mark for each valid suggestion	Max	5
(c)	1 mark for each sensible ethical issue	Max	5
			40

2

> **Tutor's hint**. Roughly one third of the marks for part (a) are for estimating the effect on EPS and share price of the merger. Also important are existing share price valuation using the dividend valuation model and a discussion of gearing. In part (b) the yield on the zero coupon bond and its estimated value need to be computed. The cash offer comments are standard. In part (c) there is one mark for each correct answer given, rising to two marks if a full answer is given for any particular defence.

(a) Since the terms of the bid involve a share-for-share swap, shareholders will be highly interested in the fundamentals underlying the current market value of shares in both companies, in the **potential economic gains** that can be made by combining the companies and the likely effect of the merger on share prices, including the proportion in which the gains are likely to be split between the two sets of shareholders.

Shareholders of Savealot are unlikely to accept unless they receive a **premium** over their existing share price, whereas Minprice shareholders will not wish to offer **too high a premium** because this will cause them to lose out. Other factors are also at play in this proposed merger, one of which is that Minprice may be seeking to reduce its high gearing by taking over the comparatively ungeared Savealot.

Existing share prices

The reasonableness of each company's existing share price can be tested against the dividend valuation model:

Latest dividend per share: Minprice: £24m/300m = 8 pence. Savealot: £5m/40m = 12.5 pence.

Share values from the dividend valuation model: $D_0(1 + g)/(K_e - g)$:

Minprice: $8 \times 1.07 / (14.5\% - 7\%) = 114$ pence

Savealot: $12.5 \times 1.08 / (13\% - 8\%) = 270$ pence

If the stock market is efficient, the companies' current market share prices provide the best indicator of the 'true' value of their shares. However, on the basis of the **dividend valuation model** (using past growth rates as an indicator of expected future growth) Minprice's actual share price of 232 pence is more than twice as high as it 'should' be. Although the DVM is a simplistic model, this might signal caution to Savealot's shareholders, whose actual price of 295 pence seems comparatively reasonable. It is clear that future growth for both companies is expected to be better than the past. This may reflect expectations of a general upturn in the sector, or may be the effect of general market feelings that mergers will be taking place.

Earnings per share are: Minprice: £50m/300m = 16.67p. Savealot: £8m/40m = 20p. The P/E ratios are: Minprice: 232/16.67 = 13.9. Savealot: 295/20 = 14.75.

Unfortunately, no P/E ratios or other statistics for the food retail industry are available for comparison. However, the P/E of Minprice, which is nearly as high as that of Savealot, seems over-rated on the basis of its poorer growth record and higher cost of equity capital.

Potential economic gains from the merger

The present value of the proposed rationalisation transactions following the merger is £7.5 million:

	£m
Warehouse sale	6.8
Redundancy	(9.0)
Wage savings for 5 years: £2.7m × 3.605*	9.7
	7.5

* The annuity factor for 5 years at 12%, the WACC of Minprice. Wage savings may last for more than 5 years, giving a higher present value.

Assuming this gain in value from combining the companies is achievable, it indicates that the merger is economically worthwhile.

The bid has not yet been made public. The effect of the potential gains from the merger terms is unlikely to have been reflected in the share prices of either company. However, it is just as probable that shareholders already have some expectations of mergers in the industry, in which case synergetic gains would already have been anticipated in share prices, even under the semi-strong view of market efficiency.

Effect of the merger announcement on share prices

There are a number of different ways of examining the effect of the merger information being made public.

(i) Assume first that shareholders had **no previous expectations** that the merger would take place and are taken totally by surprise when the synergetic gains of £7.5 million are announced.

They will estimate the value of the combined business as:

Value of firms before merger:	£m
Minprice: 300m × 232p	696.0
Savealot: 40m × 295p	118.0
	814.0
Post merger synergy	7.5
Estimated value after merger	821.5

Minprice will issue 4/3 × 40m new shares = 53.333m new shares to the shareholders of Savealot. The total number of shares in Minprice will rise to 353.333m.

The expected share price for Minprice after the merger is announced will be £821.5m/353.333m = 232.5 pence. This is only a 0.5p gain to Minprice shareholders, who will have allowed all the advantage of synergy to accrue to Savealot.

Savealot shares will be expected to reflect the announcement by rising to 4/3 × 232.5p = 310p, giving them a 15p gain, an increase of 5%.

The reconciliation of the gains is: Minprice 300m shares × 0.5p = £1.5m and Savealot 40m shares × 15p = £6m, giving a total of £7.5m.

On this assumption, shareholders of Savealot would be fairly happy with the terms of the offer and Minprice shareholders would not lose from their existing position.

Total equity earnings from the combination will be £50m + £8m = £58m, assuming that wage savings are offset against redundancy cost write-offs and before any expected earnings growth.

This will give an expected earnings per share of £58/353.333 = 16.4 pence. This represents a drop from Minprice's existing 16.67p, but Savealot shareholders would receive the equivalent of 4/3 × 16.4p = 21.9p compared with their existing 20p.

(ii)   Suppose however that shareholders had **already guessed** that the merger would take place and share prices had **already increased** to reflect expected gains (a stronger view of market efficiency).

The value of the combined business would then be £814m and the expected value of Minprice's shares after the terms of the offer were announced would be £814/353.333 = 230.3 pence, a drop of nearly two pence.

Minprice shareholders would be disappointed with the terms of the offer. Savealot shareholders would still be better off, with an expected increase in share price to 4/3 × 230.3p = 307 pence (a premium of 4%).

(iii)   As a third possibility, Minprice's shares may be **temporarily over-valued** by the market, as indicated by the high share price compared with that predicted from the DVM.

Such an over-valuation might occur, for example, if investors had false hopes of Minprice's opportunities in the merger market. A fair price for Minprice's shares based on its existing business might be 114p, giving a total value of 300m × 114p = £342m.

Then the value of the combined company would be £342m + £118m + £7.5m = £467.5m, giving an expected share price after the merger announcement of £467.5/353.333 = 132.3 pence.

This would represent very favourable merger terms to Minprice, but would be unacceptable to Savealot, whose equivalent share value would fall from 195p to 4/3 × 132.3p = 176.4p.

In summary, the merger terms appear to be fair and acceptable, provided that Minprice's shares are not temporarily over-valued by false expectations. Savealot shareholders need to evaluate the stability of Minprice's share price before accepting the offer.

309

Other factors

(i)   **Gearing**

Minprice is very highly geared. Even if only long term debt is considered, gearing (D/E) in terms of book value is 314/222 = 141% and in terms of market value is 364/696 = 52%.

By comparison, Savealot's gearing is only 17.5/54.7 = 32% in book terms and 17.5/118 = 15% in market value terms.

In addition, Minprice has high current creditors resulting in net current liabilities. While this is not unusual for a supermarket chain, it indicates that gearing in real terms is even higher. The shareholders of Minprice will favour the share issue terms for the merger with Savealot which should reduce their gearing substantially, whereas Savealot's shareholders are unlikely to see this as an advantage.

(ii) **Dividend policy**

The companies have different dividend yields and covers, which may influence the views of some shareholders.

	Minprice	Savealot
Dividend yield	3.4%	4.2%
Dividend cover	2.1	1.6

(iii) **Management plans**

The composition of the board of directors and senior managers will be fundamental to the success of the business after the merger. Savealot seems to have been performing better than Minprice recently and may be able to argue for more than proportional representation on the board. Shareholders of both companies will be interested in these plans.

(b) **325 pence per share cash offer**

For the shareholders of Savealot this represents a **premium of 10%** over the current market price of 295p and is significantly better than the most optimistic estimate of the share offer's value, which was 310 pence.

The **cash offer** gives a **risk free return** compared with the risk of shares. For this reason cash offers are usually less in value than the equivalent share offers. Since this offer is *more* than the share offer it represents good value to Savealot shareholders. However, they will suffer immediate capital gains tax on the disposal.

From Minprice's point of view, the cash offer is **unlikely** to be **feasible**, given its high gearing and weak liquidity position.

Zero coupon debenture

If Savealot shareholders accept the zero coupon debenture they could either sell it or hold it. Holding it would imply a **reduction in the risk** of their investment portfolio.

Each debenture would effectively have a cost of $10 \times 295p = £29.50$ and could be redeemed in 10 years for £100. The rate of return can be estimated from $£29.50(1+r)^{10} = £100$. Thus $1/(1+r)^{10} = 0.295$. Looking at the 10 year row in the PV tables, 0.295 implies a return of 13%. Since this is high compared with the 10% expected return on equivalent-risk corporate debt, the debenture represents good value.

To estimate its value, discount the £100 redemption value for 10 years at 10%. This gives a value of £38.60, or 386 pence per Savealot share, representing a premium of

31%. The debenture is clearly the most attractive of the three forms of offer to Savealot shareholders.

To Minprice it is less attractive than cash in the longer term but more attractive in the short term because **no cash payments** are **required** for 10 years. However, earnings per share will suffer if the cost of the debt is amortised over 10 years.

(c)   To: Board of Directors of Savealot plc
    From: Consultant

In the UK, defences made by a publicly quoted company against a takeover bid must be legal and be allowed by the City Code on Takeovers and Mergers and Stock Exchange regulations. Our advice on your proposals is as follows.

(i)   If your profits are likely to double, then **now** is a good time to **announce** the fact. You will need to substantiate your claims with clear evidence that can be verified by shareholders. This is very likely to halt the bid, or at least secure better terms.

(ii)   Stock Exchange regulations **prohibit** the alteration of articles of association to require more than a 51% majority to accept an offer for acquisition.

(iii)   This defence, which was used for example in the Guinness case, is illegal under the Companies Act, as it is tantamount to the company **purchasing its own shares**.

(iv)   As with defence (i) this can be a very effective form of defence provided that the **information** is **true** and can be substantiated, otherwise a libel action might result.

(v)   **Revaluation of fixed assets** is a good idea, provided that it is carried out by an independent valuer and the values can be **substantiated**. However, the effect on share values may be less significant than might be thought as, in an efficient market, these true asset values will already have been estimated by institutional shareholders.

Marking guide

		Marks	
(a)	Discussion of the current bid and its premium over the share price	2	
	Valuation using dividend valuation model and comment	3-4	
	Dividend policy, dividend growth and EPS growth	2-3	
	Gearing differences and risk	2	
	Estimates of expected EPS and share price	4-5	
	Other discussion	2	
		Max	15
(b)	Zero coupon yield and value	4-5	
	Cash offer and implications	2-3	
		Max	7
(c)	1-2 marks for correct comment. 2 if a full answer is given	Max	8
			30

3

Tutor's hint. In (a) (i) and (b) there are two alternative versions of the International Fisher Effect and Purchasing Power Parity formulae. Either one will give the correct result. In (a) part (ii) you must distinguish between the terms 'unbiased' and 'accurate', and state some of the assumptions behind the IFE formula. In part (b) the best type of hedge where it is uncertain whether cash is needed is a currency option.

(a) (i)   To: Managing Director
From: Financial analyst

Predictions of Euro/£ exchange rate

If exchange rates are freely floating and interest rates are also freely determined by market forces, then, according to the International Fisher Effect, interest rate differentials between two countries can be applied to the current exchange rate to give an unbiased predictor of the future exchange rate.

Using the formula $(i_f - i_{uk}) / (1 + i_{uk})$, the predicted future exchange rate would change by:

$(3.5\% - 6\%) / 1.06 = -2.358\%$. This implies that the Euro is predicted to strengthen against the pound by 2.36%.

If this happens for two years, the predicted exchange rate will be $1.667 \times (1 - 0.02358)^2 = 1.667 \times 0.97642^2 = 1.589$ Euro/£.

The non-executive director is wrong, having applied the formula wrongly as $1.667 \times (1 + 0.02358)^2 = 1.747$ Euro/£.

Tutor's hint. An alternative version of the formula gives the predicted figure as follows:

Predicted future exchange rate = spot rate $\times (1 + i_f) / (1 + i_{uk})$

This gives year 1 exchange rate as $1.667 \times 1.035/1.06 = 1.6277$, and year 2 as $1.6277 \times 1.035/1.06 = 1.589$ Euro/£, as above.

(ii)   The fact that a predicted exchange rate is **unbiased** does not make it accurate. Unbiased simply means that the rate is as likely to be above the prediction as below it. The margin of error on the prediction over two years will be very large, even if other factors remain the same, which is unlikely. Over the next two years interest rates are almost certain to change with changing economic conditions.

The **assumptions** behind the IFE model are also **unlikely to hold**. The model assumes that the currencies are freely traded on the market with, for example, no government intervention, and that the current exchange rate represents an equilibrium position. The forecast exchange rate is therefore very unlikely to be accurate.

(b)   The best form of protection against foreign exchange risk, in a situation where it is uncertain whether there will be a need for the currency to be exchanged, is a **currency option**. A forward contract cannot be avoided if the contract is lost and could create a currency loss, whereas a currency option can be allowed to lapse if it is not advantageous. The disadvantage of a currency option is the 'up-front' premium, which is non-refundable and can be expensive.

The option is needed **from the date** the **tender is made** to **the date the results are announced**. Beyond that point, if the contract is won, currency protection could be achieved by a money market hedge (borrowing Dinars on the strength of the future sales proceeds), or by another option, but forward contracts do not appear to be available.

Since the date of award of the contract is unknown, an alternative hedge would be to take out an **option** for the **whole 18 month period**. The company would purchase an option to sell (put) Dinars for Euros in 18 months time.

If no hedge is used, a prediction of the exchange rate in 18 months is needed to estimate the tender price.

The spot rate is 0.256 – 0.260 Euros per Dinar. The rate for selling Dinars is 0.256 (when you sell Dinars you will get the lower number of Dinars).

Using purchasing power parity:

The formula is $(I_\epsilon - i_D) / (1 + i_D)$.

The Euro is predicted to strengthen against the Dinar: (3% – 9%) / 1.09 = -5.505% per year.

In 18 months (1.5 years) the exchange rate is predicted to be $0.256 \times (1 - 0.0505)^{1.5}$ = 0.235 Euros per Dinar.

Purchasing power parity has been used instead of the International Fisher effect as it is regarded as more reliable.

The Euro cost in 18 months time is predicted to be 340,000. A 25% margin gives a price of €425,000.

If no hedge is used, the recommended tender price is 425,000/0.235 = 1,808,511 Dinars.

If an option hedge using today's exchange rate is used, the price should be 425,000/0.256 = 1,660,156 Dinars *plus* the cost of the option.

Marking guide		Marks
(a)	Use of IFE to estimate future exchange rate and conclusion	4
	Comments about why forecasts are not likely to be accurate	3
		7
(b)	Discussion of alternative hedgers – reward options most	3
	Calculations of tender price and conclusion	5
		8
		15

4

> **Tutor's hint**. In part (a), on hedging interest rate risk by futures contracts, the computation of basis is crucial to the solution. In part (b) you will need to assess the effective 'cap' which the swaption puts on the interest rate paid.

(a) (i) It is now the end of June. Panon **needs to borrow** in 5 months' time at the end of November, for a period of 4 months until end of March. The December futures contract will be selected as a hedge, being the contract which matures the soonest after the start date of borrowing.

To hedge borrowing, Panon should **sell December sterling three month futures** now and buy them at the end of November. The number of contracts to be sold and bought is £6m/£500,000 × 4/3 = 16 contracts.

(ii) The **basis** is the **difference** between the **futures price** and the price of the **underlying cash instrument**.

Three month LIBOR is 7.1%. The December futures price is 92.10, which converts to 100 – 92.10 = 7.9%, giving a basis of 0.8% or 80 basis points (or ticks).

By the end of December, (6 months' time) this will have reduced to zero. Assuming a smooth reduction in basis, at the end of November it will be 1/6 × 80 = 13 basis points, that is the effective interest rate on the future will be 0.13% above LIBOR.

BPP PUBLISHING

When Panon closes out its futures contract, the effective interest rate it will pay is expected to be the current futures price less 0.13% + the 1% premium it pays above LIBOR, ie 7.9% − 0.13% + 1% = 8.77%.

This interest rate will only be achieved if the **basis declines smoothly** over the 5 month period. This may not happen if, for example, there are significant movements in debt yield curves.

(b) A **swaption** gives the buyer the **right** but not the obligation to **swap from floating rate to fixed interest** at a specified rate. In the case of an American style swaption, this can be done at any time up to the maturity date of the swaption. A European style swaption may only be exercised on the maturity date.

The swaption suggested by the advisor gives Panon the right but not the obligation to swap from its floating Euro rate of EURIBOR + 1% to a fixed rate of 8.5% at any time over the next 6 months. This would benefit Panon if EURIBOR rises at some stage over the next 6 months and is expected to stay high for the duration of Panon's loan, which still has 3¼ years to run. Effectively this puts a cap on the interest rate.

Suppose, as a simplifying assumption, EURIBOR rises in three months time, midway through the swaption's life. Panon can take advantage of three years fixed interest. The swaption cost of €50,000 is 2.5% of the loan value, that is approximately 0.833% per year (ignoring the time value of money). If the swaption is exercised, the cap on the interest rate will effectively be 8.5% + 0.833% = 9.333%.

Panon is currently paying 7.2% + 1% = 8.2%. The cap is therefore about 14% (as a proportion of 8.2%) above this figure.

If the interest rate falls, the **swaption can be allowed to lapse** and advantage taken of lower interest payments. Although the swaption is expensive, its cost is the price of having the flexibility to avoid very high interest rates but take advantage of lower rates.

However, once exercised, the swaption **cannot be reversed** is interest rates fall at a later stage. Panon may wish to compare the cost of obtaining a series of short term options over the three year period.

Marking guide			Marks
(a)	(i) Correct type of hedge and illustration		4
	(ii) Current basis		2
	Future basis		1
	Expected interest rate		1
	Whether this will be achieved		1
			9
(b)	Explanation of swaption		2
	Illustration of when it would be of value		4
			6
			15

5

Tutor's hint. Part (a) is a standard dividend policy discussion. State the dividend irrelevance hypothesis and show the effect of real world factors.

(a) In financial management theory some writers (eg Modigliani and Miller) have shown that, under perfect capital market conditions, the discussion of whether cash should be paid as dividends or reinvested is irrelevant, provided that the company accepts all its profitable opportunities. The argument is based on two main premises.

- If cash is **paid** as **dividends, funds for expansion** can be **raised by share issues**.

- If cash is reinvested, shareholders can achieve their returns by **selling shares** at an **increased value**.

However, the real world factors which affect dividend policy in practice include the following:

(i) **Share issues** are **expensive, time consuming** and **require divulgence of information** to the general public. It is cheaper and more convenient to fund expansion by use of retained earnings. These factors would lead the company to prefer lower dividend payouts.

(ii) If shareholders have to **sell shares** to achieve their returns, they suffer **brokerage fees**. This may lead them to prefer higher dividend payouts.

(iii) Some shareholders may prefer to take their rewards as **capital gains** if there is a lower effective tax rate. These would prefer lower dividend payouts.

(iv) **Corporate taxation treatment** may also favour the payment of lower dividends.

(v) In the **absence of perfect information** concerning the company's prospects, shareholders may take the dividend as a **signal**. For example, an increase in dividends may be taken as a signal of higher expected future earnings.

All these factors need to be taken into consideration when formulating a dividend policy. In practice companies often aim for a **smooth trend** in dividend growth, allowing increases or decreases in borrowings to absorb the fluctuations in cash generated. In order to carry out this policy, dividend pay-out must be reasonably low, and there should be good reasons for any significant increase.

However, the above arguments assume that the company has **investment opportunities**. If it does not, then it is not advisable to allow cash to accumulate in the bank. A choice needs to be made between increasing dividends and buying back shares.

(b) The company has 40 million shares (worth a total of £160 million) and a shareholder owning 1,000 shares currently has a wealth of £4,000 cum div.

(i) If a cash dividend of 15 pence per share is paid, the expected ex div price will drop to 385 pence. The **shareholder's wealth** will be **£3,850 in share value** and £150 in cash, with the total unchanged at £4,000.

(ii) If a 5% scrip dividend is paid, the company will **issue 2 million new shares** at no charge. Since the value of the company will not change, the share price will drop to 400p × 100/105 = 381 pence. The shareholder will now have 1,050 shares worth 381p each, giving a total wealth of £4,000.

(iii) If 10% of the ordinary share capital (4 million shares) are repurchased at 400 pence each, the **value of the company** will **drop** by the £16 million cash spent to £144 million. The share price will be £144m/36m = 400 pence per share, unchanged. The shareholders wealth will be made up of 900 shares at 400 pence (£3,600) and cash of 100 × £4 (£400), giving total wealth of £4,000, as before.

These estimates may be inaccurate because they **ignore any information content** which may be contained in the company's action. For example, a share buy-back may cause investors to assume that the company has no immediate plans to expand, whereas a scrip dividend may be taken as indication of expansionary plans.

Marking guide		Marks
(a)	Look for mix of theory and practical comments	8
(b)	2 marks for each estimate	6
	Comment about accuracy	1
		$\frac{}{7}$
		$\frac{}{15}$

6

> **Tutor's hint**. Although this is nominally a straight economics question on the reduction of balance of payments deficits, to answer it well you need to be well versed in the international trade section of the syllabus, including barriers to trade, and in the work of the IMF.

A current account deficit is caused when **cash inflows** from exports of goods and services, investment income and current transfers are **lower** than **cash outflows** on equivalent imports.

If the deficit is persistent, the government may decide to finance it for a period by **running down foreign currency reserves,** or by borrowing from international banks, donor countries or international organisations such as the IMF. However, action must eventually be taken to inhibit imports or encourage exports. One or more of the following actions may be taken:

(a) **Increasing interest rates**. This will reduce the demand for local borrowing and hence for purchases (including imports), as well as attracting foreign funds to take advantage of the high interest rate.

(b) A **further reduction in the money supply** by increasing credit restrictions, or imposing wage and price controls. Decreasing government expenditure will take cash out of the economy and reduce the government's budget deficit.

(c) **Increasing taxation**. This will reduce further the demand for purchases (including imports).

(d) **Devaluing the currency,** or allowing it to float downwards, if it has previously been on a fixed exchange rate system. This will make export sales more competitive and imports more expensive.

(e) **Imposing exchange controls** (restrictions on selling the local currency), import tariffs and quotas to prevent or discourage purchases of imports. For countries which are part of the World Trade Organisation (WTO) such methods are restricted.

(f) **Subsidising exports** in a variety of ways. Again this is restricted by the WTO.

IMF

The IMF will **extend loans** (normally for up to five years) to countries needing to finance a balance of payments deficit, but attaches strong conditions concerning economic and regulatory measures. The objective of these conditions is to force the country to reduce government budget deficits, reduce imports and to facilitate efficient production and sale of exports. These conditions are often summarised as 'deflation, devaluation and deregulation'.

Of the methods described above, the IMF favours **increasing interest rates** and **reducing inflation, increasing taxation** and **reducing government expenditure** to reduce government budget deficits, and allowing the currency to float freely. In addition it favours deregulation by **abolition of exchange controls,** and **reduction of trade tariffs and quotas,** as well as **abolition of restrictive practices** and **privatisation** of state enterprises. The overall effect of the IMF's work is intended to reduce volatility in exchange rates (although this effect is often more than countered by the actions of speculators) and to improve world trade, allowing indebted countries to 'sell' their way out of their problems.

The IMF also makes special arrangements for countries with prolonged severe economic problems. In this respect there is a blurring of responsibility between the IMF and the World Bank which can cause rivalry between the two Washington-based organisations.

The effect on multi-national companies of the above economic measures taken by governments varies as to whether the local subsidiary is a **net exporter** or importer.

If the subsidiary extracts raw materials or produces goods with a predominantly local cost input, the devaluation of the currency will **lower real costs** and assist it to **increase export sales**, although local costs of taxation and borrowing will increase. However, the multinational may attempt to use transfer pricing to avoid the tax bill and may be able to **switch borrowing** to another country.

If the subsidiary is a **net importer, designed to sell goods** to the local population, it will probably find business more difficult until the reduction in demand caused by the economic measures has taken its effect. An exception is where tariffs, quotas or exchange controls are imposed, in which case the local subsidiary of a multinational will have an advantage over the restricted imports from foreign competitors. However, as indicated above, such restrictive measures are discouraged by both the WTO and the IMF.

Marking guide		**Marks**
(a)	Measures to reduce the deficit	6-7
	(For very high marks most of the alternatives must be discussed)	
	Role of the IMF	3-4
	Impact of government actions and of the IMF on multinationals	5-6
		15

BPP PUBLISHING

Mathematical tables and exam formulae

MATHEMATICAL TABLES

PRESENT VALUE TABLE

Present value of 1, ie $(1+r)^{-n}$

where   r = discount rate

n = number of periods until payment

Periods	Discount rates (r)									
(n)	1%	2%	3%	4%	5%	6%	7%	8%	9%	10%
1	0.990	0.980	0.971	0.962	0.952	0.943	0.935	0.926	0.917	0.909
2	0.980	0.961	0.943	0.925	0.907	0.890	0.873	0.857	0.842	0.826
3	0.971	0.942	0.915	0.889	0.864	0.840	0.816	0.794	0.772	0.751
4	0.961	0.924	0.888	0.855	0.823	0.792	0.763	0.735	0.708	0.683
5	0.951	0.906	0.863	0.822	0.784	0.747	0.713	0.681	0.650	0.621
6	0.942	0.888	0.837	0.790	0.746	0.705	0.666	0.630	0.596	0.564
7	0.933	0.871	0.813	0.760	0.711	0.665	0.623	0.583	0.547	0.513
8	0.923	0.853	0.789	0.731	0.677	0.627	0.582	0.540	0.502	0.467
9	0.914	0.837	0.766	0.703	0.645	0.592	0.544	0.500	0.460	0.424
10	0.905	0.820	0.744	0.676	0.614	0.558	0.508	0.463	0.422	0.386
11	0.896	0.804	0.722	0.650	0.585	0.527	0.475	0.429	0.388	0.350
12	0.887	0.788	0.701	0.625	0.557	0.497	0.444	0.397	0.356	0.319
13	0.879	0.773	0.681	0.601	0.530	0.469	0.415	0.368	0.326	0.290
14	0.870	0.758	0.661	0.577	0.505	0.442	0.388	0.340	0.299	0.263
15	0.861	0.743	0.642	0.555	0.481	0.417	0.362	0.315	0.275	0.239

	11%	12%	13%	14%	15%	16%	17%	18%	19%	20%
1	0.901	0.893	0.885	0.877	0.870	0.862	0.855	0.847	0.840	0.833
2	0.812	0.797	0.783	0.769	0.756	0.743	0.731	0.718	0.706	0.694
3	0.731	0.712	0.693	0.675	0.658	0.641	0.624	0.609	0.593	0.579
4	0.659	0.636	0.613	0.592	0.572	0.552	0.534	0.516	0.499	0.482
5	0.593	0.567	0.543	0.519	0.497	0.476	0.456	0.437	0.419	0.402
6	0.535	0.507	0.480	0.456	0.432	0.410	0.390	0.370	0.352	0.335
7	0.482	0.452	0.425	0.400	0.376	0.354	0.333	0.314	0.296	0.279
8	0.434	0.404	0.376	0.351	0.327	0.305	0.285	0.266	0.249	0.233
9	0.391	0.361	0.333	0.308	0.284	0.263	0.243	0.225	0.209	0.194
10	0.352	0.322	0.295	0.270	0.247	0.227	0.208	0.191	0.176	0.162
11	0.317	0.287	0.261	0.237	0.215	0.195	0.178	0.162	0.148	0.135
12	0.286	0.257	0.231	0.208	0.187	0.168	0.152	0.137	0.124	0.112
13	0.258	0.229	0.204	0.182	0.163	0.145	0.130	0.116	0.104	0.093
14	0.232	0.205	0.181	0.160	0.141	0.125	0.111	0.099	0.088	0.078
15	0.209	0.183	0.160	0.140	0.123	0.108	0.095	0.084	0.074	0.065

BPP
PUBLISHING

ANNUITY TABLE

Present value of an annuity of 1, ie $\dfrac{1-(1+r)^{-n}}{r}$

where   r = discount rate

n = number of periods

Periods					Discount rates (r)					
(n)	1%	2%	3%	4%	5%	6%	7%	8%	9%	10%
1	0.990	0.980	0.971	0.962	0.952	0.943	0.935	0.926	0.917	0.909
2	1.970	1.942	1.913	1.886	1.859	1.833	1.808	1.783	1.759	1.736
3	2.941	2.884	2.829	2.775	2.723	2.673	2.624	2.577	2.531	2.487
4	3.902	3.808	3.717	3.630	3.546	3.465	3.387	3.312	3.240	3.170
5	4.853	4.713	4.580	4.452	4.329	4.212	4.100	3.993	3.890	3.791
6	5.795	5.601	5.417	5.242	5.076	4.917	4.767	4.623	4.486	4.355
7	6.728	6.472	6.230	6.002	5.786	5.582	5.389	5.206	5.033	4.868
8	7.652	7.325	7.020	6.733	6.463	6.210	5.971	5.747	5.535	5.335
9	8.566	8.162	7.786	7.435	7.108	6.802	6.515	6.247	5.995	5.759
10	9.471	8.983	8.530	8.111	7.722	7.360	7.024	6.710	6.418	6.145
11	10.37	9.787	9.253	8.760	8.306	7.887	7.499	7.139	6.805	6.495
12	11.26	10.58	9.954	9.385	8.863	8.384	7.943	7.536	7.161	6.814
13	12.13	11.35	10.63	9.986	9.394	8.853	8.358	7.904	7.487	7.103
14	13.00	12.11	11.30	10.56	9.899	9.295	8.745	8.244	7.786	7.367
15	13.87	12.85	11.94	11.12	10.38	9.712	9.108	8.559	8.061	7.606

	11%	12%	13%	14%	15%	16%	17%	18%	19%	20%
1	0.901	0.893	0.885	0.877	0.870	0.862	0.855	0.847	0.840	0.833
2	1.713	1.690	1.668	1.647	1.626	1.605	1.585	1.566	1.547	1.528
3	2.444	2.402	2.361	2.322	2.283	2.246	2.210	2.174	2.140	2.106
4	3.102	3.037	2.974	2.914	2.855	2.798	2.743	2.690	2.639	2.589
5	3.696	3.605	3.517	3.433	3.352	3.274	3.199	3.127	3.058	2.991
6	4.231	4.111	3.998	3.889	3.784	3.685	3.589	3.498	3.410	3.326
7	4.712	4.564	4.423	4.288	4.160	4.039	3.922	3.812	3.706	3.605
8	5.146	4.968	4.799	4.639	4.487	4.344	4.207	4.078	3.954	3.837
9	5.537	5.328	5.132	4.946	4.772	4.607	4.451	4.303	4.163	4.031
10	5.889	5.650	5.426	5.216	5.019	4.833	4.659	4.494	4.339	4.192
11	6.207	5.938	5.687	5.453	5.234	5.029	4.836	4.656	4.486	4.327
12	6.492	6.194	5.918	5.660	5.421	5.197	4.988	4.793	4.611	4.439
13	6.750	6.424	6.122	5.842	5.583	5.342	5.118	4.910	4.715	4.533
14	6.982	6.628	6.302	6.002	5.724	5.468	5.229	5.008	4.802	4.611
15	7.191	6.811	6.462	6.142	5.847	5.575	5.324	5.092	4.876	4.675

FORMULAE

Formulae provided to Paper 3.7 candidates are set out below.

Ke   (i) $E(r_j) = r_f + [E(r_m) - r_f]\beta_j$ → $CAPM$

(ii) $\dfrac{D_1}{P_0} + g$

WACC $Ke_g \dfrac{E}{E+D} + Kd(1-t)\dfrac{D}{E+D}$

or $Ke_u \left[1 - \dfrac{Dt}{E+D}\right]$

2 asset portfolio $\sigma_p = \sqrt{\sigma_a^2 x^2 + \sigma_b^2 (1-x)^2 + 2x(1-x) p_{ab}\sigma_a\sigma_b}$

Purchasing power parity $\dfrac{i_f - i_{uk}}{1 + i_{uk}}$

Corporate beta $\beta_a = \beta_e \dfrac{E}{E + D(1-t)} + \beta_d \dfrac{D(1-t)}{E + D(1-t)}$

Call price for a European option $= Ps\,N(d_1) - X_e^{-rT}\,N(d_2)$

$d_1 = \dfrac{\ln(Ps/X) + rT}{\sigma\sqrt{T}} + 0.5\sigma\sqrt{T}$

$d_2 = d_1 - \sigma\sqrt{T}$

See overleaf for information on other
BPP products and how to order

ACCA Order

To BPP Publishing Ltd, Aldine Place, London W12 8AA
Tel: 020 8740 2211. Fax: 020 8740 1184
email: publishing@bpp.com   online: www.bpp.com

Mr/Mrs/Ms (Full name)

Daytime delivery address

Postcode

Daytime Tel   Date of exam (month/year)

	2/01 Texts	1/02 Kits 9/01	Passcards	MCQ cards	Tapes	Videos
PART 1						
1.1 Preparing Financial Statements	£19.95 ☐	£10.95 ☐	£5.95 ☐	£5.95 ☐	£12.95 ☐	£25.00 ☐
1.2 Financial Information for Management	£19.95 ☐	£10.95 ☐	£5.95 ☐	£5.95 ☐	£12.95 ☐	£25.00 ☐
1.3 Managing People	£19.95 ☐	£10.95 ☐	£5.95 ☐		£12.95 ☐	£25.00 ☐
PART 2						
2.1 Information Systems	£19.95 ☐	£10.95 ☐	£5.95 ☐		£12.95 ☐	£25.00 ☐
2.2 Corporate and Business Law (6/01)	£19.95 ☐	£10.95 ☐	£5.95 ☐		£12.95 ☐	£25.00 ☐
2.3 Business Taxation FA 2001 (for 2002 exams)	£19.95 (8/01) £10.95 ☐	£5.95 (1/02) ☐			£12.95 ☐	£25.00 ☐
2.4 Financial Management and Control	£19.95 ☐	£10.95 ☐	£5.95 ☐		£12.95 ☐	£25.00 ☐
2.5 Financial Reporting (6/01)	£19.95 ☐	£10.95 ☐	£5.95 ☐		£12.95 ☐	£25.00 ☐
2.6 Audit and Internal Review (6/01)	£19.95 ☐	£10.95 ☐	£5.95 ☐		£12.95 ☐	£25.00 ☐
PART 3						
3.1 Audit and Assurance Services (6/01)	£20.95 ☐	£10.95 ☐	£5.95 ☐		£12.95 ☐	£25.00 ☐
3.2 Advanced Taxation FA 2001 (for 2002 exams)	£20.95 (8/01) £10.95 ☐	£5.95 (1/02) ☐			£12.95 ☐	£25.00 ☐
3.3 Performance Management	£20.95 ☐	£10.95 ☐	£5.95 ☐		£12.95 ☐	£25.00 ☐
3.4 Business Information Management	£20.95 ☐	£10.95 ☐	£5.95 ☐		£12.95 ☐	£25.00 ☐
3.5 Strategic Business Planning and Development	£20.95 ☐	£10.95 ☐	£5.95 ☐		£12.95 ☐	£25.00 ☐
3.6 Advanced Corporate Reporting (6/01)	£20.95 ☐	£10.95 ☐	£5.95 ☐		£12.95 ☐	£25.00 ☐
3.7 Strategic Financial Management	£20.95 ☐	£10.95 ☐	£5.95 ☐		£12.95 ☐	£25.00 ☐
INTERNATIONAL STREAM						
1.1 Preparing Financial Statements	£19.95 ☐	£10.95 ☐	£5.95 ☐	£5.95 ☐	£12.95 ☐	£25.00 ☐
2.5 Financial Reporting (6/01)	£19.95 ☐	£10.95 ☐	£5.95 ☐		£12.95 ☐	£25.00 ☐
2.6 Audit and Internal Review (6/01)	£19.95 ☐	£10.95 ☐	£5.95 ☐		£12.95 ☐	£25.00 ☐
3.1 Audit and Assurance services (6/01)	£20.95 ☐	£10.95 ☐	£5.95 ☐		£12.95 ☐	£25.00 ☐
3.6 Advanced Corporate Reporting (6/01)	£20.95 ☐	£10.95 ☐	£5.95 ☐		£12.95 ☐	£25.00 ☐
SUCCESS IN YOUR RESEARCH AND ANALYSIS PROJECT						
Tutorial Text (9/01)	£19.95 ☐					

SUBTOTAL £ ☐

POSTAGE & PACKING

Study Texts

	First	Each extra	
UK	£3.00	£2.00	£ ☐
Europe*	£5.00	£4.00	£ ☐
Rest of world	£20.00	£10.00	£ ☐

Kits/Passcards/Success Tapes/MCQ cards

	First	Each extra	
UK	£2.00	£1.00	£ ☐
Europe*	£2.50	£1.00	£ ☐
Rest of world	£15.00	£8.00	£ ☐

Breakthrough Videos

	First	Each extra	
UK	£2.00	£2.00	£ ☐
Europe*	£2.00	£2.00	£ ☐
Rest of world	£20.00	£10.00	£ ☐

Grand Total (Cheques to *BPP Publishing*) I enclose

a cheque for (incl. Postage) £ ☐

Or charge to Access/Visa/Switch

Card Number ☐☐☐☐ ☐☐☐☐ ☐☐☐☐ ☐☐☐☐

Expiry date _____   Start Date _____

Issue Number (Switch Only) _____

Signature _____

We aim to deliver to all UK addresses inside 5 working days; a signature will be required. Orders to all EU addresses should be delivered within 6 working days. All other orders to overseas addresses should be delivered within 8 working days. * Europe includes the Republic of Ireland and the Channel Islands.

REVIEW FORM & FREE PRIZE DRAW

All original review forms from the entire BPP range, completed with genuine comments, will be entered into one of two draws 31 July 2002 and 31 January 2003. The names on the first four forms picked out on each occasion will be sent a cheque for £50.

Name: _____   Address: _____

_____

_____

How have you used this Kit?
(Tick one box only)

☐ Self study (book only)

☐ On a course: college (please state)_____

_____

☐ With 'correspondence' package

☐ Other _____

Why did you decide to purchase this Kit? *(Tick one box only)*

☐ Have used the complementary Study Text

☐ Have used other BPP products in the past

☐ Recommendation by friend/colleague

☐ Recommendation by a lecturer at college

☐ Saw advertising in journals

☐ Saw website

☐ Other _____

During the past six months do you recall seeing/receiving any of the following?
(Tick as many boxes as are relevant)

☐ Our advertisement in *Student Accountant*

☐ Our advertisement in *Pass*

☐ Our brochure with a letter through the post

☐ Our website

Which (if any) aspects of our advertising do you find useful?
(Tick as many boxes as are relevant)

☐ Prices and publication dates of new editions

☐ Information on product content

☐ Facility to order books off-the-page

☐ None of the above

When did you sit the exam? _____

Which of the following BPP products have you used for this paper?

☐ Study Text   ☐ MCQ Cards   ☑ Kit   ☐ Passcards   ☐ Success Tape   ☐ Breakthrough Video

Your ratings, comments and suggestions would be appreciated on the following areas of this Kit.

	Very useful	Useful	Not useful
'Question search tools'	☐	☐	☐
'The exam'	☐	☐	☐
'Background	☐	☐	☐
Preparation questions	☐	☐	☐
Exam standard questions	☐	☐	☐
'Tutor's hints' section in answers	☐	☐	☐
Content and structure of answers	☐	☐	☐
Mock exams	☐	☐	☐
'Plan of attack'	☐	☐	☐
Mock exam answers	☐	☐	☐

	Excellent	Good	Adequate	Poor
Overall opinion of this Kit	☐	☐	☐	☐

Do you intend to continue using BPP products?   ☐ Yes   ☐ No

Please note any further comments and suggestions/errors on the reverse of this page. The BPP author of this edition can be e-mailed at: nickweller@bpp.com

Please return this form to: Katy Hibbert, ACCA range manager, BPP Publishing Ltd, FREEPOST, London, W12 8BR

REVIEW FORM & FREE PRIZE DRAW (continued)

Please note any further comments and suggestions/errors below.

FREE PRIZE DRAW RULES

1   Closing date for 31 July 2002 draw is 30 June 2002. Closing date for 31 January 2003 draw is 31 December 2002.

2   Restricted to entries with UK and Eire addresses only. BPP employees, their families and business associates are excluded.

3   No purchase necessary. Entry forms are available upon request from BPP Publishing. No more than one entry per title, per person. Draw restricted to persons aged 16 and over.

4   Winners will be notified by post and receive their cheques not later than 6 weeks after the relevant draw date.

5   The decision of the promoter in all matters is final and binding. No correspondence will be entered into.